PSYCHOLOGICAL RESEARCH

THE INSIDE STORY

edited by
MICHAEL H. SIEGEL
State University of New York, Oneonta

H. PHILIP ZEIGLER
Hunter College of the City University of New York
and
American Museum of Natural History

Harper & Row, Publishers
New York, Hagerstown, San Francisco, London

Sponsoring Editor: George A. Middendorf
Project Editor: Alice M. Solomon
Designer: Michel Craig
Production Supervisor: Francis X. Giordano
Compositor: V & M Typographical, Inc.
Printer and Binder: The Murray Printing Company
Art Studio: Danmark & Michaels, Inc.

PSYCHOLOGICAL RESEARCH: The Inside Story

Library of Congress Cataloging in Publication Data

Main entry under title:

Psychological research.

  (Harper experimental psychology series)
  1. Psychological research.   I. Siegel, Michael H.
II. Zeigler, Harris Philip, 1931-   [DNLM: 1.   Psy-
chology.   2.   Research.   BF76.5 P974]
BF76.5.P78   150′.7′2   75-42462
ISBN 0-06-046137-3

CONTENTS

Section FOUR: Applications: Psychological Research and the Problem of Relevance   323

PREFACE

In this book, some outstanding psychologists describe how they work: how they become diverted by apparently irrelevant issues; how they make mistakes; how their plans grow, change, and mature. In short, this book attempts to describe the process of research.

It is our conviction that some sense of what it is like to do research in psychology can best be conveyed by concrete descriptions of researchers at work. Since we have also tried to make the book reflect the extraordinary diversity of research activities in psychology, our contributors have necessarily touched on many of the major research areas and dealt with many of the central problems of our field. However, we have made no attempt to achieve a systematic coverage of standard topics in psychology—that approach would be inconsistent with our main purpose. Readers who wish to learn more about the topics described might check the reference sections following most chapters for suggestions for further reading.

Of the 19 chapters included, all but 2 have been written especially for this book. The chapters by Skinner and Schachter are the exceptions, but their style and purpose fit those of the book.

We have divided the book into four sections. In the first, two of psychology's most distinguished senior scientists look back over their research careers. The second section consists of four chapters about working with animals. The third section describes the work of nine different laboratories dealing with a very wide range of problems, from perceptual development to memory, but all involving people. The fourth and final section consists of four chapters concerned with the application of research findings to a variety of specific problems faced by society. Because of the nature of the book, any chapter sequence is arbitrary, and there is no necessity to preserve the sequence proposed by the editors if another plan works better.

Michael H. Siegel
H. Philip Zeigler

INTRODUCTION

An accurate but unsatisfying definition of psychology reads: "Psychology is what the psychologist does." The difficulty, of course, is that psychologists do so many different things. The selections in this book will give you a glimpse of some of them.

Certainly, the 19 chapters constituting this book have not been written by a representative cross section of psychologists, nor do they give a complete picture of what psychologists do. What the chapters do offer is some insight into how these scientists grapple with ideas and, perhaps, why they do. All of the contributors were especially invited to participate, because their work is absorbingly interesting and important.

As you read these selections, you are bound to be impressed by the range of topics studied through experimentation in psychology. You will soon discover that each laboratory has a unique approach and style. Work from that laboratory will have an identifiable stamp and probably can be recognized rather easily. It is precisely this personal style of research and this highly individual research interest that makes it possible to read 19 separate "stories" rather than the same story 19 times. After you have read four or five of the accounts, you may be struck by some similarities. Despite differences in subject matter and the variety of approaches, there are some features common to good science, or at least good scientists. It is worth commenting on a few of these features here.

Perhaps the most frequently encountered characteristic of the good scientist is shared with other successful individuals in fields which are removed from research. This quality has variously been called perseverance, dedication, and sticking to your guns. (It has also been called other things by the wives or husbands of the individuals so afflicted.) Possibly, it is merely the final stages of the infection usually first contracted during college days and made incurable in graduate school. Having it, though, is no guarantee of success, but only infrequently can the scientist be successful without it. Whether it takes the form of forcing yourself to stay up all night to study someone's sleep pattern, placing you as an expert witness in an explosively controversial criminal trial, or requiring you bodily to restrain a mature male ram from fostering amorous attentions upon a willing ewe, the successful scientist must keep on going when it just is not fun to do so.

Another regularly occurring event in the lives of successful scientists is sometimes called serendipity. This refers to the good fortune of finding what you were not looking for. The "accident" may be merely coming across a fictionalized account of the actions of army ants during childhood or realizing that it is possible for you to add a string of numbers and still think about something else. Almost always, though, it leads scientists along paths they could not possibly have anticipated, paths they must be willing to travel even though they may actually be required to jump into a brand new area. It is this quality which is needed to make those social psychologists interested in cognitive processes and emotion see some implications for their own thinking of physiological studies of obesity in animals. What is required, evidently, is not only luck, but an awareness that something significant has been found and a willingness to wonder about it.

An analogy that appears throughout the book relates the progress of science and experimentation to a tree. Each new encounter, each experiment, provides the scientist with a choice of branches to climb. There is no way of telling when the scientist first begins work where on the tree he or she will eventually appear. Each of the people writing here had to make such decisions during his or her research program.

Other ideas appear often enough to comment on here. One is the distinction between experimentation in the laboratory and observation in the field. Both are required. Progress in experimentation calls for additional fieldwork. Ideas first encountered while observing in the field should be tested in the laboratory when feasible. The gulf generally acknowledged between the hard-nosed experimenter and the careful observer of nature seems to be narrowing.

Yet another recurring idea found in many of the chapters describes the genesis of research—the transition from a hunch to an experiment. The popular notion of just how science is done may be far more elegant, but almost all of the contributors to this book have commented that they first performed little "thought experiments," tried out an idea on their children or spouses, or ran simple, informal tests. Very rarely can the final product emerge on a first try.

One final point: Although most of the accounts related here rest on unifying, organizing principles, sometimes called theories, and although all involve some sort of search for an answer to a problem or set of problems, few, if any, describe what the popular press would regard as a breakthrough. Progress toward the solution of scientific problems comes slowly, undramatically, and in small steps. The occasional "Eureka!" experience does not provide continuing satisfaction for these people; more often satisfaction is derived from the steady, uneven, day-to-day dealing with the small details of research that lead to broader ideas and theories.

M. H. S.

H. P. Z.

PSYCHOLOGICAL RESEARCH
THE INSIDE STORY

SECTION ONE

REFLECTIONS ON A RESEARCH CAREER

The two chapters that make up the first section were written by two of the best known and most influential research psychologists, Harry F. Harlow and B. F. Skinner. The careers of both have been characterized not only by productivity, but by inventiveness and resourcefulness.

Although Harlow and Skinner have been responsible for the development of two distinctly different approaches to research in psychology, their stories show several similarities. Both are interested in understanding the nature of learning, both prefer to use animals in their research, and both have been involved with the development of instrumentation which changed the course of psychological research.

Both chapters show clearly just how ideas for research develop, how they evolve as a result both of new interests and necessity, and, how they lead to further changes in the direction of research. The final product is scarcely recognizable from its ancestors. The line connecting the most recent with the earliest research shows a completely logical progression, but one which easily could have evolved differently.

Harlow's chapter begins with his first attempts to establish an animal laboratory at the University of Wisconsin and concludes with some work intended to shed light on human mental illness. He describes the development of what has become standard equipment for primate labs, explains how he became involved in research on learning sets, and tells about his work with the development of sexuality in monkeys, which in turn led to his research on surrogate mothers.

Skinner's chapter was originally written for presentation at the Eastern Psychological Association meeting in 1955. It is organized around the development of the cumulative record, a means of showing responding which gives a particularly clear picture of the rate of response. What may appear as an attempt to grapple with a simple, technical problem, develops into the story of a research career concerned with far more than just developing instrumentation. Skinner presents a defense of studying the single organism, describes his concern for training animals, and, in short, summarizes the history of operant psychology. The applications discussed or foreshadowed extend from the study and treatment of mental illness (see also Chapter 16) to plotting the dark adaptation curve of pigeons and even to the notion of controlling human behavior.

We can ask what raised both Harlow and Skinner to their eminence. Some glimpses at an answer may be found in their chapters. Although both are interested in a wide range of research questions, they are able to concentrate all their energies upon the current issue. Certainly, luck or circumstance are important to any research career. Even more important is the ability to see what may develop into a worthwhile research area and a willingness to change direction. Skinner calls this a first principle and explains it this way: "When you run into something interesting, drop everything else and study it."

CHAPTER
1
MONKEYS, MEN, MICE, MOTIVES, AND SEX
Harry F. Harlow

IN THE BEGINNING, OR, HOW I GOT INTO THE MONKEY BUSINESS

In most psychological ivory towers there can be found an animal laboratory. Animal psychologists think of themselves as theoretical psychologists because their obligation is to discover general laws of behavior applicable to mice, monkeys, and men. These "comparative" psychologists have one great advantage over the psychologists who study humans: They can subject their subhuman subjects—rats, cats, or monkeys—to more rigorous experimental controls than ordinarily can be imposed on human beings.

In order to do so they need a laboratory. Before coming to the University of Wisconsin as an Assistant Professor, fresh from graduate school at Stanford and laboratories brimming with rats, I had been told that one of my duties was to run the Laboratory of Comparative Psychology at Wisconsin. You can imagine my dismay when I learned, upon my arrival, that the facilities for animal psychology at Wisconsin were not merely meager, they were nonexistent. Indeed, the previous laboratory had been torn down that spring.

Now, an animal psychologist without a laboratory is like a surgeon without an operating room. Fortunately, the City of Madison, Wisconsin, boasted an unusually fine zoo. In this zoo was a modern building filled with an excellent diversified collection of well-mannered primates —especially on the days when visitors were not admitted. My chairman's wife suggested that someone should test "Jiggs," a very unusual, totally tame 14-year-old orangutan. We made a round plunger and a square plunger, and gave them to Jiggs together with two blocks of wood, one with a round hole and one with a square hole. For hours on end he worked on the task of trying to insert the square plunger in the round hole, a problem symbolic of an animal who was born to be Prince of the Woods and lived out his days as Consort of the Cage. After 6 weeks of endless effort Jiggs died, apparently from psychosomatic symptoms, but I had taken the first steps toward graduating from the study of rats to the study of primates.

Dr. Harlow is Emeritus Professor of Psychology at the University of Wisconsin and is now affiliated with the University of Arizona.

Meanwhile, the sum of a million dollars—none of which I ever saw—ended the search for a laboratory. This money was appropriated to build a new U.S. Forest Products Laboratory. When the forest products people moved into their new facilities they left vacant a group of buildings, one of which was a spacious modern brick structure, complete with all modern conveniences. This wasn't the building we inherited. The building we got had been used as the box testing factory. With a borrowed pneumatic hammer, and money primarily from my own pocket, we converted this structure, 26 feet square and two stories high, into a substantial primate laboratory. The first floor was a forest of concrete pillars, two of them 6 x 3 feet thick and 16 feet high. These two would have gone through the ceiling, but there wasn't any ceiling in that half of the building. Below the half ceiling and the roof there was a maze of pipes: water, gas, steam, and disconnected. We took over a thousand feet of pipe out of that building, but when we were done, there were still enough pipes left for the occasional escapee monkey to take very safe refuge in the tangle. We feared that two monkeys might simultaneously escape and eventually establish a colony entirely independent of the rest of the laboratory.

My first important psychological discovery was made not by me, but by my wife, nee Clara Mears. She discovered Paul Settlage, who later became a double doctor—both scientific and medical and medically scientific. One of Paul's most important discoveries was his cousin, Walter Grether. The only absolute necessities in a primate laboratory beside four-legged primates are two-legged primates called graduate students. Patience, luck, hallucinations, and serendipity will get you nowhere in research without catalytic graduate students.

In this laboratory we initiated a long series of studies on learning in primates. These studies grew out of an interest in brain function, but eventually led us to a number of important new approaches to the study of learning and thinking in both human and subhuman primates.

We were studying the visual abilities of monkeys who had undergone experimental surgery designed to remove portions of the visual areas of the brain, and we needed reliable and efficient tests to measure visual function in these monkeys. Settlage and Grether had encountered the work of Kurt Goldstein, a German clinical neurologist, and we adapted some of the tests he used in the clinic with brain-damaged patients. One of these tests, the string test, is illustrated in Figure 1.1. The individual problems could be varied in difficulty so that we could study the effects of brain lesions upon both simple and complex visual tasks. In the course of these studies we found that if the cortical lesions produced a massive effect, a small number of subjects would suffice. Four subjects became our standard number. At times wisdom decreed that the results should be replicated, but if a task cannot be studied with two groups of four, it is probably a problem of little significance. This maxim, which I now name Harlow's Law, prevented

Figure 1.1. *Rhesus monkey responding to presentation of a "string-test" problem. Correct solution requires that the monkey pull in the baited chain. The problems can be varied in difficulty by varying the arrangement of the chain.*

us from working on an enormous number of problems with little or no meaning.

Like many other researchers, we struggled to construct apparatus for measuring discrimination-type problems, but all primatologists seemed bound by a rigidity of thinking into compounding the same errors over and over again. Fortunately, the discrimination problem was resolved by Dr. Heinrich Klüver, who created and recognized the importance of the monkey formboard. The formboard was a flat test tray, approximately 10 x 26 inches, with an appropriate number of wells or holes in which rewards were placed. These were covered by stimuli of any desired type, which could differ in color, form, and size, and other factors. The monkey made his choice by displacing one of the stimuli. If he was correct, he got a raisin or a peanut. If he was wrong (i.e., if his choice didn't coincide with what the experimenter had decided was correct on that trial) he found the hole empty (Fig. 1.2). We later learned that one of the reasons the formboard technique was so successful was that requiring the monkey to displace the stimulus object forced it to attend to the stimuli associated with reward.

Many of the earlier American experiments on subhuman animals were limited by the brief period of time over which the subjects were studied, and by the specificity and limitation of the problem studied.

Figure 1.2. *Monkey formboard being used in the Wisconsin General Test Apparatus (WGTA), in a test of discrimination learning. The test board is mounted on rollers, contains two food wells and is pushed to within reach of the subject to initiate each trial.*

A typical procedure with rats had been to arrange 120 rats in groups, to subject them to three different stimulus situations together with two different motivational conditions, and then to test the effects while running them meaninglessly and endlessly down a straight alley. Moreover, when rats were tested on discrimination problems, they were commonly tested on a single problem and then sacrificed. This left both the rats and the experimenters incapable of further thinking. Most of the experimenters never realized that these experiments were meaningless, although it must have dawned on some of the rats. Fortunately, monkeys are too expensive to test on a single problem and then sacrifice, so it was impossible to follow the rat learning paradigm. Indeed, we would probably never have discovered the phenomenon of *learning set* if we had worked with rats. First, because rats aren't very good at it (although it can be seen to some extent in both rats and pigeons). Second, the fact that monkeys were scarce and expensive forced us to learn all we could out of a single animal before discarding it. In this, as in so many other instances of scientific research, necessity was the instigator of invention.

THE FORMATION OF LEARNING SETS

In the late 1940s, we began to test monkeys on a long series of six trial problems. The objects presented varied from problem to problem, but for each set of problems within a series the principle of solution remained constant. Thus, in the oddity problem, the principle was

Figure 1.3. Rhesus monkey engaged in the solution of an object discrimination.

"choose the odd of the three objects," while in the object discrimination problem, the principle was simply "choose the object in each pair which had been rewarded on the last trial" (Fig. 1.3).

Our first studies of learning in monkeys took place in the 1930s, in the midst of a theoretical debate about the nature of learning known as the continuity-noncontinuity controversy. The continuity theorists maintained that even the most complex human learning was built up gradually by the process of trial and error, and the gradual accumulation of the associations between rewards and stimuli. The noncontinuity theorists argued that even the lower animals were capable of the animal equivalent of looking at a problem, saying "aha," and quickly solving it. Put another way, the noncontinuity or "insight" theorists suggested that the animal is not behaving randomly—waiting for associations to be stamped in by rewards and punishments—but is actively trying out "hunches" and following up those that pay off (Marvin Levine, a former student of mine, discusses this in Chapter 11).

When we examined the performance of monkeys over many months of testing on a variety of problems, we could see that both types of learning ("trial and error" and "insight") were present, but that they merely represented different stages in the monkeys' learning process. On a series of problems of a single type, the pattern of responses on the six trials of the early problems (intratrial comparison) resembled trial and error learning curves. After the underlying principle had been learned, the intratrial learning curves of the later problems in the series resembled curves associated with insight or noncontinuity learning. This "learning to learn" is a transfer from problem to problem which we call the formation of a learning set (Fig. 1.4).

The formation of learning sets for all problems measured is a highly predictable, orderly process. Once the monkeys have formed these learning sets they retain them for long periods and use them appropriately. This is important, because it points out that human be-behavior is not to be understood in terms of the results of single learning situations. We are changed into thinking beings through a variety of learning situations which are repeated many times in similar form. Changes are effected through multiple but comparable problems. The learning of primary importance, to the primates at least, is the learning of how to learn efficiently in situations frequently encountered.

MOTIVATION, DRIVE, AND CURIOSITY—THE CASE OF THE PEEPING RHESUS

The work on learning sets had three important effects. It created a new Harlow, a learning theorist, and buried once and for all the continuity-noncontinuity controversy. It also taught me that I owed more to the monkeys than they owed to me.

One of the many things I owe them was a demonstration that changed my whole way of thinking about the problem of motivation in general and its relation to learning in particular. The demonstration was a simple one but in order to understand its significance for me, and eventually for others, you will have to try to imagine the theoretical atmosphere in which students of animal learning carried on their research in the period between 1930 and 1950.

Beginning in the 1920s, after the behavioral revolution of Watson, the behavior theorists looked for a motivational theory to integrate with their developing S-R learning constructs. The instinct theory fell into disrepute, battered by the heredity-environment controversy and confused by different interpretations of the term instinct. The hedonistic pain-pleasure theory was discarded because of its subjective implications. Between 1920 and 1930 the outstanding work in the area of motivation related to internal, visceral drives, and drive cycles. The only important unlearned motives were considered to be such homeostatic biological drives as hunger, thirst, elimination, and sex. It was therefore only natural that the self-conscious behavior theorists should choose these available tissue-tension relief or drive-reduction hypotheses as companions to their conditioned responses. We do not question that these theses have fertilized the field of learning, but we feel that drive-reduction theory led psychologists to attack problems of limited importance. Nothing better illustrates this point than the kinds of apparatus used in such research. The single-unit T-maze is an ideal apparatus for studying the visual capacities of a nocturnal animal, and the straight alley maze enables one to measure quantitatively the speed and rate of running from one dead end to another.

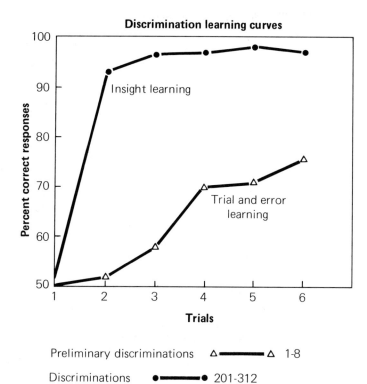

Discrimination learning curves

y-axis: Percent correct responses (50, 60, 70, 80, 90, 100)

x-axis: Trials (1, 2, 3, 4, 5, 6)

Insight learning

Trial and error learning

Preliminary discriminations △━━━△ 1-8

Discriminations ●━━━● 201-312

Figure 1.4. *The formation of a "learning set." The monkey is given a large number of six-trial problems. Note that on the early problems (1–8), improvement seems to take place slowly within each problem over the six trials. After a large number of problems, the monkey learns the "rules" of the game: "If you win, stay with it, if you lose—shift". Thus, while on Trial 1, he can do no better than 50 percent; on Trial 2, he is almost perfect. The marked difference between the kind of performance shown in the two sets of curves suggests that two different types of learning processes are involved.*

Given their emphasis on the organism's visceral drives as the sole source of motivation, it is not surprising that investigators typically tested their rats under conditions of food deprivation, maintaining them on a regime of 23 hours starvation and 1 hour of plenty. We saw that monkeys did not do well under these conditions and began feeding them shortly before the training sessions. It was then that the monkeys gave me a demonstration of the total inadequacy of the current drive-reduction theory of motivation, at least as far as primates were concerned.

The rhesus monkey is equipped with enormous cheek pouches and, consequently, many subjects would begin the educational process with a rich store of incentives crammed into the buccal cavity. Upon making a correct response, the monkey would add a raisin to the storeroom and swallow a little previously munched food. Following an incorrect response, the monkey would also swallow a little stored food. Thus, according to the S-R drive-reduction theory, both incorrect and correct responses are being rewarded equally and no learning should take place. In fact, the monkeys performed beautifully under these conditions.

There has been a constant increase in experimental evidence that the key to real learning theory is in patterns of response motivated by a large variety of external, as well as internal, stimuli. Monkeys can and do learn to solve mechanical puzzles for the sheer glee of solving puzzles. Thus, monkeys who are rewarded with food frequently abandon a problem after solving it, whereas those who are not rewarded with food keep on for the fun of it. Figure 1.5 shows a picture of an apparatus used to test the strength of the monkey's curiosity. Making a response opened a small window through which the monkey could see a wide variety of objects. In this situation monkeys sometimes responded for 18 consecutive hours or more, without ever being given a food reward for pressing the window. However, I should note that curiosity-exploratory tendencies can be measured quantitatively even in the rat.

SEPARATION, SECURITY, AND SEXUALITY, OR
THE RISE AND FALL OF A BREEDING COLONY

After a while, we were carrying on a variety of research programs. We used fewer subjects in our primate research than did the rodentologists, but we still needed a large number of monkeys. We imported most of our monkeys from India where grisly diseases were endemic. I first became scientifically interested in sex, at least in monkey sex, when I acquired the benign hope that we could produce an enormous breeding colony free of these diseases. Toward this end we separated baby monkeys from their mothers immediately after birth. We then raised these infants in total or near total social isolation. We were guided by divine ignorance and achieved the same kind of nondivine results as would the fanciers of pedigreed cats and dogs, hell-bent on maintaining the genetic purity of their lines. Little did we realize that raising mammals in total social isolation completely guarantees the purity of the line. A total lack of procreation does not leave the species with pure progeny. It leaves it without any progeny. There can be no genetic variation in a vacuum.

When these infant monkeys reached sexual maturity, as measured by anatomy and endocrinology, we attempted to set up a breeding colony. We brought selected and mature males and females together and waited hopefully for the end results. To our horror these monkeys treated each other like brother and sister, proving that two can live in complete propinquity with propriety as long as neither of them cares. When the laboratory-bred and isolated females were smaller than the males they would back away and sit down looking appealingly at the

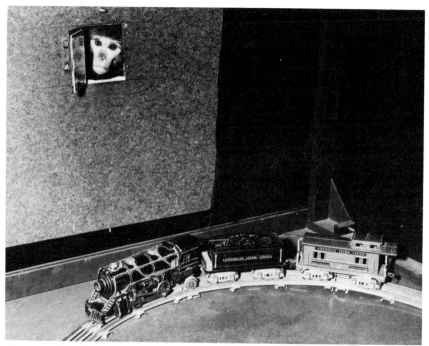

Figure 1.5. *Curiosity in the rhesus monkey.*

would-be consorts. Their hearts were in the right place even if nothing else was. Of those lab-reared males who made any attempt at amorous advances, some created bizarre sexual scenes by mounting the head of the female (Fig. 1.6), while others grasped the midbody of the female and thrust laterally, leaving them totally at cross purposes with reality (Fig. 1.7). It was not surprising that the morale of our lab-reared monkeys was not very high. Indeed, we had inadvertently created not a breeding, but a brooding colony.

In a desperate attempt to achieve our goal we then placed 15 of our mature isolate males and 15 of our mature isolate females on a monkey island at the Madison Zoo, with the pious hope that on some enchanted evening the full moon would rise over the waters of Lake Wingra and have its reputed effect on the couples. With this romantic setting we hoped that the monkeys would do something other than just seeing eye to eye, and we would reap a crop of delayed darlings. Unfortunately, the isolate males and females had not been programmed for enchantment.

In desperation we sent for our finest normal breeding male, Smiley, to test his tireless masculine energy against feminine indifference. His advent on the island was not auspicious. All 30 animals surrounded him on the island brink. Being outnumbered did not bother Smiley. He knocked the first intruder aside, pushed the face of the

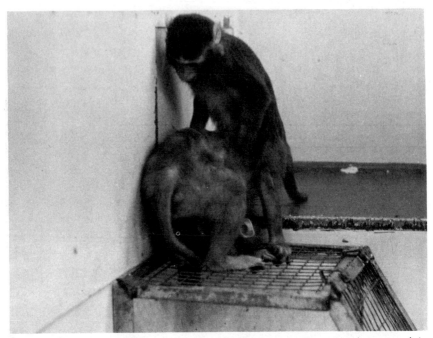

Figure 1.6. *Sexual behavior of a laboratory-reared male—inappropriate mounting responses.*

next into the concrete circles, encircled the throat of the third, without biting, and step by step moved up the island. At the top of the island he looked around. Dominance had been established.

As soon as we saw the conqueror Smiley, we waited for what was to us the inevitable advent of infants. Unfortunately we did not understand the psychology of affectional learning. To our surprise—and Smiley's—the females remained frozen, fixated on vacuity, not on virility. Smiley's role gradually changed to one of defeat and despair. He realized that these females were far more fatuous than feminine and his interest waned. It dawned on both the virile male and the experimenters that there can be no love without longing. When Smiley approached the females, they scampered away and passion without proximity leaves much to be desired.

When Smiley was returned to his normal female friends he rejected them. However, he became subsequently rehabilitated when eventually he rediscovered that all females were not feelingless and frustrating.

As often happens in science, we were much more curious about the abnormal behavior of our animals than we would have been about their normal sexual behavior. The disruption of a normal behavioral function is of considerable interest to the scientist, because it promises to give him insights into the processes which maintain the behavior in

Figure 1.7. *Sexual behavior of a laboratory-reared male rhesus—working at cross purposes with reality.*

normal animals. By rearing our monkeys in social isolation we had severely disrupted the processes underlying normal sexual and emotional development, even though their physical development was normal. This showed clearly that sexual behavior in primates is not "innate" or "instinctive"—whatever these overworked terms mean. Like other complex behaviors it must be the outcome of a long and complex process analogous in some respects to the process of "learning to learn."

LEARNING TO LOVE: THE DEVELOPMENT OF
THE SURROGATE MOTHER

In raising the monkeys in social isolation we obviously had deprived them of many types of social experience which they normally would have received: experience with their mothers, their fathers, other adult animals, and their young peers. The isolated monkeys were raised in individual cages and were given only cheesecloth diapers to serve as blankets. The attachments formed by the babies to their security blankets, and the upset shown by the infants when the diapers were removed for sanitary purposes, led eventually to the invention of the surrogate mother.

I was one of the few passengers in a plane flying from Washington, D.C., back to Madison one Saturday night. Suddenly I looked at the empty seat beside me and there I envisioned the female who was to be the cause of my being named "father of the cloth mother." Recognizing almost immediately some of her research possibilities I meditated on some potential experiments and crystallized my thoughts in a verse later to be used in my address to the APA:

> Beloved girl of wondrous charms
> Although devoid of brain and arms
> Your contact comfort holds the heart
> Though lyric love may play no part.

The form and fate of the surrogate mothers with their two faces is now a matter of history, but when I hurried to the lab the next morning I feared I would have to perform the act of creation alone. Fortunately one of the graduate students, Robert Zimmermann, caught on to my enthusiasm and we went to work on the basic surrogate mother researches, designed to extol, and at times to exploit, the possibilities of motherhood.

The creation of the surrogate mother (Fig. 1.8) took us more than 7 days and was a joint project with the infant monkeys. The mothers' bodies were nothing more than circular wire mesh frames. The cloth mother's body was draped in a terrycloth sheath, whereas the wire mother's body was unadorned. We made a serious attempt to build arms into the surrogate, but inanimate arms are without charm, as they cannot respond to the subtle responses of the infants. When we created the surrogates we were not limited by natural selection, and we were proud of the fact that we had built them according to human engineering principles. There were two mothers, but, as only one breast at a time was required, we gave each mother only a single breast. The cloth surrogate had a doll face and the wire surrogate a dog face. Intuitively we knew that monkey babies would better bask in the light of the doll face than of the dog face. To adult people, the doll face is a beautiful mother face and the dog face repugnant. The thought that these opinions do not hold for monkeys did not cross our minds. As it turned out, to babies, monkey or human, all mothers' faces are beautiful.

In spite of all our efforts, the first baby monkey to be used in any surrogate mother research was born before the doll face on the first surrogate was completed. In desperation we supplied the infant with a

Figure 1.8. *Infant rhesus monkey and surrogate mothers. (Background— wire mother, foreground—cloth mother.)*

mother whose face was a smooth, unpainted wooden ball. The infant immediately developed love for this featureless-faced female. All went well for the first 3 months. At that point carpentry caught up with creativity and we substituted for the smooth ball a doll face which had features in the front and nothing in the back or above the ears. The infant took one look at her new faced mother and screamed in terror. She fled to the back of the cage and assumed an autistic-like posture, with face on the floor and head wrapped in both arms.

We could not decide what to do about the mother. The infant monkey rapidly found the solution for us by rotating the face 180 degrees to get a blank stare. Clinical tests showed that if we rotated the ball 180 degrees back to the face the baby promptly rotated it backwards to the bare ball. This procedure could be repeated dozens of times. As far as we were concerned, this was the only solution, but the monkey was far more ingenious. We arrived one morning to find that the baby monkey had pulled the head from the mother and rolled it into the bottom of the cage.

It was obvious that consistency, or lack of change, was a far more important variable in maternal facial preference than doll or dog design. Since infants love a mother, no matter how ghastly or gruesome, the baby monkey gradually went back to the cloth mother, complete with doll face, sought succor at her breast and reveled in contact comfort.

At this point we made a great discovery, with vast possibilities of generality: When an experimenter can no longer train an animal, the animal can begin to train the experimenter.

The surrogate mothers were the end result of a long effort to break away from the homeostatic drive motivational theory of behavior. The surrogate mothers obliged by fulfilling their promise to aid in an analysis of motivation. The surrogate mothers made it possible to separate infant love for the mother from maternal love for the baby, a distinction often difficult to make due to the close physical proximity and the intimate reciprocal relationship between live mothers and infants. Furthermore, the use of inanimate monkey mothers allows the study of one variable at a time, while keeping all others constant. For instance, the primary motivating force of contact with the mother's body was studied through varying the body surface of two surrogate mothers, one with a bare body of welded wire, the other with a covering of soft terrycloth. When we raised our first Wisconsin colony, the monkeys developed such strong attachments to their cheesecloth diapers that they would wrap their entire bodies in them (Fig. 1.9). The surrogate experiments were able to show that contact comfort of the mother's body was of greater importance than breast-feeding.

The data on the surrogate mothers were crystal clear and statistically, totally significant. Contact comfort was the all important affectional variable, and activities associated with breast-feeding were relatively negligible. Obviously, infant-mother love does not have a solely liquid love basis, as the drive-reduction theory asserts. A series of experiments at the Wisconsin laboratory has demonstrated the importance of many secondary variables in addition to the primary responses to contact comfort. No important behavior is produced by a single variable, particularly in animals as complex as monkeys and humans. The infant shows more love for the mother that rocks than for one who sits firm, more love for the one who lactates than for the

Figure 1.9. *Infant rhesus and terrycloth toweling.*

nonlactating, more love for the hot mother than for the cold. In all these attributes, the infant finds solace and security.

Indeed, the mother provides much more than just contact comfort. She provides the "push" that enables the infant to establish effective peer association. In our attempt to produce a colony of breeding monkeys that were raised in isolation cages, we saw the resultant travesty of heterosexual love. The sexual behavior of the male and female chronologically adult monkeys was immature and grotesque, a pitiful distortion. These monkeys had been deprived of the experiences of maternal, infant, and age-mate love. They had not had the good fortune to exchange physical contacts with their mothers nor to continue to learn the acceptance of physical contact from other species members through peer play. In a very real way, peer play is the proving ground for subsequent successful sex, and peer love provides the opportunity to develop sexual and social roles and behaviors, in ways new and mysterious in comparison with mother's contact comfort.

Figure 1.10.   *Infant rhesus monkeys in the "partial social isolation" situation.*

However, strong as are the basic motivations of the infant love responses, infant love may be destroyed. A simple and sure way is to prevent any suggestion of any kind of love from developing. Infant love for the mother, as well as some or all other varieties of love, may be denied development as well. In the years of laboratory research, it became obvious that there is no such thing as universal love. There are at least five basic kinds of love. These five love systems are maternal love, infant love for the mother, age-mate (playmate or peer) love, heterosexual love, and paternal or father love. The complete denial of a chance for social interaction with other monkeys from birth onward will undeniably prevent any kind of love from developing.

The simplest way to prevent the development of love in monkeys is to raise them individually in bare wire cages, in what we call partial social isolation, as shown in Figure 1.10. These monkeys can see and hear other monkeys, but cannot contact them. Denied all physical contact with other monkeys from birth on, they are automatically denied all five varieties of love. The physical isolation may be termed partial, but the affectional isolation is total. It is fairly customary to see these monkeys sitting toward the front of their cages staring vacantly into outer space—a passive behavior pattern which we labeled the schizophrenic stare. Attention is turned entirely on the self, with self-mouthing, rocking and huddling, and stereotyped postures as seen in Figure 1.11.

Figure 1.11. *Typical posture and behavior of an infant rhesus reared in partial social isolation.*

Total social isolation was achieved through the use of a chamber from which the monkey could see no other animals, either monkey or human, until the predetermined period of social isolation should end. In our series of experiments monkeys were raised in isolation, either partial or total, for varying periods of time. Monkeys who were raised in total isolation for the first 90 days of life went into a stage of extreme panic or shock when exposed to the world. However, the isolates who survived the first social exposure—and not all did—made a remarkably rapid social recovery when allowed to interact with control monkeys of identical ages. These monkeys had been deprived only of maternal and infant love and had been kept in isolation only up to the stage when peer play begins to appear normally. Although we believe that no other affectional system can totally substitute for maternal love, age-mate love may be able to do so partially.

Monkeys who were raised in total isolation for the first 6 months of life failed to indicate any semblance of social adjustment when allowed interaction with normal control monkeys. Contact play was nonexistent and other social behavior might just as well have been (Fig. 1.12). Security and freedom from fear, achieved through mother, infant, and age-mate love experiences, had no chance to develop. Behavior of the unloved and unloving isolates was characterized by fear and terror reactions with no affectional bonds to ameliorate and control.

While 6 months of total social isolation produced drastic behavi-

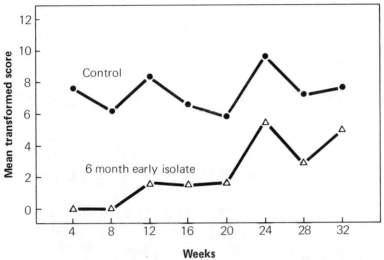

Figure 1.12. *Development of one type of social behavior (rough and tumble play)—comparison of isolates and controls.*

oral effects, monkeys totally isolated from birth for 12 months exhibited a greater frequency of withdrawal, bizarre behavior, and social incompetence than did those isolated throughout the first 6 months of life. When isolation continues through the ages in which peer play normally develops, not only is there a total deficit in social interaction, but the monkey is prone to extreme depression. The disappearance or the nonappearance of the ability to play proves itself one of the striking indicators of depression.

THE PSYCHOPATHOLOGY OF AFFECTION

Out of our researches on the several affectional systems has come a fringe benefit. Strange as it may seem, the love researches led us to study primate psychopathology with depression as the first of the models. Perhaps it is not surprising that our researches went from love to depression. Depression seldom ends in love, but love often ends in depression.

In the late 1960s, a major program was instituted at the University of Wisconsin Primate Laboratory to develop a family of behavioral techniques designed to produce psychopathology in monkeys. The goal is and has been to gain understanding and insight into both the cause and cure of human pathology.

One of the techniques used in this program is illustrated in Figure 1.13. Two sets of mothers and infants were raised in the apparatus. The infants lived with their mothers in the home cages, and they alone were allowed to play in the central compartments. At 180 days of age, plexiglas shields were inserted between the mothers in the liv-

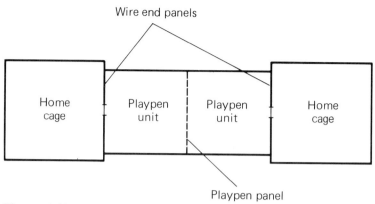

Figure 1.13. *Deprivation apparatus. Schematic diagram of the playpen situation used to study the effects of mother-infant separation.*

ing cages and the centrally located infants. These techniques have been used in subsequent research by many other investigators. The infants exhibited behavior characteristic of Bowlby's first two stages of anaclitic depression caused by the maternal separation of human infants. Prolonged protest was followed by grim despair. The monkey children were subject to crying, as illustrated in Figure 1.14, and made frantic attempts to rejoin the mother. Indeed, it reached the point where rhesus monkey babies, pigtail monkey babies, and squirrel monkey babies were subject to constant emotional jeopardy. One of our collaborators on this research, Steve Suomi, highlighted the importance of peer or age-mate separation by a series of investigations of separations of monkey infants from the ages of 3 to 9 months. The infants were isolated for a total of 20 periods involving separation for 4 days of each of the 20 weeks, and being reunited with their would-be playmates the other 3 days. During every separation period, there was clear evidence of the protest stage with exaggerated locomotion and loud vocalization. The subsequent despair was characterized by self-clasp, rock, and huddle. Beyond this, Suomi discovered a remarkable phenomenon, the phenomenon of induced behavioral infantilism. Monkey play, which should be at its height at 9 months, was absent for all practical purposes at this time, while completely infantile behaviors such as ventral clinging and self-mouthing, continued as strong at 6 and 9 months as at 3 months of age. Not only is normal development of age-mate relationships and social behavior vital for adequate affective relationships, but for any adequate personal existence at all.

Love may at times lead to depression, but depression is not a very pleasant state in which to leave a reader. The syndrome produced in monkeys through isolation from the mother, from age-mates, and even from the experimenter, leaves the monkey captured and confined within his own self-centered existence by his inability to experience and

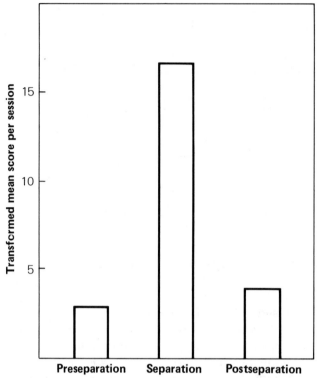

Figure 1.14.   *Effects of separation on the frequency of infant crying.*

interact with the form and fact of other animals. Recent experiments, we are delighted to report, show that under certain favorable conditions of rehabilitation therapy, these unfortunate isolates can acquire comprehension and appropriate responsiveness to other monkeys and find some joy in life.

CHAPTER 2

A CASE HISTORY IN SCIENTIFIC METHOD
B. F. Skinner

It has been said that college teaching is the only profession for which there is no professional training, and it is commonly argued that this is because our graduate schools train scholars and scientists rather than teachers. We are more concerned with the discovery of knowledge than with its dissemination. But can we justify ourselves quite so easily? It is a bold thing to say that we know how to train a man to be a scientist. Scientific thinking is the most complex and probably the most subtle of all human activities. Do we actually know how to shape up such behavior, or do we simply mean that some of the people who attend our graduate schools eventually become scientists?

Except for a laboratory course which acquaints the student with standard apparatus and standard procedures, the only explicit training in scientific method generally received by a young psychologist is a course in statistics—not the introductory course, which is often required of so many kinds of students that it is scarcely scientific at all, but an advanced course which includes "model building," "theory construction," and "experimental design." But it is a mistake to identify scientific practice with the formalized constructions of statistics and scientific method. These disciplines have their place, but it does not coincide with the place of scientific research. They offer a method of science but not, as is so often implied, *the* method. As formal disciplines they arose very late in the history of science, and most of the facts of science have been discovered without their aid. It takes a great deal of skill to fit Faraday with his wires and magnets into the picture which statistics gives us of scientific thinking. And most current scentific practice would be equally refractory, especially in the important initial stages. It is no wonder that the laboratory scientist is puzzled and often dismayed when he discovers how his behavior has been reconstructed in the formal analyses of scientific method. He is likely to protest that this is not at all a fair representation of what he does.

This paper was written for a meeting of the Eastern Psychological Association in April 1955. It was first published in *American Psychologist,* 1956, 2: 221–233. Copyright 1956 by the American Psychological Association. Reprinted by permission.

But his protest is not likely to be heard. For the prestige of statistics and scientific methodology is enormous. Much of it is borrowed from the high repute of mathematics and logic, but much of it derives from the flourishing state of the art itself. Some statisticians are professional people employed by scientific and commercial enterprises. Some are teachers and pure researchers who give their colleagues the same kind of service for nothing—or at most a note of acknowledgment. Many are zealous people who, with the best of intentions, are anxious to show the nonstatistical scientist how he can do his job more efficiently and assess his results more accurately. There are strong professional societies devoted to the advancement of statistics, and hundreds of technical books and journals are published annually.

Against this, the practicing scientist has very little to offer. He cannot refer the young psychologist to a book which will tell him how to find out all there is to know about a subject matter, how to have the good hunch which will lead him to devise a suitable piece of apparatus, how to develop an efficient experimental routine, how to abandon an unprofitable line of attack, how to move on most rapidly to later stages of his research. The work habits which have become second nature to him have not been formalized by anyone, and he may feel that they possibly never will be. As Richter (1953) has pointed out, "Some of the most important discoveries have been made without any plan of research," and "there are researchers who do not work on a verbal plane, who cannot put into words what they are doing."

If we are interested in perpetuating the practices responsible for the present corpus of scientific knowledge, we must keep in mind that some very important parts of the scientific process do not now lend themselves to mathematical, logical, or any other formal treatment. We do not know enough about human behavior to know how the scientist does what he does. Although statisticians and methodologists may seem to tell us, or at least imply, how the mind works—how problems arise, how hypotheses are formed, deductions made, and crucial experiments designed—we as psychologists are in a position to remind them that they do not have methods appropriate to the empirical observation or the functional analysis of such data. These are aspects of human behavior, and no one knows better than we how little can at the moment be said about them.

Some day we shall be better able to express the distinction between empirical analysis and formal reconstruction, for we shall have an alternative account of the behavior of Man Thinking. Such an account will not only plausibly reconstruct what a particular scientist did in any given case, it will permit us to evaluate practices and, I believe, to teach scientific thinking. But that day is some little distance in the future. Meanwhile we can only fall back on examples.

When the director of Project A of the American Psychological Association asked me to describe and analyze my activities as a research psychologist, I went through a trunkful of old notes and records and, for my pains, reread some of my earlier publications. This has made me all the more aware of the contrast between the reconstructions of formalized scientific method and at least one case of actual practice. Instead of amplifying the points I have just made by resorting to a generalized account (principally because it is not available), I should like to discuss a case history. It is not one of the case histories we should most like to have, but what it lacks in importance is perhaps somewhat offset by accessibility. I therefore ask you to imagine that you are all clinical psychologists—a task which becomes easier and easier as the years go by—while I sit across the desk from you or stretch out upon this comfortable leather couch.

The first thing I can remember happened when I was only 22 years old. Shortly after I was graduated from college Bertrand Russell published a series of articles in the old *Dial* magazine on the epistemology of John B. Watson's Behaviorism. I had had no psychology as an undergraduate but I had had a lot of biology, and two of the books which my biology professor had put into my hands were Loeb's *Physiology of the Brain* and the newly published Oxford edition of Pavlov's *Conditioned Reflexes.* And now here was Russell extrapolating the principles of an objective formulation of behavior to the problem of knowledge! Many years later when I told Lord Russell that his articles were responsible for my interest in behavior, he could only exclaim, "Good Heavens! I had always supposed that those articles had demolished Behaviorism!" But at any rate he had taken Watson seriously, and so did I.

When I arrived at Harvard for graduate study, the air was not exactly full of behavior, but Walter Hunter was coming in once a week from Clark University to give a seminar, and Fred Keller, also a graduate student, was an expert in both the technical details and the sophistry of Behaviorism. Many a time he saved me as I sank into the quicksands of an amateurish discussion of "What is an image?" or "Where is red?" I soon came into contact with W. J. Crozier, who had studied under Loeb. It had been said of Loeb, and might have been said of Crozier, that he "resented the nervous system." Whether this was true or not, the fact was that both these men talked about animal behavior without mentioning the nervous system and with surprising success. So far as I was concerned, they cancelled out the physiological theorizing of Pavlov and Sherrington and thus clarified what remained of the work of these men as the beginnings of an independent science of behavior. My doctorial thesis was in part an operational analysis of Sherrington's synapse, in which behavioral laws were substituted for supposed states of the central nervous system.

But the part of my thesis at issue here was experimental. So far as I can see, I began simply by looking for lawful processes in the behavior of the intact organism. Pavlov had shown the way; but I could

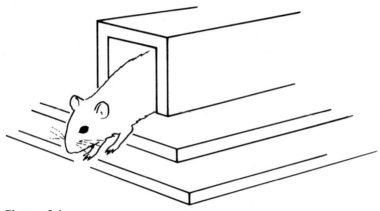

Figure 2.1.

not then, as I cannot now, move without a jolt from salivary reflexes to the important business of the organism in everyday life. Sherrington and Magnus had found order in surgical segments of the organism. Could not something of the same sort be found, to use Loeb's phrase, in "the organism as a whole"? I had the clue from Pavlov: Control your conditions and you will see order.

It is not surprising that my first gadget was a silent release box, operated by compressed air and designed to eliminate disturbances when introducing a rat into an apparatus. I used this first in studying the way a rat adapted to a novel stimulus. I built a soundproofed box containing a specially structured space. A rat was released, pneumatically, at the far end of a darkened tunnel from which it emerged in exploratory fashion into a well-lighted area. To accentuate its progress and to facilitate recording, the tunnel was placed at the top of a flight of steps, something like a functional Parthenon (Fig. 2.1). The rat would peek out from the tunnel, perhaps glancing suspiciously at the one-way window through which I was watching it, then stretch itself cautiously down the steps. A soft click (carefully calibrated, of course) would cause it to pull back into the tunnel and remain there for some time. But repeated clicks had less and less of an effect. I recorded the rat's advances and retreats by moving a pen back and forth across a moving paper tape.

The major result of this experiment was that some of my rats had babies. I began to watch young rats. I saw them right themselves and crawl about very much like the decerebrate or thalamic cats and rabbits of Magnus. So I set about studying the postural reflexes of young rats. Here was a first principle not formally recognized by scientific methodologists: When you run onto something interesting, drop everything else and study it. I tore up the Parthenon and started over.

If you hold a young rat on one hand and pull it gently by the tail, it

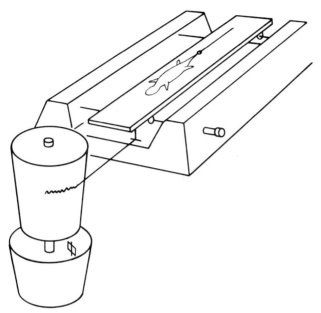

Figure 2.2.

will resist you by pulling forward and then, with a sudden sharp spring which usually disengages its tail, it will leap out into space. I decided to study this behavior quantitatively. I built a light platform covered with cloth and mounted it on tightly stretched piano wires (Fig. 2.2). Here was a version of Sherrington's torsion-wire myograph, originally designed to record the isometric contraction of the *tibialis anticus* of a cat, but here adapted to the response of a whole organism. When the tail of the young rat was gently pulled, the rat clung to the cloth floor and tugged forward. By amplifying the fine movements of the platform, it was possible to get a good kymograph record of the tremor in this motion and then, as the pull against the tail was increased, of the desperate spring into the air (Fig. 2.3).

Now, baby rats have very little future, except as adult rats. Their behavior is literally infantile and cannot be usefully extrapolated to everyday life. But if this technique would work with a baby, why not try it on a mature rat? To avoid attaching anything to the rat, it should be possible to record, not a pull against the substrate, but the ballistic thrust exerted as the rat runs forward or suddenly stops in response to my calibrated click. So, invoking the first principle of scientific practice again, I threw away the piano-wire platform and built a runway, 8 feet long. This was constructed of light wood, in the form of a U girder, mounted rigidly on vertical glass plates, the elasticity of which permitted a very slight longitudinal movement (Fig. 2.4). The runway became the floor of a long tunnel, not shown, at one end of which I

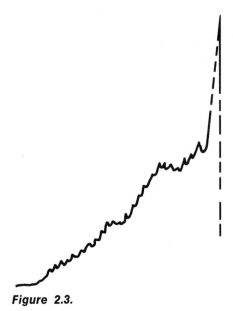

Figure 2.3.

placed my soundless release box and at the other end myself, prepared to reinforce the rat for coming down the runway by giving it a
bit of wet mash, to sound a click from time to time when it had reached
the middle of the runway, and to harvest kymograph records of the
vibrations of the substrate.

Now for a second unformalized principle of scientific practice:
Some ways of doing research are easier than others. I got tired of
carrying the rat back to the other end of the runway. A back alley
was therefore added (Fig. 2.5). Now the rat could eat a bit of mash

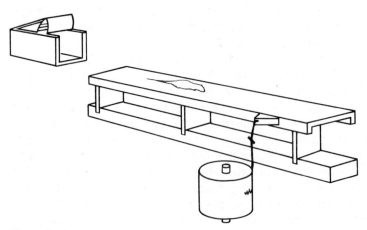

Figure 2.4.

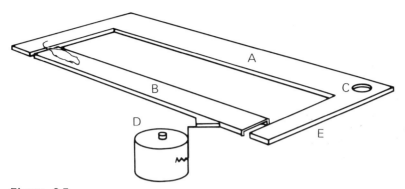

Figure 2.5.

at point C, go down the back alley A, around the end as shown, and back home by runway B. The experimenter at E could collect records from the kymograph at D in comfort. In this way a great many records were made of the forces exerted against the substratum as rats ran down the alley and occasionally stopped dead in their tracks as a click sounded (Fig. 2.6).

There was one annoying detail, however. The rat would often wait an inordinately long time at C before starting down the back alley on the next run. There seemed to be no explanation for this. When I timed these delays with a stop watch, however, and plotted them, they seemed to show orderly changes (Fig. 2.7). This was, of course, the kind of thing I was looking for. I forgot all about the movements of the substratum and began to run rats for the sake of the delay measurements alone. But there was now no reason why the runway had to be 8 feet long and, as the second principle came into play again, I saw no reason why the rat could not deliver its own reinforcement.

A new apparatus was built. In Figure 2.8 we see the rat eating a piece of food just after completing a run. It produced the food by its own action. As it ran down the back alley A to the far end of the rectangular runway, its weight caused the whole runway to tilt slightly on the axis C and this movement turned the wooden disc D, permitting a piece of food in one of the holes around its perimeter to drop through a funnel into a food dish. The food was pearl tapioca, the only kind

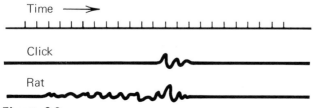

Figure 2.6.

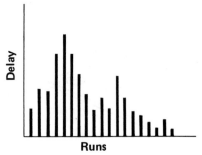

Figure 2.7.

I could find in the grocery stores in reasonably uniform pieces. The rat had only to complete its journey by coming down the homestretch B to enjoy its reward. The experimenter was able to enjoy *his* reward at the same time, for he had only to load the magazine, put in a rat, and relax. Each tilt was recorded on a slowly moving kymograph.

A third unformalized principle of scientific practice: Some people are lucky. The disc of wood from which I had fashioned the food magazine was taken from a storeroom of discarded apparatus. It happened to have a central spindle, which fortunately I had not bothered to cut off. One day it occurred to me that if I wound a string around the spindle and allowed it to unwind as the magazine was emptied (Fig. 2.9), I would get a different kind of record. Instead of a mere report of the up-and-down movement of the runway, as a series of pips as in a polygraph, I would get a *curve*. And I knew that science made great use of curves, although, so far as I could discover, very little of pips on a polygram. The difference between the old type of record at A (Fig. 2.10) and the new at B may not seem great, but as it turned out the curve revealed things in the rate of responding, and in changes in that rate, which would certainly otherwise have been missed. By allowing the string to unwind rather than to wind, I had got my curve in an awkward Cartesian quadrant, but that was

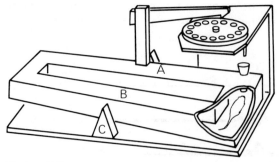

Figure 2.8.

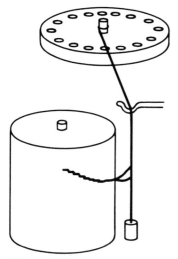

Figure 2.9.

easily remedied. Psychologists have adopted cumulative curves only very slowly, but I think it is fair to say that they have become an indispensable tool for certain purposes of analysis.

Eventually, of course, the runway was seen to be unnecessary. The rat could simply reach into a covered tray for pieces of food, and each movement of the cover could operate a solenoid to move a pen one step in a cumulative curve. The first major change in rate observed in this way was due to ingestion. Curves showing how the rate of eating declined with the time of eating comprised the other part of my thesis. But a refinement was needed. The behavior of the rat in pushing open the door was not a normal part of the ingestive behavior

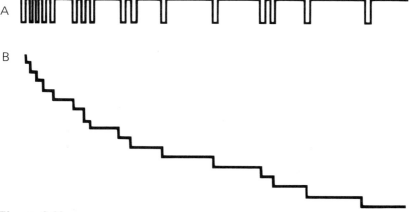

Figure 2.10.

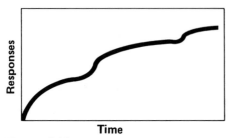

Figure 2.11.

of *Rattus rattus.* The act was obviously learned but its status as part of the final performance was not clear. It seemed wise to add an initial conditioned response connected with ingestion in a quite arbitrary way. I chose the first device which came to hand—a horizontal bar or lever placed where it could be conveniently depressed by the rat to close a switch which operated a magnetic magazine. Ingestion curves obtained with this initial response in the chain were found to have the same properties as those without it.

Now, as soon as you begin to complicate an apparatus, you necessarily invoke a fourth principle of scientific practice: Apparatuses sometimes break down. I had only to wait for the food magazine to jam to get an extinction curve. At first I treated this as a defect and hastened to remedy the difficulty. But eventually, of course, I deliberately disconnected the magazine. I can easily recall the excitement of that first complete extinction curve (Fig. 2.11). I had made contact with Pavlov at last! Here was a curve uncorrupted by the physiological process of ingestion. It was an orderly change due to nothing more than a special contingency of reinforcement. It was pure behavior! I am not saying that I would not have got around to extinction curves without a breakdown in the apparatus; Pavlov had given too strong a lead in that direction. But it is still no exaggeration to say that some of the most interesting and surprising results have turned up first because of similar accidents. Foolproof apparatus is no doubt highly desirable, but Charles Ferster and I in recently reviewing the data from a 5-year program of research found many occasions to congratulate ourselves on the fallibility of relays and vacuum tubes.

I then built four soundproofed ventilated boxes, each containing a lever and a food magazine and supplied with a cumulative recorder, and was on my way to an intensive study of conditioned reflexes in skeletal behavior. I would reinforce every response for several days and then extinguish for a day or two, varying the number of reinforcements, the amount of previous magazine training, and so on.

At this point I made my first use of the deductive method. I had long since given up pearl tapioca as too unbalanced a diet for steady use. A neighborhood druggist had shown me his pill machine, and I

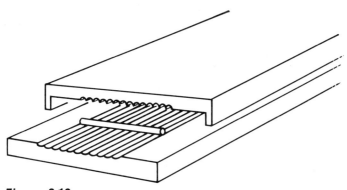

Figure 2.12.

had had one made along the same lines (Fig. 2.12). It consisted of a fluted brass bed across which one laid a long cylinder of stiff paste (in my case a MacCollum formula for an adequate rat diet). A similarly fluted cutter was then lowered onto the cylinder and rolled slowly back and forth, converting the paste into about a dozen spherical pellets. These were dried for a day or so before use. The procedure was painstaking and laborious. Eight rats eating 100 pellets each per day could easily keep up with production. One pleasant Saturday afternoon I surveyed my supply of dry pellets and, appealing to certain elemental theorems in arithmetic, deduced that unless I spent the rest of that afternoon and evening at the pill machine, the supply would be exhausted by ten-thirty Monday morning.

Since I do not wish to deprecate the hypothetico-deductive method, I am glad to testify here to its usefulness. It led me to apply our second principle of unformalized scientific method and to ask myself why *every* press of the lever had to be reinforced. I was not then aware of what had happened at the Brown laboratories, as Harold Schlosberg later told the story. A graduate student had been given the task of running a cat through a difficult discrimination experiment. One Sunday the student found the supply of cat food exhausted. The stores were closed, and so, with a beautiful faith in the frequency-theory of learning, he ran the cat as usual and took it back to its living cage unrewarded. Schlosberg reports that the cat howled its protest continuously for nearly 48 hours. Unaware of this I decided to reinforce a response only once every minute and to allow all other responses to go unreinforced. There were two results: (a) my supply of pellets lasted almost indefinitely, and (b) each rat stabilized at a fairly constant rate of responding.

Now, a steady state was something I was familiar with from physical chemistry, and I therefore embarked upon the study of periodic reinforcement. I soon found that the constant rate at which the rat stabilized depended upon how hungry it was. Hungry rat, high rate; less hungry rat, lower rate. At that time I was bothered by the practical problem of controlling food deprivation. I was working half time at the Medical School (on chronaxie of subordination!) and could not maintain a good schedule in working with the rats. The rate of responding under periodic reinforcement suggested a scheme for keeping a rat at a constant level of deprivation. The argument went like this: Suppose you reinforce the rat, not at the end of a given period, but when it has completed the number of responses ordinarily emitted in that period. And suppose you use substantial pellets of food and give the rat continuous access to the lever. Then, except for periods when the rat sleeps, it should operate the lever at a constant rate around the clock. For, whenever it grows slightly hungrier, it will work faster, get food faster, and become less hungry, while whenever It grows slightly less hungry, it will respond at a lower rate, get less food, and grow hungrier. By setting the reinforcements at a given number of responses it should even be possible to hold the rat at any given level of deprivation. I visualized a machine with a dial which one could set to make available, at any time of day or night, a rat in a given state of deprivation. Of course, nothing of the sort happens. This is "fixed-ratio" rather than "fixed-interval" reinforcement and, as I soon found out, it produces a very different type of performance. This is an example of a fifth unformalized principle of scientific practice, but one which has at least been named. Walter Cannon described it with a word invented by Horace Walpole: *serendipity*—the art of finding one thing while looking for something else.

This account of my scientific behavior up to the point at which I published my results in a book called *The Behavior of Organisms* is as exact in letter and spirit as I can now make it. The notes, data, and publications which I have examined do not show that I ever behaved in the manner of Man Thinking as described by John Stuart Mill or John Dewey or in reconstructions of scientific behavior by other philosophers of science. I never faced a Problem which was more than the eternal problem of finding order. I never attacked a problem by constructing a Hypothesis. I never deduced Theorems or submitted them to Experimental Check. So far as I can see, I had no preconceived Model of behavior—certainly not a physiological or mentalistic one and, I believe, not a conceptual one. The "reflex reserve" was an abortive, though operational, concept which was retracted a year or so after publication in a paper at the Philadelphia meeting of the APA. It lived up to my opinion of theories in general by proving utterly worthless in suggesting further experiments. Of course, I was working on a basic Assumption—that there was order in behavior if I could only discover it—but such an assumption is not to be confused with the hypotheses of deductive theory. It is also true that I exercised a certain Selection of Facts but not because of relevance to theory but because one fact was more orderly than another. If I engaged in

Experimental Design at all, it was simply to complete or extend some evidence of order already observed.

Most of the experiments described in *The Behavior of Organisms* were done with groups of four rats. A fairly common reaction to the book was that such groups were too small. How did I know that other groups of four rats would do the same thing? Keller, in defending the book, countered with the charge that groups of four were too *big.* Unfortunately, however, I allowed myself to be persuaded of the contrary. This was due in part to my association at the University of Minnesota with W. T. Heron. Through him I came into close contact for the first time with traditional animal psychology. Heron was interested in inherited maze behavior, inherited activity, and certan drugs —the effects of which could then be detected only through the use of fairly large groups. We did an experiment together on the effect of starvation on the rate of pressing a lever and started the new era with a group of 16 rats. But we had only four boxes, and this was so inconvenient that Heron applied for a grant and built a battery of 24 lever-boxes and cumulative recorders. I supplied an attachment which would record, not only the mean performance of all 24 rats in a single averaged curve, but mean curves for four subgroups of 12 rats each and 4 subgroups of 6 rats each (Heron and Skinner, 1939). We thus provided for the design of experiments according to the principles of R. A. Fisher, which were then coming into vogue. We had, so to speak, mechanized the Latin square.

With this apparatus Heron and I published a study of extinction in maze-bright and maze-dull rats using 95 subjects. Later I published mean extinction curves for groups of 24, and W. K. Estes and I did our work on anxiety with groups of the same size. But although Heron and I could properly voice the hope that "the possibility of using large groups of animals greatly improves upon the method as previously reported, since tests of significance are provided for and properties of behavior not apparent in single cases may be more easily detected," in actual practice that is not what happened. The experiments I have just mentioned are almost all we have to show for this elaborate battery of boxes. Undoubtedly more work could be done with it and would have its place, but something had happened to the natural growth of the method. You cannot easily make a change in the conditions of an experiment when 24 apparatuses have to be altered. Any gain in rigor is more than matched by a loss in flexibility. We were forced to confine ourselves to processes which could be studied with the baselines already developed in earlier work. We could not move on to the discovery of other processes or even to a more refined analysis of those we were working with. No matter how significant might be the relations we actually demonstrated, our statistical Leviathan had swum aground. The art of the method had stuck at a particular stage of its development.

Another accident rescued me from mechanized statistics and brought me back to an even more intensive concentration on the single case. In essence, I suddenly found myself face to face with the engineering problem of the animal trainer. When you have the responsibility of making absolutely sure that a given organism will engage in a given sort of behavior at a given time, you quickly grow impatient with theories of learning. Principles, hypotheses, theorems, satisfactory proof at the .05 level of significance that behavior at a choice point shows the effect of secondary reinforcement—nothing could be more irrelevant. No one goes to the circus to see the average dog jump through a hoop significantly oftener than untrained dogs raised under the same circumstances, or to see an elephant demonstrate a principle of behavior.

Perhaps I can illustrate this without giving aid and comfort to the enemy by describing a Russian device which the Germans found quite formidable. The Russians used dogs to blow up tanks. A dog was trained to hide behind a tree or wall in low brush or other cover. As a tank approached and passed, the dog ran swiftly alongside it, and a small magnetic mine attached to the dog's back was sufficient to cripple the tank or set it afire. The dog, of course, had to be replaced.

Now I ask you to consider some of the technical problems which the psychologist faces in preparing a dog for such an act of unintentional heroism. The dog must wait behind the tree for an indefinite length of time. Very well, it must therefore be intermittently reinforced for waiting. But what schedule will achieve the highest probability of waiting? If the reinforcement is to be food, what is the absolutely optimal schedule of deprivation consistent with the health of the dog? The dog must run to the tank—that can be arranged by reinforcing it with a practice tank—but it must start instantly if it is to overtake a swift tank, and how do you differentially reinforce short reaction times, especially in counteracting the reinforcement for sitting and waiting? The dog must react only to tanks, not to a refugee driving his oxcart along the road, but what are the defining properties of a tank so far as a dog is concerned?

I think it can be said that a functional analysis proved adequate in its technological application. Manipulation of environmental conditions alone made possible a wholly unexpected practical control. Behavior could be shaped up according to specifications and maintained indefinitely almost at will. One behavioral technologist who worked with me at the time (Keller Breland) is now specializing in the production of behavior as a salable commodity and has described this new profession in the *American Psychologist* (Breland, 1951).

There are many useful applications within psychology itself. Ratliff and Blough have recently conditioned pigeons to serve as psychophysical observers. In their experiment a pigeon may adjust one of two spots of light until the two are equally bright or it may hold a spot of light at the absolute threshold during dark adaptation. The techniques which they have developed to induce pigeons to do this are only indirectly related to the point of their experiments and hence exemplify the application of a behavioral science (Ratliff and Blough, 1954). The field in which a better technology of behavior is perhaps most urgently needed is education. I cannot describe here the applications which are now possible, but perhaps I can indicate my enthusiasm by hazarding the guess that educational techniques at all age levels are on the threshold of revolutionary changes.

The effect of a behaviorial technology on scientific practice is the issue here. Faced with practical problems in behavior, you necessarily emphasize the refinement of *experimental* variables. As a result, some of the standard procedures of statistics appear to be circumvented. Let me illustrate. Suppose that measurements have been made on two groups of subjects differing in some detail of experimental treatment. Means and standard deviations for the two groups are determined, and any difference due to the treatment is evaluated. If the difference is in the expected direction but is not statistically significant, the almost universal recommendation would be to study larger groups. But our experience with practical control suggests that we may reduce the troublesome variability by changing the conditions of the experiment. By discovering, elaborating, and fully exploiting every relevant variable, we may eliminate *in advance of measurement* the individual differences which obscure the difference under analysis. This will achieve the same result as increasing the size of groups, and it will almost certainly yield a bonus in the discovery of new variables which would not have been identified in the statistical treatment.

The same may be said of smooth curves. In our study of anxiety, Estes and I published several curves, the reasonable smoothness of which was obtained by averaging the performances of 12 rats for each curve. The individual curves published at that time show that the mean curves do not faithfully represent the behavior of any one rat. They show a certain tendency toward a change in slope which supported the point we were making, and they may have appeared to warrant averaging for that reason.

But an alternative method would have been to explore the individual case until an equally smooth curve could be obtained. This would have meant not only rejecting the temptation to produce smoothness by averaging cases, but manipulating all relevant conditions as we later learned to manipulate them for practical purposes. The individual curves which we published at that time point to the need not for larger groups but for improvement in experimental technique. Here, for example, is a curve the smoothness of which is characteristic of current practice. Such curves were shown in the making in a demonstration which Ferster and I arranged at the Cleveland meeting of the

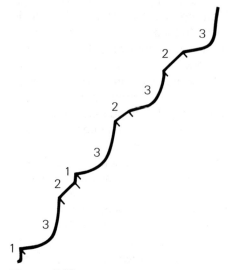

Figure 2.13.

American Psychological Association (Fig. 2.13). Here, in a single organism, three different schedules of reinforcement are yielding corresponding performances with great uniformity under appropriate stimuli alternating at random. One does not reach this kind of order through the application of statistical methods.

In *The Behavior of Organisms* I was content to deal with the overall slopes and curvature of cumulative curves and could make only a rough classification of the properties of behavior shown by the finer grain. The grain has now been improved. The resolving power of the microscope has been greatly increased, and we can see fundamental processes of behavior in sharper and sharper detail. In choosing rate of responding as a basic datum, and in recording this conveniently in a cumulative curve, we make important temporal aspects of behavior *visible.* Once this has happened, our scientific practice is reduced to simple looking. A new world is opened to inspection. We use such curves as we use a microscope, X-ray camera, or telescope. This is well exemplified by recent extensions of the method. These are no longer part of my case history, but perhaps you will permit me to consult you about what some critics have described as a *folie à deux* or group neurosis.

An early application of the method to the behavior of avoidance and escape was made by Keller in studying the light aversion of the rat. This was brilliantly extended by Murray Sidman in his shock-avoidance experiments. It is no longer necessary to describe avoidance and escape by appeal to "principles," for we may *watch* the behavior develop when we have arranged the proper contingencies of reinforcement, as we later watch it change as these contingencies are changed.

Hunt and Brady have extended the use of a stable rate in the study of anxiety-producing stimuli and have shown that the depression in rate is eliminated by electroconvulsive shock and by other measures which are effective in reducing anxiety in human patients. O. R. Lindsley has found the same thing for dogs, using insulin-shock therapy and sedatives. Brady has refined the method by exploring the relevance of various schedules of reinforcement in tracing the return of the conditioned depression after treatment. In these experiments you *see* the effect of a treatment as directly as you see the constriction of a capillary under the microscope.

Early work with rats on caffeine and Benzedrine has been extended by Lindsley with dogs. A special technique for evaluating several effects of a drug in a single short experimental period yields a record of behavior which can be read as a specialist reads an electrocardiogram. Dr. Peter Dews of the Department of Pharmacology at the Harvard Medical School is investigating dose-response curves and the types and effects of various drugs, using pigeons as subjects. In the Psychological Laboratories at Harvard additional work on drugs is being carried out by Morse, Herrnstein, and Marshall, and the technique is being adopted by drug manufacturers. There could scarcely be a better demonstration of the experimental treatment of variability. In a *single* experimental session with a *single* organism one observes the onset, duration, and decline of the effects of a drug.

The direct observation of *defective* behavior is particularly important. Clinical or experimental damage to an organism is characteristically unique. Hence the value of a method which permits the direct observation of the behavior of the individual. Lindsley has studied the effects of near-lethal irradiation, and the effects of prolonged anesthesia and anoxia are currently being examined by Thomas Lohr in co-operation with Dr. Henry Beecher of the Massachusetts General Hospital. The technique is being applied to neurological variables in the monkey by Dr. Karl Pribram at the Hartford Institute. The pattern of such research is simple: establish the behavior in which you are interested, submit the organism to a particular treatment, and then look again at the behavior. An excellent example of the use of experimental control in the study of *motivation* is some work on obesity by J. E. Anliker in collaboration with Dr. Jean Mayer of the Harvard School of Public Health, where abnormalities of ingestive behavior in several types of obese mice can be compared by direct inspection.

There is perhaps no field in which behavior is customarily described more indirectly than psychiatry. In an experiment at the Massachusetts State Hospital, O. R. Lindsley (1956) is carrying out an extensive program which might be characterized as a quantitative study of the temporal properties of psychotic behavior. Here again it is a question of making certain characteristics of the behavior visible.

The extent to which we can eliminate sources of variability be-

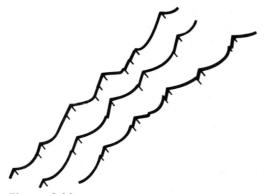

Figure 2.14.

fore measurement is shown by a result which has an unexpected significance for comparative psychology and the study of individual differences. Figure 2.14 shows tracings of three curves which report behavior in response to a multiple fixed-interval fixed-ratio schedule. The
hatches mark reinforcements. Separating them in some cases are
short, steep lines showing a high constant rate on a fixed-ratio schedule and, in others, somewhat longer "scallops" showing a smooth
acceleration as the organism shifts from a very low rate just after reinforcement to a higher rate at the end of the fixed interval. The values of
the intervals and ratios, the states of deprivation, and the exposures to
the schedules were different in the three cases, but except for these
details the curves are quite similar. Now, one of them was made by a
pigeon in some experiments by Ferster and me, one was made by a
rat in an experiment on anoxia by Lohr, and the third was made by a
monkey in Karl Pribram's laboratory at the Hartford Institute. Pigeon,
rat, monkey, which is which? It doesn't matter. Of course, these three
species have behavioral repertoires which are as different as their anat-
omies. But once you have allowed for differences in the ways in which
they make contact with the environment, and in the ways in which they
act upon the environment, what remains of their behavior shows astonishingly similar properties. Mice, cats, dogs, and human children
could have added other curves to this figure. And when organisms
which differ as widely as this nevertheless show similar properties of
behavior, differences between members of the same species may be
viewed more hopefully. Difficult problems of idiosyncrasy or individuality
will always arise as products of biological and cultural processes, but
it is the very business of the experimental analysis of behavior to devise
techniques which reduce their effects except when they are explicitly
under investigation.

    We are within reach of a science of the individual. This will be
achieved, not by resorting to some special theory of knowledge in

which intuition or understanding takes the place of observation and analysis, but through an increasing grasp of relevant conditions to produce order in the individual case.

A second consequence of an improved technology is the effect upon behavior theory. As I have pointed out elsewhere, it is the function of learning theory to create an imaginary world of law and order and thus to console us for the disorder we observe in behavior itself. Scores on a T-maze or jumping stand hop about from trial to trial almost capriciously. Therefore we argue that if learning is, as we hope, a continuous and orderly process, it must be occurring in some other system of dimensions—perhaps in the nervous system, or in the mind, or in a conceptual model of behavior. Both the statistical treatment of group means and the averaging of curves encourage the belief that we are somehow going behind the individual case to an otherwise inaccessible, but more fundamental, process. The whole tenor of our paper on anxiety, for example, was to imply that the change we observed was not necessarily a property of behavior, but of some theoretical state of the organism ("anxiety") which was merely *reflected* in a slight modification of performance.

When we have achieved a practical control over the organism, theories of behavior lose their point. In representing and managing relevant variables, a conceptual model is useless; we come to grips with behavior itself. When behavior shows order and consistency, we are much less likely to be concerned with physiological or mentalistic causes. A datum emerges which takes the place of theoretical fantasy. In the experimental analysis of behavior we address ourselves to a subject matter which is not only manifestly the behavior of an individual and hence accessible without the usual statistical aids but also "objective" and "actual" without recourse to deductive theorizing.

Statistical techniques serve a useful function, but they have acquired a purely honorific status which may be troublesome. Their presence or absence has become a shibboleth to be used in distinguishing between good and bad work. Because measures of behavior have been highly variable, we have come to trust only results obtained from large numbers of subjects. Because some workers have intentionally or unconsciously reported only selected favorable instances, we have come to put a high value on research which is planned in advance and reported in its entirety. Because measures have behaved capriciously, we have come to value skillful deductive theories which restore order. But although large groups, planned experiments, and valid theorizing are associated with significant scientific results, it does not follow that nothing can be achieved in their absence. Here are two brief examples of the choice before us.

How can we determine the course of dark adaptation in a pigeon? We move a pigeon from a bright light to a dark room. What happens? Presumably the bird is able to see fainter and fainter patches of light

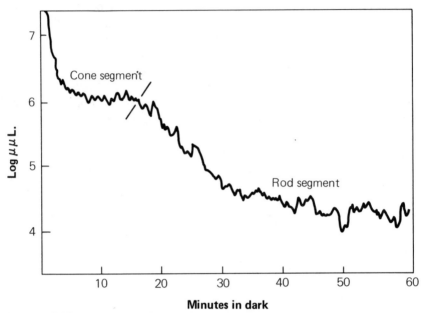

Figure 2.15.

as the process of adaptation takes place, but how can we follow this process? One way would be to set up a discrimination apparatus in which choices would be made at specific intervals after the beginning of dark adaptation. The test patches of light could be varied over a wide range, and the percentages of correct choices at each value would enable us eventually to locate the threshold fairly accurately. But hundreds of observations would be needed to establish only a few points on the curve and to prove that these show an actual change in sensitivity. In the experiment by Blough already mentioned, the pigeon holds a spot of light close to the threshold throughout the experimental period. A single curve, such as the one sketched in Figure 2.15, yields as much information as hundreds of readings, together with the means and standard deviations derived from them. The information is more accurate because it applies to a single organism in a single experimental session. Yet many psychologists who would accept the first as a finished experiment because of the tables of means and standard deviations would boggle at the second or call it a preliminary study. The direct evidence of one's senses in observing a process of behavior is not trusted.

As another example, consider the behavior of several types of obese mice. Do they all suffer from a single abnormality in their eating behavior or are there differences? One might attempt to answer this with some such measure of hunger as an obstruction apparatus. The numbers of crossings of a grid to get to food, counted after dif-

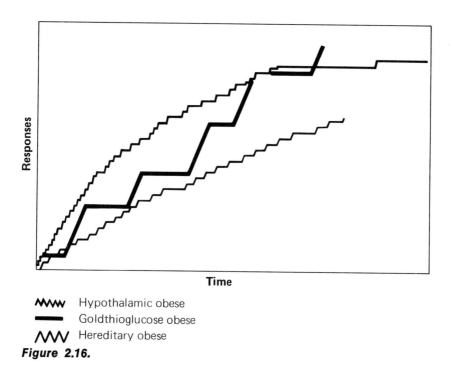

MWW Hypothalamic obese
■■■ Goldthioglucose obese
/\/\/ Hereditary obese

Figure 2.16.

ferent periods of free access to food, would be the data. Large numbers of readings would be needed, and the resulting mean values would possibly not describe the behavior of any one mouse in any experimental period. A much better picture may be obtained with one mouse of each kind in single experimental sessions, as Anliker and Mayer (1956) have shown. In an experiment reported roughly in Figure 2.16, each mouse was reinforced with a small piece of food after completing a short "ratio" of responses. The hypothalamic-obese mouse shows an exaggerated but otherwise normal ingestion curve. The hereditary-obese mouse eats slowly but for an indefinite length of time and with little change in rate. The gold poisoned obese mouse shows a sharp oscillation between periods of very rapid responding and no responding at all. These three individual curves contain more information than could probably ever be generated with measures requiring statistical treatment, yet they will be viewed with suspicion by many psychologists because they are single cases.

It is perhaps natural that psychologists should awaken only slowly to the possibility that behavioral processes may be directly observed, or that they should only gradually put the older statistical and theoretical techniques in their proper perspective. But it is time to insist that science does not progress by carefully designed steps called "experiments" each of which has a well-defined beginning and end. Science is a continuous and often a disorderly and accidental process.

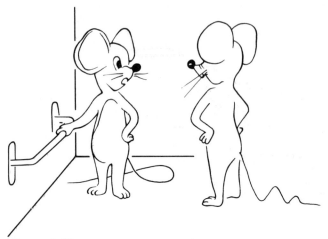

Figure 2.17.

We shall not do the young psychologist any favor if we agree to reconstruct our practices to fit the pattern demanded by current scientific methodology. What the statistician means by the design of experiments is design which yields the kind of data to which *his* techniques are applicable. He does not mean the behavior of the scientist in his laboratory devising research for his own immediate and possibly inscrutable purposes.

The organism whose behavior is most extensively modified and most completely controlled in research of the sort I have described is the experimenter himself. The point was well made by a cartoonist in the Columbia *Jester* (Fig. 2.17). The caption read: "Boy, have I got this guy conditioned! Every time I press the bar down he drops in a piece of food." The subjects we study reinforce us much more effectively than we reinforce them. I have been telling you simply how I have been conditioned to behave. And of course it is a mistake to argue too much from one case history. My behavior would not have been shaped as it was were it not for personal characteristics which all psychologists fortunately do not share. Freud has had something to say about the motivation of scientists and has given us some insight into the type of person who achieves the fullest satisfaction from precise experimental design and the intricacies of deductive systems. Such a person tends to be more concerned with his success as a scientist than with his subject matter, as is shown by the fact that he often assumes the role of a roving ambassador. If this seems unfair, let me hasten to characterize my own motivation in equally unflattering terms. Several years ago I spent a pleasant summer writing a novel called *Walden Two.* One of the characters, Frazier, said many things which I was not yet ready to say myself. Among them was this:

I have only one important characteristic, Burris: I'm stubborn. I've had only one idea in my life—a true idée fixe . . . to put it as bluntly as possible, the idea of having my own way. "Control" expresses it, I think. The control of human behavior, Burris.

In my early experimental days it was a frenzied, selfish desire to dominate. I remember the rage I used to feel when a prediction went awry. I could have shouted at the subjects of my experiments, "Behave, damn you, behave as you ought!" Eventually I realized that the subjects were always right. They always behaved as they ought. It was I who was wrong. I had made a bad prediction.

(In fairness to Frazier and the rest of myself, I want to add his next remark: "And what a strange discovery for a would-be tyrant, that the only effective technique of control is unselfish." Frazier means, of course, positive reinforcement.)

We have no more reason to say that all psychologists should behave as I have behaved than that they should all behave like R. A. Fisher. The scientist, like any organism, is the product of a unique history. The practices which he finds most appropriate will depend in part upon this history. Fortunately, personal idiosyncrasies usually leave a negligible mark on science as public property. They are important only when we are concerned with the encouragement of scientists and the prosecution of research. When we have at last an adequate empirical account of the behavior of Man Thinking, we shall understand all this. Until then, it may be best not to try to fit all scientists into any single mold.

REFERENCES

Anlinker, J. and Mayer, J. 1956. Operant conditioning technique for studying feeding patterns in normal and obese mice. *Journal of Applied Psychology* 8:667–670.

Breland, K. and Breland, Marion 1951. A field of applied animal psychology. *American Psychologist* 6:202–204.

Heron, W. T. and Skinner, B. F. 1939. An apparatus for the study of behavior. *Psychological Research* 3:166–176.

Lindsley, O. R. 1956. Operant conditioning methods applied to research in chronic schizophrenia. *Psychiatric Research Report* 5:118–139.

Ratliff, F. and Blough, D. S. 1954. Behavioral studies of visual processes in the pigeon. Report of Contract N5Ori-07663, Psychological Laboratories, Harvard University, September 1954.

Richter, C. P. 1953. Free research versus design research. *Science* 118:91–93.

SECTION TWO

BIOLOGICAL FOUNDATIONS IN PSYCHOLOGICAL RESEARCH

Most students enrolled in introductory psychology courses are interested in understanding human behavior. They are perplexed to find that so much of the data from contemporary psychology come from studies involving the use of animals. If psychology is primarily interested in the study of human behavior, why study animals at all?

Clearly, the editors of this book felt that the study of animals was important. You are about to read chapters in which the central characters are ants, sheep, cats, guinea pigs, and dogs as well as rats. When you add to this list the chapters by Harlow and Skinner

(Section 1), you will see that a substantial part of this book is devoted to the study of animals. This should lay to rest once and for all the notion that psychology is interested only in the behavior of rats and college sophomores, sometimes considered interchangeable. Still, we are left with the question, why study animals at all?

There are two different answers to that question. The first is convenience. It is possible to perform experiments upon animals which would be too dangerous or too immoral to perform upon humans. The second answer involves the issue of biological perspective. Even those psychologists who are primarily interested in human behavior, must perform their research within the framework provided by evolutionary theory. That is, the behavior of humans and of animals must be seen as products of the natural world. The study of animals enables the psychologist to avoid both the fallacy that man is nothing but an animal and its opposite—that man is something other than an animal.

Psychologists involved with animal research can be viewed as falling between two extremes. One group considers the behavior of species in their natural environment as a source of endless fascination. Their approach is often "biological" and the central question their research poses is how different species living in different environments have solved their common problems of survival and reproduction. Research is focused on differences between different species rather than similarities to human behavior. On the other hand, some psychologists are primarily interested in the study of processes such as learning, motivation and hunger, development, etc. They view the laboratory animal as simply a convenient replacement for a human subject.

Perhaps the clearest examples of the two extremes in this book are the chapters by Skinner (Chapter 2) and Topoff (Chapter 3). Skinner is not interested in the pigeon and the rat as they exist in nature, but rather, in understanding the factors which control the probability of certain classes of response. By contrast, Topoff is interested in the specific social behavior of army ants as it occurs in nature. He would define a successful laboratory experiment by the degree to which it accounted for the behavior he saw in the field, not by its help in explaining some aspect of human behavior.

Although these two approaches differ radically, a recurring theme in several of the chapters indicates that both are needed. Some of the recent work of "reinforcement" psychologists has made it clear that many so-called "universal" laws of behavior will have to be amended to take into account the particular environments within which these animals evolved. Topoff's study of social behavior in ants also contributes to the understanding of the evolution of social behavior throughout the whole animal kingdom. The chapters by Bermant, Collier and his associates, and Fuller (Chapters 4, 5, and 6) fall somewhere between the two extremes. Fuller, who uses an animal as a model for developing organisms in general and human children in particular, is also aware that the same environmental events may have different effects in different species. In fact, he uses different breeds of dogs to explore this problem.

Throughout this section, as elsewhere in this book, you will find that the whole course of a scientist's research program may be totally reshaped by unexpected and seemingly trivial events. For example, whether or not subjects remained in a transport cage turned out to be a critical factor for Fuller's research. As a result of this issue, almost accidentally raised, Fuller acquired an important insight into the nature of developmental processes.

The two remaining chapters in this section reflect the growing interest among psychologists in the study of ecology, that branch of biology concerned with the interrelationships of animals with their natural environments. Whether it is feeding behavior, as in Collier's chapter, or sexual behavior, as in Bermant's, the form which that behavior takes reflects the nature of the animal's environment. That environment includes social as well as physical features and, for humans, it includes language. Instead of looking for "universal" laws of behavior applicable across species, it may be more profitable to understand the behavioral strategies peculiar to a given species.

When Bermant discusses the Coolidge effect in sexual behavior of animals and man, it is clear that the effect is different in different species and that its magnitude seems to be related to the social organization of the species and not simply to its physiology. Although he has no doubt that man is an animal, Bermant's conjectures about experiments on human sexual behavior make it clear how important that larger social context is and how critical are the differences between species. Thus, paradoxically, it is to the student of animal behavior that we may yet owe our fullest understanding of what is uniquely human about human beings.

THE SOCIAL ORGANIZATION OF ARMY ANTS: INTEGRATION OF FIELD AND LABORATORY RESEARCH
Howard Topoff

FROM BROOKLYN TO THE TROPICAL RAIN FOREST

The night of July 10 was particularly uncomfortable for sleeping, and I awoke at 5:00 A.M. The temperature was 83 degrees and the humidity a thick 94 percent. My bed was located on a screened porch, and through the darkness of the tropical night I could hear the chugging of cargo ships and oil tankers moving across Gatun Lake in the Panama Canal. This was my second night on Barro Colorado Island, a research station of the Smithsonian Institution, situated in the Panama Canal Zone of Central America (Fig. 3.1).

The climate of the island is tropical, with a dry season from December to May, and a wet season from May to November. The heavy rains fall during July and August, and I wondered how long it would take for my body to adjust to the unrelenting dampness. My pillow, mattress, and clothes constantly felt as if they had been removed from a dryer that was turned off after completing only half a cycle.

It was now 5:30 A.M. and I had to hurry. I dressed quickly and headed for the laboratory to assemble my field equipment. In the lab, I put on a pair of heavy leather boots that had been waterproofed with silicone paste. Next I checked my knapsack to make sure that it contained all of the materials I would need that morning: compass, camera, forceps, measuring tape, collecting jars, small shovel, plastic bags, magnifying glass, field markers, water canteen, and a topographic map of the island. I secured the knapsack tightly across my back. Then I positioned a headlamp firmly on my forehead, and clipped the lamp's battery pack to my belt. Finally, I sprayed my clothes, boots, arms, hands, and neck with a copious dose of mosquito repellent. Heavily laden, I trod out of the laboratory and headed

Dr. Topoff is in the Department of Psychology, Hunter College of The City University of New York, and Department of Animal Behavior, The American Museum of Natural History. Supported by a grant (#1723) from the Research Foundation of The City University of New York.

Figure 3.1. *View of the boat dock and laboratory (above) of the Smithsonian Tropical Research Institute on Barro Colorado Island.*

for Wheeler Trail, one of the many narrow paths that radiate outward from the laboratory clearing across the 3-mile wide island (Fig. 3.2).

It was still quite dark on the floor of the tropical forest, and I could just detect the first soft glow of morning light penetrating the incredibly thick canopy of trees that rose 200 feet above me. I walked approximately 1 mile along the mud-soaked trail, slapping continuously at the hordes of mosquitoes that encircled my head and kept pace with me along the entire route. I finally came to an orange plastic flag which I had placed as a marker on the trail the day before. At the flag I made a right turn, left the trail, and untangled my way through the forest underbrush. I was able to orient only by following a series of orange flags that fluoresced under the projecting beam of my headlamp. I penetrated the lush growth of the forest for approximately 85 meters and finally came to the last flag. I stopped, turned off my headlamp, and stood motionless. Just ahead was a sight that

Figure 3.2. *Wheeler Trail, extending from the laboratory across Barro Colorado Island. There are only a few places along the trail where sunlight can penetrate the thick canopy of trees and reach the forest floor. During the rainy season, with a rainfall of well over 100 in., the trails are muddy and very slippery.*

few human beings have ever seen: a nest of the Central American army ant *Eciton hamatum*. And what a sight it was! A cylindrical nest almost one meter in diameter suspended from beneath a hanging log, and composed of the interlocked bodies of almost 500,000 ants (Fig. 3.3). I moved slowly toward the nest, and as I approached to within a few meters of it, I could see the nest pulsate as thousands of ants began to shift their position in preparation for the start of their morning activities. As I watched them, I recalled the circumstances that brought me to the tropics to study the social behavior of these fascinating animals.

As a teenager in junior high school, I was not one of those precocious "scientific-type" kids. As a result, my first exposure to army ants did not come from reading natural history books. On the con-

Figure 3.3. *Cylindrical bivouac of the army ant,* Eciton hamatum, *suspended from beneath a fallen log. The nest is composed of the interlocked bodies of approximately 500,000 ants. This temporary nest serves the colony as a base for raiding, a shelter, and an incubator for the developing brood.*

trary, I first heard about these insects when my English teacher assigned a short science fiction story entitled *Leinengen Versus The Ants,* by Carl Stephenson. The story was based upon old legends of huge armies of ants in the Amazon valley of South America. I was totally captivated by this tale of man-against-insect, and even today I can still recall many of its passages. One particularly vivid scene opens with a Brazilian District official rushing to Leinengen to warn him that the ant army will reach his plantation in two days, and he pleads with Leinengen to abandon the area.

> *"Leinengen!" he shouted. "You're insane! They're not creatures you can fight—they're an act of God! Ten miles long, two miles wide—ants, nothing but ants! And every single one of them a fiend from hell; before you can spit three times they'll eat a full grown buffalo to the bones. I tell you if you don't clear out at once there'll be nothing left of you but a skeleton picked as clean as your own plantation."*

But Leinengen was stubborn. He had devoted many hard years to building up his plantation, and was not about to turn it over to a swarm of ants. He was banking on the protection of a water-filled ditch which he had constructed around his property. When the ants found this obstacle to be but a momentary barrier, Leinengen poured gasoline into the moat. When this tactic also failed, he had no choice but to reach the dam and flood the entire plantation, a decision that forced him to run for 2 miles through the swarming ants. Leinengen was saved, but the plantation was not.

Many years later, when I left Brooklyn and began studying army ants professionally, my main sources of information shifted to the more traditional (but less exciting) scientific literature. The first thing I discovered was that the massive predatory raids of army ants were well known and had been described by naturalists more than 100 years ago. Furthermore, even in real life, army ants were evidently among the most notorious of all animals. In fact, many descriptions of their behavior in the scientific literature were not altogether unlike my image of them as conveyed in the science fiction stories I had read years earlier. For example, the field naturalist Henry Bates observed the movements of army ants in the Amazon forest in 1863, and described them as follows:

> *Wherever they pass all the rest of the animal world is thrown into a state of alarm. They stream along the ground and climb to the summits of all the lower trees, searching every leaf to its apex, and whenever booty is plentiful, they concentrate all their forces on it, the dense phalanx of shining and quickly-moving bodies looking like a flood of dark red liquid. All soft-bodied and inactive insects fall an easy prey to them and they tear their victims to pieces for facility of carriage.*

Many of the early naturalists were particularly struck by the analogy of army ants to human armies; they could not describe the movements of army ant colonies without using strong military metaphors. Consider, for example, this description by A. Hyatt Verill, another explorer of animal life in South America:

> *In all the world, the army ants of the tropics are the most remarkable in many ways. Utterly blind, yet they move in vast armies across the land, overcoming every obstacle other than fire and water, maintaining perfect formation, moving with military precision and like a real army having their scouts, their engineering corps and their fighting soldiers.*

Needless to say, the accounts of the behavior and ecological devastations of army ants by the early naturalists (not to mention those of science fiction writers) are grossly exaggerated. On the other hand, the movements of army ant colonies are so spectacular in tropical habitats that it is quite understandable why these insects have fascinated so many generations of scientists. But this is the twentieth century, not the nineteenth. The days of the pith helmet and bushjacket safaris into the innermost regions of the "jungle" to seek out the mysteries of nature are just about over. As a result, any student taking introductory psychology would be perfectly justified in wondering why a professional psychologist would leave the comfortable confines of a laboratory in New York City, and travel 3000 miles to a rain-soaked and mosquito-infested tropical forest to study the behavior of these insects. The answer to this question lies in the very nature and goals of the science of psychology.

PSYCHOLOGY AND EVOLUTION—IS THE MARRIAGE A BLESSING OR A CURSE?

Psychology is a science that objectively studies the behavior of organisms. It is a discipline that attempts to understand how behavior is influenced by processes taking place within the organism and by external events in the organism's physical and social environment. This is a very broad definition indeed, and the goal is a difficult one to achieve when we realize that there are well over a million living species of organisms within the animal kingdom.

Many beginning students of psychology do not seem to appreciate why it is important for psychologists to study the behavior of many species of vertebrate and invertebrate animals, and not to restrict their studies only to human beings. In a real sense we owe a debt of gratitude to Charles Darwin for educating us in this respect. After the publication of Darwin's two most important works, *The Origin of Species* and *The Descent of Man,* scientists accepted the notion that human beings belong within the animal kingdom, and that humans share some kind of evolutionary relationship with all other species in the kingdom. Darwin also pointed out that the theory of evolution encompasses not only the evolution of body structures; it also attempts to account for the progressive changes in patterns of behavior that have enabled species to adapt to their environment. But comparing the biology and behavior of different species within the framework of evolutionary theory is not as easy as it sounds. To see why this is so, let's consider as an example the evolution of the primates. The fossil record clearly shows that human beings and other primate species, such as the chimpanzee, have evolved from a common ancestor. As a result, both humans and chimpanzees possess characteristics that categorize them as primates, such as five fingers and toes, well developed eyes, and a clavicle (or collarbone), to cite just a few. We must not forget, however, that human beings did not evolve from any *living* group of chimpanzees. On the contrary, since the ancestral populations diverged, humans and chimpanzees have been evolving different characteristics for millions of years. The result is that although humans and chimpanzees share some characteristics, they are totally unique with respect to others. For example, comparative anatomists have found that the clavicle is structurally very similar in all living species of primates, including humans. In addition, paleontologists have shown that the clavicles of living primates are also very similar to those found in extinct fossil primates. As a result, we may safely conclude that the clavicle has not changed appreciably throughout the evolutionary period since the separation of humans and their closest living relatives.

Psychologists are not terribly interested in clavicles; they are very interested, however, in behavior. Is it logical for psychologists to conclude that because the clavicle is so similar in all living and extinct primates, the behavior of all primates must be at least as similar? The obvious answer to this question is no, but the reason may not be so obvious. Behavior is very much influenced by the structure and function of the nervous system. Although some structures, such as the clavicle, may have remained relatively unchanged throughout primate evolution, other structures, such as the nervous system, evolved at a much higher rate and along considerably different routes among all species of primates. Taxonomists separate the human species from all other primates by placing humans in a separate family, the Hominidae. This separation is hardly based on structural characteristics, but on the fact that human behavior is so different from that of all other primates. The moral of this example is clear. Evolutionary theory tells us that patterns of behavior often evolve at a different rate from that of structural characteristics. As a result, we have to be very cautious about extrapolating the results of behavioral studies from one species to another, no matter how similar the species may be morphologically.

To complicate matters even more for the psychologist, let's turn the question around. If it is true that closely related species may indeed have very different behavioral patterns, is it also possible that two species may exhibit apparently similar behavioral patterns which are caused by very different structural and functional characteristics? The answer to this question is yes! To understand why, consider the following example. Suppose your instructor sets up a microscope demonstration of the unicellular protozoan ameba. You look through the microscope and observe the animal approach a particle of food, surround it with pseudopodia, and ingest it. If your instructor asks you to name this pattern of behavior, you would probably call it feeding behavior. Now consider what name you would give to the pattern of human behavior that involves the ingestion of a steak dinner. Again, you would probably call it feeding behavior. Suppose your instructor asks you whether the mechanisms of these patterns of behavior are the same for the ameba and for the human being? Your answer would undoubtedly be an emphatic no! The point is that we all understand that the term "feeding" is a descriptive term which we, as human beings, assign to patterns of behavior in other species of animals if their behavior *looks* similar to what *we* do when we feed. Psychologists understand that the label "feeding behavior" merely calls attention to an adaptive behavioral pattern that has evolved in every species of animal. We must always keep in mind, however, that a *descriptive term* is not an *analytic term;* that is, it does not provide any information about the similarities and differences in the mechanisms that cause the behavior in different species.

There are many descriptive terms that psychologists apply to the behavior of many species of animals, including human beings. Can you think of any? How about aggressive behavior, sexual behavior, or social behavior? In each case the principal goal of the psychologist is to go beyond the mere labeling of patterns of behavior. The scientist must determine to what degree patterns of behavior in human beings and other species have similar causes, and to what degree their behavior is determined by structures and physiological processes that are unique to each species. To achieve this goal, psychologists must not restrict their studies to human beings and the white rat. They must expand their horizons and study the similarities and differences in the causes of behavior in as many species of invertebrate and vertebrate animals as possible.

THE SOCIAL BEHAVIOR OF ARMY ANTS

For the past 10 years, I have been interested in the evolution and development of social behavior, a phenomenon certainly characteristic of human beings. Social behavior is based on the tendency of individuals to form relatively permanent associations with other members of their species. By almost every criterion imaginable, human societies are organized through some of the most complex biological, psychological, and cultural processes that exist in the animal kingdom. Nevertheless, complex patterns of social behavior have also evolved many times among invertebrates, especially among the insects. Permanent societies of insects are found in the termites, and in many species of bees and wasps; however, invertebrate social behavior has evolved its greatest degree of complexity among the almost 10,000 species of ants, which comprise the insect family Formicidae (from the Latin word *formica,* which means "ant"). I will discuss the social behavior of a group of species popularly known as army ants. These ants comprise the ant subfamily Dorylinae (so named from the Greek word *dory,* meaning spear, which probably alludes to their potent sting). There are several hundred species of doryline ants in the world, most confined to tropical habitats. Several species have evolved adaptations for living in more temperate climates.

Colonies of army ants typically consist of a single queen, a brood of developing young, and a great population of adult workers. The queen is the sole reproductive agent in the colony, and is therefore ultimately responsible for the massive size of the colony. In many species she is approximately twice as large as the biggest workers and also much stouter (Fig. 3.4). The bulk of her weight is concentrated in her abdomen, the site of her immense reproductive capacity. At regular intervals her abdomen swells with fatty tissues and eggs, as

Figure 3.4. *Queen of the army ant* Neivamyrmex nigrescens *attended by worker ants.*

she enters the gravid (or physogastric) state. During this interval, which lasts approximately one week, she may lay well over 100,000 eggs.

The brood passes through four successive stages of development: embryo, larva, pupa, and finally the adult ant, which on emergence from the pupal stage is lightly pigmented and readily recognizable as a callow worker. The brood and adult worker populations consist of sterile females whose sterility is due to underdeveloped ovaries. In some species of army ants, the workers developing from a given batch of eggs typically vary in size and structure, a condition known as polymorphism (Fig. 3.5). Adult ants, differing in size and structure, exhibit contrasting patterns of behavior in their societies, so that a "division of labor" is established within the colony. For example, in the genus *Eciton* of Central America, the smallest workers (as little as 3 mm in length) spend most of their time in the nest feeding the larval broods. Intermediate sized workers, which constitute most of the colony's population, participate predominantly in raiding. The largest individuals (over 14 mm in length) have huge heads and long, powerful jaws (Fig. 3.6). If these major workers become aroused during a predatory raid, they assume a characteristic position in which they rear upward with their front legs off the ground, vibrate their antennae, and rhythmically open and close their huge jaws. These ants are popularly called "soldiers." The analogy is a good one, in the sense that the behavior of the majors undoubtedly affords the colony protection against predators. The "soldiers" not only look formidable, they are! Their large heads house an enormous musculature that operates their extremely sharp mandibles. The tips of the mandi-

Figure 3.5. *The diagonal ribbon in this photograph is formed by the raiding column of the African army ant genus* Dorylus. *The ants orient in the column primarily by following a chemical trail deposited from the hindgut of each ant participating in the raid. Note that the ants differ greatly in size, a condition known as polymorphism. In this species the ants range in size from major workers (15 mm in length) to minor workers (5 mm in length). The photograph was taken by Dr. William Gotwald of Utica College.*

Figure 3.6. *Major worker of the Central American army ant* Eciton hamatum. *The majors have long, sickle-shaped jaws. The tips of the jaws are extremely sharp and are curved backward; if the ant bites a human being, the jaws easily penetrate the skin and are very difficult to remove.*

bles are curved backwards, and are therefore very difficult to remove once they have penetrated the skin.

The notoriety of army ants is based upon the fact that all species possess some truly outstanding characteristics. First, they have large colonies and consequently very impressive feeding habits. Edward Step, a science writer who made a career of describing the marvels of insect life, depicted army ants as a terror to all other creatures.

They march in such enormous numbers that everything which desires not to be eaten has to fly before them; from the cock-roach and the mouse to the huge python, the elephant, the gorilla, and the war-like native man, the story is the same.

Army ants are almost exclusively carnivorous. Although it is true that some species of Latin American and African dorylines occasion-ally eat small vertebrates such as lizards and snakes, the typical diet consists predominantly of other species of insects. The amount of food they consume is enormous. After carefully observing the forag-ing behavior of many colonies of *Eciton burchelli* in Central America, Carl Rettenmeyer estimated that a colony may take back to the nest over 100,000 arthropods every day. It is not surprising, therefore, that army ants are among the most important predators in the ecological communities in which they live.

Another unique feature of army ants is the nature of their nests. Colonies of most other ants make their own nests by settling in pre-formed cavities in trees, or by excavating tunnels and chambers in the soil. Whether the nest is fabricated, dug, or even taken over from other insects, the same nest generally serves as shelter from an early stage in the colony's life until its end. Army ants, by contrast, do not have permanent nests, and the nests of some species are composed entirely by thousands of ants clustering together and interlocking their long legs (Fig. 3.3). At the beginning of nest formation, worker ants form hanging clusters which dangle like strings from beneath a raised object, such as a fallen log. As other ants are attracted to these clusters, the newcomers run downward along the strands and extend it toward the ground by fastening themselves to other ants. As more and more ants stream into the forming nest, strands become ropes and the ropes eventually fuse into a heavy fabric of ants.

Another characteristic behavior of army ants is the tenacity with which they conduct all their behavioral functions in well-organized groups. Even the most casual observers of army ants in the field have been impressed by the tight cohesiveness of the ants belonging to a colony. Unlike most species of ants from other subfamilies, army ants do not forage for food individually. Instead, all raiding activities, as well as all emigrations to new nesting sites, are conducted by columns of individuals closely following a chemical trail deposited continuously

Figure 3.7. *Callow major worker of* Eciton hamatum *immediately after emerging from the pupal stage of development. The callow majors have white heads and golden yellow bodies. Note the darkly pigmented eye which stands out on the white head. Most army ants lack the well-developed compound eyes that are found in other groups of ants. In army ants, the eye is reduced to a single facet.*

by each worker ant as she runs along the ground. In army ants particularly, the success of the large scale raids and emigrations depends upon the ants' ability to deposit and follow these chemical trails. This is so because most army ants lack the well-developed compound eyes that are found in other species of ants. In most species of dorylines, the eye is reduced to only a single facet (Fig. 3.7). These photoreceptors enable the army ants to respond to changes in the intensity of illumination, but it is doubtful whether the eyes can function as image-producing organs.

Perhaps the most striking aspect of behavior common to army ants is their periodic shifting of nesting sites. These movements, or emigrations, involve the entire colony—workers, brood, and queen. The new nest may be several hundred meters from the old one, and it may take the colony 12 hours or more to complete the move. Practically all of the naturalists of the last century who reported on the behavior of army ants included some reference to the ants' peculiar behavior of periodically moving to a new nesting location. No one, however, could explain why. Over the years, two rival hypotheses were put forward to explain the movements of the ants. The first suggested that the emigrations were caused by physical conditions of the environment, such as temperature, humidity, air pressure, or even phases of the moon. The second hypothesis suggested that the stimulus for emigrations might simply be depletion of the food supply in the area around the ants' nest. According to this idea, a colony would stay at one site, where it would gather all of the available insect food; after depleting the local resources, the colony would move on to a new area.

The first truly systematic investigation of this problem was conducted in 1932 by T. C. Schneirla. By the end of his first field trip to Barro Colorado Island, he had gathered enough evidence to show that both of the prevailing hypotheses concerning the movements of army ants were wrong.

Imagine for a moment that you were Schneirla, setting out for the tropics in 1932 to find out why colonies of ants, containing up to one million individuals, periodically leave one nesting site and emigrate several hundred meters to a new location. From what you have just read about the life history of army ants, what kinds of evidence would you have had to gather to test the two hypotheses?

Suppose it were true that the emigrations are controlled by some aspect of the ants' physical environment, such as the phase of the moon. In this case, one should be able to predict that all colonies in a given area will be synchronized. That is, all colonies subjected to the same physical environment should be emigrating at the same time. But when Schneirla observed several dozen colonies of *Eciton hamatum* and *E. burchelli,* he found that there were always some colonies emigrating and some that were not. Clearly this observation is not consistent with the hypothesis that army ant emigrations are regulated by events in the ants' physical environment.

The second hypothesis, the one that suggested food exhaustion as the cause of emigrations, sounded much more reasonable. But another of Schneirla's observations showed that this hypothesis also had to be dismissed. On several occasions, Schneirla noted that a colony of army ants moved into a nesting site that had just been vacated by another colony, and the newcomers would remain at this site for up to 3 weeks. Obviously, the food supply near the nest had had not been depleted by the previous colony.

Perhaps the most important of Schneirla's observations was that the emigrations of both species were not random and sporadic at all. Instead, they occurred at intervals that were quite predictable. Schneirla noted that colonies of *E. hamatum* and *E. burchelli* exhibit cycles of activity that can be divided into two distinct phases. The first is the nomadic phase, during which a large proportion of the adult workers go out on daily raids and forage for food. In *Eciton* the raids begin at dawn. The ants pour out of the nest and form several columns, each column subsequently dividing into a network of branches. By midmorning the raiding columns of ants have overrun an area extending up to 100 meters from the nest. At the front of the raid the ants attack insects and other arthropods, biting and stinging the prey, pulling it apart, and carrying the softer parts back to the nest. The raiding column, therefore, is really a two-way stream, with some ants advancing from the nest and others returning with their prey. As evening approaches, the raid turns into an emigration, with the colony moving over one of the principal raiding trails of that day. This daily routine of massive raids and emigrations from nest to nest continues for approximately 2 weeks. Then, more or less abruptly, the colony settles down to a much quieter period, which I call the statary phase. During this phase, which lasts approximately 3 weeks, the raids are much less intense than during the nomadic phase, and relatively little prey is taken back to the nest. Finally, throughout the statary phase, the colony does not emigrate, but instead remains at the same site for the entire 3-week interval.

In addition to showing that army ant emigrations occurred only during one particular phase of a behavioral cycle, Schneirla also noted a very interesting correlation between the behavioral phase of the colony and the developmental condition of its immense brood. Whenever a colony was emigrating during the nomadic phase, the brood being carried by the adult workers was always in the larval stage of development. When emigrations ceased and the colony entered into the statary phase, Schneirla had to obtain his samples of brood from inside of the nest. Significantly, every brood sample from statary colonies consisted only of individuals in the pupal stage of development. Furthermore, whenever a colony was observed through the transition from the nomadic to the statary phase, the behavioral transition always coincided with the period during which the larvae were spinning cocoons and entering into the inactive pupal stage. This correlation between colony behavior and brood development provided the first suggestion that the alternations between the nomadic and statary phases were regulated by processes within the colony itself.

When this correlation was repeatedly observed for many other colonies of *E. hamatum* and *E. burchelli,* Schneirla formulated a theory of army ant behavior based upon fluctuations in the intensity of excitatory interactions between the colony's developing brood and the adult worker population (Fig. 3.8). According to this theory, when a mature pupal brood completes its development, the individuals emerge as lightly-pigmented callow workers. The behavior of the older workers indicates that the callows are highly excitatory to them. The older workers respond to the callows by manipulating them, licking them, and dropping pieces of food on them. This intensive social stimulation is transmitted throughout the bivouac by communication among the older workers, and the result is a massive raid that is followed by an emigration. The nomadic phase has begun! As the callows mature, their excitatory effects wear off. However, nomadic activities in the colony are now maintained by comparable stimulation imparted to the

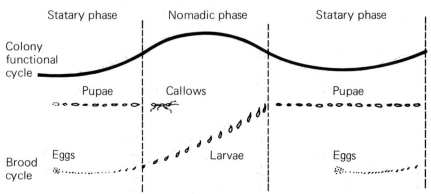

Figure 3.8. *The army ant genera* Eciton *and* Neivamyrmex *exhibit alternating phases of behavior. The nomadic phase begins when a brood of pupae emerges as callow workers, and is maintained by stimuli arising from a brood of developing larvae. For approximately 17 days, the colony sends out daily large raiding parties for obtaining food. At the end of the raid, the colony shifts to a new nesting site. During the nomadic phase, the queen's abdomen remains contracted. When the larvae enter the pupal stage of development, the statary phase begins. During this phase, the colony remains at the same nesting site for 3 weeks, and the raids are much smaller. During the statary phase, the queen's abdomen enlarges, and she lays a new batch of eggs. When the pupae emerge as callows and the newly laid eggs hatch into larvae, another nomadic phase begins and the cycle is repeated.*

adult ants by a brood of developing larvae, which by now have hatched from the eggs laid by the queen during the previous statary phase. As the larvae grow and mature, their excitatory effect on the rest of the colony steadily increases. Consequently, there is a steady increase in the intensity of raiding throughout the nomadic phase. Then, after about 2 weeks of development, the larvae cease feeding, begin to spin cocoons, and soon metamorphose into relatively inactive pupae. As pupae, the brood imparts very little stimulation to the adult worker population. This, in turn, causes the entire colony to lapse into a prolonged statary phase with very small raids and no emigrations. Midway through this phase, the queen becomes physogastric and starts laying another batch of eggs. These eggs hatch into larvae at approximately the same time that the present pupal brood emerges from their cocoons. The emergence of the new population of callow workers initiates another nomadic phase, and the cycle is repeated.

CONDUCTING PSYCHOLOGICAL RESEARCH IN THE FIELD
At this point, stop and think for a moment about the scientific procedures used by Schneirla to generate his theory of army ant behavior. Note particularly that he accomplished this task by studying the behavior of the ants in the field and not in the laboratory. This

might seem a bit strange to you at first, because most students in introductory psychology are accustomed to the idea that the only way theories can be formulated and tested is by conducing elaborate experiments in laboratories stockpiled with osciloscopes, computers, and other sophisticated electronic apparatus. If this is the only approach to science to which you have been exposed, let's see if we can clear up some misconceptions.

In studying behavior and attempting to explain its causes, psychologists typically take every measure possible to insure that their procedures lead to reliable and valid conclusions about the natural world. The procedures used to accomplish this are called *controls.* Because the laboratory is traditionally the place where the scientific study of phenomena can proceed without the intervention of too many outside variables, many students (and scientists too) have the erroneous impression that adequate control can be achieved only under laboratory conditions. This is not always the case; often it is advantageous for studies of behavior to proceed in carefully designed stages. At first, the investigator may want to observe the behavior of the species under study in the field environment. This type of field study is important because it enables the scientist to become familiar with the entire pattern of the animals' behavioral adjustment to its environment. This, in turn, is necessary before the investigator proceeds to the second stage of laboratory study, where environmental variables are systematically manipulated. At each stage of the investigation, the scientist must insure that adequate controls are used, even though the type of control used in the field and in the laboratory may differ. When field observations of behavior are made, reliability and validity may be increased in several ways. Experimenter-caused disturbance can be reduced by viewing the subjects from a blind. During the period of study, the accuracy of the psychologist's observation may be increased by using binoculars, as well as cameras, tape recorders, and other recording devices.

As a small exercise, let's review how Schneirla studied the social organization of army ants. Schneirla first observed many colonies of ants that staged large daily raids and nightly emigrations. Throughout these periods of observation, he noted that each colony had a large brood in the larval stage of development. These preliminary observations led Schneirla to hypothesize that an excitatory effect from the larval brood was responsible for the overall arousal of the ants during the nomadic phase. As a test of this hypothesis, he continued his observations of the ants' behavior until the larval brood pupated. He found that precisely on the day when the brood of grown larvae was enclosed in cocoons, the adult ants were considerably less excitable. Each colony began to stage very small raids, and emigrations ceased to occur. In this phase of the study, the maturation and pupation of the larval brood constituted a kind of *control* that was selected by the observer to determine whether or not the larval brood was indeed responsible for the large raids and emigrations. Another control was provided when the pupal brood emerged as callow workers and another brood of larvae had hatched from the egg stage. At this time, all colonies began once more to stage massive daily raids and nocturnal emigrations. Thus, through prolonged and detailed observations of the changes in the behavior of colonies of army ants as their broods passed through successive stages of development, Schneirla's hypothesis was well on its way to being confirmed.

As you can see, the first stage of the field study relied heavily on observation and controls selected by observing; no environmental variables were directly manipulated by Schneirla. But sometimes, research conducted in the field is criticized for this very reason—because environmental variables are impossible to manipulate in the field, the scientist can do nothing but wait for events to occur (just as Schneirla had to wait for the larval brood to pupate). By contrast, the psychologist in the laboratory can easily manipulate the important variables. In other words, the laboratory investigator can literally make events occur, and thereby facilitate the establishment of causality.

This criticism of field research is also not always warranted. Thus, think for a moment about an experiment that Schneirla could have done to test his hypothesis further, an experiment that would have involved a direct manipulation of environmental variables in the field. If, according to the hypothesis, stimulation from the developing larval brood causes the colony to become nomadic, then what should happen to the large daily raids and emigrations characteristic of the nomadic phase if the investigator removes the larval brood from the colony? Schneirla located two colonies of *E. hamatum* during the nomadic phase. In one colony (the experimental colony) he tore open the bivouac and removed approximately 85 percent of the larval brood. In the second colony (the control colony), he again tore open the nest, but removed no larvae. Within 3 days all nomadic activities had ceased in the colony from which the larval brood had been removed. The intensity of daily raids dropped sharply, and all emigrations ceased. In the control colony, nomadic behavior continued normally until the larval brood pupated.

INTEGRATING FIELD AND LABORATORY RESEARCH

Schneirla's analysis of social organization in army ants provides an excellent illustration of how psychological studies can be conducted in the field. By selecting this example, I do not mean to imply that field research is more important than research conducted in the laboratory. On the contrary, the ideal program for many behavioral studies is one that involves a coordination of field and laboratory investigation. Field studies can offer an opportunity to become acquainted with the animal's full pattern of activities under a range of natural environmental conditions. Once we know both the typical behavior of the species under these conditions, and the range of natural conditions to which the species is capable of adjusting, we often are in a better position to proceed to the next stage—laboratory study. Let me illustrate the advantages of coordinating field and laboratory studies by discussing some of my own research concerning the orientation of army ants.

The social organization of army ants is maintained by behavioral interactions among all the individuals of the colony. The principal goal of my research has been to clarify how these interactions enable a colony consisting of hundreds of thousands of ants to function as an integrated unit. Perhaps the best illustration of social organization in army ants is the collective behavior of the workers during the colony's predatory raids.

Several years ago I spent the summer months at the American Museum of Natural History's Southwestern Research Station in Arizona, studying the raiding behavior of the army ant *Neivamyrmex nigrescens.* The behavior of this species is very much like that of *E. hamatum* of Central America. It exhibits distinct nomadic and statary phases, and all raiding and emigrations are conducted by ants running in narrow columns as they follow a chemical trail deposited from the hindgut of each ant in the column. It differs from *Eciton,* however, because the raiding and emigrations take place at night. When one looks closely at individual ants in the raiding column, it can be seen that the ant's antennae are arched forward and downward, with the antennal tips just skimming the ground. The observer gets the impression that the ants are using some kind of "scanning" process to follow the trail, locate food, and maintain contact with other individuals in the raiding column. The overall impression is that the ants are extremely dependent upon chemical and tactile stimuli for orienting on the trails (which is not surprising when we recall that their eyes are vestigial and their raids take place at night). The sense of touch seems to be used in two ways: contact with other ants on the trail, as they palpate each other with their antennae, and with objects in the physical environment. The importance of this second form of contact is evidenced by the fact that the raiding columns do not usually advance across flat, open areas of the ground. Instead, the ants typically run along the edges of rocks, branches, and fallen tree trunks.

After observing the behavior of the ants in the field for several nights, and mapping the distance and direction of their meandering columns, I became interested in how the ants utilize chemical and tactile stimuli during the predatory raids and emigrations. Specifically, I wanted to know if the ants could successfully orient in an environment that contained the chemical trail, but did not contain tactile cues from rocks, logs, and other physical objects. Conversely, would the ants be able to run along the edges of physical objects if no trail

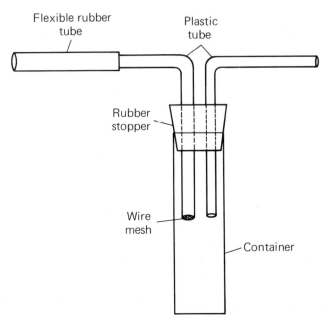

Figure 3.9. *Aspirator used to collect ants in the field. Suction is applied to the flexible rubber tube, and the ants are drawn through the plastic tube at right and into the lower container. The disc of wire mesh prevents the ants from being aspirated into the collector's mouth.*

were present for them to follow. To answer these questions I would have to compare the ability of the ants to orient in an environment that contained either chemical cues or tactile cues, but not both. But this presents a problem: in the ants' natural environment, both classes of stimuli are always present, and it would be impossible to separate them. It is possible, however, to set up an environment in the laboratory that permits the ants to use only one kind of stimulus at a time. Here, then, is a case in which a question about behavior that arose from observing the ants under natural conditions in the field can best be answered by carefully controlled experiments conducted in a laboratory setting.

I began by collecting several thousand workers from a raiding column in the field. This was accomplished by using a collecting device called an aspirator (Fig. 3.9). The ants were taken to the laboratory and placed in a large holding container. My first task was to assess the ants' ability to orient using only their species' chemical trail. For this I needed a large quantity of the trail chemical, which I obtained quite easily by washing the ants in an organic solvent such as petroleum ether. The ether dissolves the trail chemical present on the surface of the ants, and the solution can then be used to redeposit the trail in a quantifiable manner. To deposit the trail, I poured the ether extract into a small buret, which I suspended above the turntable of a phonograph. The turntable was set spinning, and the buret opened for the duration of one rotation. This simple procedure enabled us repeatedly to deposit a uniform circular trail onto a disc of absorbent filter paper. We adjusted the position of the buret to deposit a circular trail that was 480 mm in circumference. Within 5 seconds after the trail was deposited, the ether solvent evaporated, leaving behind an invisible residue of the trail chemical.

The last step of the procedure was testing the ants for trail following. To do this, the disc of filter paper was removed from the turntable as soon as the ether solvent had evaporated, and placed on top of a circular template. A black circle was drawn on the template, so that it coincided exactly with the position of the invisible chemical trail on the filter paper above it. Because the black circle was visible through the disc of filter paper, we could easily determine whether a test ant was indeed following along the trail. To test the ants for trail following, I constructed a plastic "starting gate" that was used to introduce the ants onto the trail extract. This consisted of a circular holding chamber and a curved tunnel that opened onto the trail (Fig. 3.10). Each test ant was initially placed in the holding chamber. From the chamber, the ant entered into the tunnel, ran along a small segment of the trail inside the tunnel, and then left the tunnel to continue running along the trail. For this experiment, we randomly selected 15 intermediate-sized worker ants from those in the large holding container. Each ant was tested once. After each test, the plastic "starting gate" was washed thoroughly to remove any odor left behind by the previous ant, and a new piece of filter paper was placed upon the template.

The results of this experiment showed that the workers of *Neivamyrmex nigrescens* had no difficulty in orienting on the chemical trail, even though no physical objects were present to provide additional tactile cues for them to use. Each ant zipped out of the tunnel and ran rapidly around the circular trail without stopping or turning around. As each ant ran around the course, it moved its head rapidly from side to side, thus enabling its antennae to repeatedly touch the trail. We conducted this experiment twice, each time using ants from a different colony of *N. nigrescens*. Table 3.1 shows the results of this experiment. In the first colony, the median time it took for the 15 ants to complete the 480 mm circular course was 10.5 seconds. The median time for the ants from the second colony was 13.0 seconds.

Once we were convinced that the ants had no difficulty orienting on a chemical trail without the presence of additional tactile cues, we reversed the question. How well would the ants orient over a comparable circular course if strong tactile cues were available to guide them, but no chemical trail was deposited for them to follow? To answer this question, we needed an entirely different experimental

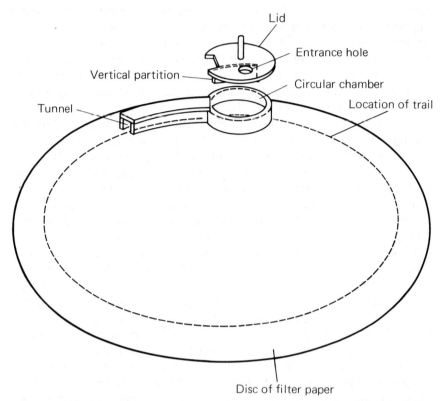

Figure 3.10. *Apparatus used to test army ants for trail following ability. The test ant is introduced into an entrance hole in the lid of the holding chamber. The ant leaves the chamber, enters into a tunnel in which it runs along a small segment of the trail, and then leaves the tunnel to continue running along the trail.*

apparatus. I took a piece of transparent plastic and cut a large hole out of its center. I then took another piece of plastic and cut out a circular disc. The diameter of the disc was slightly less than that of the hole. As a result, when the disc was placed inside of the hole, the gap between them created a circular tunnel (Fig. 3.11). By cutting discs and holes of varying diameters, I was able to vary the size of the

TABLE 3.1 MEDIAN TIME FOR 15 ANTS TO COMPLETE A 480 mm CIRCULAR COURSE WHEN CHEMICAL TRAIL IS PRESENT

	Time (sec)
Colony no. 1	10.5
Colony no. 2	13.0

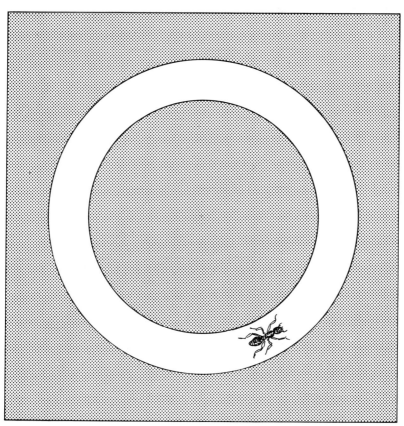

Figure 3.11. *Circular tunnel used to study orientation of army ants in an environment containing tactile cues only, provided by an inner and outer wall. If a chemical trail were present, the ant could complete the circular course in approximately 10 sec. Under conditions of this experiment, when only tactile cues were available, most ants required over 500 sec to complete the course.*

gap between the inner and outer walls of the circular tunnel. I was careful to make sure that the circumference along the midline of the tunnel was always 480 mm, regardless of the size of the gap.

I constructed four circular tunnels, each with a different size gap. The distance between the inner and outer walls of the first tunnel was 5 mm (which is the width of an intermediate-sized worker ant). In this tunnel, the ants can run quite normally and have no difficulty turning around. The second tunnel had a gap of only 3 mm. In this tunnel the ant could move only by holding its legs tightly against the sides of its body. It could turn around, but only with difficulty, by bending sharply at its waist, thus forming its body into a "V" shape. The third and fourth tunnels had gaps of 7 and 9 mm respectively. The distance between the inner and outer walls of these tunnels was so great

TABLE 3.2   MEDIAN TIME FOR 15 ANTS TO COMPLETE 480 mm
CIRCULAR COURSE WHEN CHEMICAL TRAIL IS NOT
PRESENT

	Width of Gap (mm)	Time (sec)
Colony no. 1	3	486.5
	5	725.5
	7	786.5
	9	735.5
Colony no. 2	3	515.3
	5	594.8
	7	609.3
	9	603.9

(relative to the ants) that the ants could turn completely around
without touching either of the walls.

For this experiment, we used ants from the same two colonies
that were used in the previous experiment. For each of the two colonies, we set aside four groups of ants, each group consisting of 15
workers. The ants in Group 1 were tested in the tunnel with the 3 mm
gap. The ants in Groups 2, 3, and 4 were tested in a similar manner
with the 5 mm, 7 mm, and 9 mm gap respectively. The results of this
series of experiments are shown in Table 3.2. As you can see from
the table, the amount of tactile stimulation present in the ants' environment does influence their ability to orient. The time it took for the
ants to complete the circular course within the 3 mm wide groove
was significantly less than the time for completing the course when
the gap was wider. However, the results of this experiment clearly
show that the absence of a previously deposited chemical trail significantly retards the ants' ability to orient in the circular test chamber.
Just compare the median time in Table 3.1 and Table 3.2. The fastest
median time for any group of ants in the apparatus that contained no
chemical trail was 486.5 seconds, which is more than 46 times slower
than the fastest group of ants using a chemical trail.

The reason for the striking differences in the ability of the ants
to orient with a chemical trail or without one became evident when
we looked closely at the behavior of the ants in the circular arena
under the two contrasting conditions of testing. When a trail was
present, the ants typically ran around the entire circular course without stopping or turning around, but their behavior was totally different
when no trail was present. When placed between the inner and outer
walls of the circular tunnel at the start of a test, the ant would
"freeze" momentarily. After a few seconds, the ant stretched its
antennae straight out in front of its head and started to palpate the

substrate very rapidly. Next, it huddled tighly against one of the walls of the chamber and pressed the ventral surface of its body close to the floor of the arena. In this crouched and "tense" position, the ant crept slowly forward for a few centimeters. Then, abruptly, it turned around and ran back over the path it had just taken. On the return run the ant ran quickly, without clinging to the walls or pressing its body to the floor of the arena. The reason for this change in the ant's behavior was obvious. When the ant initially moved from the starting position to the point where it turned around, it was depositing its own chemical trail. As a result, when the ant turned around and started back, it could move rapidly by following along its own trail. It did not seem to depend so heavily on the tactile stimulation provided by the walls of the chamber. As the ant continued on its return journey, it soon passed the starting point and the trail ended. Now the ant's behavior changed again. It stopped momentarily, straightened its antennae, huddled against the walls of the tunnel, pressed its body close to the ground, and slowly advanced for a few more centimeters. Then, just as before, it abruptly turned around again and ran quickly over its own chemical trail in the other direction. Each ant repeated this pattern of behavior over and over again. Every time an ant turned around, it ran back over its previous route by following its own chemical trail, and then extended the route by advancing along the walls of the chamber. By extending its route a few centimeters during each back and forth run, the ant eventually completed the entire circular course.

OUT OF THE LABORATORY AND BACK INTO THE FIELD

The research project I have just described began by observing the behavior of army ants in the field during their predatory raids. In the field, the ants run in columns and orient by responding to a combination of chemical and tactile stimuli. This observation resulted in a question concerning the relative importance of chemical and tactile stimuli for the ants' orientation. Because it is impossible to separate these stimuli in the field, I decided that the question could best be answered in the laboratory where the important variables could be readily manipulated. The laboratory experiments revealed that the ants could orient much more efficiently when a chemical trail was present. When a chemical trail alone was present, the ants ran rapidly around the entire circular course. In the circular tunnel containing vertical walls, the orientation of the ants was also greatly affected by the presence or absence of a chemical trail. It was clear that the importance of tactile cues from the walls of the experimental chamber increased greatly when the ants had no chemical trail to follow.

With the information I had gained from this laboratory study, I was finally ready for the last step of the project. I still had to answer a very important question. Have the results of this series of experiments provided any increased understanding of the ants' behavior in their species-typical field environment? In the laboratory, I had shown that the ants' behavior is strikingly different in the presence or absence of a chemical trail. But in the field, both kinds of stimuli are always present. As a result, I was a bit perplexed as to how to relate my laboratory study to the behavior of the ants in the field. Almost immediately, a question came to mind that could shed some light on the problem. Perhaps there were circumstances in the field where army ants would have to orient without a chemical trail. I took another look at Schneirla's field notes in which he described the railding behavior of *Neivamyrmex,* and it wasn't long before I found the all-important clue. I had indeed overlooked a very important aspect of the ants' raiding behavior. I had always made my observations when a full scale raid was already in progress. As a result, I only observed the behavior of the ants when a strong chemical trail was present for them to follow. Schneirla, however, began his observations earlier in the day, before the ants had left the nest, and consequently he was able to describe the behavior of the ants at the very start of raiding when no chemical trail was present on the ground. According to Schneirla's notes, a sort of relay trail laying activity develops at the start of raiding. There are no permanent scouts that deposit the advancing trail; instead, all ants near the raiding front contribute to some degree to the new trail. When an ant reaches the outer boundary of the trail, its behavior changes abruptly. The ant stops momentarily, presses its body firmly to the ground, and increases the frequency of antennal tapping on the ground. In this position, the ant advances slowly for a few centimeters, stops, turns around, and retreats quickly back toward the main column. In the meantime, ants coming up behind the first ant follow along the small section of trail that it has deposited, and they, in turn, extend it in a similar way for a few more centimeters. In this way the raid steadily advances, with each group of ants taking turns at trail laying as it reaches the front. The overall advance of the raid depends upon the number of ants participating, their degree of excitement, the amount and location of food sources, and the nature of the terrain.

I was immediately struck by the similarity between Schneirla's description of army ants at the raiding front and the behavior of the ants in the laboratory test chamber. In the laboratory experiment, when an ant was running through a portion of the tunnel on which it had previously deposited its own chemical trail, it behaved like an ant running in the middle of an established raiding column in the field. It oriented by following the chemical trail and made little use of tactile cues from physical objects. When the test ant entered a segment of the tunnel that contained no trail, its behavior approximated the behavior of an ant at the head of a raiding front in the field. It pressed its body down on the substrate, huddled close to the walls of the tunnel, and advanced slowly for a few centimeters before turning around and running back into the main column.

The series of experiments described above, together with our observations in the field, show that the behavior of army ants changes abruptly when they pass from an environment containing a chemical trail into one that contains no trail. The fact that the ants rely heavily on tactile cues in the absence of a chemical trail clarifies why large sections of the raiding columns are located along the edges of rocks, logs, and other physical objects. It is also clear that this pattern of behavior is very adaptive for the entire colony, because it enables all the ants to forage efficiently and with a minimum of disruption. This is so because army ants are extremely sensitive to air currents; even the most gentle of breezes is enough to disrupt a raiding column and send the ants scurrying off in all directions. The edges of rocks and logs provide an excellent shelter against these disturbances.

All of our research on army ants seems to substantiate the fact that the social organization of these ants differs from that of other species in many respects. It is clear, however, that it is their group behavior that makes them truly outstanding. All nesting, foraging, and emigrations are conducted by the integrated behavior of many thousands of ants. The success of these group activities depends upon complex behavioral interactions among all members of the colony, with the result that the colony is able to function as a coordinated social unit. Like many species of social insects, army ants rely heavily on the senses of olfaction and touch for communicating with each other and for orienting within their environment. By studying how the individuals of army ant colonies use chemical and tactile stimuli to adjust to their environment, we, as psychologists, hope to gain a better understanding of their social organization.

SEXUAL BEHAVIOR: HARD TIMES WITH THE COOLIDGE EFFECT
Gordon Bermant

Students sometimes suspect that psychologists enjoy giving unfamiliar names to well-known facts in order to create the illusion of erudition where in fact there is at best common sense. Particularly in the early days of psychological investigation, there was a tendency to name a significant relationship or phenomenon after the investigator who brought it to attention or who clarified its nature, thus we have Weber's Law, Stiles-Crawford Effect, von Restorff Effect, Emmert's Law, and (my personal favorite for its mellifluous sound) the Pulfrich Pendulum Effect. A curious feature of this labeling by name is that it provided an air of legitimacy, one might even go so far as to say dignity.

What are we to expect, then, when we come across "The Coolidge Effect?" Here is a label that includes the name of the thirtieth president of the United States, Calvin Coolidge, and refers to an aspect of the sexual behavior of male animals. What can be made of this? A number of possibilities spring to mind, mostly salacious. Imagining what arcane sexual secret is hidden behind the dour visage of our thirtieth president is an intriguing way to pass the time. The unlikely combination of Coolidge and explicit talk of sex provides a cognitive tension within which the imagination can work to create a spiral of increasingly bizarre fantasies.

The truth, it turns out, is more prosaic than any of your fantasies are likely to be. We can uncover some information about the label and what it labels by telling the following fable:

One day President and Mrs. Coolidge were visiting a government farm. Soon after their arrival they were taken off on separate tours. When Mrs. Coolidge passed the chicken pens she paused to ask the man in charge if the rooster copulates more than once each day. "Dozens of times" was the reply. "Please tell that to the President," Mrs. Coolidge requested. When the President passed the pens and was told about the rooster,

Dr. Bermant is affiliated with Battelle Seattle Research Center and The University of Washington.

*he asked "Same hen everytime?" "Oh no, Mr. President, a
different one each time." The President nodded slowly, then said
"Tell that to Mrs. Coolidge."**

While not exactly a thigh-slapper, the story has its merits. To
begin with, it points out an obvious but interesting fact about chickens,
namely that under normal barnyard conditions one rooster copulates
with more than one hen. Why this fact strikes us as interesting needs
a bit of examination.

Look at it this way. The idea that one man should have more
than one wife was so repugnant to the accepted American morality
of 1857 that President James Buchanan sent troops against the
polygamous Mormons of Utah. The Federal Government's fight with
the Mormons over polygyny continued for a number of years, with
the question of Utah's status as a state hanging in the balance.
Between 1862 and 1887 the Congress and Supreme Court of the
United States cooperated fully in drafting and upholding legislation
that prohibited multiple marriage. In fact, Utah was not admitted to
the Union until 1896, after the president of the Mormon Church publicly declared in 1890 that polygyny was no longer the official doctrine
of the church.

The message is that as a nation and a society we have been
strongly committed to the notion that monogamy is the only acceptable form of marriage. But this notion of ours did not follow from a
rational analysis of alternative life styles followed by democratic procedures of decision making and careful regard for the rights of the
dissenting minorities. Rather it was a continuing view of the relation
between sex, marriage, and society that had prevailed in this country
from its beginning, as part of "civilized morality" (Hale, 1971).

What do President Buchanan and civilized morality have to do

---

*If an outrageously complete history of psychology is ever written, it will record
that this story was entered into our discipline by Professor Frank A. Beach of the
University of California. Some of the events leading up to this occasion are described
in context later in the paper. However, lest historians of the future fall to feuding
over the correct chronology, let me list it here as kindly transmitted to me by the
hand of Dr. Beach in a letter dated June 29, 1973: Following the publication by
Beach and Jordan (1956), A. E. Fisher presented a paper at the Eastern Psychological Association outlining the basic effects of female novelty on the copulatory
behavior of male rats. Beach and Richard Whalen repeated this work in Berkeley
in 1959, and Whalen reported the results at the Western Psychological Association
meetings of that year. Whalen's WPA address provided the opportunity to relate this
story, for the chairman of that particular session was Professor David Krech, whose
ability to appreciate a joke is well known. So at the critical moment, just before
Krech ascended the podium to introduce Whalen, Beach shot him a note with the
request to introduce the talk under the heading of "The Coolidge Effect." Krech
complied.

This completes the history of the phrase in the oral tradition. The first pub-
lished reference is on page 641 of Wilson, Kuehn, and Beach (1963), as follows:
"This phenomenon, which has been termed the Coolidge Effect, is not limited to
Rattus norvegicus. . . ." And thus, gentle reader, did science march on.

with President Coolidge and rutting roosters? One answer might be that our American history of sexual repression and suppression has so attuned us to double entendre and other indirect ways of dealing publicly with our sexuality that even jokes as poor as the one about President Coolidge will be told and retold if they say anything at all relevant about human sexual experiences. And that gets us to the second interesting point about the story, which is that it is as much about people as it is about chickens.

A closer look at the story reveals a little bit about the dark side of the informal sex education of many American males. It has to do with sexual capacity, in particular the rate at which the male can achieve ejaculations. When Mrs. Coolidge makes her sly remark to the farmer she is saying, in the story behind the story, "Show that rooster to the old boy, will you? Now there's a *real* cock. It'll put the old boy in his place to see that rooster in action." Against this attack on his ejaculatory capacity the President counterattacks laconically and by indirection. He points out that the rooster's sexual prowess is due at least as much to the variety of hens available to him as to anything else. The implication is that if he, the President, had the same opportunities that the rooster had for variety, then he might do just as well.

It is the rooster's capacity for multiple sexual contacts in a brief period of time that catches the First Lady's attention. It is the rapid recurrence of copulatory capacity (called potency, or virility, in various guises) that impresses. Male concerns about this facet of sexual psychology and physiology are widespread in sexual humor. Here, for example, is a relatively innocuous story collected by Legman:

> *A man who is able to have intercourse thirty times a night (or with a hundred different women) is only able to get up to twenty-six the night his friends are betting on him. "I can't understand it," he says later, "it went perfectly at the rehearsal this afternoon" (1968, p. 313).*

This story could interest us for a number of reasons. Most relevant to the Coolidge Effect is the inclusion, in parenthesis, of mention that more ejaculations are possible when the identity of partners is varied.

The story about President Coolidge and his wife represents one variation in the large class of stories dealing with male ejaculatory capacity and how it is influenced by changes in the number of available females. By deflecting the focus of concern from humans to animals, the story takes on a cleaner character than more direct stories. It is a story which even very proper people might find "cute" or at least inoffensive.

What began as a disguise to enter the parlor can be used as a means to raise some interesting psychobiological questions. First, what is it about roosters and hens that makes them the focus of the story? Why wasn't the story told about some other animal? Do all male animals behave like roosters? Second, why is this story not told about female animals? Are females different from males in regard to their sexual response? If so, what are the biological foundations of this difference, and what can experiments in comparative and physiological psychology tell us about them? Third, while it is a fact that roosters behave as the story indicates, there is an open question whether people would behave the same way given the same opportunity. Folklore is one thing, facts may be another. What do we know about the facts?

I am not going to answer all these questions in the sections that follow. I cannot do that, at least not in a definitive way. Rather, I will outline some general aspects of psychology and biology that are relevant to providing complete answers, and I will talk about what it was like to do some of the experiments that attempted to arrive at these answers.

ENTER RATS

I will now perform the psychologist's typical magic trick: instead of pulling a rabbit out of the hat, I will pull a rat. Specifically, I am going to talk about how the Coolidge Effect has been studied in the laboratory version of *Rattus norvegicus.* At this point, I suspect, readers might feel that I am stretching their credulity beyond its snapping point. How can this discussion about rats get us back to the interesting questions and answers about human conduct? As I mentioned above, I am not sure that it can, but it may get us somewhat along the way, and it will surely give insights into how problems in the experimental study of sexual behavior are formulated and solved. In any case, the reader can feel he or she has a legitimate IOU from me to fill in the gaps contained in the arguments made here—it shouldn't take more than one or two lifetimes to make the debt good.

The story begins in the laboratories of the Psychology Department at Yale University in 1956. During that year, Frank A. Beach and Lisbeth Jordan (Beach and Jordan, 1956) published a careful analysis of sexual exhaustion and recovery in the male rat. In order to understand what they meant by this, it is necessary to have some idea about how rats copulate. It turns out to be somewhat different from what you are used to. So here is a brief digression on the fundamentals of rat sex.

Figure 4.1 shows a pair of rats engaged in the three sexual events in which rats typically engage: a mount without vaginal insertion, called a *mount,* a vaginal insertion, called an *intromission,* and an *ejaculation.* During a mount the male thrusts against the female's perineal area but does not achieve intromission, either because his

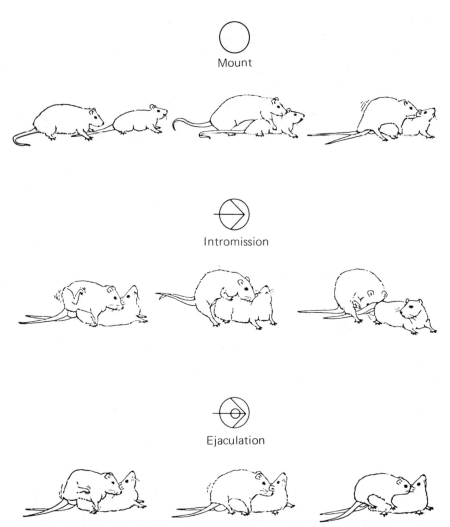

Figure 4.1. *The three events characterizing copulation in rats. The raised hind leg characterizes the occurrence of penetration. Intromission is terminated by a rapid dismount. (Courtesy of Gordon Bermant, Ph.D., from his article* Copulation in Rats *in* PSYCHOLOGY TODAY *Magazine, July, 1967.)*

erection is insufficient or because his penis is incorrectly placed. When the tip of the penis does contact the vaginal opening, other things being equal, the male will perform one deep thrust into the vagina then throw himself off the female immediately—the intromission typically lasts between one-third and one-half of a second (Bermant, Anderson, and Parkinson, 1969). The intromission terminates when the male pushes vigorously away from the female and in a characteristic balancing gesture, spreads his arms wide as he falls backward. When you've been spending hours watching the animals copulate, this gesture takes on a mildly annoying self-congratulatory air. Between intromissions the pair of rats remains unconnected for 15 seconds to 1 minute (a period called the *intercopulatory* interval or *interintromission* interval—it takes almost as much time to say it as the rats take to do it). The important thing to remember is that the male rat has not yet ejaculated: the intercopulatory interval ends when the pair of rats engages in another successful intromission. As shown in the time line graph (Fig. 4.2), the first ejaculation of the given session occurs after several intromissions. The number varies within and between individual rats, but it usually is between 7 and 15 intromissions. The ejaculation is noticeably different from the intromissions that have preceded it. To begin with it lasts longer: the pair remain coupled for approximately 5 seconds. Second, the male moves off the female slowly, deliberately, with none of the flamboyant *joie de vivre* that characterized his dismount after an intromission. Third, and most importantly for our concerns, the ejaculation has a definite effect on the length of time it takes the animals to start copulating again. Whereas the interval between two ordinary intromissions lasts from 15 seconds to 1 minute, the interval between an ejaculation and the next intromission (called the *postejaculatory interval)* is approximately 5 minutes long. Moreover, the second ejaculation occurs after fewer intromissions than the first; most male rats will ejaculate the second time after 4 to 7 intromissions instead of after 7 to 15 as in the first time around.

This brief description is sufficient for an appreciation of the experiment that Beach and Jordan reported in 1956. They had two purposes: (1) to measure the course of sexual exhaustion in male rats who had not copulated for 2 or 3 weeks and who therefore were completely rested, and (2) to plot the course of recovery from exhaustion by varying the time between exhaustion and the male's next opportunity to copulate, and measuring the behavorial differences manifested at different times.

At this point the most important question is, what did Beach and Jordan mean by "exhaustion"? Their criterion was completely explicit: "A male was judged to be exhausted when he allowed 30 minutes to elapse without mounting the incentive female" (Beach and Jordan, 1956, p. 123). As mentioned above, the first postejaculatory interval is typically about 5 minutes long. When Beach and Jordan made 30 minutes their criterion, they were saying that a rat who hasn't resumed copulation after one-half hour (six times longer than he would normally take after one ejaculation) is "exhausted" for all scientific and practical purposes. I am emphasizing this detail in order to point up that (1) operational definitions such as this always have a certain arbitrariness about them, but that (2) without *some* explicit specification we might go on arguing for a long time whether the male was "really" exhausted or not. As we will see, the question of what con-

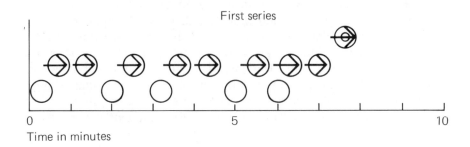

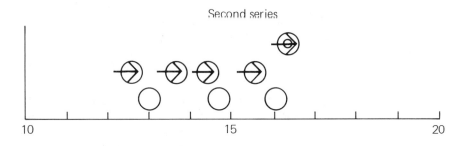

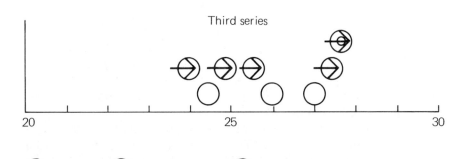

Figure 4.2. *The time course of three successive bouts of copulation lead-ing to ejaculation. The behavior leading up to each ejaculation is called an ejaculatory series. The number of intromissions in the first series is greater than the number of intromissions preceding the second or third ejaculations. (Courtesy of Gordon Bermant, Ph.D., from his article* Copulation in Rats *in* PSYCHOLOGY TODAY *Magazine, July, 1967.)*

stitutes sexual exhaustion comes up in more substantive fashion anyway, so it is important that there be no confusion on semantic grounds.

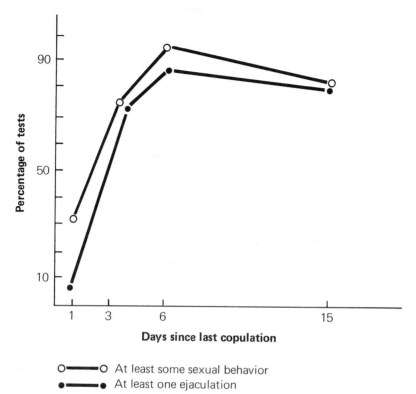

O━━━O At least some sexual behavior
●━━━● At least one ejaculation

Figure 4.3. *Sexual recovery of male rats after extended copulation with a single female. (Drawn from Table II of Beach and Jordan, 1956).*

The most important feature of the Beach and Jordan experiment for our concerns is that once a male and female were placed together, they stayed together until the 30-minute criterion of exhaustion was reached. Exactly why this methodological detail was important will become clear shortly. When the criterion of exhaustion was reached, the male and female were separated. The next time a male got a chance to copulate was after 1, 3, 6, or 15 days. When his turn did come up again, he almost always was paired with a female different from the last one he had been with.

The results of the experiment were quite clear. During the initial exhaustion tests, males ejaculated on the average seven times before reaching the criterion of exhaustion; the range was from five to ten. The postejaculatory intervals grew progressively longer after successive ejaculations; after the last ejaculation, by definition, the interval was 30 minutes.

Figure 4.3 describes two aspects of the behavior observed after the various periods of recovery. The first thing to notice is that sexual activity generally increased from 1 day's recovery to 15. Thus after 1 day of recovery, only 31 percent of the tests included any sexual behavior at all, and only 6 percent included an ejaculation. After 6 days' recovery, however, 96 percent of the tests showed at least some sexual behavior and all but two of those included at least one ejaculation. Only one rat ejaculated after 1 day's recovery, and he did so only once. After 6 days, however, the median number of ejaculations was five (range from four to six), and after 15 days it was six (range from five to eight).

In general, then, the results suggested that these male rats took about 2 weeks to regain approximately maximum ejaculatory response. Most importantly for our current concerns, they were simply nonejaculatory after 24 hours of rest.

The Experiment of Alan E. Fisher

One psychologist who read the report of Beach and Jordan was Alan E. Fisher, who noted that each male had been paired with a single female for the duration of a single test. On the basis of anecdotal evidence (recall the earlier discussion) and some scientific reports on the behavior of dairy bulls (which will be mentioned again later), Fisher wondered what would happen if he exhausted the male with one female and then put a new sexually receptive female in *immediately* instead of waiting for a minimum of 24 hours as Beach and Jordan had done. He set up an experiment that would compare the behavior of males left with one female until they reached a criterion of exhaustion (45 minutes without a mount) with their behavior when, after 15 minutes without a mount, the original female was replaced by a new one. Thus the males would have the opportunity to mate with a novel female every time they allowed 15 minutes to elapse without mounting the female already in the testing cage. The session was terminated when the male finally allowed 45 consecutive minutes to pass without mounting.

The results of the experiment were striking. When new females were not introduced, the males averaged 7 ejaculations (range 5–10); when new females were introduced the males averaged 13 ejaculations (range 7–22). Thus the introduction of new females at a time when the males were reducing their rates of copulatory behavior led to substantial increases in the numbers of ejaculations they achieved before going 45 minutes without a mount.

Here, demonstrated in a relatively dramatic way by a normally undramatic animal, were the effects of changing the identity of the sexual partner on sexual performance. The most obvious conclusion to be drawn from the results was that what appeared to be exhaustion, in the sense of physiological fatigue of the ejaculatory process or mechanism, was instead satiation with the erotically arousing properties of a single female rat; when a new female was introduced, the male was capable of rearousal and additional ejaculation. The distinction between exhaustion and satiation reflects a difference between processes occurring in the neuromotor response mechanisms and processes occurring in the neuromechanisms involved with the analysis and integration of stimuli.

NEW DEPARTURES

Following Fisher's initial report, several investigators sought to answer some of the basic questions posed by the puzzling fact that male rats appeared to copulate more earnestly with a fresh receptive female immediately after being sexually satiated than they did if given a 24 hour rest. A number of studies dealt with the characteristics of the female that were necessary and/or sufficent for changing the satiated male's behavior (Fowler and Whalen, 1961; Wilson, Kuehn, and Beach, 1963; Hsiao, 1965, 1969). The ins and outs of these studies are manifold and too complex to be described here in any detail. Three generalities should be mentioned, however: (1) If the novel female has herself just mated, the male may not exhibit quite so much copulatory behavior as he would if she were receptive but not recently mated. Different studies have found different degrees of the effect of "freshness." (2) If females are changed after each of the male's ejaculations, there is relatively little effect, i.e., it is as if the females were not changed at all. Thus it appears that the effect, at least in rats, depends upon a "rebound" from accumulated satiation. (3) Different investigators have found different degrees of ejaculatory improvement when new, fresh females are introduced. Generally speaking, the doubled ejaculatory frequencies reported by Fisher (1962) have not been achieved by the rats performing in other laboratories.

Temporal Characteristics of the Coolidge Effect

Sometime in 1965 my colleague Dale Lott and I were sitting around the coffee room in the Psychology Department of the University of California at Davis, talking about sex. There was in itself nothing unusual about that. It is one of the glories of academic life that one can sit around and talk about things like sex and be working withal, provided of course one adopts a suitably serious mien. On this occasion Lott and I were discussing the Coolidge Effect generally, and specifically the paradoxical nature of the male rat's change in sexual responsiveness within the first 24 hours after satiation. What kind of process was it that allowed the male more sexual activity immediately after satiation, when the new female was introduced, than 24 hours later? We decided that one approach to understanding more about the process was to trace its time course precisely over the 24-hour period. Our plan was to satiate male rats with one female, then wait no time at all before introducing the new female (as Fisher had done), or wait either 1½, 3, 4½, 6, 12, 18, or 24 hours (24 hours being the shortest time Beach and Jordan had worked between females). In this way we would bridge the gap between the Fisher and Beach-Jordan experiments, and show how the Coolidge Effect waned over time. Such was our intention.

There was nothing particularly clever about thinking up this experiment. Our idea was to plot the time course of a phenomenon, and nothing in science is more basic or generally more simple than that. The trick came in the details of the operation. To understand why that was tricky you need to know a bit more about sexual behavior, particularly in rats.

To begin with, consider the female rat. Up to this point the female has been described as if she were an adjunct to the process of copulation rather than a fully sharing partner. There are reasons for this sexist bias, however, which are not obvious and which are understandable only when the relevant biology is made clear. The female rat is normally receptive to sexual behavior for a period of several hours once every 4 or 5 days. Her sexual receptivity is closely tied to the occurrence of ovulation. In fact, the hormonal events which lead to ovaluation are the same as those which affect the nervous system and lead to receptivity (see Bermant and Davidson, 1974, for an account of these events). Of course, if a normally receptive female copulates, she will most likely become pregnant. Once she becomes pregnant she stops cycling through her periods of receptivity (*estrus cycles*) until the young are born—a period of 3 weeks. As a practical matter, then, an experimenter interested in studying the sexual conduct of male rats cannot afford to use normally receptive females, because he can't use them often enough. The practical solution is to fool the female's nervous system by injecting hormones into the female that bring about sexual receptivity but not ovulation. With this technique the female never becomes pregnant and can participate in copulation every 2 weeks or less, at least for several sessions, without undesirable side effects. But one does not have complete freedom about the timing of the hormone injections. Experience has shown that very good results are achieved if the female is injected with one hormone (estrogen) 72 hours before she is to copulate and injected with another hormone (progesterone) 4–6 hours before.

With this in mind, reconsider the design of our experiment. We were planning to test satiated males at eight different intervals, ranging from 0 to 24 hours after satiation.* We needed fresh females for each of these intervals, which meant that both 72 and 6 hours before that time, as well as 72 and 6 hours before the satiation sessions, we had to inject enough females with hormones to insure sufficient supply. The practical significance of this will become clear in a moment.

---

*Males were not tested at all of these intervals each time, but only at one of them. They then were given two weeks rest, allowed to copulate to satiation again, then tested after a different interval, and so on.

The second thing to consider is that rats copulate more actively in the dark than in the light (Larsson, 1956). If you want to study copulation in rats you have two options: either work at night or work during the day having first fooled the rats into behaving as if day were night. If you take the first option, you may learn a lot about rat copulation but your own social life is likely to suffer. In order to take the second option, you need a room that you can make dark during the day and light at night. This "reversed day-night cycle" as it is technically called, is preferred by most nonmonastic students of rat copulation; after a while the rats don't know the difference, and the people involved like it a lot better.

Our laboratory was arranged so that we normally tested animals between 3:00 and 6:00 P.M., a generally comfortable but not terribly productive part of the day, well-suited for sitting in a dark room to watch animals copulate.

As a brief digression, I should mention that anyone worth his salt in the rat sex business watches four pairs of rats, in separate cages, copulating at the same time. The behavior of the four pairs is usually recorded on four channels of a machine called an event recorder, which is basically a motor driving a sprocket attached to a spool of paper. The paper is pulled under four ink pens at a constant rate. Each pen can be "twitched," (electrically deflected) through a switch set into a box placed near the experimenter's hand. The experimenter punches the switches as the events occur. A single twitch signals a mount without penetration, a series of rapid twitches signals an intromission, and a long twitch signals an ejaculaton—a simple, suitable symbolism. Often, after I had watched four pairs of rats for hours on end and faithfully recorded their couplings, my mind would wander to the possibility of hooking my switches up to powerful fountains and colored lamps, creating a water dance choreographed by copulating rats. The idea had esthetic merit, I thought, but insufficient scientific promise to warrant its funding by the National Science Foundation, which was supporting my research at the time.

Now, let us return to the practical problems facing us as we planned our experiment. We had space to watch four pairs at a time. Experience suggested that these four pairs would become satiated (i.e., reach a point of approximately a 30-minute postejaculatory interval), after 90 minutes of copulation with a single female. If we started our satiation sessions at 3:30 P.M. we would finish at about 5:00 P.M. We decided to allow the male 90 minutes with the new female whenever she was presented. Thus, if we presented the new female immediately after removing the old one, we would be finished by about 6:30 P.M. Under the conditions of our next shortest prearranged delay, which was also 90 minutes, we would begin the test with the new female at 6:30 P.M. and be finished at 8:00 P.M. It didn't take a genius to see that we were going to be working some strange hours.

For example, at the 12 hour delay we would start testing at 5:00 A.M. and finish at 6:30 P.M.

We wanted a total of 12 males in the experiment. That meant we would have to test four a day for 3 days, every other week, until the experimental design was completed.

When the testing schedules were combined with the hormone injection schedules, things really got complicated. Seventy-two hours before use, a female needed to receive estrogen, and 6 hours before use, she needed to receive progesterone. These calculations led us to a single, inescapable conclusion: we needed help. It was our good fortune, just then, that a graduate student named Linn Anderson entered the picture. Not only did he understand just what we were doing and why, but he had the stamina to do the bulk of it. Linn hired on for the experiment and we were off and running.

Some months later the experiment was completed. The three of us, with Linn the most bleary-eyed from the seemingly endless round of hormone injections and sex testing at all hours, gathered to see what the rats and we had accomplished. To begin with, we had male rats who averaged between five and six ejaculations during their satiation tests. When the new female was introduced immediately after satiation, most of these males achieved only one ejaculation in 90 minutes, and none achieved more than three. The average for all 12 males was 1.5 ejaculations, hardly the kind of ejaculatory performance with a new female that we had been led to expect from reading Fisher's paper. However, as mentioned above, several investigators, in particular Hsiao (1965; 1969), had not been able to coax large numbers of additional ejaculations out of their male rats by presenting new females to them. We do not understand completely which variables differentiated the animals or conditions in Fisher's experiment from others—the genetic background of the animals, their ages at time of testing, the lighting conditions in the room, or the time of day at which they were tested are only some of the possibilities.

It may be useful to note at this point that large differences in results between laboratories are not as unusual as beginning students of psychology or animal behavior might imagine. It is for this reason that researchers take pains to write up their methods and procedures in great detail and accuracy, so that others, wishing to repeat the experiment or make particular modifications, will know how to proceed. Concern for replicability and the social confidence in an experimenter's ability are the reasons for the exercises in report writing that students of psychology so often complain about in their laboratory courses. Like it or not, much of what goes on in a laboratory is simply paying careful attention to relatively uninteresting detail, and faithfully transmitting it to others.

We compared the numbers of ejaculations males achieved when

the new female was introduced immediately with their performances 24 hours later, and found that there had been only a slight improvement, to an average of about 2.2 ejaculations. Average ejaculation frequencies measured at the intermediate times, from 1½ to 18 hours after satiation, ranged between one and two ejaculations; there had been no major spurts of performance in the middle of the night. In general, judging on the basis of ejaculatory frequency alone, the Coolidge Effect in rats was about as exciting as last week's TV Guide. We had gone to elaborate lengths to find out that there was nothing to find out.

This glum view did not correspond with our total impressions of how our males had responded to the introduction of the new female. Their behavior had seemed quite a bit different when the delay of the new female's introduction was relatively short, say less than 6 hours, than when the delay was relatively long. Here the story got somewhat more interesting. Consider, for example, the time the males took to achieve their first intromission after the introduction of the new female. When the introduction was made immediately after the satiation period, the males achieved penetration in about 20 seconds. After the 24-hour delay, however, the males took 10 times longer to achieve their first intromission. Measured in terms of intromission latency, then, the Coolidge Effect was sizeable if not exactly staggering. Intromission frequency also showed sizeable changes over the 24 hour period, as did the postejaculatory interval.

When we put all our effects and lack of effects together in one package, we concluded that the Coolidge Effect in the male rat was primarily a heightening of sexual arousal rather than a restitution of capacity for sexual performance. In other words, if we allow ourselves the luxury of speaking in ordinary English, the rats appeared to want to copulate with the new female, particularly when she was introduced immediately after the old one was removed, but this desire was not accompanied by a major restitution of ejaculatory performance. Put another way—even if the spirit was willing, the flesh was not. As Beach and Jordan had already pointed out, complete recovery was likely to take 2–3 weeks.

A few years later Edward Cherney and I performed an experiment to work out a way to distinguish between sexual arousal and sexual performance that harmonized with the available experimental evidence. Readers with a continuing interest in the Coolidge Effect in rats are referred to this paper (Cherney and Bermant, 1970). But we have other fish to fry or, more accurately, sheep to shear. For no matter what the final scientific story about the Coolidge Effect in rats turns out to say, it is unlikely that it will be as interesting as the Tale of the Chubby Checkers: Speedy, One-Horn, and Short Stuff (Go on ewe, he said sheepishly).

Factors Affecting Copulatory Satiation in the Ram,
Ovis aries; or, How to Make a Horny Pickle and a Sweet Pipe

Sheep are stupid—make no mistake about that. But they have certain redeeming features, including their enormous importance in commerce and agriculture, for both wool and meat. Any bit of knowledge that contributes to increased efficiency in sheep breeding can have useful consequences. It was partly with this idea in mind, and partly for a more fundamental scientific reason, that I became interested in the copulatory behavior of sheep and, in particular, their performance in a Coolidge Effect experimental setting.

I received my first education about sheep in 1965 from Professor M. T. Clegg, then of the University of California, Davis. Clegg and his colleagues and students had already done a good deal of work on the hormonal control of sexual behavior and reproduction in ewes. Specifically, they had shown that a particular section of the ewe's brain was involved uniquely in the regulation of her sexual receptivity. After that section of the brain was removed surgically, the ewe never again became sexually receptive, even though apparently normal hormonal cycles still continued. There were two possible interpretations for this phenomenon. First, that part of the brain (which is in an area of the hypothalamus, just anterior to the optic chiasma) might function normally as the nervous system's monitor of circulating hormonal levels. It is known that nervous system activity leading to sexual receptivity depends upon proper hormonal functioning, particularly in nonprimate mammals like sheep. If the place where hormone levels are monitored is surgically removed, sexual receptivity will not occur. A second interpretation would be that the brain area in question was involved in sexual receptivity, but was completely independent of hormonal control. When it was destroyed sexual receptivity ceased, but *not* because the nervous system could no longer "read" the levels of circulating hormones.

At that time, some rather elegant ways of experimenting to decide between these alternatives were becoming available. For example, had we removed the ewe's source of sex hormones (her ovaries), she would have stopped expressing sexual receptivity. Then we could have replaced the hormones *locally,* right at the brain site in question, by lowering a probe with the appropriate hormone on the tip of it. If sexual receptivity reappeared following this implant, we could conclude that this brain area was indeed involved in monitoring hormonal levels.

However, we did not do this experiment. For various reasons we turned our attention to the behavior of the ram, and asked ourselves whether the brain area which controlled the ewe's behavior controlled the ram's behavior as well. Would surgically removing the same area of a ram's brain stop him from behaving sexually? That was the question we set out to answer. Here, as is true for all other research in which I have been involved, the reasons for getting involved in a particular experiment or project always seem clear at the time but are fuzzy in retrospect. If I am atypical, it probably means that I am not a very good experimentalist; if I am typical, it probably means that a lot of research gets done for fuzzy reasons. As the following account will show, not only the inception but also the eventual direction of research can take unexpected turns.

In order to establish a proper baseline level of sexual responsiveness against which to measure the effects of the selective brain lesions, we set out to standardize our methods of measuring sheep copulations. As suggested above, rat sex watching has achieved a high degree of technical sophistication, if not artfulness. We needed to bring some of this to bear on the measurement of behavior in the ram. Some work had already been done by Banks (1964), and by Pepelko and Clegg (1965). In addition to Clegg and myself, Wes Beamer, then a graduate student in psychology, joined our effort and became a full contributor.

The first step was to insure that the ewes with whom our experimental rams copulated were fully receptive during the tests. First, as with the rats, this involved injecting the females with the proper hormones. Then, just before the ewes were to be used in the experiment, testing their receptivity with a sexually active, nonexperimental ram. These nonexperimental rams which were used to check the ewes' receptivity we called "checkers." By individual name they were Speedy, One-Horn, and Short Stuff. Each possessed the peculiar sort of witless individuality so often observed in sheep. Take Short Stuff, for example. He was a runt. One consequence of his runtiness was that he couldn't stand tall enough to insert his penis into the vagina of an adult ewe. Not that this inability bothered him. Whenever we brought him in to check the ewe's receptivity, he comported himself with a sort of calculated insouciance, indicating that as far as he was concerned any form of sexual contact other than interfemoral was decidedly *déclassé*. Shorty had mastered the adman's ploy of turning deficiency into an asset.

Speedy was our champion checker. He was a big ram, close to 300 lb, very muscular, and completely devoted to his task. His devotion often worked some hardships on us. At the beginning of our experiments, for example, we had the ewes penned in small groups in a barn while the rams lived in an adjoining pasture.

We would begin our day's work by placing a potentially receptive ewe into a separate pen, then sliding open the barn door to the pasture. The rams usually were congregated at the far end of the pasture, where there was a water trough and shelter. During the first few days, we had to walk out to the rams and drive them back to the door in order to get one ram in to check the ewe. Within a week, however, we no longer had to make the trip. All we had to do was slide the door open and stand there waving our arms and whistling until we caught the rams' attention. Then the race was on, as one after another, the checker rams stopped tugging at the grass long enough to look our way and then, slowly at first but with gathering momentum made their ways over to us.

Speedy was usually first to make the door. By the time he reached us he was in full gallop. Our job was to stop him before he crashed through the wooden pens separating different groups of ewes. Unrestrained in the barn, Speedy's ardor knew no bounds, so it was imperative that we channel his activity toward the ewes scheduled to participate in the experiment that day. Thus as he breached the door, Wes Beamer and I would hurl ourselves on him and wrestle him over to the appropriate pen. This was actually rather fun, recapturing as it did thrills of high school football scrimmage. Things were different when it had been raining—there is no fun in wrestling a 300 lb. sopping wet ram. One comes away from the contact covered with water, lanolin, and impacted sheep dung—an unsavory combination.

One day as we tusseled with Speedy, my favorite pipe fell from my pocket and immediately became obscured by the combination of wet straw, spilled food, and dung covering the floor of the pen. I didn't notice I had lost it until the evening, and when I retraced my steps, it was nowhere to be found. It wasn't until 6 months later, when we were moving all our animals and equipment to another barn, that I spied the pipe, now only partially covered by the layers of accumulated glop on the floor. Overjoyed by the reunion, but apprehensive about what changes time and circumstances might have made, I gathered the pipe up and returned it to its place in the rack on my desk. Very soon, however, the odor that had accumulated on it over the months forced me to exile the pipe to a bottom drawer where it lay forgotten for several more months. When finally I discovered the pipe again the odor had almost completely disappeared. The challenge was obvious. So, after cleaning the bowl with copious quantitites of cheap gin and several dozen pipe cleaners, I inserted a new stem, stoked it, and smoked it. Marvelous. It had always been a decent pipe, of course, but the long rest under unusual conditions had accentuated all its virtues and eliminated the sharp edges of bad breeding that inevitably characterize inexpensive pipes. Perhaps pipe manufacturers should look into the possibility of regularly curing their pipes under these conditions. I suspect sheep ranchers would supply the necessary material at reasonable prices, at least until the word got out and the market became competitive.

During the summer our sheep needed to be sheared. When Speedy's turn came and the wool began to fall off of him under the skillful hands of the shearer, we saw that our favorite checker had been afflicted with a skin problem. The hay in the barn contained many little foxtails, which had worked their way through Speedy's wool and into his skin, causing bumps and welts all over his body. When the last wool fell away and Speedy stood there naked, with the air of offended dignity that sheep sometimes affect, he looked like nothing so much as a pinkish four-legged pickle, if you can imagine it. It turned out that his ardor was undiminished by the shearing; if anything, his checking became even more vigorous than before. We had created a horny pickle.

Perhaps I am creating the impression that all was fun and games in the sheep barn. Much of it was, of course; the best thing about research in animal behavior is that it often is fun. But the fun stopped abruptly when we had collected baseline copulatory behavior data from enough rams to begin the surgical part of the experiment. It is one thing to wrestle a horny ram to the ground and later count his ejaculations; it is quite something else to drive a smoking drill through his thick skull and then lower an electrode into what you hope is the correct portion of his brain, in order to destroy it. Any one who thinks *that* is fun is sick. The scientific justification for the research should be very secure before such research is undertaken, even on so vague and stupid a creature as a sheep. And sometimes, even when your scientific justification is clear and you've done all you reasonably can to insure technical efficiency and generally sound procedure, you end up with some sorry, messy situations and uninterpretable results.

Basically, that's what we did end up with after operating on about a dozen rams. Among other unhappinesses, Speedy's life was forfeited in our search for a better surgical procedure. But even the rams that lived long enough and well enough after surgery to make us believe they were *generally* healthy, were too variable in their sexual behavior to allow us an unequivocal conclusion about the effect of the brain lesion on copulation. In general, then, we killed about a dozen sheep and learned nothing of scientific value.

These were low times for Beamer, Clegg, and myself. We decided that we would not operate on any more animals unless and until we could convince ourselves that we had improved the procedures sufficiently to warrant it. Part of the problem was in localizing the place in the ram's brain toward which to aim our electrode. There is no atlas describing the sheep brain in stereotaxic coordinates similar to those for the rat, cat, and rhesus monkey. Thus we had to locate our spot by injecting a radio-opaque substance into one of the brain's ventricles (passages for cerebrospinal fluid) and quickly, before the substance sank to the bottom of the spinal canal, take an X-ray of it. Then we would have to develop the X-ray immediately and try to locate the appropriate brain location by an astute reading of the shadows and light places on the film. Clegg was very good at this, but he was fighting an uphill battle for several reasons. First, because of the thickness and irregularities of rams' skulls, it was difficult to drill through the skull with great precision. Second, the rams' necks were so strong that, even while virtually immobilized with anesthetic, a tremor of their musculature moved their heads in our apparatus, thereby rendering our precise measurements meaningless. And third, the spot we were trying to locate was so deep in the brain that we needed very long electrodes which tended to bend as they made their way downward. This nest of problems, coupled with bad reactions to our general anesthetic, were causing the bulk of the difficulties.

After staring at our data for some time and pondering the general nastiness of nature, it finally dawned on us that although our adventure into the brain had failed, we still had about 14 rams with well-known sexual histories that could serve as baseline data for further behavioral experiments, including some with the Coolidge Effect. So we changed the focus of our interest at that point and started some Coolidge Effect experiments.

The first thing to understand about the Coolidge Effect in sheep is that it is a very large effect. It is so large that no experimenter has as yet published a result showing the maximum number of ewes a ram will ejaculate with before giving up. A couple of years before we did our work, a student of Clegg's named Bill Pepelko exchanged ewes 13 times in a row. At the end of that time the ram looked pretty much as good as new, but Pepelko was exhausted (Pepelko and Clegg, 1965). We repeated that experiment through the presentation of 12 ewes, exchanging them after each ejaculation. The rams' behavior in this situation, contrasted with their behavior when the same ewe was left with them without exchange, is shown in Figure 4.4.

Rams left with one ewe didn't get beyond five ejaculations, while rams given a fresh ewe after each ejaculation had hardly slowed down after a dozen introductions. Here then is the Coolidge Effect in all its glory, clear and unabashed. Our next job was to try to figure out what was bringing it about. More precisely, we tried to figure out why the rams slowed down when a single ewe was left with them.

We started out with the simple idea that it was something about either the *sight* or the *smell* of the single ewe, left with the ram over time, that produced his sexual satiation. We also recognized the possibility that it might be both, working together. In any case we decided to try to fool the ram by making it as difficult as possible for him to tell whether a ewe was "new" or "old." This we did by dressing the ewes in what are called "show bags and hoods," a Klannish outfit used by sheep showers when they have groomed their sheep but before the animals have been judged. We fit these outfits on blackfaced ewes who looked, to us, as much alike as any we could find. The result of our efforts at ovine haberdashery are shown in Figure 4.5.

We assumed that there are obvious visual characteristics of "sameness" that grow on a ram as he spends time with a single ewe. We also assumed that there are similar olfactory properties which are sufficiently volatile to be picked up from the ram's and ewe's bodies and get placed on the bags that the ewes wear. If so, as we

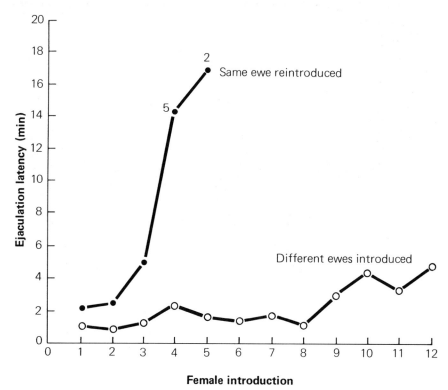

Figure 4.4. *The Coolidge Effect in sheep. The numbers on the top line are the numbers of rams, out of 6, that achieved that ejaculation frequency. (Data from Beamer, Bermant, and Clegg, 1969).*

put in new ewes after each ejaculation but dressed them always in the same, progressively smellier and familiar bag and hood, the ram should start responding to the bag and hood instead of to the ewe underneath and slow down his rate of ejaculation. On the other hand, it might be that the ram uses very specific cues from the physiognomy of ewes to identify "sameness" or "difference," and in the absence of these cues he responds to any ewe-like object as he would to a "new ewe." In this case, the same ewe reintroduced in an always-fresh bag and hood should receive the same prompt attention a truly fresh animal would receive. We didn't know which of these ideas, if either, would turn out to be accurate.

The design of our experiment follows: rams were exposed to 1. repeated introductions of a single ewe wearing the same bag and hood; 2. repeated introductions of a single ewe wearing a freshly laundered bag and hood after each ejaculation; 3. introductions of a fresh ewe after each ejaculation, each ewe wearing the same bag and hood; 4. introductions of a fresh ewe after each ejaculation, each ewe

Figure 4.5. *Ewes dressed in show bags and hoods. (From Beamer, Bermant, and Clegg, 1969).*

wearing a freshly laundered bag and hood. The behavior of primary interest was the time taken between the introduction of the ewe and the ram's ejaculation (ejaculation latency).

The results of our experiment, as diagrammed in Figure 4.6, are very simple to understand. The rams were not fooled one bit by the outfits. When the same ewe was reintroduced, the rams slowed down regardless of the newness or oldness of her outfit; if new ewes were introduced, the rams did not mistake them for the same female reintroduced.

At this point, then, we do not know how the rams discriminate among ewes, but we can say a little bit about the mechanisms they do not use. They do not use whatever visual characteristics are obscured by show bags and hoods. The question of olfactory cues must remain open because our experiment didn't deal with olfaction in a completely satisfactory fashion. Other investigators, however, using dairy cattle as subjects (cattle behave much as sheep in this kind of situation) found that when they smeared strongly smelling substances over their animals they still could not fool the bull (Almquist and Hale, 1956).

Another experiment in this series is worth mentioning briefly. We decided to find out whether rams needed to ejaculate with a ewe in order to become tired of her, or whether simply being presented to her and allowed to mount but not ejaculate would have the same effect. To accomplish this we tied an apron around the ram's middle.

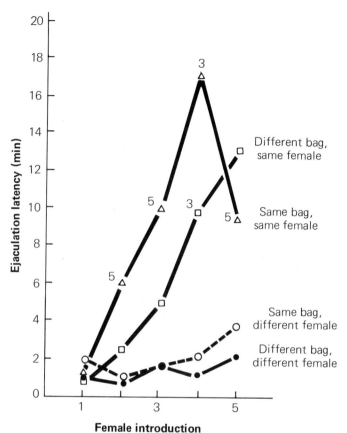

Female introduction

Figure 4.6. *Rams were not fooled by the clothes on the ewe. (Data from Beamer, Bermant, and Clegg, 1969).*

Thus when he mounted the ewe the apron would fall between the animals and prevent penetration without hindering mounting activity. We measured the intervals from the introduction and repeated reintroduction of a single ewe to the ram's first mount. Grabbing the ewe out from under the determined, aproned ram was not the easiest task we had ever undertaken, but we persevered until we had collected a respectable amount of data.

The results seemed clear cut: the aproned ram did not lose interest in the ewe. We could take her out and put her back in many times, and each time the aproned ram would approach and mount her within a minute or less. Our first conclusion was that ejaculation was necessary for sexual satiation; heavy petting wasn't enough. But then Wes Beamer noticed something strange, which was that there was semen smeared on the aprons at the end of a session. It appeared that the rams were emitting semen during these sessions;

whether they were going through an entire ejaculatory reflex was unclear. What we did to investigate a little further was to change aprons every time the ewe was removed and reintroduced, and check for semen each time; we found it present in about 60 percent of the cases. The probability of a ram emitting semen onto his apron was about the same whether the same ewe was reintroduced or a new ewe was introduced each time. By the time the semen got onto the apron and smeared around it was virtually impossible to measure its quantity. Hence we do not know whether the amount emitted was equivalent to the amount emitted during a regular ejaculation (1.0–1.5 cc). But we are left with the possibility that it is *penetration* of the ewe, and not necessarily ejaculation, that is necessary for the development of sexual satiation.

CONCLUSIONS
What are the Differences Between Species
in Regard to Sexual Satiation and Rearousal
Produced by Changing the Sexual Partner?

As a general rule, the rearousing effects of new female partners appear to be most pronounced in those species where the male typically guards, tends, defends, or otherwise deals with a group of females under natural conditions. Sheep on the range often fall into groups in which one male has more or less exclusive sexual control of a female. What we know about the life of wild rats, on the other hand, suggests that there is little in the way of harem formation. Barnyard fowl also organize themselves into groups wherein one rooster dominates the sexual activities of several hens, indeed this is the fact that got the whole story started. Another species with a pronounced tendency to this form of social organization is the elephant seal. Le Boeuf (1972) has presented data showing that a single bull elephant seal can account for almost 50 percent of all the mating taking place in a colony during a single season, and that four bulls in the colony accounted for between 60 percent and 90 percent of the copulations in 3 successive years. If one could ever figure out a way to deal with these enormous animals in an experimental setting, as we are able to deal with sheep and rats, then the prediction would be that they would behave like sheep and not like rats, i.e., they would show major ejaculatory enhancement with the presentation of novel females after each ejaculation. Thus the Coolidge Effect makes good biological sense for those species that are organized on a one male-many female basis.

Is the Coolidge Effect Restricted to Male Animals, or
Does Something Similar Exist for Female Animals as Well?

To the extent that the Coolidge Effect relates to the frequency with which sperm and semen can be emitted, it obviously makes sense with regard to male animals only. If, on the other hand, sexual *arousal* is being altered by the availability of continuously novel sexual partners, then it is reasonable to look for the effect in females as well.

Very few experiments so far have searched for an equivalent of the Coolidge Effect in female animals. In part this may be due to a sexist bias on the part of the people who study sexual behavior; until recently, virtually all researchers have been men, and it is somewhere between frightening and thrilling for a man to believe that females do not discriminate the identity of their sex partners. However, we know, for example, that female mice can distinguish between indivdual males on the basis of odor alone (Parkes and Bruce, 1961). More immediately to the point, we know that female beagle dogs exhibit definite preferences for certain males at the expense of others. Moreover, the "preference list" of these female dogs is not necessarily the same when they are in heat as when they are not (Beach, 1970). It has also been known for some time that if the opportunity is provided, female rats will actively regulate their participation in sexual intercourse. Thus, they will press a lever to regulate the presentation of a male who, after performing a single intromission, is removed until the female presses the lever again (Bermant and Westbrook, 1966). As far as we can tell from these experiments, the identity of the male is not important, but the amount of stimulation delivered to the female is: The greater amount of genital stimulation delivered, the longer the female waits before pressing the lever again. However, experiments designed explicitly to test for a "personal preference list" have not as yet been designed with this technique. Fluctuations in short-term receptivity associated with exposure to different male partners, superimposed upon the basic receptivity produced by changing hormonal levels, is the equivalent in females of the Coolidge Effect in males.

Studies of the sexual behavior of nonhuman primates under natural conditions and in the laboratory have generally concentrated on the relationship between the social status (dominance) of a male and his frequency of copulation. Generally speaking, dominant males are more likely to ejaculate than subdominant or low-ranking males. Most of the descriptions I have read emphasize the behavior of the males in determining the relationship between status and copulatory frequency (e.g. Conoway and Koford, 1965; DeVore, 1965; Hanby, Robertson, and Phoenix, 1971; Kummer, 1968). However, it is conceivable that females are more likely to initiate sexual behavior with high-ranking males than with lower-ranking ones. The closest analog to a Coolidge Effect situation here would be if a female's receptivity to copulation were greater to a new male than to continued copulation with her current consort. Testing this possibility would be difficult under natural field conditions, because the original consort typically fights off, or at least tries to fight off, any new male who attempts to copulate. Whether or not the female is more greatly aroused by the new male, the old male often reacts as if she were.

What is the Relationship Between the Coolidge Effect in Nonhuman Animals and the Sexual Behavior of People?

This is our final question. In some ways it is the hardest to answer, in other ways it is not. To begin with, we must clarify the kind of relationship we are looking for. Do we really want to know whether men and women, for example, if treated just as rats and sheep have been treated, would behave just as rats or sheep have behaved? Just imagine what the experiment would be like: a man and a woman engage in sexual intercourse as often as possible until the man's post-ejaculatory refractory period reaches some arbitrary criterion. All the details of behavior during and between copulatory sequences is carefully monitored and recorded by the experimenters. As soon as the criterion is reached, the woman stands up and walks rapidly out of the room. On her way out she passes the "new female," who walks in and begins immediately to attempt to arouse the male to a new erection and ejaculation. This woman remains until the criterion is once again reached, when she leaves in favor of woman number three, and so on. Of course, adequate control conditions would be required. This means that on some occasions the first woman would need to leave the room, then immediately reenter and resume sexual activity. Moreover, a "novel but used woman" control condition would be required, in which women would move from copulation with one man to copulation with another, in order to ascertain if their prior exposure affected their ability to arouse their second partner.

This experiment would be easier to do with people than it was to do with sheep. Moreover, there is no doubt in my mind that the experimenters could easily find both men and women volunteers for these procedures. Although some might ask for financial compensation for their participation, others would participate simply because the idea appealed to them. In fact the idea as described above is really very similar to the kind of "plot line" that typifies today's hard-core pornographic film. The important question about the experiment is, *what valuable knowledge would one gain about human sexual behavior after the results were in?* We already know from pornographic films that some people could perform in this experiment in a number of different ways, depending upon what the film's director told them to do. For example, there is one famous male actor in pornographic films who claims that he can copulate more or less indefinitely without ejaculation, but can ejaculate within about 14 seconds after being instructed to do so by the film's director. Now this may be unusual ability, but perhaps with the right training procedures many other men could achieve this kind of control over ejaculation. Certainly the results of the Masters and Johnson treatment program for premature ejaculation (Masters and Johnson, 1970), as well as other experiments on developing voluntary control of erection (Laws and Rubin, 1969) suggest that men can increase voluntary control over both of these aspects of their genital response. In any case, there would be a sufficiently great self-selection factor in the subjects participating in this experiment that results might have but little generality to the rest of the population.

Somehow this was not really what we wanted to know about people anyway. It seems to me that the Coolidge Effect joke and related matters have more to do with concerns about monogamy and adultery than they do with interest in the kind of rapid-fire ejaculatory capacity that sheep display. Some important questions, for example, might be framed as follows: Is it a basic part of human sexual biology that a man who has lived with one woman for a given period of time (1 year, 5 years, 30 years) finds that woman less sexually arousing than he did before? Are the qualitative characteristics of that couple's copulatory behavior different from those observed when the man copulates with another woman? (For example, is he more enthusiastic and attentive, thereby increasing his partner's pleasure?) Is he more aroused by other women as time goes by? Do the same answers hold for women? What are the ranges of individual differences for men and women in this regard?

These are important psychological questions because they relate to behavior that has profound social consequences. Our rules and expectations about marriage and divorce, fidelity and adultery, monogamy and polygamy, have been conditioned by our basically non-scientific, intuitive responses to such questions. These are questions that have to do not so much with erections and orgasms per se, but with the social contexts in which these sexual events take place. It is the *contexts* of orgasms, not their *frequency* which are of primary importance in human sexual conduct.

As I emphasized at the beginning, there is a sexual tradition in our society that the availability of several female partners will enhance a man's sexual performance. The data of Kinsey and associates (1948) showed that married couples gradually decreased the frequency of their sexual contacts. Masters and Johnson (1965; 1970) claim that "psychological factors" are often responsible for declining sexual responsiveness in older men. In a very different type of society, the preliterate Pacific Island group described by Davenport (1965), the men complained that when the colonial authorities took away their concubines (women from other islands who served as sexual partners for the men in a single "club"), they found it difficult to maintain sexual interest in their wives.

Taken all together, these findings suggest that sexual variety might indeed have an enhancing effect on male sexual performance and interest. The same may very well be true for women. Perhaps it is true that, for many married couples, the quality and quantity of sexual experiences within the marriage would be enhanced by participation in sexual behavior outside the marriage. *But this does not mean, necessarily, that the marriage would be strengthened.* Before any conclusions about the advisability of extramarital sexual experience could be drawn from the realization that something like the Coolidge Effect exists in both men and women, a number of additional considerations would have to be dealt with. I am not about to deal with them here. I am not sure I would know how. Any reasonably serious student of the problem can generate a list of important considerations without difficulty. Rather I will close this chapter with the statement of Shah Zaman, who, in John Barth's novel *Chimera*, speaks of having sex with 2000 women in 2000 consecutive nights. Here is what the Shah concluded:

> *Tall and short, dark and fair, lean and plump, cold and ardent, bold and timid, clever and stupid, comely and plain—I bedded them all, spoke with them all, possessed them all, but was myself possessed by nothing but despair. Though I took many, with their consent, I wanted none of them. Novelty lost its charm, then even its novelty. Unfamiliarity I came to loathe: the foreign body in the dark, the alien touch and voice, the endless* exposition. *All I craved was someone with whom to get on with the story of my life, which was to say, of our life together· a loving friend; a loving wife; a treasurable wife; a wife; a wife (Barth, 1972, p. 52).*

Good luck to you.

REFERENCES

Almquist, J. and Hale, E. 1956. An approach to the measurement of sexual behavior and semen production in dairy bulls. *Proceedings of the Third International Congress on Animal Reproduction.* Cambridge, England: Plenary Papers, pp. 50–59.

Banks, E. 1964. Some aspects of sexual behavior in domestic sheep, *Ovis aries. Behaviour,* 23:249–279.

Barth, J. 1972. *Chimera.* New York: Random House.

Beach, F. 1970. Coital behaviour in dogs. VIII. Social affinity, dominance and sexual preference in the bitch. *Behaviour,* 36:131–148.

Beach, F. and Jordan, L. 1956. Sexual exhaustion and recovery in the male rat. *Quarterly Journal of Experimental Psychology,* 8:121–133.

Beamer, W.; Bermant, G.; and Clegg, M. T. 1969. Copulatory behavior of the ram, *Ovis aries.* II: Factors affecting copulatory satiation. *Animal Behavior,* 17:706–711.

Bermant, G. 1967. Copulation in rats. *Psychology Today,* July 1967:52–61.

Bermant, G.; Anderson, L.; and Parkinson, S. 1969. Copulation in rats: Relations among intromission duration, frequency, and pacing. *Psychonomic Science,* 17:293–294.

Bermant, G. and Davidson, J. M. 1974. *Biological Bases of Sexual Behavior.* New York: Harper & Row.

Bermant, G.; Lott, D.; and Anderson, L. 1968. Temporal characteristics of the Coolidge Effect in male rat copulatory behavior. *Journal of Comparative and Physiological Psychology,* 65:447–452.

Bermant, G. and Westbrook, W. 1966. Peripheral factors in the regulation of sexual contact by female rats. *Journal of Comparative and Physiological Psychology,* 61:244–250.

Cherney, E. and Bermant, G. 1970. The role of stimulus female novelty in the rearousal of copulation in male laboratory rats. *Animal Behavior,* 18:567–574.

Conoway, C. and Koford, C. 1965. Estrous cycle and mating behavior in a free-ranging band of rhesus monkeys. *Journal of Mammalogy,* 45:577–588.

Davenport, W. 1965. Sexual patterns and their regulation in a society of the Southwest Pacific. In F. Beach (ed.), *Sex and Behavior.* New York: Wiley, pp. 164–207.

DeVore, I. 1965. Male dominance and mating behavior in baboons. In F. Beach (ed.), *Sex and Behavior.* New York: Wiley, pp. 266–289.

Fisher, A. 1962. Effects of stimulus variation on sexual satiation in the male rat. *Journal of Comparative and Physiological Psychology,* 55:614–620.

Fowler, H. and Whalen, R. 1961. Variations in incentive stimulus and sexual behavior in the male rat. *Journal of Comparative and Physiological Psychology,* 54:68–71.

Hale, N. 1971. *Freud and the Americans.* New York: Oxford University Press.

Hanby, J.; Robertson, L. T.; and Phoenix, C. H. 1971. The sexual behavior of a confined troop of Japanese macaques. *Folia primatologia,* 16:123–143.

Henson, D. E. and Rubin, H. B. 1971. Voluntary control of eroticism. *Journal of Applied Behavioral Analysis,* 4:37–44.

Hsiao, S. 1965. Effect of female variation on sexual satiation in the male rat. *Journal of Comparative and Physiological Psychology,* 60:467–469.

Hsiao, S. 1969. The Coolidge Effect in male rat copulation: failure to replicate Fisher's results. *Psychonomic Science,* 14:1–2.

Kinsey, A., et al. 1948. *Sexual Behavior in the Human Male.* Philadelphia: Saunders.

Kummer, H. 1968. *Social Organization of Hamadryas Baboons.* Chicago: University of Chicago Press.

Larsson, K. 1956. *Conditioning and Sexual Behavior in the Male Albino Rat.* Stockholm: Almqvist and Wiksell.

Laws, D. and Rubin, H. 1969. Instructional control of an autonomic sexual response. *Journal of Applied Behavioral Analysis,* 2:93–99.

Le Boeuf, B. 1972. Sexual behavior in the Northern Elephant Seal, *Mirounga angustirostris. Behaviour,* 41:1–26.

Legman, G. 1968. *Rationale of the Dirty Joke.* New York: Grove Press.

Masters, W. and Johnson, V. 1965. *Human Sexual Response.* Boston: Little, Brown.

Masters, W. and Johnson, V. 1970. *Human Sexual Inadequacy.* Boston: Little, Brown.

Parks, A. S. and Bruce, H. M. 1961. Olfactory stimuli in mammalian reproduction. *Science,* 134:1049–1054.

Pepelko, W. and Clegg, M. T. 1965. Studies of mating behavior and some factors influencing the sexual response in the male sheep, *Ovis aries. Animal Behavior,* 13:249–259.

Wilson, J.; Kuehn, R.; and Beach, F. 1963. Modifications in the sexual behavior of male rats produced by changing the stimulus female. *Journal of Comparative and Physiological Psychology,* 56:636–644.

CHAPTER 5

ENVIRONMENTAL DETERMINANTS OF FEEDING BEHAVIOR OR HOW TO TURN A RAT INTO A TIGER

George H. Collier
Robin Kanarek
Edward Hirsch
Alan Marwine

The history of comparative psychology reflects a continuing controversy between those investigators whose work emphasized the study of animals in their natural environments and those who viewed the laboratory animal as a convenient model for the study of general processes such as motivation or learning. The fieldworkers were concerned with the adaptation of animals to specific environments, while the laboratory workers were trying to develop "universal" laws of behavior to account for these general processes. The two groups often have used very different methods and carried out very different kinds of research.

OF MODELS AND MECHANISMS

In their thinking about behavioral processes, psychologists, like physicists, chemists, or economists, often are aided by developing analogies or *models* which attempt to account for the observed facts. Let me begin by describing the model which is most widely used by psychologists to account for the facts of feeding behavior as they relate to the organism's intake and expenditure of energy.

When we examine the feeding behavior of any animal, including humans, two of its characteristics are immediately striking. First, eating is intermittent. Even when food is constantly available—as it is to humans and to laboratory animals on an *ad libitum* schedule—the animal ingests its daily food intake in a series of discrete meals,

George H. Collier is affiliated with the Department of Psychology, Rutgers University, New Brunswick, N. J. Robin Kanarek is with the Department of Nutrition, Harvard School of Public Health, Harvard University, Boston, Mass. Edward Hirsch is on the faculty of the Department of Psychology, Mount Holyoke University, South Hadley, Mass. Alan Marwine is affiliated with the Department of Animal Behavior, American Museum of Natural History, New York, N. Y.

interrupted by other activites. Second, despite very great variations in the day-to-day expenditure of energy and considerable variation in energy intake, the body weight of animals and humans is remarkably constant from day to day.

We have, then, variable energy intake and variable energy expenditure, but a constant end product in the form of body weight. These facts immediately suggest the presence of a mechanism for *regulation* —some process which detects energy expenditure and operates upon feeding behavior to insure a food intake sufficient to compensate for the loss of energy. In other words, information about energy depletion or energy expenditure is monitored by the body and this information is available as *feedback* to those portions of the nervous system controlling food intake. The greater the depletion—so this model assumes—the greater the hunger and the more prolonged or intense will be the feeding behavior.

This "model" of hunger motivation is a familiar one and reflects the way most of us think about hunger, even in humans. Moreover, by now the notion of a feedback mechanism is very familiar. The most common of these mechanisms probably is the thermostat which regulates the temperature of our houses. The operation of a thermostat involves the constant monitoring or measurement of room temperature and the feedback of temperature information to a device which turns the furnace or air conditioner on or off in order to maintain a constant level of temperature in the room. The analogy of the thermostat with prevalent modes of hunger motivation is complete when we recall that just as the desired temperature can be preset and maintained constant, so is body weight maintained constant by the operation of the hypothetical weight sensing mechanism.

This cybernetic model of hunger derives historically from the physical sciences and more recently from physiology. It is based upon a mechanistic conception of nature dating back to the work of the seventeenth century philosopher, René Descartes. Descartes viewed animals as reflex machines pushed into motion by external energy sources in the form of stimuli. In the nineteenth century, the French physiologist Claude Bernard developed the concept of the *milieu interne*—the internal environment—and pointed out that a variety of physiological mechanisms existed which maintained various bodily constituents within relatively constant values. In the early part of the twentieth century, the American physiologist Walter Cannon investigated these mechanisms in more detail and coined the term *homeostasis* to refer to the processes which maintain the constancy of the internal environment. If homeostatic mechanisms can physiologically regulate the amounts of sugar, salt, or water, in the blood, or the ratio of acids to bases, it seemed reasonable to assume that similar mechanisms would account for the control of food and water intake and the regulation of body weight.

As this model of motivation was refined over the years, it has given us the simple, elegant framework of a mechanical, homeostatically motivated automaton whose optimum state is quiescence. It is from within this framework that much of the research on hunger has been carried out. Investigators have completed vast numbers of studies in search of some physiological factors which can be correlated with hunger and satiety, that is, with the initiation and termination of feeding. It has also led to a careful examination of the effects of food deprivation and body weight loss upon hunger, as measured either by feeding behavior itself or by the probability of engaging in food-reinforced instrumental behaviors such as bar-pressing. The approach taken by these investigators has been characterized as the "refinement experiment," and in many ways it copied the approach of the earlier physicists. The logic of these experiments has been to make them as "pure" and "controlled" as possible in an attempt to eliminate "extraneous" factors. Animals used in such studies are raised in a sterile, stimulus-impoverished environment, and isolated from interaction with other animals in an attempt to guarantee that they are "naive." The testing situation is designed to limit both stimulus and response possibilities. The experimenter controls both the initiation and termination of test sessions, the kind and amounts of food available, and the rate at which it is made available. Such studies usually are carried out with deprived animals in order to insure that the animal will respond in the test situation—it is presumed that the animal is goaded into action by various internal forces resulting from depletion. Finally, the unit of response in such experiments is generally something called the feeding (or drinking) response—whether this response is a lick at a drinkometer or feedometer or a bar press. It has been assumed that the laws obtained in such artificial, highly constrained situations are fundamental and can be combined to provide a description of more complex behaviors in more elaborate environments.

It is true that this approach has generated precise, reproducible functions in many cases. Thus, body weight loss (produced by water or food deprivation) has been shown to effect bar pressing for food (or water) in an orderly way across several species (Fig. 5.1). Similar results have obtained for other measures of hunger. However, this approach runs into several problems when we compare feeding behavior in the natural situation or in the free-feeding laboratory animal with that seen in the kinds of experimental studies I have been describing.

To begin with, the most obvious characteristic of feeding behavior in an unconstrained situation is that feeding occurs in meals. This being the case, it is necessary to ask whether the *meal* is a more appropriate unit for the analysis of hunger than is the feeding *response*. From the time scientists such as Curt Richter first began studying meal patterns, they found that the most useful units of analysis

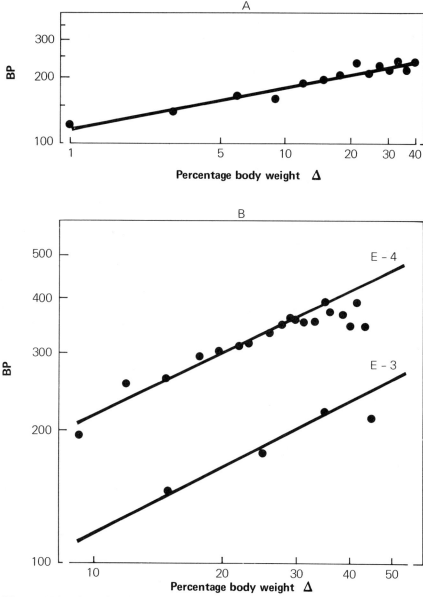

Figure 5.1. *Log bar-press rate as a function of log percentage body weight (A) in hungry rats, and (B) in thirsty rats.*

(or parameters) were the frequency, the duration, and the rate of eating, as well as the interval between meals. Moreover, they studied meals in the *free-feeding* situation, where the subject initiated and terminated the meals and thus had control of these parameters. These early studies showed that meals occurred with a characteristic frequency and had a characteristic distribution over time. Thus, for example, the rat takes most of its meals at night and ingests his entire daily food ration in about 8–14 meals per day.

In attempting to explain these meal patterns in terms of the homeostatic model, workers such as LeMagnen have hypothesised that the beginning and ending of each meal is correlated with fluctuations in the level of some circulating metabolites correlated with depletion or satiation. Other workers have tried to uncover relations between metabolic processes, brain mechanisms, and meal patterns.

On the other hand, it is hard to account for such meal patterns by the homeostatic model of depletion and repletion alone. It is well known that these patterns are related to environmenal factors such as the light-dark cycle, past experiences with food availability, and opportunities to engage in activities other than eating. Moreover, it is hard to see any obvious connection between such short-term inake patterns and depletion or deprivation. That is, it seems unlikely that any significant degree of depletion is taking place in the relatively brief intermeal intervals. If this were the case, there would be no information about depletion to be fed back and initiate a new meal.

It would seem that in addition to homeostatic aspects, there are several other factors to be considered in trying to explain feeding behavior. To begin with, as Wynne-Edwards has pointed out, deprived animals are seldom observed in nature. Both in the field and the lab, the meal pattern of many animals is such that it is unlikely that they undergo short-term depletion. The most obvious examples are ruminants, such as cows. The nature of their digestive process creates a situation in which the gut acts as a large reservoir and the input of nutrients across the intestinal lumen is essentially constant. Examination of the stomach contents of freely feeding rats and guinea pigs in our laboratory reveals a similar phenomenon, because we have never observed a completely empty stomach, again suggesting a nearly constant input of nutrients. It appears that at least some animals eat in such a fashion that they are never hungry in the depletion sense of the term. How then are we to account for the existence of relatively precise and consistent feeding patterns?

ECOLOGY AND HUNGER:
THE NATURAL HISTORY OF FEEDING PATTERNS

A possible answer to this question was suggested to us by the literature on ecology as it relates to the nutrition and feeding behavior of animals living in their natural habitats. It often has been pointed out that the density of animals in intact ecological systems tends to match the exploitable resources. In addition to matching their numbers to the available resources, species have specialized in exploiting specific food items and they occupy different positions in the food chain. Animals have evolved to occupy and exploit certain types of environmental niches. Behavior, no less than structure, is selected and refined by the same iron law of "reproductive potential." An animal's feeding behavior must somehow be appropriate to the niche it occupies. In its broadest sense, the niche includes not only the food the animal eats, but social, physical, climatic, ecological, and nutritional factors. To see how some of these variables may participate in the control of feeding behavior, let us consider what has been called the *feeding chain* and the feeding *strategies* which form the links of this chain.

DIETARY DIMENSIONS AND FEEDING STRATEGIES

In thinking about the characteristics of the foods eaten by different animals, we can arrange them in three categories—availability, caloric density, and nutritional quality. Similarly, we can arrange animals in three categories with respect to their major sources of food—herbivores, carnivores, and omnivores. Now, it becomes immediately obvious that two of the three types of animals specialize in foods which differ with respect to the three categories. Thus, the herbivore's diet of vegetable matter is highly available, but is low in caloric density and nutritional quality. The carnivore's diet is relatively low on availability by comparison with the herbivore's, but compensates for its low availability by its high nutritional quality (i.e., it is a replica of the animal's bodily composition and therefore needs little digestive reprocessing). It is also of relatively constant caloric density. The diet of omnivores is notable primarily for the fact that it varies in availability, caloric density, and nutritional quality. All items of food ingested in this diet will not be equal in nutritional quality or caloric density as will be the relatively uniform diets of the herbivore and carnivore.

With these differences in the properties of the foods they eat, each group of animals faces certain problems in relating energy intake to energy expenditure. It would not be surprising to find, therefore, that they exhibited what may be called different *feeding strategies* to deal with these problems. Moreover, these strategies must be sensitive not only to the quality of the diet, but to such factors as whether the animal is primarily preyed upon or is itself a fairly invulnerable predator preying on others.

When the term *strategy* is applied to human behavior, it implies a choice among several available courses of action in order to achieve a goal most efficiently. As used to describe the feeding behavior of animals in different ecological niches it is, of course, a metaphor. But it is a useful metaphor, because it focuses on the fact that feeding behavior involves the interaction of a number of basic characteristics or parameters. None of these parameters are fixed, and they may be combined in different ways to achieve the same goal. Analysis of free-feeding indicates that there are three obvious parameters which determine the amount of food eaten: frequency (number of meals), duration (length of meals), and intensity (rate of feeding). Since the same total food intake may be achieved by different arrangements of these parameters, animals may be said to exhibit different strategies in meeting their nutritional and energy needs.

As we have already noted, the location of an animal on the food pyramid produces certain environmental constraints or restrictions. We might expect animals with different types of diets to exhibit different strategies. Thus, animals at the bottom of the food pyramid exploit the readily available plant food. Although they have developed an extremely efficient digestive process for extracting the maximum nutritive value from their low quality diets, these animals pay a price for this easy access—of reduced caloric density and lesser nutritional quality. Herbivores are thus faced with the problem of ingesting large quantities of readily available plant food to achieve the same caloric and nutritional value they might achieve from smaller quantities of a diet with high caloric density and high, frequent meals of long duraton and low intensity or rate.

At the top of the food pyramid, the carnivores have sacrificed availability and gained foods of constant caloric density and high nutritional quality. This feeding habit requires a careful matching of the carnivore density to the density of prey, and a careful rationing of energy expenditure in discovery and capture of the prey. This has led to a pattern of relatively infrequent eating among carnivores. If they are large (say lions or tigers), and thus not threatened by other predators, they take large, long duration meals at a low rate of feeding and then let a long interval go by before they go out to hunt their next meal. However, small, social, and/or scavenging carnivores, such as hyenas and dogs, who are themselves potential prey or who compete with one another for prey, eat large meals at high intensity.

The omnivore, whose food varies enormously in quality and availability, has developed an opportunistic pattern of feeding which allows a wide choice of habitats. Moreover, the omnivore's food is likely to come in very different size packages and there is no obvious relationship between package size and caloric density or nutritional quality. It must thus develop some mechanisms which enable it to compensate effectively for variations in the deficiencies or excesses of calories which it may encounter.

There is another environmental constraint which may be important in determining an animal's feeding strategy. Seeds form the major portion of the diet of many animals, especially birds, and the seed represents a food "package" in which nutrients are available in units of different sizes, but of constant quality. However, the rate of ingestion is limited by the rate at which these packages may be procured and ingested. Seed eaters might then be expected to employ a strategy in which the rate of feeding, that is, the number of units taken in a given time, is varied to maintain the required nutritional inputs.

IMPLICATIONS FOR THE HOMEOSTATIC-DEPLETION MODEL

In thinking about the kinds of considerations which arise out of the animal's ecological situation, it seemed clear that the constraints of an animal's environmental niche must necessarily influence its patterns of feeding behavior. That is, one would expect animals occupying different ecological niches to exhibit different feeding patterns. The data taken under naturalistic conditions seemed to bear this out. It also seemed clear that one could not just dismiss such considerations even when studying the feeding behavior of highly domesticated species such as those used in the laboratory. In fact, the ecological data seemed to offer a serious challenge to the homeostatic model which suggested that feeding behavior was turned on and off by fluctuations in nutritive state, was related primarily to depletion processes, and depended upon feedback.

First of all, data on free feeding, whether acquired in the laboratory or in the field, suggested that the appropriate unit for the analysis of feeding behavior is not the feeding response per se, but the *feeding cycle*—the characteristic pattern of meal distribution shown by the animal. Second, these patterns appear to operate so as to prevent the kinds of depletion which are so important to the homeostatic model. The feeding patterns do not seem to be related to depletion in any obvious manner in the free-feeding situation. Finally, at least on a short-term basis, feedback does not seem to be involved, and the patterns of feeding are matched to environmental constraints so as to be appropriate to these constraints. That is, by some means as yet unclear, animals develop the response patterns appropriate to their ecological niche. Unless there are drastic changes either in the nature of the external environment (such as a natural disaster which changes food availability), or in their internal environment (such as pregnancy), this pattern successfully "anticipates" their nutritional requirements and is thus meshed to their niche, relatively dependent of feedback or depletion.

It is within this framework that we have now come to view the problem of feeding. If we are to bolster this framework with hard evidence, however, it is necessary that we develop experimental analogs for critical aspects of the environment, so that we can test the validity of our predictions about the relation of environmental factors to feeding patterns. In other words, we must construct laboratory analogs of availability, caloric density, nutritional quality, danger and/or effort involved in obtaining food, package size, etc. We could then explore the effects of these variables on the feeding patterns of different species.

ECOLOGICAL DETERMINANTS
OF FEEDING: EXPERIMENTAL STUDIES

While we cannot review all the experiments we have done within this framework, it might be interesting to examine the effects of three different environmental situations: first, the free-feeding situation; second, a situation in which availability is varied by varying the effort required to obtain a meal; and third, the effects upon patterns of feeding of putting the diet in packages of different sizes.

We chose as subjects three species: rats, cats, and guinea pigs —representing omnivores, carnivores, and herbivores. They were housed in separate cages and given an appropriate laboratory version of their typical diet, while their daily meal patterns, food intake, and body weight were recorded. In this free-feeding situation, there were no restrictions designed to influence feeding patterns, and we expected the animals to show the patterns characteristic of their species. In this respect we were not disappointed.

Caged young (and probably unhappy) house cats in this fairly homogeneous environment ate 9–10 meals per day. They ate the bulk of their meals at night and the largest meal following their exercise period. If we diluted their diet so that greater food intake was required to maintain equal caloric intake, they did not increase intake and lost weight over 2–3 months. They seemed to be treating their diet as if its caloric density and nutritional quality were constant (as it usually is for carnivores in the wild), and had no mechanisms for reacting quickly to variations in these qualities.

Caged rats ate 12–15 meals per day, with their largest meals just after and just before the daily maintenance period. They too showed a strong nocturnal pattern of feeding. Unlike cats, they responded to dilution or concentration of their nutrients by changing the meal frequency and increasing or decreasing their total intake as required. Thus, they fit the patterns suggested earlier for omnivore feeding and were able to compensate for variability in the quality of the diet just as they do in nature.

Caged guinea pigs, eating a laboratory version of a herbivorous diet, ate 22–25 meals per day. They showed no diurnal cycle, and were very regular in the pattern and amount of intake. They showed no increase in intake to a diet diluted with celluflour, and stubbornly refused to lose weight at any but the most diluted diet. In this respect, they were like other herbivores in showing an ability to extract nutrients from substances of very low nutritional quality, probably by increasing their utilization.

Thus, our three species gracefully fitted the predictions we had made which were based on an attempt to view them against their ecological backgrounds. Encouraged by these results, we pursued the study of their feeding patterns in several other directions. Our next study was designed to see what the effect of effort or availability might be upon the feeding strategies of these animals. In exploring this problem, we also were able to gather data on two problems which have puzzled students of food patterns for some time. First, widely different values have previously been reported for the daily frequency of meals for rats. Our results, on the other hand, had shown that meal frequency was quite stable and seemed to be characteristic of the individual animal. Differences in nutrient structure and composition (liquid versus solid) seem to be possible variables, but more intriguing was the possibility that it was the difficulty in obtaining the meal that might affect meal frequency. Richter had suggested earlier that the more difficult it was for a rat to obtain a meal, the less frequently he would eat.

The second puzzle arose from the implication of the depletion-repletion model of meal taking, that intermeal interval and meal size should be correlated. According to this, the longer an animal waited before initiating a meal, the hungrier it should be, and, consequently, it will consume a larger meal. On the other hand, larger meals would be followed by longer intervals of not eating. We have failed to find either correlation. No one has reported evidence of the intermeal-interval–meal-size correlation. The meal-size–intermeal-interval correlation is more of a problem. Several investigators have reported it; others have failed to obtain it. There is a possibility that significant values are the result of computational artifacts. The best strategy seemed to be to try to manipulate meal size and intermeal interval experimentally and examine the correlations. As stated above, increased effort to obtain a meal had been conjectured to reduce meal frequency and increase meal size. We decided to explore the relation systematically by introducing an instrument to which the animal would have to respond in order to get food. The response would involve various degrees of exertion which could be regulated prior to or during the meal. This would allow us to explore the meal-intermeal correlations and perhaps to explain the discrepancies in meal frequencies reported by different investigators.

Our apparatus consisted of a food magazine which was made available when the animal completed a required number of bar-presses. The animal controlled the size of its meal after obtaining the magazine. When the animal had stopped eating for a fixed period of time (10 min.) the magazine was removed and once again the animal had to make the required number of responses in order to feed.

The results for rats are shown in Figures 5.2, 5.3, and 5.4. They indicated that the rat is a very commonsensical animal. When food becomes more difficult to obtain, rats eat less frequently, but consume larger meals and in this manner maintain food intake and thus, body weight. The number of bar presses—5120 per meal—that the rat performed before he was reduced to one meal per day, is surprisingly large. These animals spent 2–3 hours of unremitting bar pressing in

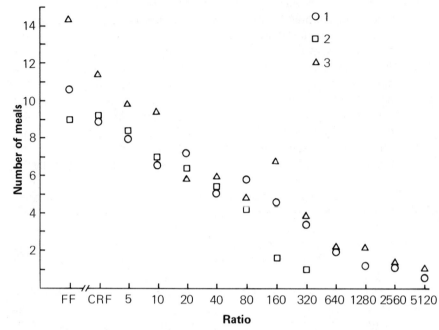

Figure 5.2. *Number of meals as a function of ratio size for each animal.*

order to complete the ratio run at the highest fixed-ratio values. The rat would do it in a leisurely fashion without increasing its rate of responding. Another surprise was that reducing meal frequency did not affect the meal-intermeal correlations. Neither correlation, when calculated on the data for a particular ratio size, approached significance.

The cat and guinea pig turned out to be as reasonable as the rat. The guinea pig data are exhibited in Figures 5.5–5.8. Again, at least some guinea pigs were able to sustain response requirements as high as 5120. They were in a greater hurry to get their meals, and increased their rate of responding and eating as the ratio size grew larger. Again, they managed to maintain intake over most of the range, although when their food intake started to fall, they still did not lose weight, somehow making more out of less. The cat results are shown in Figures 5.9–5.12. As befits a carnivore, the cat was able to sustain ratios as high as 10,240 which reduced it to a meal every 3–4 days. Even on this feast and famine routine, the cats were able to maintain average intake and thus body weight. Neither the cat nor the guinea pig showed the LeMagnen correlations at any ratio, although the cat showed occasional significant correlations between intermeal interval and meal size.

These results have quite serious implications for a depletion-repletion model. First, they show that variables exist, which are not

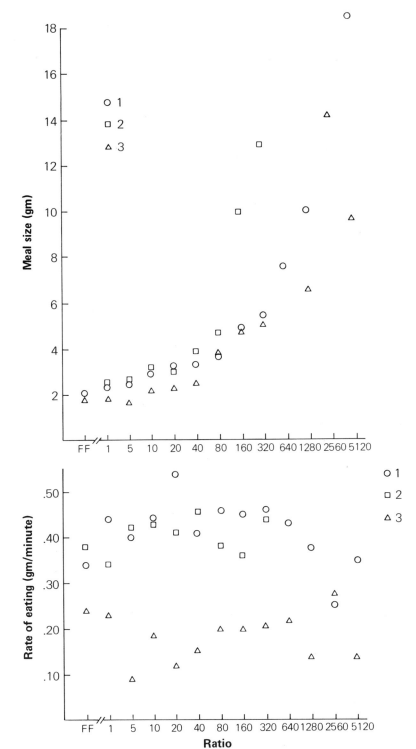

Figure 5.3. Meal size (above) and rate of eating (below) as a function of the ratio size for each animal.

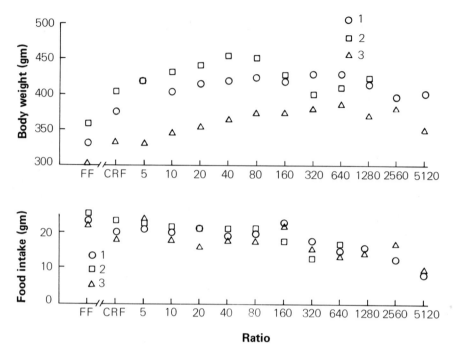

Figure 5.4. *Body weight and food intake as a function of ratio size for each animal.*

internally determined, which cause the animal voluntarily to change its pattern of feeding. Food availability appears to be an important determinant of this pattern. Second, changing the frequency of feeding does not appear to affect the meal-intermeal correlations as one would expect if the major determinants of initiation and termination of meals were the level of circulating metabolites or hormones, and the gastrointestinal load. The results show that these animals can change their pattern of regulation to reflect their environmental circumstances.

To assure ourselves that these results were not simply some peculiarity of bar pressing, the experiment was repeated using rats running in wheels to obtain their dinner. Again, meal frequency fell and meal size increased as the distance was increased. Similarly, when rats were made to work for water they reduced their frequency of drinking (one to two bouts per day at the highest requirements), increased bout size, and maintained intake and body weight. The pattern of food intake was unaffected by this change in pattern of drinking. These surprising results are less surprising when one remembers that at times the waterhole is difficult to get to, and it is a dangerous place for an animal in the wild. These factors would seemingly discourage frequent visits.

When constraints are placed on feeding by manipulating the

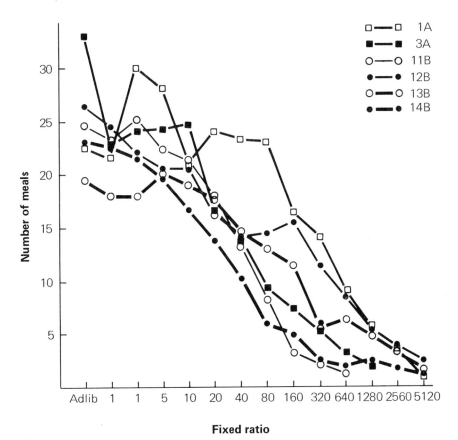

Fixed ratio

Figure 5.5. *Frequency of feeding as a function of ratio size.*

effort required to obtain the meal, animals will compensate by changing their pattern of feeding. Even more striking is the fact that the animal can sustain unexpectedly large instrumental requirements in order to effect this change in pattern. In all the cases presented, animals were "running" larger ratios than have been previously reported, and doing it when they were not deprived. This fact suggests that animals are capable of anticipating their requirements, rather than merely responding to them.

In the preceding experiment, the animal could maintain a constant intake in the face of decreased food availability (increased effort) by reducing the number of meals it ate, and increasing the size of each meal. In other words, the environmental constraint or restriction was availability, and the appropriate feeding strategy involved variation in the parameters of frequency and duration. Thus, we faced all three species with the environmental constraints normally faced by tigers—and they all behaved like tigers.

Having turned them all—temporarily—into tigers, we next asked

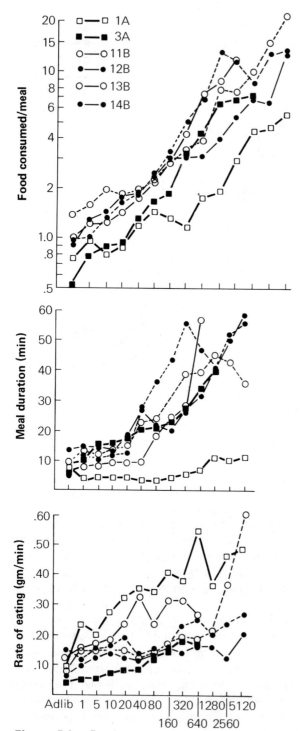

Figure 5.6. *Food consumed per meal (above), meal duration (center), and rate of eating (below) as a function of ratio size.*

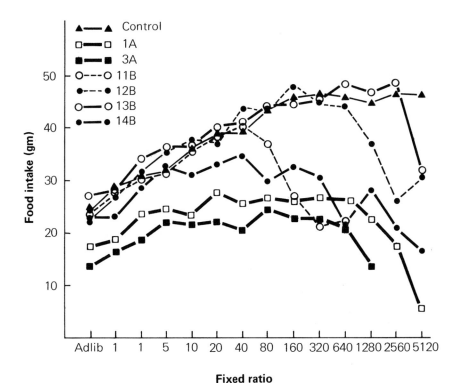

Figure 5.7. *Daily food intake as a function of ratio size.*

if we could turn them into pigeons. That is, we attempted to face our subjects with one of the constraints faced by many birds whose diet consists primarily of seeds or berries. In such a diet, the nutrient is packaged in units of constant size and quality, but different types of seeds or berries might have different nutritive values. In this situation, the rate of ingestion is limited by the rate at which these "packages" can be located and procured. In order to maintain a constant nutrient intake in the face of variations in package size or ease of procurement, the appropriate feeding strategy would involve variations in the *rate* of feeding, i.e., the number of individual feeding responses per unit time.

The experimental analog to this environmental situation involves presenting the food in small units and either varying the nutrient quality of each unit or varying the amount of behavior required of the animal between each unit. To do this, we used a standard operant situation (a fixed ratio schedule) to deliver a fixed portion of food (such as a .045 gm food pellet) for the performance of some fixed number of responses. Thus, using a free-feeding condition in which the animal has food available over 24 hour periods but must make one bar-press for each pellet, rats will eat approximately five pellets per minute during each of their meals.

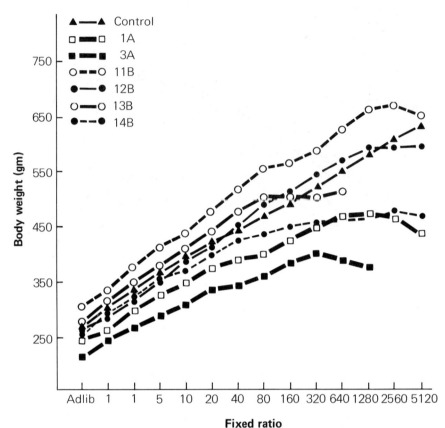

Fixed ratio

Figure 5.8. *Body weight as a function of ratio size.*

There are two ways in which the rate of eating can be constrained in this situation. First, additional responses can be interpolated between each pellet. For example, if the schedule is changed to FR 5, the time between each pellet will increase. A second constraint can be accomplished by changing pellet size, e.g., from .045 to .022 or .090 gms, thus changing the amount consumed per ingestive act. If an animal has a "natural" ingestive rate, which it will defend, it can be predicted that any behavior which will enable the animal to accomplish this normal rate of eating will be increased. Thus, it would be expected that increasing the number of responses between pellets or decreasing pellet size would increase rate of responding. Figures 5.13–5.15 show the results for rats freely feeding when the number of bar-presses per pellet is increased. Normally, the rat eats about 500 pellets per day, .045 gm each. If it were to maintain its intake at this level as the number of bar presses increased from 1 to 200 bar-presses per pellet, the rat would have to increase the total number of responses from

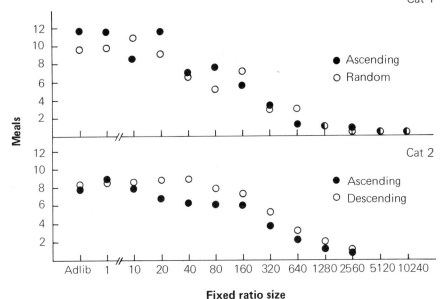

Figure 5.9. *Number of meals as a function of ratio size.*

500 to 100,000. The rat does not quite reach this total, asymptoting at approximately 70,000, and suffering a small decline in food intake. As expected, rate of responding during a meal increases from 5 bar presses per minute to almost 120 per minute (7000 per hour). This astonishing increase in rate should be compared with the results from the previous situation in which rate of responding did not change as the number of responses to accomplish feeding increased. Number of meals does not change in this paradigm, since change in meal frequency does not affect rate of ingestion. Body weight does not fall below 6 percent of initial weight even at the highest ratios. Similar results were found for guinea pigs showing that this effect is not specific to the rat. Here again, we find the rate of eating, as well as frequency, are primary meal parameters.

There are no data on manipulation of duration of meals in the free-feeding situation, but it could be expected that such a manipulation would affect frequency and/or rate of eating. That is, a constraint on one parameter would produce an appropriate variation in other parameters to maintain a constant intake.

ECOLOGY, HOMEOSTASIS, AND MOTIVATION: TOWARD A MORE COMPREHENSIVE FRAMEWORK FOR THE STUDY OF FEEDING BEHAVIOR

The basic assumption of the homeostatic theory of motivation is that motivation to eat is a function of the time elapsed since the last eating, and is the result of the depletion which takes place during

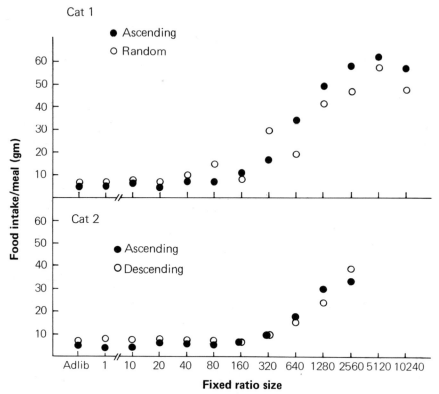

Figure 5.10. *Food consumed per meal as a function of ratio size.*

that interval. It is a fact that animals deprived of food lose body weight. Under normal conditions, rats lose about 3 percent of their body weight per 24 hours during starvation (Fig. 5.16). However, numerous studies show that animals do not exhibit a relation between instrumental response parameters (such as rate of responding for food) and body weight loss until they have lost 7–10 percent of their body weight—until almost 2 days of starvation. The implication of these facts is that the intermeal interval is not an important determinant of free feeding until the animal is in an emergency situation. This conclusion contradicts the classic view in that it suggests that there are two independent processes controlling food intake. The first of these controlling processes is based on patterns of food intake expressing the species adaptation to its ecological niche (its feeding strategy); these prevent the animal from undergoing depletion by utilizing the reserve maintained in the gastrointestinal tract. The second controlling process is based on body weight loss, and acts as an emergency system. One set of variables controls intake when the animal is freely feeding and has not undergone substantial body weight loss (less than that produced by 1–2 days starvation); a second

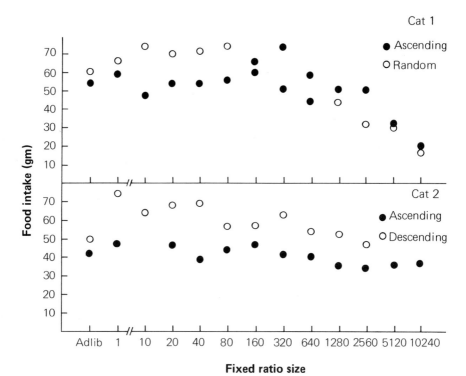

Figure 5.11. *Total food intake as a function of ratio size.*

set of variables takes control when body weight loss is substantial. It would seem that the amount of behavior that can be generated in anticipating needs, in terms of size of FR tolerated or speed of responding, for example, is much greater than that generated by the emergency response. To construct adequate accounts of motivation, we must consider the problems the animal is trying to solve in its commerce with this physical and social environment, as well as its momentary physiological state.

Returning to the question of homeostasis, it would seem profitable to divide regulatory processes into three categories. First, it seems clear that there are homeostatic mechanisms relating the circulating metabolites to the animal's reserves. This is an entirely internal system which maintains the nutritional milieu of the cells. Second, it also seems clear that there is a long-term mechanism relating intake and reserves, in such a fashion that constancy of body weight and composition are maintained. Finally, it would seem that there is a short-term mechanism in which environmental variables determine the pattern of intake, so that the average intake anticipates average expenditures in all but emergency circumstances.

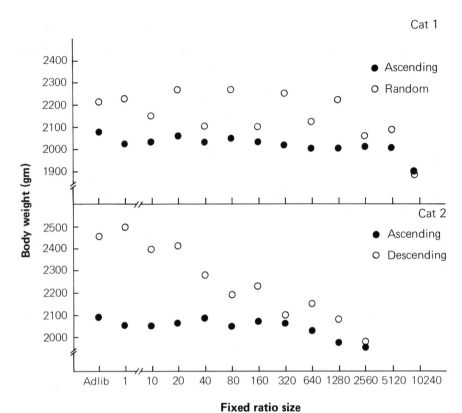

Figure 5.12.   *Body weight as a function of ratio size.*

The approach we have taken in this paper has some implications for our ways of thinking about reinforcement processes, particularly as they are studied in operant conditioning situations. The Skinner-box situation has always been viewed as studying the effect of reinforcement on response patterns. The assumption is that delivery of the reinforcer acts directly on response probability. The density and distribution of reinforcement (schedules) summate in some fashion to give rate of responding. Most important is the assumption that the fundamental dimension of responses is number; i.e., that the basic unit of analysis is the individual response. A different way to view this situation is to regard the typical Skinner-box *session* as a meal, one which the experimenter initiates and terminates and in which he controls the rate of ingestion. The manipulandum, the object manipulated by the animal (Skinner-box bar, lever, or key) can be viewed as a feeding utensil, a fancy fork. Within this framework, the experimenter can now be viewed as studying the effects of various constraints (schedules) on the structure of the meal, that is, on the pattern of ingestive responses.

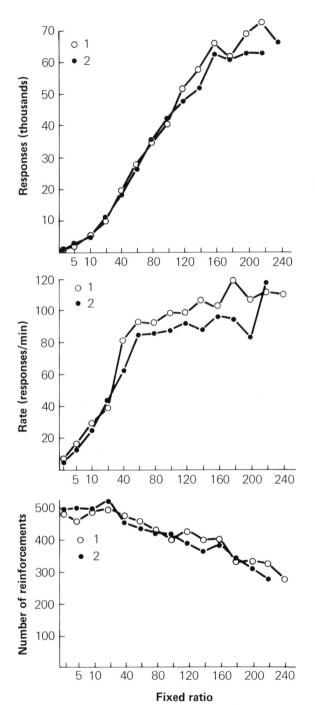

Figure 5.13. *Number of responses (above), rate of responses (center), and number of reinforcements (below) as a function of the ratio size for each animal.*

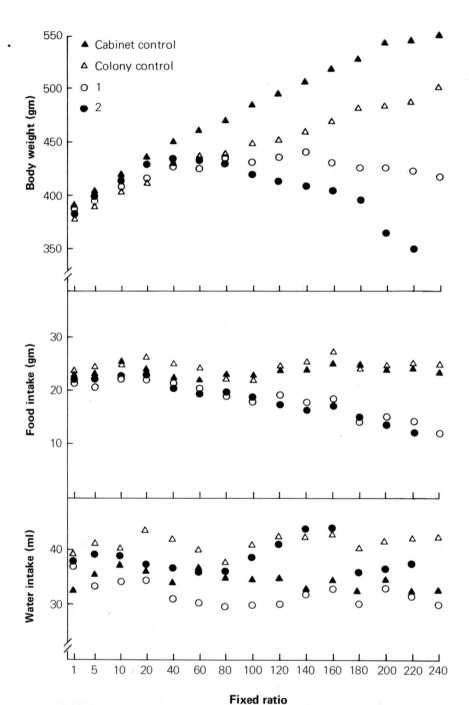

Figure 5.14. *Body weight, food intake and water intake as a function of ratio size.*

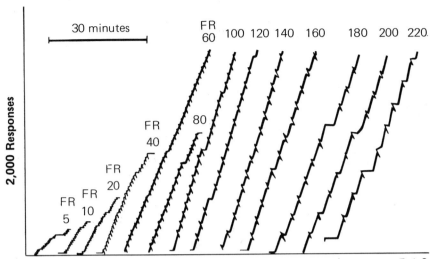

Figure 5.15. Samples of cumulative records taken at each ratio for Rat 2.

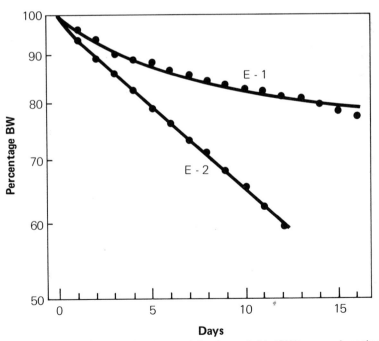

Figure 5.16. Log percentage of body weight (BW) as a function of days on a water ration (Experiment 1) and without water (Experiment 2).

LABORATORY AND FIELD STUDIES:
RESOLUTION AND FUTURE PROMISE

The quarrel between field and laboratory workers has a long and stormy history, and has led to the development of two disciplines —ethology and comparative psychology. Both are concerned with animal behavior, but there is only fragmentary communication between them. As we have seen, field and laboratory are not necessarily contradictory. It is the intention, if not the the accomplishment, of the present set of studies to bring field-derived concepts into the laboraory, by constructing simplified analogs of important field (relevant) variables. It is the assumption of this approach that one cannot understand either regulation or reinforcement without understanding their role in the total economy of the animal, nor can one discover laws without manipulating variables.

CHAPTER
6
THE K-DOGS
John L. Fuller

We called them the K-dogs because their life histories were reminiscent of the semilegendary Kaspar Hauser, the bewildered boy of about 16 who was found wandering the streets of Nuremberg one May afternoon in 1828. His story, as pieced together from contemporary accounts, included a long period of confinement in a barren room where he was tended by invisible jailers who visited his cell only while he slept. Somehow he escaped (or was released), and was forced to adapt to the life of a small German town. For a while the boy seemed to be cut off from communication with other persons, but gradually he became more and more verbal—eventually forming strong attachments to his mentors. His rehabilitation was cut short when he was stabbed to death while walking in a park.

The story of Kaspar was a sensation throughout Europe. Some thought the whole affair was a hoax; others considered this boy to be the rightful heir to a minor German principality, who was abducted from the court, probably when he was 3 or 4 years old, so that a rival contender could take his place. We shall probably never know the truth. However, Kaspar and others who have been subjected to extreme stimulus deprivation at an early age, can throw light on important psychological issues. We stress the importance of early stimulation for the intellectual, emotional, and social development of infants. Implicit in this concern with the first part of life is the notion that a person's future is built upon a foundation established during infancy and early childhood. Anselen van Feuerbach, writing of Kaspar Hauser in 1833, voiced this view as follows:

> Besides, one of the chief moments, which ought not to be
> overlooked, is this: since childhood and boyhood are given and
> destined by nature for the development and perfection of our
> mental as well as our corporeal life, and since nature overleaps
> nothing, the consequence of Kaspar's having come into the
> world as a child, at the age of early manhood, is, that the
> different stages of life which in other men are formed and
> developed gradually, have in him, both now and forever, been

John Fuller is Professor of Psychology at State University of New York, Binghamton.

displaced and improperly joined together. . . . He will, throughout his life, remain as regards his mind, less forward than his age.

A more modern expression of the importance of early experience was provided by Hebb in 1949:

It is proposed that the characteristics of learning undergo an important change as the animal grows . . . ; that all learning tends to utilize and build on any early learning instead of replacing it, so that much early learning tends to be permanent; and finally, that the learning of the mature animal owes its efficiency to the slow and inefficient learning that has gone on before, but may also be limited and canalized by it. . . .

The K-dogs enabled me and my co-workers, notably Lincoln Clark, to explore some of the consequences of early experiential deprivation and to evaluate the efficacy of various kinds of rehabilitation. Some of these findings may have implications for human beings, though one must always be cautious in transferring results from one species to another. Actually our first experiments were directed at a practical problem for which we adopted the puppy as an animal model for infant organisms in general. Puppies turn out to be especially attractive animals to work with, not only because of their attachment to humans, but also because of the importance of social behavior in their development. They also mature much more rapidly than chimps, which are another attracive species.

Partial isolation, hence a degree of experiential deprivation, was chosen as a technique for a psychopharmacological study. The experiments were carried out in the late 1950s when the drugs popularly known as tranquilizers were fairly new. Concern was expressed that deleterious residual effects on psychological competence might follow the treatment of overactive children with these substances. The early use tended frequently to subdue individuals so much that behavioral variety was severely restricted. It was hypothesized that tranquilization might curb undesirable behavior at the cost of interfering with the basic early learning emphasized by Hebb. Thus, its effects could be similar to those of sensory and social deprivation imposed by environmental restrictions.

DOES TRANQUILIZATION EQUAL DEPRIVATION?

We had problems in designing an experiment to test the drug-induced deprivation hypothesis. Keeping the puppies constantly drugged might impair their health and would have involved an inordinate amount of handling; furthermore, the additional contacts with the experimenter during administration could have disruptive effects in their own right. So we developed a situation of semi-isolation: The puppies were weaned at 3 weeks of age (when they can feed themselves). We know that even at this early age puppies have had many experiences and may have learned a great deal about the world. The puppies were placed in large, well-ventilated cages where they could be fed and watered through a porthole without seeing their caretakers. We could observe them, without being seen, through half-mirrored glass. Wastes fell through a perforated floor into a pan and were removed daily. The puppies thrived physically in these cages and, important to us, behaved normally when removed to a 10 ft square arena five times a week for a standard set of observations. Thus we could see and record all the social and manipulative behavior of our subjects for the duration of the experiment. In general, the isolation period ended at 16 weeks of age when normally reared puppies in our dog colony had acquired a behavioral repertoire which was substantially adult, although it did not include courtship, mating, or parental care.

The tranquilization study had a rather complex design, involving several combinations of drugged and drug-free groups, and permissive or disciplined rearing. The drug, chlorpromazine, was given orally 2 hours before the arena observations began. The arena experiences doubled as a source of data on behavioral development, and as an opportunity to treat the puppies in different ways. In the disciplined condition one of the arena toys was electrified, and the experimenter swatted the puppy firmly with a newspaper when it came too close during an off-limits period, to give just two examples. At other times the puppy was called and petted on approach. Clear signals were provided so that the subjects could distinguish between the "safe" and "not safe" times for social interaction with a human. In the permissive condition the puppy was never punished.

The outcome of the experiment did not confirm our hypothesis that tranquilization would interfere with behavioral development. To be sure, the drugged puppies were lethargic and a bit unsteady in the arena. They spent less time investigating the inanimate features of the arena, sniffing in corners, following a ball, and the like. But when a tranquilized and a nontranquilized puppy were placed together, their behavior was indistinguishable as they wrestled and chased each other in play.

Disciplined puppies quickly learned to avoid the experimenter during off-limits periods, but they showed no diminution in approach and play behavior during safe periods. Chlorpromazine-treated pups found it easier to unlearn avoidance habits when shifted from a disciplined to a permissive rearing procedure. This was expected, since a tranquilizer is supposed to operate by reducing fear—hence lowering the motivation to avoid a potential source of punishment.

The final appraisal of the effects of style of rearing and drug administration involved a series of runway dominance tests in which four members of a litter, each with a different type of rearing, competed for access to petting by an experimenter. No reliable differences, attributable to permissive versus disciplined rearing, or to chlorpromazine were found. In a way, then, the experiment failed since the hypothesis under test was not confirmed. Other tests or other procedures might have given different results, but the dominating impression for me was the robustness of the development process. The pups reared under semi-isolation behaved essentially like their cousins reared in litters by their mothers. This was surprising to me, since more than 99 percent of the period of most rapid behavioral maturation had been spent in isolation. How much could one reduce their visits to the arena without producing canine Kaspar Hausers?

A Dose-Response Study

Pharmacologists often perform dose-response studies in which a drug is administered in varying amounts and its effects measured on a quantitative scale. I decided to apply this concept to experience and rear puppies in my isolation chambers for a 12-week period with zero, one, two, or four excursions into the arena during each week. These subjects are hereafter referred to as Groups 0, 1, 2, and 4.

A fifth group (2-delayed) was isolated, like the others, at 3 weeks of age, placed on the zero schedule for the first 6 weeks and on the biweekly schedule for 6 more weeks. Thus they had the same amount of experience as pups tested once a week for the entire period. At 16 weeks of age all subjects were tested four times a week for 4 additional weeks. Behavior directed toward the experimenters, toys, and another puppy of the same breed and treatment were recorded along with activity. Ten beagles and 10 wire-haired fox terriers were subjects.

Whether the pups had one, two, or four arena visits per week had no effect on the frequency of their contacts with each other. Such contacts increased rapidly between the fourth and sixth week, and remained relatively stable for 9 more weeks. But the intensity of their interactions varied according to "dosage of experience." Group 4 puppies played tug-of-war when a towel was thrown between them; often one pup took full possession of the towel and defended it vigorously against his subordinate companion. Group 1 puppies spent much time together, but competition was seen only rarely. Group 2 puppies were intermediate. (See Figs. 6.1 and 6.2). Striking differences between the groups were also seen in amount of play with a bell. Perhaps the highly stimulating value of another puppy is attributable to an imprinting or conditioning process during the 3 weeks of group living with the mother. Further, it is possible that a live animal which moves spontaneously is a stronger eliciter of behavior than a bell which moves only when pursued. Regardless, the dose of experience needed to produce a puppy which plays vigorously with toys and competes with another puppy for possession of a well-chewed

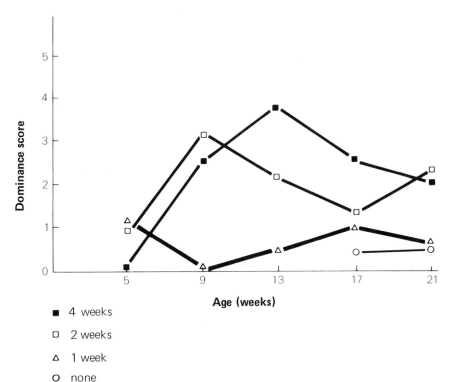

■ 4 weeks

□ 2 weeks

△ 1 week

○ none

Figure 6.1. *Effect of dosage of experience on average dominance behavior scored as amount of time spent competing for possession of a towel. Circles designate number of arena experiences per week from 4th through 15th week. All subjects were given four weekly trials during rehabilitation period (weeks 16–19).*

towel (apparently a great status symbol) is greater than that needed to produce a socialized puppy who plays sedately with its friend. One might ask if the puppies with smaller doses of experience are simply lethargic. No, indeed. The arena floor was marked off into nine squares and the number of movements between squares counted. Activity scores were about twice as great for Group 1 as for Group 4; Group 2 was intermediate. In fact, Group 1 puppies reminded us of some hyperkinetic children who flit from object to object, giving superficial attention to each (Fig. 6.3).

What happens to these puppies when they, along with the full-isolates, are given arena experience 4 days a week from age 16 to 19 weeks? This period of rehabilitation should indicate whether there is a critical age for the development of investigative, manipulatory, and social skills.

At the end of the rehabilitation period some striking breed differences in behavior were noted. Taking terrier scores as 100, beagles

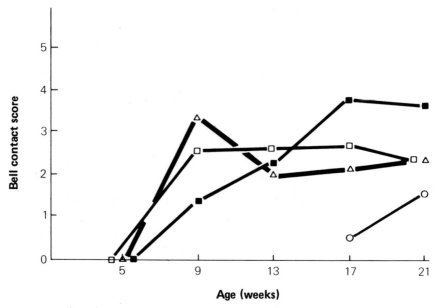

■ 4 weeks

□ 2 weeks

△ 1 week

○ none

Figure 6.2. *Effect of dosage of experience upon amount of play with a suspended bell. Generally, more experience produces more play, although there is little difference between the effects of one and two arena experiences per week.*

scored 45 in strong contacts with the experimenter (pawing, chewing clothes, etc.), 30 on strength of dominance in the towel test, and 60 in number of squares entered. On each of these measures the dosage of experience also had a powerful effect. Taking the scores of Group 4 as 100, the scores of Group 0 (full isolation for 12 weeks) were 12 for strong contacts with experimenter, 8 for dominance, and 300 for squares entered.

A number of other behavioral measures were practically identical in beagles and terriers, and these measures were also less influenced by the amount of arena experience. This occasioned some surprise. One might expect that environmental differences would predominate when genetic influences were small, and vice versa. But the opposite was found. It may even be true that behaviors with a strong experiential component, social dominance for example, may be particularly sensitive to modifications by genes. Certainly, results such as these expose the futility of arguments as to whether variability in a particular form of behavior is due to heredity or experience.

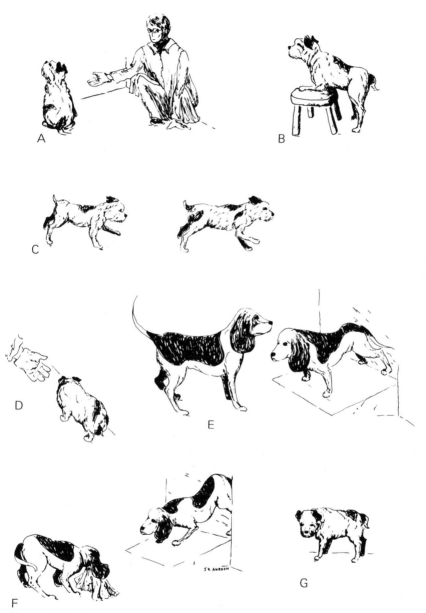

Figure 6.3. *A. K-dog orients away from experimenter. B. Rigid postures were maintained over long periods by many K-dogs, never by pets. Here is one characteristic pose. C. When first placed in the arena, K-dogs ran with a stiff-legged gait; here a male and female mechanically circle the arena together. D. Tail down, head-averted, body slumped, all characteristics of a K-dog. E. K-dog in transport cage orients toward pet in arena, but does not emerge completely. Note postural differences. F. Towel play. G. Karla before rehabilitation.*

MODIFIED ISOLATION

We had demonstrated a quantitative relationship between "dosage of experience" in the early postweaning stage and behavior of young "adolescents." A surprisingly small amount of time spent in the arena counteracted the more severe effects of isolation. I concluded that Hebb might have overstressed the slowness of perceptual learning; one minute per week was enough for puppies to acquire a suitable set of responses to a bell or to another puppy. Four minutes per week (spaced over 4 days) was still better, the responses being more vigorous if not more frequent. The observers of these partial isolates, all of them familiar with puppies reared in the ordinary fashion, were united in the opinion that brief breaks in isolation produced essentially normal puppies.

Actually, the puppies with four arena visits per week were almost supernormal. Their play was more intense and more continuous than usually seen, as though they had developed a hunger for social and manipulative experience during the long intervals spent in solitary confinement. Animals placed on a rigid schedule of feeding behave similarly when food is placed before them. We did not follow up this lead, but it supports the idea that there is a need for external stimulation which has some features in common with needs for food and water.

The direction we actually took was the qualitative rather than the quantitative modification of isolation. Beagle pups were transferred at weaning into one of five conditions. An isolation (I) group lived for 12 weeks under our Kaspar Hauser condition; an object experience (O) group had rubber toys like those used in the arena test placed in their isolation cages; a visual experience (V) group was allowed to look out at the laboratory and the people in it for 10 minutes twice a day; each member of a comparison (C) group shared an oversize isolation cage with a littermate; and a pet-reared (P) group was taken from isolation twice a day and allowed the run of the laboratory, during which time they could interact with people.

The modifications were effective. O puppies chewed their toys and had to be supplied with replacements; V puppies looked out of their windows and responded to the voice and gestures of the experimenters; C puppies played together in their cages; P puppies raced about the laboratory (they were not allowed in the arena) came on call, engaged in destructive activities from which they were firmly but gently dissuaded, and were in general much like ordinary lively housepets (Fig. 6.4).

It is convenient to evaluate the effects of modified isolation by comparing the O, V, and C pups with full isolates and with pet-reared animals. Here it is important to note a variation in our procedure. The basic test was unaltered; we recorded behavior directed toward a human, toys, and other puppies in a standardized order. But whereas

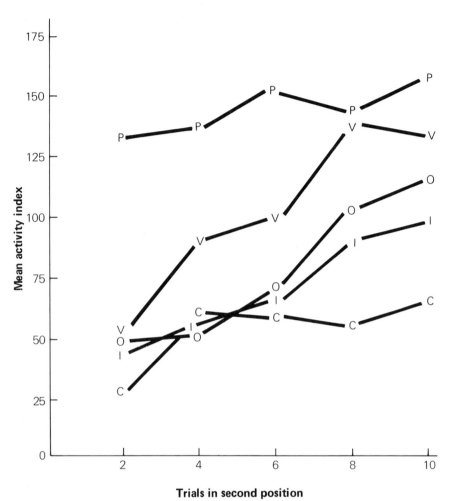

Figure 6.4. *The effect of variable kinds of modified isolation upon activity levels in the arena test during successive trials. Because of the test procedure, only alternate trials were comparable between individuals; hence, the 10th trial in second position is actually either the 19th or 20th exposure to the arena. Pet-reared (P) controls were essentially unchanged over the 5 weeks of observation. Visually-experienced (V) subjects eventually reached the same level. Object-experienced (O) and individual isolates (I) increased gradually, but companion-reared (C) subjects were more retarded than Is.*

previously we had carried subjects from their cages and lowered them gently into the arena, now we wheeled them to the scene of action in a transport cage with an overhead door. When the cage was aligned with an opening in the arena wall, the door was raised and the 7-minute observation period began. With this arrangement a pup could decline to participate and could remain in the transport cage without ever becoming involved with the test stimuli. The act of emergence, therefore, was critical for all scores and variation in the latency of emergence turned out to be the sensitive index of the effectiveness of our treatments. Thus, the use of this transport cage, which represented only a minor change of procedure, allowed us to see something important. Whether or not the animal *chose* to leave the cage and enter the arena could now be determined.

An experiment of this kind yields an immense amount of data. To make it more manageable I designed two indexes; one for activity (AI) and another for directed responses (RI). The activity index was a composite based upon the number of times subjects were observed lying down, standing, walking, running, or jumping. The response index was based upon the number of times the pup was seen to orient toward, approach, sniff, contact, or manipulate (with paws or jaws) one of the stimuli presented. High scores on these indices denote more vigorous activity or directed responses. The indices are not wholly independent; a nonemerging pup (low AI) could not obtain a high RI. But vigorous activity would not insure a high RI; some pups ran and jumped in rather aimless fashion and seemed to be little affected by the changes in stimuli which we provided.

The percentage of time spent in the arena gives a measure of the propensity of each group for interaction with a variety of stimuli. These values were: pet-reared, 95 percent; visual-reared, 29 percent; object-reared, 22 percent; full-isolates, 20 percent; and companion-reared, 12 percent. The pups with "enriched isolation" were closer to full isolates than to pets. In fact, there is a strong suggestion that companion-rearing has more severe aftereffects than solitary-rearing. Visuals did better than the above figures indicate. Although they were slow to enter the arena, they spent a great deal of time on the ramp leading down from the transport cage, and visually explored their environment more than any of the other isolate groups. Over the 5 weeks of observations their activity and number of directed responses came close to that of the pets. On both AI and RI, the companion-reared puppies were consistently lowest.

All of these data supported our view that the deficiencies of K-dogs are due primarily to the stress of emergence and not to a need for becoming familiarized with the specific stimuli used in the arena test. The records of individual pups confirmed the fact that, once a K-dog (of type I, O, V, or C) emerged and began to interact with people, toys and other pups, it distributed its responses almost identically with pets. Contacts with people, toys, and other puppies appeared to be reinforcing, although they had never been associated with the satisfaction of such biological needs as food and water. The K-dogs responded less vigorously than pets, but once involved in the arena they behaved in a normal manner. I interpret this as indicating that the K-dog's problem is not inadequate perceptual learning experiences, but inadequate habituation to complex stimulus fields. Sudden exposure to the arena floods the K-dog with many stimuli and it has no way of closing down some inputs and responding to a selected few. *Experience is at least as much a process of shutting down neural pathways as opening them up.*

REDUCING EMERGENCE STRESS

If our hunch were correct, then reducing the impact of emergence would make K-dogs more like their pet-reared brothers and sisters. Essentially there are two ways of doing this—by modifying the procedure so that isolates are gradually habituated to the arena, or by altering the internal state of the subjects. In one experiment we compared three groups of beagle puppies who were isolated at three weeks of age. One group (distributed experience) was brought to the arena once a week for 16 weeks. These puppies, even with such brief exposure to the outside world, behaved essentially like ordinary laboratory-reared dogs. They interacted vigorously with toys, people, and each other.

The other two groups were isolated until they were 16 weeks old—then they were brought to the arena four times weekly until they, too, had completed 16 tests. One group received chlorpromazine in their food just before each test; the second did not. Pups of both delayed-experience groups were less active and responsive in the arena than their littermates with the same amount of experience spread evenly through the experimental period. The delayed-experience puppies were not "perceptually blind." Persons, dogs and other puppies elicited orienting reactions, but relatively few approaches and contacts. In addition, there were reliable effects of the drug. Chlorpromazine-treated pups were more responsive than nondrugged pups, and our clinical judgment placed them closer to the distributed experience group than to the standard K-dogs.

These data tended to support the emergence-stress hypothesis—and this was encouraging. We planned an experiment to evaluate two modes of reducing stress in eight pairs of beagle puppies isolated for 12 weeks under our standard procedure, and then observed for 20 arena tests given over a period of 5 weeks. One member of each pair was stroked for 5 minutes following each test. Four of the pairs received chlorpromazine (CPZ) about an hour before going to the arena. We were particularly interested in differences in emergence time; more rapid emergence was interpreted as an indicator of reduced stress. The results appear in Table 6.1.

At first this seemed to be a puzzling and disappointing result. Why had the drug failed to facilitate emergence? More seriously, why had it actually inhibited emergence in the nonhandled group? A careful comparison with the procedures of our earlier experiment provided a cue. Because we had only one transport cage in our early stages,

TABLE 6.1 EFFECT OF CHLORPROMAZINE AND HANDLING ON EMERGENCE INTO ARENA

Treatment			
Handled	CPZ	First Eight Trials	End of Experiment
Yes	No	Learned to emerge, 3 min	Emerging in 6 sec
Yes	Yes	Learned to emerge, 3 min	Emerging in 6 sec
No	No	Learned to emerge, 4 min	Emerging in 12 sec
No	Yes	Remaining in transport cage	Emergence rare

we had to push the first tested puppy of each pair into the arena so that we could wheel the cart back to the cage room for the second. Thus, these animals were pressured gently into becoming involved with novel stimuli. In the second drug study we had two carts—subjects could remain there throughout the test and most of the drugged nonhandled puppies did just that. Favorable effects of chlorpromazine were thus contingent upon simultaneous exposure to handling. One might call it canine psychotherapy. Whether the drug was beneficial or detrimental with respect to behavioral development following experiential deprivation depended upon a procedural detail which we had overlooked.

ARE ALL DOGS ALIKE?
Individual variations in behavior were marked in all these experiments. Each subject had its idiosyncrasies: whirling, cautious approach to a toy followed by a quick avoidance, cuddling up to the experimenter, or chewing so vigorously that the handlers had to wear gloves and heavy coveralls for self-protection. Even animals with similar treatments had distinctive personalities. But the influence of such variables as schedules of experience, handling, and drug administration was powerful enough to show through the complex background of individual variation.

Nevertheless, the possibility of a genetic basis for differential vulnerability to experiential deprivation was constantly in our minds. The laboratory in which I worked was traditionally concerned with genetic analysis of behavioral variation. And so we carried out a number of experiments comparing the effects of experiential deprivation on beagles and wire-haired fox terriers. Terriers are more active and aggressive than beagles; they have higher heart rates, greater muscle tension, and larger adrenal glands. We had used both breeds in some of our early experiments, and were under the impression that isolation produced less drastic effects (or at least different ones) in terriers.

TABLE 6.2 CONDITIONS FOR TESTING TERRIERS FOR EFFECTS
OF ISOLATION

Group	Rearing	Testing in Arena
Companion-reared	With littermate in large cage	With companion
Isolation A	Standard isolation cage	With another isolate
Isolation B	Standard isolation cage	With a pet-reared littermate
Pet-reared	Isolation cage with run of lab for one hour daily	With isolated littermate

It was time, then, to put this idea to a formal test. Table 6.2 outlines the procedure. The isolation B group was introduced to see whether or not exposure of a K-dog to a pet-reared companion would have a beneficial effect—perhaps helping the isolate to recover more quickly from the effects of experiential deprivation. We knew that human intervention could facilitate emergence into the arena and considered it possible that a peer of essentially normal social behavior would be even more effective.

"Peer therapy" did not occur. Encounters with a pet-reared puppy in the arena were no more effective than companion-rearing in changing the behavior of K-dogs. For all practical purposes we had only four groups: isolated and pet-reared beagles, isolated and pet-reared terriers.

The K-beagles were less active than pet-beagles for 2 or 3 weeks, but by the fifth week the groups came together with average scores of about 140 on a scale with 360 maximum. K-terriers were less active than pets for the first week, but thereafter scored about 210 on our scale as compared with 160 for pets. Experiential deprivation, therefore, resulted in increased activity in the genetically more mobile terriers, and decreased activity in the more placid beagles. K-terriers were reminiscent of hyperkinetic children with short attention span. K-beagles, in contrast could be described as shy and retiring. We also, as in earlier experiments, measured the frequency and strength of responses to our standard stimuli: people, pups, and playthings. Again experiential deprivation affected the breeds differently. K-beagles averaged 230 points as against 302 for their pet-reared littermates. But K- and pet-reared terriers were practically indistinguishable with scores of 288 and 308 respectively. We could really see no lasting effects of experiential deprivation in these animals.

There can be no doubt that genes affect the recovery from isolation. Somehow K-terriers recover more rapidly from the condition we have called emergence-stress. They continue to be hyperkinetic but respond in normal fashion to social and physical stimuli. As expected, pets always won in dominance tests involving competition between pets and isolates, but the dominance differences were much less pronounced in terrier pairs than in beagle pairs. In our test (possession of a towel), the maximum possible margin of victory was 40 points; terrier-pets won by an average of 20 points; beagles by 33 points. This is the more remarkable because dominance hierarchies in standard reared terriers are more clearly defined than in beagles.

ARE K-DOGS UNINTELLIGENT?

The effects of isolation described thus far are related to social behavior, investigative play, and level of activity. The arena test cannot be considered a measure of intelligence. If more resources (people, money, space) had been available I would have tested all the K-dogs and their controls on a variety of learning tasks. However, we were able to test extensively only 16 isolation-reared and 6 pet-reared beagles. The subjects were between 23 and 26 weeks old when training started. All had recently been observed in 20 arena tests.

Their task was to push a slide with their noses to obtain a spoon-ful of commercial dog food. This was apparently so desirable a reward that it was unnecessary to deprive them of their ordinary dry chow before testing. There were two slides, one of which was locked, and the dog's task was to learn whether the right or the left one was movable. Once the task was learned satisfactorily, correct and incorrect slides were reversed until each subject had mastered 12 problems. This task, sometimes called reversal learning, has previously been found to be a good indicator of learning capacity, because it requires that the animals master a principle—choose the one, regardless of physical characteristics, which was last rewarded.

The scatter of scores among both groups was enormous (Fig. 6.5). On the very first task the poorest subject made 21 errors before meeting the criterion and the best made 2 errors. Both were K-dogs. On this first round the two groups differed insignificantly. Errors went up on the second and third rounds, significantly more in the K-dogs, but from then on the two groups could not be differentiated by standard statistical criteria. Most subjects became so adept that they made zero to three errors per series; the best performer of all was an isolate-reared female.

Insofar as this relatively simple task measures dog intelligence, we found no important effect of isolation. K-dogs, like Harlow's isolated monkeys (see Chapter 1) are deficient in social skills, often display bizarre behavior patterns, but most are still capable of per-forming well in formal learning tests. This experiment demonstrates that the immediate effects of experiential deprivation were counter-acted to a marked degree by a series of 20 arena tests. To the extent

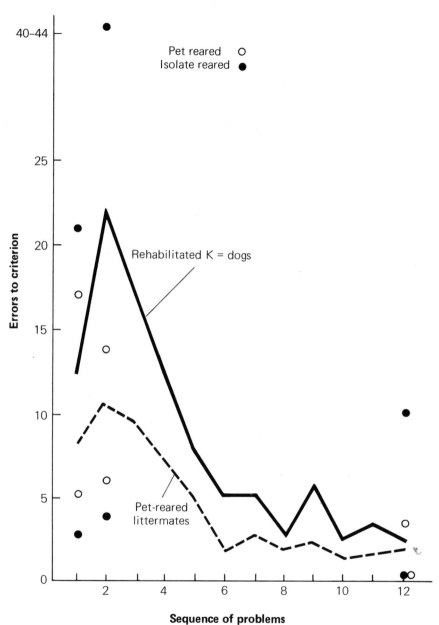

Figure 6.5. Average number of errors on successive reversals for a spatial discrimination task. The circles represent for selected problems the best and worst performance in each group. In each instance, both the individual with most and the individual with least errors was isolate-reared.

that the results might be transferrable to humans, this finding should promote optimism. But such a hopeful view must be tempered by other facts.

Three of the 16 K-dogs continued to perform poorly on the reversal problem. These animals did not appear fearful, but they could not shift their responses readily. On a statistical basis, we can say that K-dogs as a group were performing like pets by the end of the study; however, if we are concerned with individuals, it is clear that three of them were still retarded. Again, there is evidence that individuals differ greatly in their vulnerability to the isolation experience.

PERCEPTUAL DEFICIT OR EMERGENCE-STRESS

The series of experiments described in this chapter were initiated within a theoretical framework which emphasized the need for a long period of slow perceptual learning as a necessary predecessor for the rapid processing of sensory information and the execution of appropriate behavior. Using this model, the deficits in K-dogs could be attributed to an inadequately organized nervous system; recovery could be explicable by postulating a critical, or at least an optimal, age for such organization.

On the other hand, some of our data, particularly that from the chlorpromazine experiments, suggested that adequate perceptual and response capacities were present in K-dogs, but that the animals were simply too disturbed to perform. These two ways of looking at the results are somewhat similar to current debates about the nature of long-term memory.

It is well established that after loss of consciousness from electroconvulsive shock, a blow on the head, or anesthesia, individuals cannot recall events just prior to the traumatic event. This phenomenon, called retrograde amnesia, has been attributed to failure to "consolidate" into long-term memory incidents which occurred immediately previous to the loss of consciousness. Since no memory was stored, nothing can be recalled. Consolidation in the memory field may be compared with neural organization in the developmental area. If perception and stimulus processing have not matured because of experiential deprivation, the machinery for adaptive responses is not available for activation.

There is, however, another explanation for forgetting, which is not based on the consolidation theory. Perhaps the memory is stored, but its retrieval is somehow blocked. Many experiments have been performed which indicate that animals can be reminded indirectly prior to a test, and then demonstrate memories which seemed to have been lost. Such theories correspond to our emergence-stress explanation for the failure of K-dogs to participate in the arena test and for their occasional bizarre behavior when they do emerge. The following case study illustrates the point.

Theron and Kaspar: A Case Study

Experimental behavioral science is based upon studies of samples large enough to yield results which can be called "statistically significant." Single cases cannot be used as the basis for a general scientific theory, but sometimes observations on one or two individuals provide a striking demonstration of a principle. And so I shall conclude with an account of two brothers, Theron and Kaspar, wire-haired terriers who were male leads in a film made to illustrate our techniques and results.

Both dogs were isolated for 12 weeks beginning when they were 21 days of age and were treated exactly alike except that Theron received a moderately heavy dose of chlorpromazine on the first and second days only of his arena test. On his first emergence day Kaspar was removed from his cage and brought to the arena. The occasion was stressful for subject and experimenter alike. Kaspar screeched, tried to bite, urinated and defecated, and struggled to escape from the experimenter, an experienced and capable dog-handler. In the arena he alternated between leaping at the barrier, an awkward stiff-legged walk, and immobility. Neither the experimenter, the toys, or another puppy elicited any direct response. Here was a K-dog of the most extreme sort.

Theron on first emergence day was a dramatic contrast. He was relaxed as he was carried to the scene of action; he first stayed near a seated person and then followed closely when the experimenter walked about the arena. When called from across the arena, Theron ran quickly toward the caller. Later he played actively with a ball and a swinging pendulum, and wrestled playfully with another puppy. An observer, not aware that Theron was really a K-dog, would have judged him a normal puppy with previous arena experience.

Over a 5-week period the differences between Theron and Kaspar lessened, but in a dominance test at the end of the observations, Theron was clearly the top dog. It is worth noting that continued drug administration was not required for him to function well in the arena. Overcoming the initial block was the crucial factor; after that the arena situation itself sustained behavior.

Theron and Kaspar had identical experiential backgrounds; hence Kaspar's troubles cannot be explained by his prior deprivation. What then did cause them? One might seek an answer at several levels: psychological, physiological, or biochemical. It is plausible that Kaspar's problems arose because he was literally flooded with stimulation when suddenly taken from his safe, dull cage. The commonplace arena was as stimulating to him as exploding firecrackers and flashing lights might be to a more sophisticated dog. And so Kaspar had a full-blown fear fit. His trouble was not inability to perceive his new environment— he perceived it unselectively and totally. With the benefit of weekly exposure he would have learned to tune out some of the input and concentrate on the humans, toys, and puppies, the optimal sources of reinforcement.

As for Theron, the most interesting facet of his behavior is his immediate recognition of humans, dogs, and mobile toys as the most fruitful objects for investigation. Theron spent little time sniffing at the floor and walls of the arena. These simply were not as attractive as our carefully planned stimuli. In contrast, Kaspar commenced his slow progression toward more normal activity, by extensive investigations and contacts with the stationary, inanimate appurtenances of the arena. I speculated that he was seeking an optimal level of arousal and that our standard stimuli for many days elicited an unpleasantly strong response.

Isabelle and Anna: Modern Human Case Histories

Kaspar Hausers are fortunately rare, but they still appear from time to time. Kingsley Davis (1947) reported the story of Isabelle who was confined to a small, dark room with her deaf-mute mother up to the age of 6 years. When she was discovered and placed in a foster home she was rachitic, and could not understand the simplest speech. She was "like a wild animal" in the company of strangers, particularly men. Standard tests showed that her hearing and eyesight were normal, but she was classified as uneducable. Fortunately, some of her caretakers did not accept this evaluation and made an effort to teach her. A dramatic change occurred. Within 2 months Isabelle was putting sentences together; after 11 months she could identify words and sentences, write well, add to 10, and retell a story. Two years after removal from isolation Isabelle had regained her lost ground and was functioning at the intellectual level appropriate to her age. And there she stayed. At the time of the Davis report there was every indication that she would have a life much like the rest of her schoolmates, successful but not distinguished. I learned of Isabelle long after the K-dog experiments were finished, and I am impressed by the similarities. There are differences, of course, but both the human and the dog retain the ability to recover from long periods of isolation.

Not all cases of human isolation have as happy an outcome. In the same paper Davis reported on Anna, who remained severely retarded during 4 years after she was taken away from a situation similar to Isabelle's. It is possible that Anna had a genetic defect, or an injured brain and would have been retarded under the best conditions. We shall never know.

AFTERTHOUGHTS

To me the significance of the dog experiments and the human case histories is that prolonged environmental deprivation need not cause permanent retardation, at least in the cognitive sphere. Perhaps we have been too hasty in attributing the defective cognitive skills of many poor children to experiential deprivation. After all, their environments are much more complex than those of Theron, Kaspar, Isabelle, and Anna.

More likely, the critical factor is in the qualitative rather than the quantitative aspects of their experience, and in the acquisition of behavior patterns which are adaptive to poverty but not to affluence. We could make an analogy to our isolated K-dogs. They appeared to be well-adjusted to life in an isolation cage, in which an ordinary laboratory-reared and socialized dog would have whined and yelped incessantly.

How long a period of isolation can be tolerated after which rehabilitation still is possible? We do not know for either humans or dogs. I kept two terriers in isolation cages for 24 weeks instead of 12, and they made good progress. My expectation is that beagles would not have done as well judging from the long-term effects of 12-week isolation in many individuals of this breed.

I have already mentioned other features in the behavior of K-dogs which may have human counterparts. Psychologists and psychiatrists who observed them noted resemblances both to hyperkinetic (over-active) and autistic (severely withdrawn) children. To the extent that these similarities are fundamental rather than superficial, it is reasonable to believe that rehabilitation techniques successful with dogs could be modified for humans. If humans differ in inherited vulnerability to experiential deprivation as greatly as beagles and terriers do, we may have an explanation for the familial concentration of certain behavior problems. Perhaps the most fruitful next step would be the discovery of the physical basis for this genetic difference in susceptibility. The answer can come only from a joint effort by geneticists, neuroscientists, and psychologists.

REFERENCES

v. Feuerbach, A. 1833. Caspar Hauser (tr. from German). London: Simpkin and Marshall. Reprinted in Singh, J.A.L. and Zingg, R.M. 1942. *Wolf-Children and Feral Man.* New York: Harper & Row.

Davis, K. 1947. Final note on a case of extreme isolation. *American Journal of Sociology,* 52:432–437.

Hebb, D. O. 1949. *Organization of Behavior.* New York: Wiley.

BIBLIOGRAPHY

Fuller, J. L. 1967. Experiential deprivation and later behavior. *Science,* 158:1645–1652.

Fuller, J. L. and Clark, L. D. 1968. Genotype and behavioral vulnerability to isolation in dogs. *Journal of Comparative and Physiological Psychology,* 66:151–156.

SECTION THREE

EXPLORATIONS IN EXPERIMENTAL PSYCHOLOGY

In 1890, when psychology was still very young, one of the new discipline's dominant figures was Harvard's William James. His textbook, *Principles of Psychology* devoted only a single chapter to the new field of Experimental Psychology which had arisen recently in Germany. James' lack of sympathy for the new development can be judged by his comments:

Within a few years what one may call a microscopic psychology has arisen in Germany, carried on by experimental methods,

*asking of course, every moment for introspective data, but
eliminating their uncertainty by operating on a large scale and
taking statistical means. This method taxes patience to the
utmost, and could hardly have arisen in a country whose natives
could be bored. (vol. 1, p. 192.)*

The experimental psychology that James was referring to is
psychophysics—an area which is devoted to studying the relation
between internal sensory events and external stimuli. At the time
James wrote, experimental psychologists had not yet made serious
attempts to study other fields. We still have psychophysicists, although
James hardly would recognize the field of experimental psychology
today. The selections presented in this section reflect some of the
diversity of interests and methods of those psychologists who are
attempting to apply the experimental method to the study of human
behavior. Hopefully, these selections will show that experimental
psychology need not be dry or boring, and that it is capable of making
a contribution to the study of such complex processes as memory,
thinking, personality, dreaming, and appetite, as well as to a psychophysics far more complex than James could have imagined.

The first three selections, although they are in the psychophysical
tradition, illustrate the application of that tradition to the study of
complex perceptual processes. The chapter by Girgus and Coren
describes their research in visual illusions, perceptions which do not
accurately represent this information. The goal of their research is
"to understand the normal functioning of the visual system." It may
seem inappropriate to work with mistakes, but, as they point out,
one of the best ways to study a process is to discover when it isn't
working smoothly. The paper by Robert Sekuler, too, is concerned
with visual perception. The surprising, but seemingly simple finding
that simultaneous visual events may not seem simultaneous at all, led
Sekuler through a series of experiments and to an ever narrowing
set of possible explanations. The formulation, testing, and refining of
his successive hypotheses illustrate a process which is typical of
much work in any experimental science. The chapter by Harris and
Strommen is concerned with the ability of older children and adults
to distinguish between the front, back, and sides of things. The
investigators realized that this ability reflects the mastery of fairly
complex and sophisticated concepts of space and orientation. However, like other developmental processes, the mastery of such
conceptual or perceptual skills takes place subtly and imperceptibly
and is rarely commented upon even by parents. For this reason, the
paper by Harris and Strommen is an excellent example of how good
researchers will see an important problem in situations which most
other people take completely for granted. In addition to explaining
some of the problems peculiar to working with children, the research

described has implications for the study of personal space (see Sommer's chapter on Environmental Psychology in Section Four of this book) and for the use of language.

Lloyd Peterson's chapter describes his contribution to the experimental psychology of memory, a persistent problem in the history of experimental psychology. In fact, Peterson's discussion of immediate and short-term memory is reminiscent of the distinction between recollection and primary memory made by William James:

> *An object which is recollected, in the proper sense of that term, is one which has been absent from consciousness altogether, and now revives anew. It is brought back, recalled, fished up, so to speak, from a reservoir in which, with countless other objects, it lay buried and lost from view. But an object of primary memory is not thus brought back; it was never lost; its date was never cut off in consciousness from that of the immediately present moment. (James, pp. 646–647.)*

The procedure Peterson developed is a simple one, but it represents an important step in the experimental study of memory because it permitted him to study the time course of forgetting as it occurs over relatively brief intervals. Furthermore, like the earliest experimental psychologists that James mentions, Peterson was not reluctant to make use of a sort of introspection to provide him with clues as to his own mental processes. As a result, what started out as a series of experiments on simple memory processes developed into a research program on some of the more complex aspects of thinking.

Marvin Levine's paper also is concerned with the study of thinking, but his approach to the problem grew out of previous work on discrimination learning. Like Peterson, Levine notes that serving as one's own subject sometimes is a good experimental strategy in the early stages of research. In fact, one of the things which led Levine to formulate what he calls "hypothesis theory" was his willingness to listen to the things he was saying to himself as he went about solving problems. If the first step in his work was the recognition that a previously well entrenched theory was inadequate, the experiments with which he followed up this insight were equally important. One test of a good experimenter is his ability to bring an important problem into the laboratory without either distorting or oversimplifying the processes involved, so that they no longer resemble the processes involved in the original problem. Levine's ingenuity in developing a set of simplified procedures for the study of hypothesis formation in humans under laboratory conditions is evident in his account of his work.

The social psychologist and the physiological psychologist

represent two very different research traditions—traditions which are rarely bridged. In his chapter, Stanley Schachter examines the issue of obesity from the perspective of a social psychologist, but he also relates his findings to physiological studies. The "tantalizing analogies" he describes present a consistent pattern both with respect to external stimulus control of eating in rats and people, and a possible locus in the brain which accompanies such control.

Hypnosis has been a topic which has captured public fascination. The presence of two chapters on hypnosis in this book indicates the persistence of this interest. Some of the stage atmosphere of hypnosis has been dispelled by serious experimenters such as Leibowitz and Barber. In this section, Leibowitz describes a series of experiments in which hypnosis apparently influenced the extent of visual illusions or the presence of near-sightedness. The implications of these findings go beyond the walls of the laboratory. They extend to the influence of advertising, or indeed, any authority, upon human behavior.

The chapter by John Antrobus describes his research program on sleeping and dreaming. Long before Freud's writings, people were intrigued with these topics, but experimentalists have attacked the problems only recently. Antrobus writes not only about his research interests, but also about some unexpected hazards in setting up a sleeping and dreaming laboratory.

The final chapter of this section is by Wayne Holtzman. It describes how and why he developed his own version of the well known ink blot test. Holtzman begins with his earliest research predicting some personality traits from responses to the Rorschach technique, goes on to describe machine scoring of the test, and even muses about a possible ink blot test scored, analyzed, and interpreted by computer.

James wrote almost a century ago, "Even in the clearest parts of psychology our insight is insignificant enough." Certainly, experimental psychology has much work ahead; however, the writers in this section and the book as a whole demonstrate the many different areas which have been probed, and the degree of success achieved in these studies.

SEEING IS DECEIVING
Joan Stern Girgus
Stanley Coren

"Seeing is believing" is one of those sayings everyone knows. Despite the fact that magicians can fool us easily with sleight of hand, we continue to believe that what we see represents "what is really out there." The classical philosophers, even before the birth of Christ, apparntly held to this viewpoint. Thus, we find Lucretius asking "What can give us surer knowledge than our senses? With what else can we distinguish the true form from the false?" This faith in our senses, particularly in sight, has remained unshaken through the years. "First of all a man must see, before he can say," was Thoreau's way of putting it.

We rely continually on the accuracy of our sense of sight. We use it to estimate how far we must jump to get across a puddle without getting wet. We use it to determine how far away a car is, and how fast it is moving so that we can cross the street safely. We use it to tell the size, distance, and shape of objects, or their direction of movement. Usually, our sense of sight doesn't lie to us. If someone looks like he's 6 feet tall, it usually turns out that indeed he is 6 feet tall. Perhaps this is why everyone finds visual illusions so fascinating and why configurations designed to "fool the eye" appear with such great regularity in Ripley's *Believe It or Not* as well as on the backs of cereal boxes.

Visual geometric illusions are line drawings whose *actual* size, shape, or direction are quite different from their *apparent* or *perceived* size, shape, or direction. Let us look at some of the most famous visual illusions. Figure 7.1A shows the well-known "arrowhead" illusion. Psychologists call this the Mueller-Lyer illusion after the man who first published it in 1889. (Naming illusions after their discoverers or the first person to publish or investigate them is a common practice.) If you ask most people which horizontal line looks longer, they will answer that the line on the right looks longer. If you take out a ruler and measure the two lines, however, you will find that both are the same length. Figure 7.1B shows the Wundt-Hering illusion, named

Joan Stern Girgus is affiliated with the City College of the City University of New York. Stanley Coren is at the University of British Columbia.

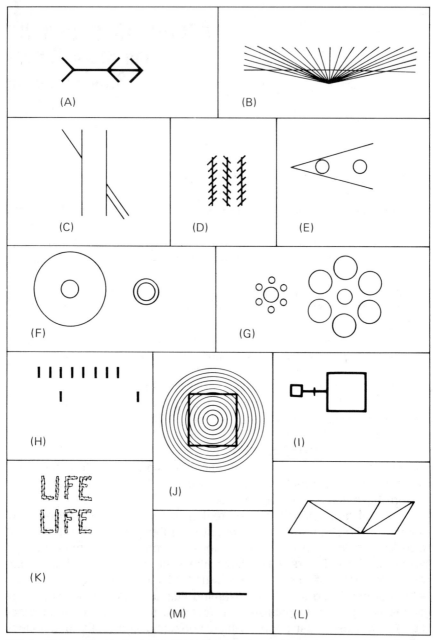

Figure 7.1. *Classical visual illusions. (A) Mueller-Lyer figure, (B) Wundt-Hering illusion, (C) Poggendorff illusion, (D) Zoellner illusion, (E) Ponzo illusion, (F) Delboeuf illusion, (G) Ebbinghaus illusion (Titchener's circles), (H) Oppel-Kundt illusion, (I) Baldwin's figure, (J) Orbison figure, (K) Twisted cord illusion, (L) Sander's parallelogram, and (M) Horizontal-vertical illusion.*

after two of the early giants in the study of perception who studied this figure. Most people see the horizontal line in this configuration as curved when in fact it is straight. Figure 7.1C is called the Poggendorff illusion. Here most people see line B as the continuation of line X, when it is actually line A that is the extension of X. Figure 7.1D shows the Zoellner illusion. Here, the vertical lines are absolutely vertical and parallel, although most people see them as leaning in different directions. Figure 7.1E is called the Ponzo illusion—both circles are physically the same size, but the one nearer the vertex of the angle usually appears larger. Figure 7.1F is the Delboeuf illusion, another distortion of apparent size. The circle surrounded by the larger concentric circle is generally seen as smaller than the circle surrounded by the smaller concentric circle. Figure 7.1G is called the Ebbinghaus illusion or Titchener's circles. In this illusion, the two center circles are the same size, but the one surrounded by large circles is seen as smaller than the one surrounded by small circles. Figure 7.1H is the Oppel-Kundt illusion in which the divided space seems longer than the undivided space, and Figure 7.1I is the Baldwin illusion in which both halves of the divided line are equal, although the side next to the large square looks smaller. Figure 7.1J represents a form of shape distortion. It is one of many figures invented by Orbison. In this particular figure, the sides of a square seem bowed inward although they are, in fact, all quite straight. In Figure 7.1K we find a distortion in direction. It is one of a series of twisted cord illusions. In this one, the letters which spell the word "life" are actually straight up and down, although they appear to be tilted toward or away from each other. Figure 7.1L is Sander's parallelogram in which lines AB and BC are actually the same length even though AB appears to be much longer than BC. Even in the simplest of patterns we seem to find perceptual errors. In 7.1M, for instance, we find that the vertical line seems longer than the horizontal, while they are, in fact, equal in length.

Many of the most eminent visual scientists during the last century studied these patterns and tried to find out why such perceptual distortions occur. Why has so much research time and effort been devoted to these simple line drawings? It is doubtful that they are studied merely because they are interesting or amusing (although that is why they appear on the backs of cereal boxes). Actually, these illusion figures illustrate a very important point about perception: An exact, miniature replica of the world is continually being registered on a photosensitive surface at the rear of the eyeball, whenever the eye is open and there is sufficient light. Visual illusions indicate that this miniature version of the world registered by the eye is not transmitted intact to the brain and turned directly into a perception since, if this were the process, the horizontals in the Mueller-Lyer illusion

(Fig. 7.1A) would look equal. Thus, some transformation or processing of the stimulus information must take place between the representation of the external world that is imaged on the back surface of the eye and the final conscious percept. We might say that visual illusions demonstrate that perception is not simply a matter of taking a snapshot of the world with our eyes—we actually perceive with our brain rather than with our eyes. Many investigators have reasoned that if they could figure out why the perceptual processing for some kinds of configurations resulted in illusions, they would then understand why perceptual processing usually leads to an accurate visual interpretation of the world.

You may be wondering why we choose to do our research on illusions rather than directly on normal, accurate perceptual processing. If you think about it, you probably will realize that it is hard to figure out what makes something work as long as it is functioning properly. One of the easiest ways to find out what makes something "tick" is to disrupt it in some way. This is a technique frequently used by experimental psychologists, as well as by other scientists. Perceptual illusions can be seen as naturally occurring disruptions in accurate perceptual functioning. Our research has been designed to try to isolate the place or level of processing that is responsible for this breakdown in accuracy.

Unfortunately, one rarely embarks on a program of research for scientific reasons alone. There always are other reasons, some of them practical and others more personal. In the case of our research on visual illusions, the primary impetus probably was simple curiosity. How could one help but be fascinated by such striking and puzzling phenomena? The urge to understand why these distortions occur is a very powerful one that we share with many of the great workers in the field of perception.

Actually, the reasons for doing the first couple of experiments were even more mundane than simple curiosity. One day, about 4 years ago, the two of us found ourselves severely limited with respect to the kind of research we could do. Much research in perception requires complicated equipment—and complicated equipment costs money. But money for research is always hard to come by, increasingly so in the recent past. At the time we were brand new PhDs, and no one was willing to risk limited research money on two unknowns. Thus, we decided we'd better find a way to do some research that didn't require complicated, expensive equipment. Another problem that young, impoverished researchers face is lack of laboratory space, especially when the new laboratory space is "still being built" or "not yet allocated." So we decided we'd better do some research that required little in the way of either space or money.

One afternoon, during a casual chat over a cup of coffee, we began to talk about an interesting observation which had been made

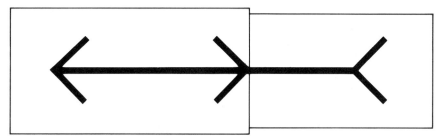

Figure 7.2. *A cardboard tongue and groove apparatus for measuring the Mueller-Lyer illusion.*

by a psychologist named Judd around 1900. Judd had been interested in visual illusions, particularly the Mueller-Lyer illusion illustrated in Figure 7.1A. In the course of his research, he noticed that the strength of the illusion actually began to decrease after he had looked at it for a while. Judd became very interested in this phenomenon because it seemed to indicate that the visual system has a built-in mechanism to correct for visual errors such as those found in illusions. We began to speculate about this self-correcting mechanism and about how we could begin to investigate its nature. The equipment problem was solved quite readily. A little quick rummaging through the desk produced a manila folder, a pair of scissors and a can of rubber cement. A few cuts and bends, and a little glue, produced a flattened cardboard sleeve with a tab which slid freely in and out of the sleeve. Using a heavy black pen, we drew one-half of the Mueller-Lyer figure on the sleeve and the other half, with an extra-long shaft, on the tab. (Later we learned to make our stimulus figures out of black drafting tape rather than ink which has a tendency to run.) Finally, we pasted a measuring tape to the back of the tab so that we could read off the length set by the subject. The basic piece of apparatus (Fig. 7.2) works quite simply. The observer is asked to slide the tab in and out, thus exposing more or less of the line on the right. He is told to continue to move the tab in and out until satisfied that both halves of the horizontal line appear equal in length. Since the right half of the illusion in Figure 7.1A usually is overestimated relative to the left half (that is, the right half of the illusion looks longer than the left half), the observer usually sets the line on the right (on the tab) so that it is physically shorter than the line on the left (on the sleeve). The amount by which he is in error serves as a measure of the extent of the illusion. For example, if the subject sets the right half of the illusion (the part on the tab) to 6.4 cm while the actual length of the left half of the illusion is 8.0 cm, the subject is showing an illusion magnitude of 1.6 cm or 20 percent of 8.0 cm. Thus, this apparatus, which cost practically nothing to construct, will provide a direct measure of the illusion. Furthermore, it was portable enough to be carried around and tried out on subjects wherever we could find them. The whole world could be our laboratory!

Of course, there was no guarantee that our rough-hewn little machine would be capable of measuring anything as exotic as the disappearance of an illusion with inspection. (Having been brought up on chrome and electronic laboratory instruments, we had our doubts.) So we immediately set about finding out. Our first subjects were all the people who were unlucky enough to pass by our office door during the next few days. With each observer, we used the same procedure. First, we asked the subject to set the right half of the illusion figure so that it looked equal to the left half. Then, we set the two horizontals to actual equality and let the observer look back and forth along the figure for five minutes. Once every minute we would set the horizontals so that they were obviously unequal and ask the subject to reset them to apparent equality. A typical result of this procedure for one subject is shown in Figure 7.3. The ordinate or vertical axis of the graph represents the amount of illusion (in millimeters) which we measured. The abcissa or horizontal axis of the graph represents the amount of time that the subject has observed the illusion pattern (with 0 representing the first measurement). Thus, we see that initially there is a distortion of 1.9 cm (19 mm). After only 1 minute of viewing the figure, the magnitude of the illusion has dropped to 15 mm. After 5 minutes of inspection, the illusion has dropped to 10 mm, only half of the original illusion strength.

By this time, we had accomplished two things. First, we had verified Judd's observation that the Mueller-Lyer illusion decreased in magnitude with inspection. Second, we had shown that, with only cardboard, ink, and paste, a piece of apparatus could be created which was accurate enough for research purposes. Now we had a tool to investigate some of the implications of this phenomenon of illusion disappearance.

The first thing we wondered about was whether the disappearance of an illusion with inspection was a general characteristic of most illusion patterns or was a special property of the Mueller-Lyer figure. A number of people had worked with illusion decrement (the technical term for reduction of the illusion) in the Mueller-Lyer pattern, but no one had worked with the majority of other visual illusion figures. Once again using cardboard as our basic material, we created adjustable versions of the Wundt-Hering (Fig. 7.1B), the Zoellner (Fig. 7.1D), and the Poggendorff (Fig. 7.1C) illusions as well as the Mueller-Lyer. With our apparatus in hand, we began to prowl the City College campus, accosting students in cafeterias, hallways, and out on the lawn, asking them to "lend" us 5 minutes of their time. Basically, we repeated the procedure of the first afternoon using 10 different subjects for each of the four different illusions.

As the data began to amass, some very clear trends began to

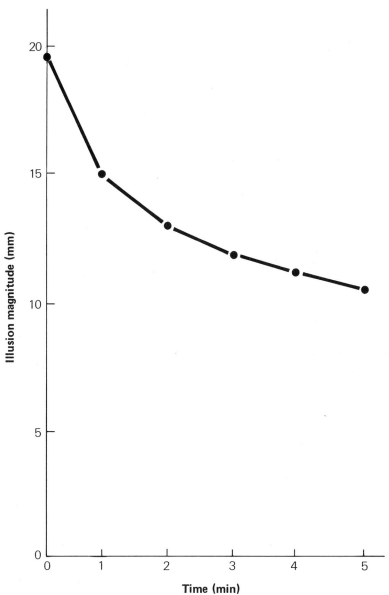

Figure 7.3. *The gradual decline in the strength of the Mueller-Lyer illusion for one subject measured over a 5-minute period.*

emerge. First, it was obvious that *all* of the illusions decreased in strength over the 5 minutes of inspection. However, it was equally clear that much of the illusion still remained after this period had elapsed. Thus, for our single subject in Figure 7.3, at first the illusion disappears quite rapidly, but soon it seems to be leveling off at a point slightly higher than half the original strength. If it is true that only about 40 or 50 percent of an illusion will disappear during inspection, then, we reasoned, there must be at least two psychological processes underlying these four illusions: one that changes during inspection and another that does not change and still remains after inspection.

The data from this experiment raised two new questions. (Data always seem to raise more questions than answers.) The first is "Why do the illusions diminish or decrement at all, when all the observer has done is look at them?" and the second is "Why doesn't the illusion diminish until it is completely gone?" Actually, if you think about it, this boils down to the following single question: "Why do some aspects of the distortion disappear and others do not?" After considerable discussion, we found we could not agree on a hypothesis to answer the first question. Our problem was that we could think of too many equally good answers and had no way of ascertaining which one was most likely to be correct. But we did have what seemed to be a single good idea for the answer to the second question.

The reason we thought the illusions failed to disappear entirely had to do with the structural properties of the eye. Let us consider some of the characteristics of this remarkable optical instrument. As you can see in Figure 7.4, the eye is basically a simple chamber, much like a camera. It has a variable opening, the pupil, which, like the diaphragm on a camera, regulates the amount of light that can enter the eye by constricting or expanding. The lens is found behind the opening in this diaphragm. This lens varies in curvature in order to focus the light on the retina—the surface lining the rear of the chamber. The retina contains photosensitive cells and serves much the same function as that of the film in a camera. In addition to registering the intensity and distribution of the light in the visual image, the retina's complex network of neural elements preprocesses and sharpens the visual image before transmitting the information to the brain.

There are, of course, differences as well as similarities between an eye and a camera. One of the principal differences between them lies in their respective optical quality. Helmholtz (an influential physicist and physiologist of the mid-nineteenth century who worked on problems of visual perception) once said that he would throw out any optician who brought him an optical instrument as poor as the human eye. This statement deserves some explanation: to function efficiently, a camera has a lens which has been carefully ground to focus all parts of the scene evenly on the film surface. Without this careful grinding parts of the image would be blurred. The curvature of the lens of the eye deviates considerably from such an ideal lens. This is called the *spherical aberration* of the lens, and it leads to a blurring of the light on the retina. Furthermore, even a two-dollar camera has

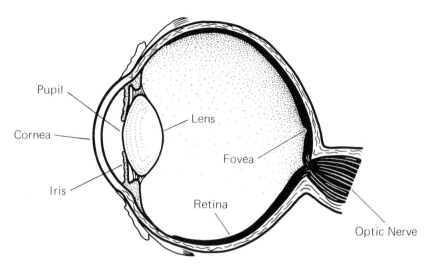

Figure 7.4. *The human eye.*

a coating on its lens which allows light of various colors to come to a focus at a single point. The lens of the eye lacks such a coating and bends blue (shorter) rays of light more than red (longer) rays. Thus, the shorter wavelengths come to a focus in front of the longer wavelengths. Thus, when the eye is *accommodated* (or focused) for the blue light rays, the red rays are not in focus. This shortcoming in the optical quality of the lens is called *chromatic aberration.* (You may illustrate this in a rather spectacular way by clipping a heart-shaped piece out of very bright red paper and placing it on a very bright blue background. As you stare at it, you will begin to see the heart pulsate and appear to float unsteadily above the blue. This occurs because the eye first focuses for the red rays and finds the blue out of focus, then it focuses for the blue rays and finds the red out of focus, and so forth. As the eye desperately tries to accommodate accurately, the blue and red alternately come into focus and the heart appears to flutter. This principle has been used by a number of "op" artists to produce some spectacular visual effects.

These lens aberrations cause blurred images on the retina. However, as the world rarely looks blurred to us, it is obvious that the visual system usually corrects for the blurring on the retina. Let us see how this might be done.

Think about a blurred line such as the ones that make up the letter A as you move down the left column in Figure 7.5. Obviously, blurred contours are darkest in the middle and get lighter toward the edges of the contour line. This is the same as saying that a blurred contour line on the retina stimulates fewer and fewer receptor cells as you move outward from the center of the line to its edges. Now, suppose the visual system usually just chooses the points of maximum

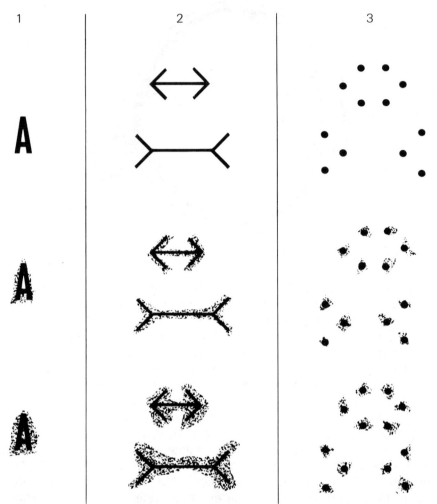

Figure 7.5. *Effect of blurring of the eye upon several patterns. Note in (1) that the letter A merely becomes illegible, while in (2) as we increase the amount of blur, we increase the size of the illusion. If we eliminate the contours from the illusion figure (3), the illusion does not increase as we make the figure more blurred.*

stimulation, and assumes that they represent the actual contour. This would explain why the world usually looks sharp and clear despite the fact that the lens aberrations generally lead to blurred retinal images.

This kind of a rule can, however, lead to a problem when two lines meet at an angle (as in the arrowheads of the Mueller-Lyer illusion). In this case, the edges of the blurred contours can overlap on the retina. This overlapping could lead to a point of maximum stimulation at the point of overlap rather than at the centers of the two contour lines. If this overlapping point of maximum stimulation is seen as the vertex of the angle, the apparent location of the vertex will seem to be displaced into the angle. This might make the distance between two such angles (again, note the Mueller-Lyer figure) look longer or shorter than it really is.

The center column in Figure 7.5 is designed to demonstrate this process, using blurred contours to exaggerate the process. As you move down the column, the image is blurred more and more. Notice that, as we do this, the lines that make the angles or arrowheads begin to run together, causing the segment with the turned-in wings to look even shorter and the segment with the turned-out wings to look even longer. This has caused some people to suggest that the Mueller-Lyer illusion is due, at least in part, to the blurring on the retina that is caused by the poor optical quality of the eye.

In fact, such an explanation can be proposed for any illusion configuration that contains intersecting or converging line elements such as the Wundt-Hering illusion, the Zoellner illusion, or the Poggen-dorff illusion. (See if you can work out for yourself how this might occur.) Such a suggestion is particularly attractive because it is based on measurable physical changes rather than on "fuzzy" psychological processes.

It seems reasonable to assume that no amount of training, viewing, or exposure will ever lead to a percept more accurate than the image projected on the retina. One would not expect that this contribution to the initial illusion strength would diminish through simple inspection of the pattern. It seems likely that this source of illusory distortion is the part which remains after the inspection procedure. Thus, the amount of illusion which persists after inspection might represent the part of the distorted percept which arises from structural factors in the eye. It is extremely important to note that such optical contributions to the illusion depend upon the presence of converging lines in the figure. In the absence of such converging lines we would expect the size of the illusion to be comparably reduced. This is seen in the right column of Figure 7.5, where we have modified the basic Mueller-Lyer pattern by removing all of the converging lines and replacing the line ends and vertices with dots. A glance at this column will show that the illusion is still present in the dot form, although it is considerably weaker. Now we begin to blur this configuration, just as we did with the standard form of the illusion in the center column of Figure 7.5. Although the dots look fuzzier and fuzzier, the impressive increase in illusion strength that we found in the center column is not present in the right one. In fact, the dot form of this illusion seems relatively unchanged by this blurring procedure.

This line of reasoning led us directly to a prediction which we hoped would help us understand how illusions arise and why some of the illusion still seems to remain after the inspection period. We argued in the following fashion: if structural factors play a role in forming the illusion, and if such effects depend upon having lines in the pattern which converge or intersect with each other, we ought to be able to vary the amount of illusory distortion by varying whether or not converging lines appear in the figure. The more converging lines present, the more opportunity there should be for these structural interactions, and hence the stronger the illusion should be both initially and after a period of inspection.

For this experiment, we used a number of illusory patterns which differed in terms of the number of converging lines, but which were all variants of the same illusion. We chose the Mueller-Lyer illusion because so many variations of it were already known and available; also, we were comfortable with it by now. The actual configurations we used in this experiment are shown in Figure 7.6. It is clear that as we move from Figure 7.6(A) to 7.6(B), we have one less pair of converging lines, and that Figure 7.6(C) has one less pair than Figure 7.6(B). Figures 7.6(E), 7.6(F), and 7.6(G) have no converging lines at all, and hence should not be affected by the optical blurring factor, while Figure 7.6(D) should be somewhere in between 7.6(C) and 7.6(E) in terms of how much it would be affected if the configurations were blurred.

Once again, the apparatus used was the adjustable cardboard illusion apparatus (Fig. 7.2). A separate illusion apparatus was constructed for each illusion pattern. In this experiment, the portability of the apparatus was particularly important. Since we could not ask an observer to work on more than one illusion, we had to find a new batch of observers for each of the seven variants. This meant that we required no less than 70 observers. The fact that the apparatus could easily be slipped into a pocket meant that we could hunt for observers in their natural habitats (also called the library and the cafeteria), rather than wait until they came to us.

Happily, the results for both initial amount of illusion and amount of illusion decrease were exactly as we had predicted. Figures 7.6(A), 7.6(B), and 7.6(C) produced the largest amount of initial illusion in exactly that order, while 7.6(E), 7.6(F), and 7.6(G) produced the least amount of initial illusion, with 7.6(D) somewhere in between. This means that increased opportunities for the involvement of structural factors led to larger perceived illusions. But there was an additional fact about the data in this experiment. Although the illusion forms varied in the amount of initial distortion, the amount of decrease in illusion strength that occurred during the inspection period was identical for all seven configurations!

If the amount of illusion is represented by the height of each point on a graph, and if the illusion decreases with inspection (see Fig. 7.3), we expect the line connecting the points to slant downward.

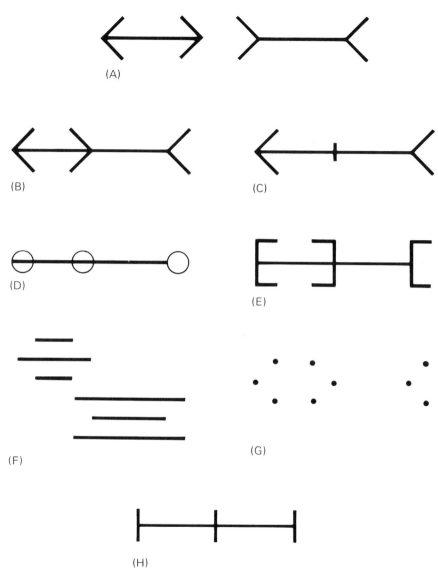

Figure 7.6. *A variety of Mueller-Lyer illusions which differ in the number of converging lines present.*

If two illusions decrease at the same rate and to the same extent, the lines on the graph should have the same degree of tilt downward. The degree of slant in the line is called its *slope*. If two lines have the same slope but different starting points, we get two parallel lines. Thus, line F, in Figure 7.7 represents the strength of the illusion pattern shown in Figure 7.6(F) and line E represents the strength of the illusion pattern in Figure 7.6(E). Note that illusion F has a greater initial

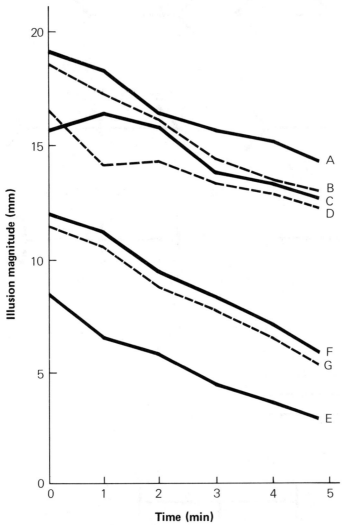

Figure 7.7. *The decrease in the strength of a number of forms of the Mueller-Lyer illusion. Each observer viewed one of these configurations for 5 minutes, with measurements each minute. (The letters refer to the results for a specific illusion form shown in Figure 7.6.)*

strength than illusion E. This is illustrated by the fact that the starting point for line F is higher than for line E. The fact that the two lines are parallel means that both illusions have diminished to the same extent during the 5-minute inspection period. As we look at the lines representing the strength of the seven variants of the Mueller-Lyer illusion over the entire viewing period, it is clear (within the limits of experimental variability or what the experimenter usually calls measurement error), that all the lines are parallel, indicating that all the illusions diminished to the same degree, regardless of their initial strength. Remember that the initial illusion strength was varied by altering the opportunity for structural factors to contribute to the illusion. Now we find that this had no effect on the rate of disappearance of the distortion. Therefore it seems likely that whatever is causing the disappearance of the illusion is independent of structural factors. We came to the conclusion that, although structural factors contributed to illusion strength, the disappearance of the illusion with inspection probably has something to do with the way in which the visual information is processed higher up in the nervous system.

We then began to consider what kind of processing might occur after the visual information has left the confines of the eye. We were looking for the types of errors that might be made in the processing of this information, which would account for the nonstructural component of the illusion.

One possibility is that these errors might simply reflect patterns of judgment that we have developed over the years. Thus, in Figure 7.1(G) (the Ebbinghaus illusion or Titchener's circles), we may be seeing the central circle surrounded by large circles as smaller, for much the same reason that a 5-foot 10-inch TV sports announcer looks small when surrounded by 7-foot tall basketball players. When the central circle is surrounded by small circles, it is as if that same announcer were surrounded by racehorse jockeys; both the center circle and the announcer appear larger as compared to the nearby objects. Thus, this illusion may simply reflect the fact that we judge objects not only on the basis of their own qualities, but also in the context of the qualities of nearby objects (near in terms of time and space). There is a story of a man who was amazed to see the circus strongman lifting the circus ponies onto the circus train. "Aren't they heavy?" he asked. "Not if you've just lifted three elephants!" came the reply. In much the same way the central circle is large in the context of the small circles, but small in the context of the large. This phenomenon is frequently called size *contrast*.

There are other ways in which errors in interpretation may arise during the normal processing of stimuli. Let us consider a representation of the real world that might be found on your retina. In Figure 7.8(A) we see a picture of a road receding into the distance. Now, it is quite clear to anyone looking at this picture that the log marked A is the same size as the log marked B. Yet, consider the actual dimensions of the stimulus for a moment. If you take a ruler and measure A you will find that it is considerably shorter than B. In the real world, when an object is farther away, its image, as projected into the eye, is considerably smaller than the image of a closer object of the same size. We correct for the size of the image in the eye by taking into account the distance of the object. In Figure 7.8(A) there are a number

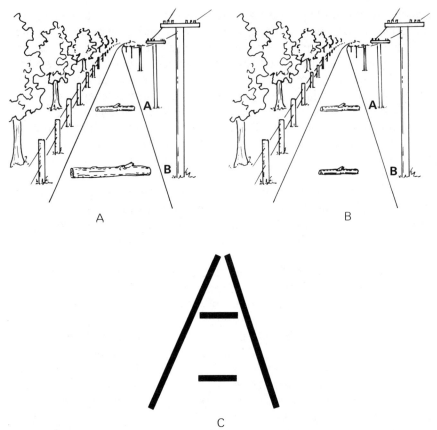

Figure 7.8. *The influence of depth cues upon perception of size. (A)— logs appear to be the same size, but measuring them will show that log A is considerably smaller. (B)—logs are physically the same size but appear to be different because they are apparently at different distances. (C)—all of the cues to distance have been removed, except the main perspective lines which are apparently sufficient to cause us to judge line A as longer than line B, although they are, in fact, the same length.*

of cues which indicate that A is farther away than B. Perhaps the most convincing of these cues is the converging lines represented in the telegraph lines and fence posts on the edge of the road. These converging lines are referred to by the artist as perspective lines. They serve as cues or clues to distance. We apparently use these cues to estimate the distance of the logs in Figure 7.8(A) and adjust the size of the retinal image accordingly. This leads to the accurate perception of size when there are real logs in a real road.

By using these distance cues to adjust the apparent size of a target, it is clear that we avoid a number of gross perceptual errors. Thus, a man does not appear to change his size as he walks nearer or farther away from us, although his image on the retina is getting constantly larger as he walks nearer, and constantly smaller as he walks farther away. Since his apparent size remains constant in spite of continual changes in image size, this psychological mechanism is called size *constancy.*

Suppose we now alter Figure 7.8(A) a little. In Figure 7.8(B), there are also two logs lying on the road. Now it is quite clear to our perceptual centers that log A is larger than log B. However, if we measure these logs with a ruler, it becomes obvious that they are, in fact, the same size. Why the apparent difference in size? This may be the operation of the size constancy mechanism. In Figure 7.8(B), the perspective cues make log A seem farther away than log B. But since A is the same actual size as B, and since they are both on the same piece of paper, log A must have the same size image on the retina as log B. In the real world, if two objects have the same size retinal image but one is farther away than the other, the farther object must be larger than the nearer one. If this were a real world situation rather than a pictorial representation, this would lead to an accurate perception of the relative size of the logs. But in Figure 7.8(B), the constancy mechanism may make a correction, based on the fact that log A *looks like* it is farther away than log B. Since log A is actually at the same distance as log B, this leads to a totally inaccurate perception —it leads to an illusion where two figures of the same size are perceived as being of unequal size. In Figure 7.8(C) we have a picture composed of two converging lines with two horizontal lines between them. There has been no attempt here to represent objects receding into the distance, or to draw a two-dimensional representation of the three-dimensional world. Nonetheless, line A looks longer than line B. Perhaps the constancy mechanism has assumed that the converging lines represent perspective cues, and that line A is thus further away than line B. The mechanism might then inappropriately correct the apparent length of the lines using size constancy. Thus, an illusory distortion has been created here because of the operation of a mechanism which, under most circumstances, helps make our perception an accurate representation of the external world. [Notice that Figure 7.8(C) is a variant of the Ponzo illusion shown in Figure 7.1(E).]

When we proceeded to tackle the problem of judgmental factors in the formation and disappearance of illusions, we decided to avoid the more complex processes—size contrast and size constancy— and to start with something that seemed even more obvious. Turn back to Figure 7.6(A). You've already observed that the segment of the Mueller-Lyer figure with the outward turned wings looks longer than the segment with the inward turned wings. That is the illusion. If you measured the *total* length of the figure (that is, from the extreme right-hand point to the extreme left-hand point), you would find that the configuration with the outward turned wings is actually longer than the segment with the inward turned wings. Now, if the observer, for one reason or another, fails to separate the horizontal line from the wings when he makes his judgment, and instead relies upon his impression of the total length of the figure, the observed illusory distortion could result. Suppose now, that as the subject views the figure over a period of time, he begins to focus his attention more accurately on the horizontal test element. In psychological jargon, we would say that he is learning to *differentiate* the test element (horizontal line) from the inducing elements (wings). This restriction of attention should gradually wipe out that portion of the illusion associated with the initial confusion of wings and line. Thus, the illusion might be said to be diminishing because the observer is learning to look at the pattern in a new and more precise way, which could account for illusion decrement.

Suppose this differentiation of the wings from the shaft leads to the diminution of the illusion with inspection. Then we should be able to help the observer by making the point where the shaft ends and the wings begin more perceptually obvious. If we can do this, it should speed up the entire decrement process. We decided to do this in two different ways: by introducing a small gap between the shaft and the wings, and by making the wings and the shaft two different colors. If the observer usually confuses the wings and the shaft, these perceptual differentiations should reduce the initial strength of the illusion by accentuating the place where the line ends and the wing begins. In addition, if decrement is the result of isolating the components of the figure, we have already done that work for the observer before the start of the experiment. Hence, he should show less illusion reduction with inspection.

The results of this experiment were a little puzzling. Differentiating the wings from the shaft by means of spatial separation or color differences indeed reduced the magnitude of the illusion, just as we had predicted. But over the 5-minute inspection period, the rate and amount of illusion decrement were the same with these new configurations as they were with the standard form of Mueller-Lyer. This result seems to indicate that confusion of the wings and the shaft plays a part in the formation of the Mueller-Lyer illusion. But illusion decrement does not seem to be caused by learning to ignore the wings and focus only on the shaft.

These data left us with two choices: We could admit that we were wrong in our initial theorizing about the cause of illusion decrement; or we could hypothesize that the ways in which we separated the wings from the shaft actually failed to affect the way in which the observer attended to the stimulus figure. We decided to opt for the latter possibility since we were rather fond of our notion of differentiation as the cause of illusion decrement.

With this in mind, we began to look for another procedure that might force the observer to direct his attention to the shaft and reduce the likelihood that the wings would intrude upon his consciousness and distort his judgment. After much discussion and many suggestions for complicated procedures, we finally decided to do this in the most direct possible way (a tactic which has proved most useful over the years). We simply instructed one group of subjects to focus their attention on the shaft and ignore the wings and gave another groups of subjects the usual instructions. We hoped that the focusing instructions would induce subjects in that group to redistribute their attention voluntarily. This would involve a process of selective attention similar to that functioning at a cocktail party, where you easily can "listen" to one conversation and avoid all the others around you. Thus, if all that is involved in causing the illusion to diminish with inspection is the way in whch the observer learns to differentiate the wings from the shaft, then we should expect considerably less illusion for any group of subjects who are instructed to focus their attention on the shaft and ignore the accessory lines. In addition, since they have already accomplished the necessary focusing of their attention at the beginning of the inspection period, we should find less reduction of the illusion as a function of continued viewing of the figure.

The data were quite easy to collect. All that was required was that subjects inspect the Mueller-Lyer figure, making settings by adjusting the cardboard figure every minute to measure the distortion. We collected the data, and compared the judgments from the group of subjects who had been instructed to ignore the wings of the stimulus and focus on the shaft, with those of the group who had been given the usual, neutral instructions. This comparison revealed that the voluntary restriction of attention certainly had reduced the initial strength of the illusion, but the rate and amount of decrease in illusion strength during the 5-minute inspection period was again the same for both groups.

With the last two experiments giving us identical results that were contrary to our hypothesis, it became clear that the explanatory mechanism that we had suggested for illusion decrement would not survive. We had learned, as had many researchers before us, that one of the great tragedies of science is the way in which beautiful theories are destroyed by ugly data. If we were to make any further progress, it was clear that we needed some new information about the nature of illusion decrement. In addition, the lack of confirmation of our most recent theoretical approach seemed to argue for a change in direction for our research. Since there are many more wrong hypotheses than right hypotheses in research, one learns very quickly to move on to a new problem when one has failed to solve a problem after several attempts. Frequently, researchers will then return to the old problem some time later, with a new approach, but it is usually necessary to work on something at least slightly different for a while before it is possible to find a new approach to an old problem.

Thus, we now turned to the question of the scope of illusion decrement. Specifically, we wondered if a person is less susceptible to other illusions after having inspected a particular illusory pattern until the distortion has weakened or disappeared. We discussed the possibility that, during illusion decrement, the brain may conclude that there is something peculiar about this particular figure, correct the perception of this array, but leave everything else unaffected. Under these circumstances, there would be no carry-over or *transfer* from the experience of inspecting this particular figure to the experience of inspecting any other pattern. But it would be much more spectacular if the experience of viewing one figure led to the conclusion that a wide range of percepts required correction. As a rather extreme example of this, the decrement procedure on an illusion such as the Mueller-Lyer figure might lead the brain to conclude that our view of the visual world is distorted in a way that all objects to the left of the center of the eye are being overestimated, and all objects to the right are being underestimated. If the brain were to reach this rather remarkable, general conclusion, illusion decrement would, in effect, represent a change in our perception of everything in the visual world. Logic and good sense argued that illusion decrement was much more likely to represent a specific correction on a particular figure, but the scent of a spectacular result sometimes swamps logic and good sense. If the whole visual world became distorted because the perceptual system had learned to correct one simple illusory distortion —what a bombshell that would be!

  With a massive dose of unsupported (and unwarranted) optimism, we worked out the implications of this hypothesis. If, after 5 minutes of viewing, our perception of all objects was now being adjusted to compensate for the distortion of the Mueller-Lyer configuration in Figure 7.6(B), we would expect that all objects to the left would be seen as slightly longer after exposure to the illusion than before such exposure, and all objects to the right would be judged as slightly shorter after exposure to the illusion than they had been judged before such exposure. We therefore, decided to measure the apparent length of the shaft in Figure 7.6(H) both before and after a 5-minute inspection period on Figure 7.6 (B). If all objects to either side of the center of the eye are influenced by the decrement procedure, we would expect the left side of Figure 7.6(H) to look longer, and the right side of Figure 7.6(H) to look shorter after the inspection of the distorted form in Figure 7.6(B). Such an *aftereffect* would represent the generalization of the correction to other nonillusion configurations.

  The data were speedily collected. Unfortunately, the results resembled a bomb more than a bombshell. The illusion [Fig. 7.6(B)] obediently diminished with inspection, as we had demonstrated dozens of times before, but there was absolutely no change in the perception of the straight line [Fig. 7.6(H)]. We gained only one thing from this experiment: it brought us back to our senses. Once again, we realized that it is better to eat in small bites than in gulps. We had to proceed more slowly and deliberately if we were to make progress.

We returned to the hypothesis which we should have addressed in the first place—given the rapidity of the diminution in the perception of the illusion, it seemed likely that the information obtained during the decrement procedure was encoded by the brain as an indication that something was distinctly peculiar about this one configuration. The percept then need only be changed for this particular configuration and the system can assume that most, if not all, of its previous percepts have been fairly accurate especially after years of dependence upon them. If we reason in this way, an interesting prediction emerges: If a figure looks very similar to the illusion figure which the observer has been inspecting, the brain may encode the configuration as being "like that strange one." If, on the other hand, the configuration is quite unlike the original illusion configuration, it seems improbable that the visual system will make much of a connection between it and the inspected figure. This reasoning led us to hypothesize that the decrease in illusion magnitude would carry over to perceptually similar figures, but not to perceptually dissimilar ones.

Testing this particular hypothesis required a two-stage experiment. First, we had to find a way to measure the amount of perceived similarity between illusion configurations. Once again, we used our old friend the Mueller-Lyer figure. Ten different versions of this illusion were presented to subjects, who were simply asked to compare the standard form of the illusion [Fig. 7.6(A)] with each of the other nine versions, and tell us whether the two illusion configurations were extremely similar, similar, fairly similar, medium, fairly different, different, or very different. This method of asking subjects to make judgments is called a rating scale. In this part of the experiment, a judgment of "extremely similar" was given a value of 1, a judgment of "extremely different" was given a value of 7, and each of the other labels was assigned the appropriate number between 1 and 7. The numbers assigned to each variant by the subjects were averaged after all the subjects had been run. The average rating for each form of the illusion indicates the perceived similarity of that pattern to the standard pattern. Once we had obtained the mean similarity rating for each of the 10 variants, we selected five of the configurations for use in the second part of the experiment. We chose these five variants so that their mean similarity ratings ranged from "very similar" to "very dissimilar."

In Figure 7.9 you will see the five patterns we selected. The pattern marked A is, of course, the standard Mueller-Lyer figure; pattern B is seen as very similar to A, C is slightly less similar, D as already quite different, and E as very different indeed. We tested five groups of observers. Each group was tested on one of the illusion variants to determine the amount of initial illusion. Following this test, everybody in the experiment inspected the standard configuration [Fig. 7.9(A)]

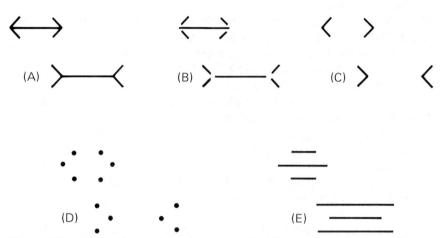

Figure 7.9. *All subjects viewed the standard form of the illusion (A) and were tested afterwards on one of the other figures (B–E).*

for 5 minutes. As usual, we found that the strength of the standard form of the illusion decreased over the exposure period. Next, we asked whether the reduction in illusion magnitude would transfer or carry over to the other forms of the illusion. This may be assessed directly by remeasuring the observer on the originally tested illusion form. Any reduction in illusion strength on this form from the initial to the postdecrement judgment represents a transfer of decrement from the inspection of the standard form. Our guess was that the more dissimilar the alternate configuration and the standard form had been judged previously, the less effect the decrement of the standard form should have. This should lead to a smaller difference between the pretest and the posttest on that variant. In other words, the greater the difference between the two configurations, the less transfer there should be.

The results of this experiment are shown in Figure 7.10. It is clear from this graph that less and less transfer occurred as the figures seemed more and more dissimilar. This would seem to imply that corrections for illusory distortions are largely confined to the single illusion configuration being inspected. Furthermore, when these corrections are extended to other illusion patterns, it is apparently done solely on the basis of how similar to the inspected figure they appear to be. Thus, the correction seems to be made in a very limited and specific way.

At this point, the number of unanswered questions still seem to be increasing rather than decreasing: Are there any illusions which do not disappear with inspection? How can we speed the decrement process? How permanent are the changes?

The actual procedures by which the perceptual centers correct the initial illusory distortion remain a mystery, although we now can

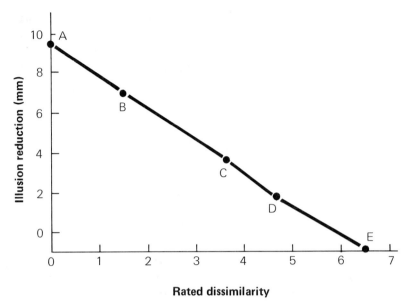

Rated dissimilarity

Figure 7.10. *The amount of illusion reduction which is transferred from one figure to another after inspection. If the figure were rated as less similar to the standard form of the Mueller-Lyer, we found less transfer of illusion decrement. The letters refer to the illusion figures tested (Fig. 7.9).*

say several things about illusions. To begin with, they appear to be caused by a variety of different factors. These include structural factors associated with neural and optical operations within the eye itself, and cognitive processing factors (such as the confusion between the total extent of the figure and the size of one element in the pattern). Both types of factors seem to contribute to the initial strength of the Mueller-Lyer illusion. In addition, it is clear that the perceptual system does not passively tolerate illusory distortions; on the contrary—it actively strives to correct them. This correction is not done with a broad stroke, but is rather confined to the specific patterns which have been shown to be in error (the proper cure for the proper disease).

It is comforting to know that the answers to these unanswered questions may emerge from equipment built of cardboard, paste, and ink. It is, after all, not so much the elegance of the equipment which determines the result, but the elegance of the ideas. With homemade apparatus, the cooperation of many people who are willing to spare a few minutes or even a few hours for research, and little else, we have made progress. This progress is slow, often halting and erratic, but is visible nonetheless. The ultimate aim is to understand the normal functioning of the visual system. The approach we have taken is somewhat unconventional; yet if we are ever to understand why visual perception is so accurate, we must first understand why, sometimes, it is not.

"You actually *study* perception? You're kidding!"

I've never found a short, simple, but polite response to that remark—one that could be heard and understood over the din of the cocktail party, where it usually comes up.

It seems that everyone considers himself an expert in visual perception, my area of research. I guess the feeling is natural. After all, day after day, everyone has millions of perfectly good perceptions. Most people can't figure out why I need courses, books, lectures, journals, computers, and experiments to understand a process that seems natural and automatic.

I'm going to try to do two things in this chapter. First, without the handicap of cocktail party noise, I'll try to explain briefly why perception *needs* studying. Second, I'll guide you through a series of experiments my students and I have been doing. The purpose of this tour is to show you how a typical research project in perception develops. I'm not claiming that they are the best experiments that anyone has ever done—they're not even my own best. It just so happens that these experiments make it easy for me to demonstrate some important things about doing research.

Perception is like most things in that when it works well it's taken for granted. Unlike most things, perception actually does work well most of the time. It's so reliable that when it fails we are quite surprised. Thus, we're surprised when we see or hear things that aren't really there, or don't see or hear things that really are. This is embarassing when your perceptions are obviously out of line with those of people around you.

While it usually does a good job, the perceptual system can be fooled if you know how it works. (See Chapter 7 for good examples by Girgus and Coren of how the system can be fooled.) The mistakes of perception teach us that the way the world looks or sounds is not a straightforward, true reflection of the way it actually is. Perception is a translation of the external world. Discrepancies between the input to a translator and its output betray the biases and quirks of the

Robert Sekuler is affiliated with Northwestern University, Evanston, Ill.

translator. As you know, in translation something must be lost, or at least changed. We can use the mistakes of perception—if we choose the right ones—to tell us about that talented translator, our sensory apparatus.

Perception depends upon a delicate balance among three sets of factors—genetic, maturation, and experience. Although this division among the three kinds of factors is arbitrary, the categories are good for organizing our thoughts. Let's discuss, very briefly, how each of the factors influences perception. First, consider the genetic material given to a creature. Until recently, psychologists have not paid much attention to genetics, although this situation is beginning to change. For example, any good ophthalmology textbook gives you an idea of the importance of genetics. The genetics of certain kinds of color blindness is well established. It now seems likely that abnormalities in stereovision (needed for good depth perception) are also heritable. In fact the range of visual defects that can be inherited is amazing. They include relatively harmless defects such as *heterochromia* (one eye blue and one eye brown); less harmless defects such as *myopia* (nearsightedness) and *hyperopia* (farsightedness); and some very serious defects, such as some cases of congenital blindness. A broad example of the genetic influence can be seen in the fact that Jews, Arabs, Chinese and Japanese tend toward myopia, while blacks in the U.S. tend toward hyperopia.

Once we are born we start getting old. This maturation causes certain changes in our perceptual machinery. Age brings changes in the shape of our eyeballs and a loss of flexibility in their lenses. These produce changes in the eye's optical responses. In addition, the lens loses some of its transparency. In the retina, old parts of photoreceptors (rods and cones) are sloughed off and replaced by newer parts. In our other senses we lose our ability to hear high pitched sounds; old taste buds die, new ones take their place. Contrary to the claims of the television commercial, we're not getting better, we're just getting older.

The experiential effects on perception are the most interesting of all because we can alter them as necessary. Since psychology textbooks are filled with demonstrations that experience alters perception we'll consider only two examples here. First, take a serious and permanent effect of experience. Imagine that an infant (say, less than 2 years old) scratches the cornea of one eye. Until quite recently, antibiotics would have been prescribed and an eye patch kept on that eye for several weeks. Basic research with kittens and monkeys has alerted us to the dangers of this treatment: Patching an infant's eye for a period of even a few weeks leads to permanent, irreversible loss of good acuity in that eye. The technical term for this loss of acuity, which cannot be attributed to some optical defect in the eyeball, is *amblyopia*. The human visual system, like that of other mammals, is extremely vulnerable to the effects of unusual experience or deprivation during the early stages of its development. Even though the child's genetic program may have specified "good acuity," the absence of proper stimulation for a brief period during a critical part of its development thwarts this program forever. Briefer exposures to unusual patterns of stimulation, even after the critical developmental period, can have effects lasting far beyond the stimulation itself. Sensitive tests show the visibility of a target, its apparent shape, or its apparent orientation can be affected by what you have seen just before the test.

Perception *is* critically dependent upon the balance among your genetic program, your developmental state, and what your whole history of exposure to the visual world has been. It's really quite remarkable that perception, for the most part, works so well.

Cars used to be simple, unencumbered by emission control devices, automatic transmissions, and electrically operated panels to hide the headlights in daytime. When cars were simple they had less inclination to break down. In the same way, the *simple* tasks that perception performs are carried out flawlessly; when it has to do complicated things, errors are more frequent. The most complicated thing perception has a part in is reading. No wonder that many children, and adults, have difficulties with reading.

I'd like to describe a series of studies, related to reading, that we have begun in my laboratory. The indirectness of our approach might strike you as odd—none of the experiments I'll describe ever required anyone to actually *read* anything, at least not in the usual sense of "read." Similarly, the vast bulk of scientists working on what they hope will be a cure for cancer never actually treat anyone who has the disease. Instead, most of them have chosen some biochemical preparation with which they hope to get insight into the disease process. This kind of preparation or model, if properly chosen, can be immensely helpful. It permits the scientist to work on the disease process without getting bogged down in the complications of having to work with actual sufferers of the disease. Of course the relevance of the preparation to the disease must be tested when the experimenter tries to *apply* what he found out.

This is what we have done in the study of reading difficulties. We did not collect kids with reading problems, catalog their problems, and try to build a theory from that catalog of observations. Instead, we tried to set up a situation which might be a simplified version of reading. In fact, most of our observations have been on people who normally don't have much trouble reading. We do not know yet whether we have chosen the right prototype—we're just beginning to work with young children who have difficulties in reading. Initial results seem promising, but it's too early to tell.

I offer the following, then, so that you can see how I try to work.

I don't offer it as a solution—even a partial one—to reading disabilities, the perceptual problem on which we are working.

TEMPORAL ORDER EFFECT: A NEW DISCOVERY

Look at reading as a perceptual task. Reading requires skilled integration of two kinds of information—spatial and temporal. A reader has to (a) keep track of which information "belongs" with what other information on the page (in space) and (b) keep track of the sequence (in time) in which he picked up various information. Without the two kinds of processing, reading would degenerate into a random hodgepodge.

A major type of reading disability—usually known as *dyslexia*—is characterized by errors in both spatial and temporal processing. For example, dyslexics tend to confuse "saw" with "was." They also may reverse or distort sequences of digits or letters they are asked to repeat. While this general diagnostic category may actually cover several different symptom clusters, enough children are dyslexic to make it a problem of major proportions.

In searching for a good prototype for reading, I remembered something that Richard Warren and his colleagues at the University of Wisconsin had found in a study of hearing. They took four different sounds of a certain kind and repeated them one after another in a cyclical fashion (1–2–3–4–1–2–3–4, etc.). Even though subjects distinctly heard each and every one, they couldn't report the *order* in which the sounds occurred.

The remarkable problems the Warren procedure caused subjects in temporal processing caught my attention, and I thought that a visual analog to Warren's effect could serve as a good prototype for the study of reading. I persuaded an undergraduate student, Eugene Levinson (recently converted from social psychology to the study of vision) to program our laboratory computer to make visual displays that might give us an analog to the Warren effect.

Levinson first tried a program which displayed four letters, each briefly flashed one after the other. An observer viewed these events on a cathode ray tube. Just before presenting the repeating cycle of letters, the computer chose a set of letters and ordered them randomly. This kept the subject from knowing ahead of time what the order would be. As it turned out, this effort was a complete flop. It was easy to name the letters as they appeared, and then to use the stored labels to identify the sequence correctly. Provided the letters were visible, subjects had little trouble in reporting their order.

To make the task more difficult, Levinson programmed the letters to be presented in different spatial positions. First, the computer selected the four letters for a trial and arranged their temporal order. Then it selected the location at which each letter would be shown

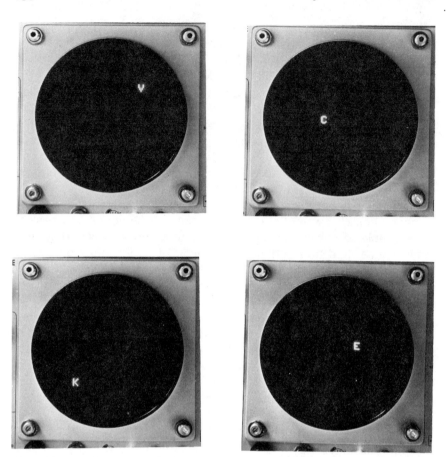

Figure 8.1. *Composite photograph showing cathode ray display at four different times during a typical trial. In the example, the subjects would first have seen the letter V, then C, K, E, V, C, K, E, V, etc. After 10 complete cycles of these four letters, the subject had to identify the order in which the letters appeared. On each trial the particular letters used and their positions on the cathode ray display were randomized.*

when its turn in the sequence came up. It should be noted that all the letters were small (about the apparent size of your pinky finger tip when your arm is fully extended), and appeared in a square region on the cathode ray display, a region about as big as your fist (Fig. 8.1). The subject watched the repeating cycle of letters jumping around the screen, and after 10 complete cycles of the four letter sequence, the subject typed on the computer console what he thought the temporal order of the letters had been. Each letter was presented for 10 msec (1/100 sec), followed by a 10 msec dark period before the next letter came on.

A careful observer, Levinson quickly discovered that his new display played weird tricks on the eyeballs and brain. When two temporally adjacent letters happened to be presented on opposite sides of the screen, one right and one left, their order, over the many repetitions of the stimulus cycle, seemed to fluctuate greatly. On one cycle the left one would seem first; on another cycle the right would seem first. As a result of this apparent fluctuation, subjects made many errors when they tried to report the correct temporal sequence of the four letters. In fact, they tended to make one particular kind of error—when the right stimulus preceded the left, they frequently reported that the left seemed to have been first; when the left preceded the right, they made few errors.

After spending several days making sure that this left-right Temporal Order Effect (TOE) was not some artifact of the computer program, we decided to study it in detail. The temporal order effect was so striking and perplexing that we didn't have much choice. We had stumbled on a surprising asymmetry between the way we see visual information given in two different orders. Before going on with the chronology of this research, two informative digressions might be in order.

Digression 1: Left to Right

There has been a recurring interest in left-right asymmetries in visual information processing. A number of people, beginning with Heron in 1957, have proposed that visual information which is presented simultaneously is processed serially, from left to right. Many lines of evidence (summarized well in Haber and Hershenson, 1973) suggest a definite directional component to the processing of visual information. For example, if a row of letters is briefly flashed, with some of them to the left of fixation and some of them to the right, subjects will be able to report the letters at the left more accurately than those at the right.

We know that not all the information in a large collection of items can be taken in one large gulp and digested by the visual system. Rather, the information seems to be nibbled on, piece by piece; the nibbling is very rapid to be sure, but still it's nibbling. This strikes us as strange. We don't have any feeling that this is what we are actually doing.

Some fancy experimental tricks are needed to make this serial processing show up clearly. Let's look at these tricks. We take a sheet of paper and type about a dozen capital letters on it. The letters are arranged in four rows of three each. The paper is placed in a special apparatus that permits us to light up the paper for any interval we want. Only when the paper is illuminated can the subject see it. We illuminate the paper very briefly—about the same length of time that a flash from an electronic photographic flash lasts (a few msec). Most subjects will be able to read about three or four letters of the dozen we typed.

Let's figure out how good this performance is. To make the arithmetic simple, let's assume that the flash lasted 2 msec (1/500 of a second). If a subject could read four letters in 2 msec, he should be able to read 500 times as many letters in a whole second—2000 letters. Going at that rate a subject would be able to read this entire chapter in about 30 seconds (not counting time to turn pages).

Now I've got a problem. I said before that perception is serial, that we nibble on the input one piece at a time. But 2000 letters per second certainly is not nibbling. If anything, it is gluttony of a kind not seen since Cronus, the Titan, swallowed whole five of his children and a large rock (which he mistook for his newborn son, Zeus). The catch here is that our subject didn't *really* pick up anything like four letters in 2 msec. In fact, he didn't even pick up one letter in that time. Let me explain. Instead of reading the four letters *during* the 2 msec, our subject read the letters after the flash was over. He read them from an iconic (picturelike) store. This can be proved if you arrange a second flash which can erase the image of the letters. The second flash illuminates a field filled with short, randomly placed line segments (visual noise). This flash will mask the afterimage of the letters and prevent further read-out from the afterimage.

By varying the delay between the first (informative) flash and the second (masking) flash you can control exactly how long the iconic store remains legible. The shorter we make this interval between flashes, the fewer letters the subject can read. In fact, when the interval reaches about 30 msec he can read only one. What does this mean? The original performance, four letters from a single, short flash, was an artifact. The effective stimulus actually lasted far longer than 2 msec—probably around 20 msec—in the form of an iconic store. If we curtail this image by presenting a masking stimulus we find that it takes about 30 msec to read just one letter. This kind of experiment shows that subjects pick up one letter at a time. That's what I call nibbling. But many studies show that adults in our Western culture don't just nibble at random from a display of letters. They tend to nibble in the same direction they read: scanning the display from left to right.

As we began our experiments on the left-right TOE (temporal order effect), the concept of scanning mechanism was controversial; today it remains so, even though, as we shall see, the TOE may provide additional support for the idea.

Digression 2: Philosophy of Science

As you probably know already, it is the scientist's lot that one experiment begets another. Since we enjoy doing research, this is pleasurable rather than upsetting. I believe, however, that the genealogy and pedigree of experiments is an important business. There should be vigilant population control. We do not want random and unplanned begetting of experiments. There are optimal ways to organize experiments so that you get the most information in the shortest possible time. One of the guiding principles which scientists ought to use is that of "strong inference" (Platt, 1964). The series of experiments I'm about to describe makes pretty fair use of strong inference—for a psychologist.

Look at the problem at hand. We came upon a new and peculiar phenomenon, the left-right TOE, quite by accident. We decided to try and explain it, since that's what science is all about. Now what exactly is involved in *explaining* a perceptual phenomenon? First, we must acknowledge that there are many competing, alternative hypotheses (or "stories," as I like to call them at this immature stage of their development) which we could cook up to explain the TOE. Each experiment we do ought to eliminate one possible explanation. If we're really clever, an experiment will eliminate more than just one alternative.

In this view, science is a treelike structure—a decision tree. Each experiment provides a choice point. The results of each experiment direct us out along the limb in the appropriate direction. However, if you subscribe to this view you can't sit down at the beginning of the study and say with certainty exactly what experiments you'll do. The sequence of experiments is determined as we go along, mandated by the pattern of the outcomes we have. Hopefully, the results of well-designed and executed experiments will give us ever better successive approximations to truth.

A sequence of experiments requires a set of hypotheses. These are intuitions about the likely effect of various experimental manipulations. The hypotheses are based both on the data of a specific, previous experiment and on our background knowledge about the system or processes we're investigating. At the start, we had two explanations for the temporal order effect. One was very complex, the other simple. Both require some understanding of the way information from the eye travels to the brain. So let's consider some simple facts about our visual system.

Digression 3: The Visual System

Each one of our eyes has about 200 million light-sensitive receptors (that's about one receptor for every man, woman, and child in the United States). Particles of light are absorbed by the photoreceptors. The result is an electrical signal whose strength varies with the intensity of the light. These electrical signals are passed along from the receptors to other neural cells. Figure 8.2 illustrates the simplest and most direct pathways. Signals go from the receptors to bipolar cells and then on to retinal ganglion cells. Most of the axons (output fibers) of the retinal ganglion cells travel along together. As a group the axons run to the lateral geniculate nucleus of the thalamus. The outputs of the geniculate cells then run to the visual projection areas

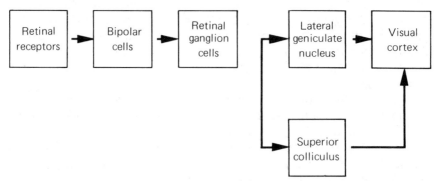

Figure 8.2. *Diagram of the information flow from photoreceptors of one eye to the brain. Comparison with any good, recent physiology text will reveal that this diagram is highly simplified.*

of the brain and elsewhere. Remember, the electrical signals at each stage are proportional to the strength of the light which fell on the receptors.

Now we know enough about the visual system to consider a simple explanation for the left-right temporal order effect. We know that it takes some time for the neural effects of visual stimulation to travel from the retina of the eye to higher centers of the brain. Work on visual processes in lower animals shows that different parts of the retina may differ in their relative latencies—time taken for stimulation to be transmitted to higher stages of the system. While there isn't much evidence for this *particular* kind of retinal latency difference, suppose that there is a latency difference between the part of the retina near our nose (nasal retina) and the part near our temples (temporal retina). It could be that the temporal order effect occurs because stimuli falling on one half of the retina are transmitted to the brain faster than stimuli falling on the other half. We could test the truth of this latency hypothesis by an experiment in which both stimuli fall on the *same* half of the retina, either nasal or temporal. If the Latency Hypothesis were true, there'd be no TOE when both stimuli fall on the same side of the retina. We tested this prediction. But before telling you how it came out, let's consider another, more complicated and interesting explanation for TOE which we tested in the same experiment.

To explain this second hypothesis we need some more visual anatomy. Let's go back to the retinal ganglion cells. To facilitate binocular vision and the appreciation of depth, each eye's retinal ganglion cell axons are separated into two halves. Roughly, fibers carrying information about the *left* half of the visual field project to the *right* geniculate and, after a synapse (a junction between two nerve cells), that information is passed along to the *right* hemisphere

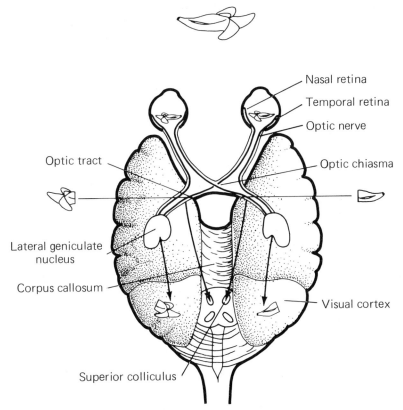

Figure 8.3. *A simplified diagram of information flow from the photosensitive surface (retina) of the eyes to the brain in a monkey. The diagram assumes that the monkey in question is staring straight ahead, at the center of the banana. This causes information about the left side of the banana to be sent to the right side of the brain and information about the right side of the banana to go to left side of the brain. The "image" of the banana in each eye is the reverse of the actual target (the optics of the eye act on the target just as any other lens would).* Note: 1. Information from the left half of each eye's retina projects to the left side of the brain; information from the right half of each eye's retina projects to the right side of the brain. To accommodate this division of labor the fibers carrying information from the nasal half of each retina must cross over to the opposite side of the brain; this occurs at the optic chiasma. 2. Only the major terminations of the optic tract are shown here.

of the brain. Ganglion cell fibers carrying information about the *right* half of the visual field project to the *left* geniculate and, ultimately, the *left* hemisphere. This is true for both left and right eyes, as shown in Figure 8.3.

What does all this mean? Hold your eyes still and fixate on some point in space. Visual information about areas to the left of that point goes to the right side of your brain, information about things to the right of fixation goes to the left side of your brain. After reaching the visual projection areas of the brain, information from each side of the field has a chance to cross over to the opposite side or hemisphere of the brain. The transfer from hemisphere to hemisphere goes along a very large collection of nerve fibers called the corpus callosum. The callosum is the major connection between the two sides of the brain. As an aside I must tell you that when people or animals suffer a lot of damage to the corpus callosum they show bizarre deficits in their behavior. To put it somewhat overdramatically, damage to the callosum produces a person with essentially two brains—a left and a right—separate and unequal. Without the ability to communicate with one another, each hemisphere is forced to operate without the assistance of the other. Some functions are localized in just one hemisphere. Language, for example, is typically a left hemisphere exclusive. With his callosum cut, a person has difficulty naming objects whose visual representations project to the right hemisphere. While he can *see* the object perfectly well, naming that object requires the cooperation of the left hemisphere—the left, "naming," hemisphere doesn't have access to the visual information in the right hemisphere. Gazzaniga (1970) describes work on these "split-brain" animals and people in an interesting and readable way. But, for us this is just an aside.

TESTING THE HYPOTHESES: PHYSIOLOGICAL POSSIBILITIES

Here's the explanation I proposed when Eugene Levinson first told me of TOE. Imagine, that before a person can judge which of two targets came on first, the neural representations of both targets have to arrive at a single center in the nervous system. Also assume that this "simultaneity center" happens to be located in the right hemisphere of the brain. These two assumptions are sufficient to account for the TOE.

How? Because of the anatomy of the visual system, a stimulus in the left half of the field projects more directly to the "simultaneity center," in the right hemisphere, than would a stimulus in the right half of the field. A stimulus in the right half of the field would project first to the left hemisphere; it would reach the "simultaneity center" only after crossing the corpus callosum. This detour *delays* its arrival at the simultaneity center.

Make this argument a little more concrete. Imagine two stimuli, one to the left of fixation and one to the right. Both are flashed briefly at exactly the same time. If there were a right hemisphere simultaneity center, these simultaneous stimuli would appear sequential. Because of its longer route to the simultaneity center, the right stimulus would arrive *after* the left stimulus. In fact, for two stimuli to appear simultaneous, the right side stimulus would have to be given a headstart of some tens of msec. How can we actually test this admittedly ad hoc story of a right hemisphere simultaneity center? Unfortunately, a story is no more than entertainment if it is not testable. An untestable story might be good science fiction, but it is not good science. The benchmark of testability is disconfirmability—you can tell that there is some good way to test an hypothesis if you can imagine some outcome (result) of your test that would make you abandon your hypothesis.

We needed a test which would, in principle, lead us to reject the idea of a right hemisphere simultaneity center. Here's what we came up with. If *both* stimuli, left and right, fall in the left half of the visual field, both will project directly to the right side of the brain and to the alleged simultaneity center. There should be no transcallosal delay and no TOE. If both stimuli, left and right, fall in the right half of the field, both project to the left side of the brain. Both would be delayed by the same amount in arriving at the alleged simultaneity center. Again, no TOE.

We designed a single experiment to test two explanations of TOE: one that postulated a simultaneity center in the right hemisphere and attributed TOE to delay in reaching it, and a second that put the blame on latency differences between the halves of the retina. We used the simplest stimulus arrangement we could devise: two letters were displayed on each trial, one to the left of fixation, one to the right. We varied the order of the letters randomly from trial to trial, and recorded the subject's judgment of which one came on first.

Let me describe the details of the experiment from the subject's point of view, since that is the most interesting perspective. After covering his nonpreferred eye with an exotic looking eye patch, the subject sat in a dark room, 57 cm from the cathode ray tube.*

Here's what the subject sees on each trial. The first event is the presentation of a large rectangle, 10 degrees on the horizontal, by 0.8 degrees on the vertical. This rectangle is made up of lots of separate points, as, in fact, are all of the items (including letters) which subjects see in this series of experiments. A small vertical strip, in the center of the rectangle (about 0.5 degrees wide) has no dots and is left blank. The subject is supposed to keep his eyes fixed on this small black region. The rectangle remains on the screen for 1 second. It goes off and 0.1 second later two letters are presented, one

---

*We use this peculiar viewing distance, 57 cm, because it saves some trigonometry. Frequently it's important to give the stimulus size in units related to the size of the image on the subject's retina, rather than in centimeters or inches. Size on the retina is determined partly by the stimulus size and partly by how far from the stimulus the subject is. The kind of units we want are degrees of visual angle. Such a measure takes into account *both* stimulus size and the viewing distance. When a subject sits 57 cm from our display, each cm on the face of the display subtends about one degree visual angle. In terms of distance on the subject's retina, the light-sensitive portion of his eyeball, one degree corresponds to about 0.3 mm.

after the other—either left letter first followed by right, or vice versa. In this first experiment there is virtually no delay (actually, 4.5 microseconds) between the letters; each letter is presented for 10 msec.

I'll have more to say about the spatial position of the letters a little later in the chapter, but now let's follow the temporal sequence of events on a given trial. One-tenth second after the second letter has gone off, the rectangle of dots returns for 1 second, as before. Now the subject has to indicate his response. He does this by entering on a keyboard the letters he thinks he saw, in the order in which he thinks they appeared. On each trial, the computer chose two letters of the alphabet and presented one of them to the left and the other to the right. Finally, the computer chose randomly which one, left or right, would appear first.

We assumed at the beginning of this first experiment that we'd be able to reproduce the left-right effect noted in our first, informal observations (with four letters sequenced in a recycling manner). Using the "decision tree" way of doing research we decided to use the first experiment to test several alternative explanations of the left-right TOE.

The experiment was run with three kinds of spatial arrangements, randomly intermixed in the session. In one arrangement, the "left-hemifield" condition, both letters appeared in the left portion of the field. In another arrangement, the "right-hemifield," they appeared in the right portion. In the third or "center" arrangement the letters appeared one on the left side of fixation, one on the right side. Regardless of the arrangement, however, each letter was about 2 degrees visual angle from its neighbor—one to the left and one to the right. If the idea of a right hemisphere simultaneity center were correct, we'd expect TOE only when the letters are in the center condition—so that they project first to opposite hemispheres. If the idea of a latency difference between left and right sides of the retina were correct, we'd also get TOE only when stimuli appear on opposite sides of fixation.

Luckily, the results from 12 volunteer subjects were clearcut. Regardless of hemifield of presentation (left, right, or centered about fixation) they got about 69 percent of the trials correct when the trials were left first, then right, and about 33 percent correct when trials were right first, then left. It did not make any difference *where* we presented the two stimuli. When they came on left-then-right they looked left-then-right 69 percent of the time; when they came on right-then-left they looked left-then-right 67 percent of the time (100 — 33). The results tell us TOE occurs regardless of whether stimuli project to the same or opposite sides of the brain. The results eliminate the right-side simultaneity center and transcallosal delay as an explanation for the TOE. They also eliminate the possibility that TOE is the result of a latency difference between the left and right halves of the retina.

TESTING THE HYPOTHESES:
PRACTICE, "ORDER OF REPORT," AND HANDEDNESS

Next, two other undergraduates, Judy Mundie and Debbie Mack tried their hands at TOE. They thought that we might simply be accustomed to seeing things left-right and that, with enough practice on the opposite order, the effect might disappear. In addition, being interested in sex differences, Mundie and Mack insisted on seeing whether males and females had different TOEs.

The basic experiment was nearly the same as the one just described. Half our subjects this time were male, half female—all college students. Moreover, each subject was run for several hundred trials: enough to tire all but the most motivated subjects. Luckily, they were all students in one of my classes and they were extremely well-motivated. The results? First, the TOE persisted. The size of the effect was essentially as before, provided there was no interval between the two stimuli. When that gap was extended to 40 msec the effect, not surprisingly, disappeared—with subjects getting virtually all such trials correct. Second, there was no evidence of a sex difference on the TOE. Third, there was no evidence that the size of TOE changed, even after several hundred trials. We concluded that the TOE is restricted to short intervals between the stimuli, and that whatever causes TOE, males and females have it in about the same amount—a finding of rather minor significance in the ongoing struggle for sexual equality. Having made this contribution, Mack and Mundie retired undefeated.

At this point, Paul Tynan, a graduate student in my laboratory became interested in TOE. Tynan's interest coincided with the emergence of several new alternative hypotheses, some difficult to test. Several people have previously suggested that what appeared to be left-right differences in perception were merely artifacts associated with "order of report." In all our experiments the subject indicated a judgment by typing the letters on a keyboard. Suppose that regardless of the apparent temporal order of the letters, the subject always typed or reported the letters in the order left first then right. Perhaps years of training constrained our subjects to report the letters to us—not in their *temporal* order, as we'd asked them to do—but in their *spatial* order, from left to right. This kind of order-of-report artifact is something you always have to worry about in experiments of this kind. Such an order-of-report artifact would be most likely when subjects are tested with letter stimuli, which they'd long since been used to reading from left to right. We decided therefore to compare TOE with letter and nonletter stimuli.

Up to this point all our observations had been with letters as stimuli. Since some earlier studies of differential sensitivity in left and right hemifields suggested that such effects hold only for letters, we became concerned that our TOE might also be critically dependent upon alphabetic stimuli. To test this, Tynan ran an experiment in which TOE produced by letters was compared to TOE produced by (of all things) a Cross of Lorraine as a stimulus. Francophiles among the readers will know that the Cross of Lorraine is a vertical bar with two shorter horizontal crossbars near its top.

Subjects were run in two kinds of trials. In one kind, two letters appeared in the same spatial arrangement used previously—either in the left half of the field, the right half of the field, or centered around fixation. Each came on for 10 msec and one followed the other without delay. As usual, either the leftmost came on first then the rightmost, or the opposite. Instead of asking the subject to type the letters on a keyboard, we eliminated order-of-report effects by asking the subject simply to hit one key if the stimuli seemed "left first, then right" and hit another key if the order seemed the reverse. The other kind of trial presented two Crosses of Lorraine instead of letters—otherwise they were identical to the letter trials. The findings were straightforward—TOE persisted. The subjects judged the temporal order correctly on 62 percent of the left-right trials but only on 39 percent of the right-left trials. This effect was essentially the same for both letters and Crosses of Lorraine.

One final point related to this experiment. It often had been suggested that the hand a person prefers to use is largely determined by differences between the left and right half-brains. Handedness, the argument goes, is related to performance on various perceptual and language-related tasks. Although this is not the place for a full scale discussion of handedness and laterality, I should point out that the two sides of the brain differ in their abilities to mediate functions such as language, music, and space perception and that a brain's lateral specialization is related to its owner's handedness. Tynan and I wanted to see whether handedness could be related to the TOE.

Since nearly all the subjects tested previously were right-handed, it was possible that the left-right TOE was peculiar to their right-handed brains. Perhaps, if we looked closely, the reverse effect would show up in the left-handed brains. To test this possibility we used half left-handed and half right-handed subjects. Each was tested with his preferred eye—usually the eye corresponding to his preferred hand. To make this long story very short: we found no evidence of a handedness effect on TOE. Both left-handed and right-handed subjects showed the left-right TOE in virtually identical amounts.

TESTING THE HYPOTHESES: RESPONSE BIAS

Some folks are hard to convince. When they heard about our peculiar findings they were skeptical. Since I was one of that skeptics band, I am delighted to report my conversion by a final experiment. Even after all the experiments I've described here, it might still be possible to claim that regardless of the way things look, subjects are biased to report that left stimuli precede right stimuli.

I'm using the term "bias" here in a technical sense that needs amplification. A subject shows *response bias* when his responses to stimuli are only loosely determined by the stimuli we give him. A subject would show one kind of response bias if the response he gives on some trial is partly (or completely) determined by the responses he himself made on previous trials. One example of this kind of response bias is the response frequency equalization principle: If the subject has two responses in some experiment, "yes" and "no," on those trials when he isn't sure of the correct response he'll give that response which tends to equalize the number of times he's used the two responses.

There's another kind of response bias that you can measure yourself. Ask some friends to imagine they're flipping an "honest" coin. Write down how the imaginary coin comes up (heads or tails) on each of about 25 imaginary tosses. There are certain things you'll find true of the imaginary coin tosses. First, there are no long strings of one type of outcome (say, head-head-head-head-head), even though probability theory tells us such strings will occur every now and then. Second, there are *lots* of alternations between heads and tails or between tails and heads. Again, you almost certainly have far more alternations than probability theory predicts. Finally, most people will give very nearly equal numbers of heads and tails. These tendencies are so very nearly universal that B. F. Skinner (1942) once proposed the absence of these response characteristics suggested mental illness. Although I doubt the validity of that proposal, the universality of these response biases is impressive. Here's the point then: Although we don't understand them well, there are processes that make some responses more probable than others. This is *response bias*. Since our knowledge of a subject's perceptions comes only from his responses, such biases may distort our idea of a subject's perceptions.

Response bias, whatever its origins, might account for TOE in all our experiments. This would turn the study of TOE from a perceptual problem into a problem of abnormal psychology. To give a solid and convincing demonstration, Tynan and I set up a forced-choice test of TOE's existence. Forced-choice procedures are used when it becomes important to objectify measurement of sensory function. Since this idea is hard to explain, let's consider some examples of forced-choice testing.

Digression 4: Forced-Choice Testing

You want to find out if a subject can see a certain very dim light; you want to measure his visual sensitivity. In the traditional approach you'd present that light and ask the subject to answer "yes" or "no" to the question "Do you see it?" Most of the time this simple approach works well. But what if the subject himself isn't sure if he sees it? Under such conditions he might adopt a conservative criterion for saying "yes." This means that our measure of sensitivity (sensory response) will be disturbed by criterion or motivational factors.

Other kinds of motivational factors can influence the *apparent* sensitivity of human subjects. Take the well-known, fictitious case of the Brothers H. During World War II, one of the brothers, Gary, wanted desperately to get into the Marine Corps; the other, Arthur, wanted desperately to remain on the homefront, out of uniform. Unfortunately, Gary, who wanted to get into the Marines, had a major hearing loss which should have made him unfit for the Marines. Just as unfortunately, Arthur had no physical disabilities to keep him out. At their hearing tests in preinduction physicals, the two H. brothers tried to fool the examiners. Although he could hear hardly anything, Gary kept on saying "Yes, I hear that" every time he thought a test stimulus was presented. The examiners were taken in—his hearing was judged superior. He was allowed into the Marines where he met an untimely end in basic training when he failed to hear and avoid some terminal stimuli sent his way. The other brother, Arthur H., was a superb malingerer during his physical: He denied hearing anything, including the orders to get undressed. He was sent home and prospered during the early years of the war. Later he was imprisoned for counterfeiting gas-ration coupons. These are two more dramatic examples of how measures of sensitivity can be subverted by motivational factors.

One good way around this subversion is a forced-choice procedure—instead of asking the subject to give a "yes" or "no" to a dim light, we give him *two* stimulus presentations and ask him to compare the two. One time (don't tell him *which* ahead of time!) show the light; the other time show nothing. The subject's task is to identify the interval, first or second, that contained the stimulus light. Here no criterion is involved—all he has to do is compare what he experiences during the two presentations. If the subject consistently identifies the interval, first or second, that contains the light, you must assume he can detect it. Look how this would have affected the Brothers H. The examiners should have divided each trial into two halves, presenting a soft tone in one half, and nothing at all in the other. Gary H., who had the hearing loss, couldn't have passed simply by saying he heard something. He would have been forced to identify in which half of the trial—first or second—the tone sounded. If his hearing loss were severe, and the tone quite soft, he would have had to guess randomly. His percent of correct answers would have been a most unimpressive 50—chance performance.

I'm afraid that the other brother, Arthur, might still have been clever enough to convince the examiners he couldn't hear adequately.

If he really did hear every tone and knew in which half-trial it occurred, he could arrange to make the wrong "guess" on half the trials— making the examiner think he couldn't hear the tone. The forced-choice procedure can't do too much to help us identify clever malingerers, but it *is* excellent for use with most nonmilitary, clinical, and laboratory subjects.

The general idea behind the forced-choice is that you present the stimulus in only one of two half-trials. The subject has to identify that half-trial which contained the stimulus. You can show rather easily with this procedure that lights so dim that subjects literally swear they can't see them, are actually quite detectable. Similar procedures have been adapted for many important clinical problems. To consider only one, David Nash, Robert Armstrong and I developed a forced-choice procedure to help physicians measure recovery of "touch" sensitivity in cases of nerve damage. In the past, according to medical books, physicians, and their patients, such measures were subjective and hit-or-miss. Patients with nerve damage are very poor judges of what they do or don't "feel." A forced-choice testing procedure gives sensitive and objective measures in these patients. To go along with our new procedure Armstrong invented some new ways of calculating the odds that a patient's sensory response is actually improving.

Now we can return to our story after this rather lengthy, but needed detour. Paul Tynan set up a forced-choice test of TOE. He used the same apparatus as before but restricted all stimuli to repetitions of the letter O—one to the left of fixation and one to the right. Each trial was divided into two distinct halves: in one half the two letters were presented sequentially, either left-then-right or the reverse. In the other half-trial, the two letters were presented simultaneously. While each letter appeared for 10 msec in the sequential presentation, *both* letters appeared for 10 plus 10, or 20 msec in the simultaneous presentation (Fig. 8.4). Sometimes the simultaneous presentation was the first on a trial; sometimes the sequential was the first. All the subject had to do was say *which* was the sequential presentation, the first or second. He did not have to judge the temporal order in the sequential pair. A tone sounded when the subject was wrong, encouraging him to do the best he could. A delay was introduced between the two letters in the sequential presentations. The length of the delay was randomly set by the computer to 2, 4, 8, 16, or 32 msec. The various delays might give us additional insights into the limits of TOE, assuming, of course, that we could reproduce TOE with these new, forced-choice procedures.

To introduce the results, consider two kinds of trials: one on which the sequential pair was left-then-right, the other one which the sequential pair was right-then-left. For all the delay values we used, subjects found it easier to tell the sequential from the simultanous

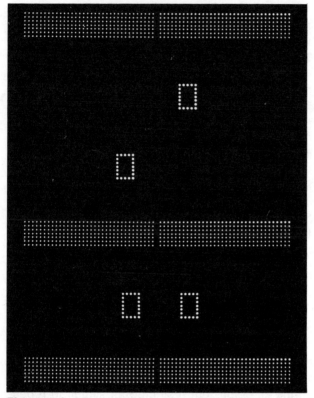

Figure 8.4. *A composite photograph of the cathode ray display as it looked to a subject in the forced-choice experiment. Starting at the top of the photograph we see each one of the six different components of a typical trial. 1. A large rectangle of dots appears. The break in the middle of the rectangle helps the subject orient his gaze. 2. A single letter O is presented to the right of center. 3. A single letter O is presented to the left of center. 4. Rectangle reappears, followed by 5. two Os. These Os, one to left and one to the right of center, come on and go off at the same time. 6. After their disappearance the rectangle returns. At the offset of the rectangle the subject must judge which of the two sets of letters, the first or the second, was the successive pair. In this trial the first pair of letters came on one after another (successively); the second pair came on at the same time (simultaneously). The correct response for this trial would have been "first pair." This sequence was just one of several with which subjects were tested.*

presentation when the sequential was left-then-right rather than right-then-left. In other words, a left-then-right sequence seemed more clearly sequential. Figure 8.5 shows the data from this experiment. The vertical axis shows the percent of times the subject correctly identified the sequential stimuli. The horizontal axis shows the delay between stimuli in the sequential pair. The filled circles give the data for trials where the sequential presentation was left-right; the

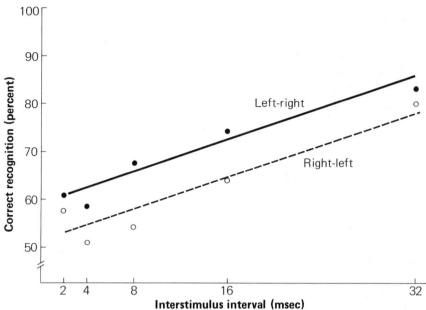

Figure 8.5. *Data from the forced-choice experiment on temporal order. The delay between members of each successive pair of letters is shown on the horizontal axis. The percent correct identifications of the simultaneous pair on each trial is shown on the vertical axis. Higher scores mean that subjects were better able to tell successive from simultaneous. Results are shown separately for two kinds of trials. The "left-right" line refers to trials in which members of the successive pair came on left first, then right. The "right-left" line refers to trials in which members of the successive pair came on right first, then left. Note that at each delay between members of the successive pair, performance is better for "left-right" than "right-left."*

unfilled circles give the data for trials on which the sequential presentation was right-left. The fact that, at every delay value, the left-right point is above the right-left point means that the left-right seemed more clearly different from its associated simultaneous pair—that is, it seemed more clearly sequential in character. The fact that both sets of data points increase in height as we move toward longer delays means that with longer delays it gets easier to tell the sequential pair from the simultaneous pair. The lines drawn through the data points are mathematically determined approximations to the data.

Several things should be said about these results. First, each point plotted is the average of performance on about 350 separate trials. This number is large enough so that we can consider performance at all delays, including the shortest—2 msec—to be reliably above chance (50 percent). Our forced-choice procedure shows that subjects are able to discriminate between a simultaneous 20 msec presentation of two letters and a sequential presentation which differs only by having a 2 msec gap inserted between the letters. This is better sensitivity than had previously been thought possible. Second, as we had hoped, there was a systematic and reliable difference between left-right and right-left trials. This difference is consistent with the TOE we had been working with all along. Finally, the results give us a new quantitative idea about TOE. The horizontal distance between the straight lines in Figure 8.5 estimates the time differential between left-right and right-left pairs. To make both pairs appear equally sequential (and equally discriminable from the simultaneous presentation), a 10 msec delay would have to be introduced into a right-left pair.

TEMPORAL ORDER EFFECT: SCANNING LEFT-TO-RIGHT?

Let me summarize up to this point. We had discovered, by accident, a new anomaly of perception. We tried to test, one after another, a set of possible explanations for this anomaly. Along the way we found out some of the conditions with which the TOE was associated, and others that proved to be unrelated to it. At this point the only hypothesis still in the running was the original idea of some kind of left-right scan or read-out. Let's discuss this scan idea, because I'm afraid that that is the explanation we're stuck with at this point.

The famous neuroscientist, Karl S. Lashley, suggested that when visual information is presented in a brief flash, we read out from an image (icon) of that information by shifting our attention. The existence of this ionic postexposure storage is now well established, but the idea of a scan or read-out by attention remains controversial. As we mentioned earlier, Heron proposed a scanning mechanism which reads out from the visual image, starting at the left side and working progressively rightward. Suppose, as Heron did, the scanning mechanism, or "attention," has an idle or rest position near fixation. When a stimulus is presented the scanner jumps first to the leftmost end of the stimulus array. During the rightward procession of the scanner which follows, information from the left portion of the array is read out slightly ahead of information from the right portion. A stimulus sequence, like some we studied, that was actually right-then-left, with a very short interval between the two stimuli, would appear left-then-right.

Where might this line of study go from here? We'd like to know whether this left-right scan, if that indeed is what we have, is trainable. Is it the product of experience with left-to-right reading patterns in Western cultures? There are two ways to answer this, one cheap, one expensive, both important, both difficult. The cheaper approach asks these questions: Does TOE exist in children in our culture before they have learned to read? Does TOE's development parallel, in some way, the development of reading skills? We've begun to study children of various ages, but it's still too early to guess at the answer. The expensive approach asks: Does TOE exist to some extent in adults in other cultures (e.g., China, Japan, Israel), where left-right reading habits do not exist? Do such cultures have TOEs in directions other than left-right?

What we've looked at is just one way of experimenting, the way I like best. There's only one serious drawback to this sequential, searching procedure for science: You can't count on doing one single, grand experiment with an easily summarizeable "yes" or "no" outcome. Instead you end up with a series of small experiments, each determined by its predecessors. This strategy for science makes heavy demands on an investigator's patience and trust. You have to trust that as you go from branch to branch in the decision tree, a weak limb won't snap off with you and your data sitting on it. But even if a crash occurs or a dead-end is reached, the lure of discoveries among the branches of a neighboring tree should make you dust yourself off and start another climb.

REFERENCES

Gazzaniga, M. S. 1967. The split brain in man. *Scientific American,* 217:24–29. Also reprinted in R. Held and W. Richards (eds.), *Perception: Mechanisms and Models.* San Francisco: W. H. Freeman, 1972.

Gazzaniga, M. 1970. *The Bisected Brain.* New York: Appleton-Century-Crofts.

Haber, R. N. and Hershenson, M. 1973. *The Psychology of Visual Perception.* New York: Holt, Rinehart and Winston.

Heron, W. 1957. Perception as a function of retinal locus and attention. *American Journal of Psychology,* 70:38–48.

Lashley, K. S. 1951. The problem of serial order in behavior. In L. A. Jeffress (ed.), *Cerebral Mechanisms in Behavior.* New York: Wiley. Also reprinted in F. Beach, D. O. Hebb, C. T. Morgan, H. W. Nissen (eds.), *The Neuropsychology of Lashley.* New York: McGraw-Hill, 1960.

Platt, J. R. 1964. Strong inference. *Science,* 146:347–353.

Sekuler, R.; Nash, D.; and Armstrong, R. 1973. Sensitive, objective procedure for evaluating response to light touch. *Neurology,* 23:1282–1291.

Sekuler, R.; Tynan, P.; and Levinson, E. 1973. Visual temporal order: A new illusion. *Science,* 180:210–212.

Skinner, B. F. 1942. The processes involved in the repeated guessing of alternatives. *Journal of Experimental Psychology,* 30:495–503. Also reprinted in B. F. Skinner, *Cumulative Record.* New York: Appleton-Century-Crofts, 1959.

Sperling, G. 1960. The information available in brief visual presentations. *Psychological Monographs,* 74, No. 498 (whole issue).

Warren, R. M.; Obusek, C. J.; Farmer, R. M.; and Warren, R. P. 1969. Auditory sequence: Confusion of patterns other than speech or music. *Science,* 164:586–587.

CHAPTER
9

UNDERSTANDING "FRONT," "BACK," AND "BESIDE": EXPERIMENTS ON THE MEANING OF SPATIAL CONCEPTS
Lauren Jay Harris
Ellen A. Strommen

How do we tell the difference between the front, back, and sides of things? How are we able to say that something is in front of, or in back of, or beside something else?

Some roots of our interest in these questions can be found in a prior study by one of us (L.J.H.) on children's knowledge of left and right. In this study, kindergartners and second-graders were asked first to indicate their own and then the adult's left and right hands; then, shown a pencil and rubber band affixed side by side on a board, they were asked to say which object was on the left and which on the right. All the second-graders, but only half of the kindergartners, answered correctly. The children then were asked to describe the spatial positions of three objects—a pencil on the left, a matchbox in the middle, and a penny on the right. The critical question was, could they correctly describe the matchbox as simultaneously to the right of the pencil and to the left of the penny? Of the kindergartners who answered the previous questions correctly, almost none could do so, and only a few second-graders were able to. But when the same children were asked comparable questions about front and back, the picture was very different. All the kindergartners and all the second-graders knew which was the front and which was the back of their own and the adult's body, and they all correctly said which of two dolls in a column was in front, which in back. When asked to describe the spatial position of a column of three objects, lined up

Lauren Jay Harris and Ellen A. Strommen are on the faculty of the Department of Psychology, Michigan State University, East Lansing, Mich.

The research described here was supported in part by faculty grants to both authors from Michigan State University, and by National Science Foundation Bio-Medical grants to L.J.H. The data analysis for the study of "personal space" was supported by National Institute of Health Grant MH–24234–01 to L.J.H.

face to back—a boy doll in front, a chair in the middle, and a mother doll behind the chair—most of the kindergartners and all the second-graders answered correctly that the chair was simultaneously behind the boy and in front of the mother.

DOING "THOUGHT" EXPERIMENTS

These results showed that children learn front-back differences earlier and better than left-right differences. But just because children know front and back before they know left and right does not mean that front and back are simple concepts, or that we understand all the ways in which front and back might be used. In fact, we suspected that the tests used in this study might reflect only a small part of children's—or adult's—understanding of front and back. So we decided to try to clarify for ourselves what we meant when we said "front" and "back." What are the various ways in which these terms are used? We were not searching deliberately for contradictions and complexities, but often we found them as we talked together. We were doing "thought experiments"—experiments in our imaginations—asking "What if?" questions. We found it helpful, often crucial, to model a great variety of situations with toys and other ordinary objects.

The front-back, left-right study had measured two different but related aspects of front and back, and therefore had posed two different but related developmental questions. The first, relating to the "absolute" sense of front and back, was can the child label the fronts and backs of objects, including his own body? The second question, that of the "relational" sense of the terms was, can he use these labels in describing the spatial relations among objects?

We believed that acquiring the first kind of skill would be fundamental to acquiring the second. Thus, we assumed that a child who has not learned which is the front and which is the back of his own body, would not be able to use the same terms accurately to describe spatial relations among objects, including the relations between objects and his own body. The results of the left-right, front-back study bore out this analysis: Every child who had answered the three-object in-front-of, in-back-of questions correctly had known the front and back of his own body.

This sort of analysis fits well with the ideas of the late developmental psychologist Heinz Werner. Werner believed that the most important clue to the source of the major systems of spatial coordinates—above-below, in front-behind, left-right—is the body itself, with "objective space" evolving from this "primitive" (i.e., fundamental) orientation. One piece of evidence is in language. Almost every language has terms expressing spatial relationships which either stand for, or refer directly to, parts of the body. For example, the Mande (African) group of languages expresses "behind" by the term "the back," the word "before" is the same as the word for "eye," "on" is the same as "neck," "in" is the same as "stomach," and so forth. Werner calls these body words "anthropomorphic substantives." Such anthropomorphic substantives can be found in English too. Two outstanding examples are the terms "in back" and "face" which simultaneously designate a part of the body and a spatial relation.

This analysis implies that the child who can follow the instructions to "put the block in front of you" and "in back of you" must first know where his own front and back are. How, then, do children learn their own fronts and backs? Think of a human body: The front and back look different and do different things. With so many clear differences it should be a simple matter for even a young child to learn the difference. As we expected when we asked children how they could tell their fronts from their backs, many of them did mention appropriate body parts. But many also mentioned items of clothing. And so we began to think about the front and back of clothing.

Generally, front-back differences are continued in clothing, with pockets and buttons marking the difference. We would assume that, as soon as the child can recognize the front of the garment, he should be able to put it on correctly. The parent therefore has to teach the child to locate the front, and since the child already knows where his own front is, this would be sufficient to enable the child to dress. Where front-back differences in clothing are subtle, as in pull-over sweaters and T-shirts, we would expect children to make more mistakes and, in many cases, put on these garments backwards. Unfortunately, the facts are not so simple. Any parent or nursery school teacher knows how frequently children put their pants, sweaters, or coats on backwards, although the children may know perfectly well where the fronts of these garments are. Why? It must be that another skill is involved, and that our first analysis was incomplete.

How, then, does the child put on his underpants or trousers correctly? He must first hold them (in front of his body) so that they and his body face in the same direction. In this orientation, he then must make a same-side movement—placing his left leg in the left trouser leg, and his right leg in the right. The same movements to trousers held in a front-to-front relation to the body will get the garment on backwards. So for the child, as for the adult, four different factors (three about front-back, and one about left-right) are involved in the seemingly simple act of putting on trousers: (1) holding the trousers on the front side of the body, (2) learning which side of the trousers is the front, (3) holding the trousers so that the back of the trousers is closest to one's own front, and (4) putting one's legs in the same-side trouser legs.

Factor (1) probably comes naturally. Since the eyes are on the front side of the body, and the arms extend more easily forwards than backwards, the child more naturally holds objects in front of his body than behind it. Factor (4) probably comes naturally too: Several investigations have shown that a young child (under about 6 years of age), asked to identify the left and right hands of a person standing opposite him, is very likely to call the other's person's left hand his right, and his right hand his left. In other words, the child makes a same-side response even when an opposite-side, or cross-over, response is correct. The child does not yet understand that the relation between left and right is reversed for someone standing opposite him. Similarly, the child will imitate a simple gesture in this "mirror" fashion. If the person standing opposite him touches his own right cheek, the child will touch his own left cheek; some adults will respond in similar manner. Therefore, if the trousers are held in just the right position, the child is more likely than not to get his feet in correctly.

The remaining factors clearly require more learning. Factor (2) requires the child to learn something absolute about the garment—the location of its front side. Factor (3) requires the child to learn something relative—to hold the garment so that its front side is facing in the same direction as the child's own body. The child therefore can put his trousers on backwards either because he has not learned one or the other.

The problems involved in putting on sleeved upper garments correctly are somewhat different. To put on a coat, the child must put his left arm in the left sleeve, his right arm in the right. But now, contrary to the case of trousers, the child must orient the front of his own body to the front of the coat if he is putting on the coat by himself. To get his left arm in the left sleeve, and his right arm in the right sleeve, he actually must mentally rotate either the coat or himself, for the sleeve nearest his left arm is the coat's right sleeve, and the sleeve nearest his right arm is the coat's left sleeve. The child, therefore, must cross over, or "transpose," his movements. As we have just said, this is very hard for a young child (and even for some adults) to do.

So the problem in putting on a coat correctly is really not so much learning front from back as learning left from right. Until a child can correctly carry out a cross-over instruction, such as "touch your left hand to your right ear," he is likely to have trouble putting a coat on correctly.

Nursery school teachers, being very clever about such problems, teach the children to lay their coats on the floor button-side up and upside-down relative to their bodies, then to bend down and put their arms in the sleeves, and finally to flip the coat up and over their bodies. Since the coat is upside-down, the child has only to place his arms in the same-side sleeves to get the coat on correctly.

Having discovered so many complexities involving front and back in the act of dressing, we fully expected to find many more as we considered other behaviors. We wondered about judgments of front and back of different types of objects. For instance, what about objects which have front-back features but unlike animal forms, lack eyes or faces? Does the child's understanding of front-back for, say, chairs and other pieces of furniture, or bicycles, cars, and other vehicles parallel his understanding for animal forms? Does it make a difference whether the objects are typically mobile (e.g., dolls, toy cars) or immobile (e.g., furniture)? How does the child judge something to be "in front" or "in back" when the objects are, say, blocks or glasses which have no front-back features? Do circumstances limit application of the judgments of "in front"? How far away can something be and still be judged in front? What if a barrier is put up? (Think of people on opposite sides of a wall or door. Can one be in front of the other?) How far from midline, or how far to the side, can something be and still be judged "in front"? Does "in back" simply mirror "in front," or are the limits of "in back" different from "in front"? Does the position of one's own body influence judgments of whether one of two objects is in front of the other?

We soon had far more questions than we could study formally. We therefore were faced with the somewhat agonizing problem of choosing among them.

SOME GENERAL METHODOLOGICAL CONCERNS

In addition to thinking about what to study, we had to decide whom to study. There is a critical question here: What is the relation between age and the growth of knowledge? Is it uniform across age, or is it greater at some periods than others? Are the changes merely in degree, with older people simply knowing more than younger? Or are there also "qualitative" changes, changes in *how* people know? This is the question that we are asking about knowledge of the spatial concepts "in front of," "in back," and "beside." By this reasoning, we would have to look at people of all ages. Practically speaking, this is very hard to do. To save time and resources, we must pick and choose. Whatever we know about cognitive development in general should help us focus on age periods when the most important changes are likely to take place. A variety of studies indicate that the age period from about 4 to 10 years is a period of major change in cognitive skills, with the most important changes occurring between 4 to 7 or 8. Therefore, we hoped to maximize our chances of finding interesting differences by picking 4- to 8-year-olds for our first study.

HOW CAN PEOPLE TELL US WHAT THEY KNOW?

If our question is, what do people understand "in front" and "in back" to mean, why not simply ask them? We should, and we have, but for developmental psychologists in particular, there are problems with this method. Children don't talk too well. Indeed, young children learn all sorts of things before they actually can talk about them. While older children talk much more and much better, they may be shy and have difficulty using language to express what they know. For example, when we asked children to tell us the difference between their fronts and their backs, some children said scarcely a word but could respond correctly to our own descriptive statements. Even the least verbal child strongly disagreed, for example, if we said, "The nose is in back." Therefore, we tried to design test situations which place as little demand as possible on verbal ability, and confront our subjects with these situations.

Our main procedure was very simple: We would ask each child to make a series of "in front," "in back," and "beside" placements of ordinary objects like toy cars and doll-house chairs. We would then see whether placements changed or stayed the same when children were asked to place different types of objects, or were given different kinds of instructions.

One problem was that the children perceived our task as having right answers, and were concerned with being right. Nearly all subjects in psychological research—children as well as adults—want to be helpful and cooperative and not to make mistakes. On occasion, we have heard teachers say to their classes, before a psychological experiment, "Now, children, I want you to do your best in this test and show everyone that Room 103 is the best in the school!" What does it mean to do one's best in a psychological experiment (not a *test*) in which there are, strictly speaking, no correct answers in the first place? This teacher might have motivated the children to listen carefully to the experimenter and follow the instructions and, perhaps, not break the apparatus. However, in saying this, the teacher might have made the children reluctant to respond for fear of being "wrong."

This being the case, we had to communicate the idea that any kind of response to the task was acceptable; what mattered was what the child thought, not what he believed that *we* thought. We therefore began by putting one object (say, a car) in front of the child, then giving him another (a truck), and asking him to place it in reference to the car. We told the child, "You can put the truck here (indicating the area on the near side of the car), over here (indicating the far side), here, or here (indicating the left and right sides), wherever you think it should go. OK, here's the truck. Put it in front of the car." Then we asked him to place the truck behind and then beside the car, varying the order of the instructions. With these instructions we hoped that the child would understand that he could place the object on any part of the board that he felt was appropriate.

Another question was what to do after each placement? We did not want to appear to be approving a particular placement, so, of course, we did not verbalize approval or disapproval. However, some children expect an approving statement from an adult when they perform a task correctly. To these children, saying nothing could mean that they have done something wrong. To other children, saying nothing could mean that they are doing something right. We therefore tried to be supportive and friendly throughout the session, regardless of what the child did.

HOW ARE OBJECTS PLACED
IN SPATIAL RELATION TO OTHER OBJECTS?

Once our initial methodological decisions had been made, we were ready to begin. The children in our first study were 40 boys and 40 girls ranging in age from 4 years, 6 months, to 7 years, 6 months. We decided to show the children pairs of objects which included objects representing living things both human and nonhuman by reason of their having eyes (dolls and toy turtles), objects which had the capacity for self-propelled movement but were not alive and lacked faces (toy cars and trucks), and nonliving inert objects which lacked faces (doll-house chairs).

Object Referent Placements

On trials we call *object referent trials,* the experimenter placed an object (the "stationary" object) on a board in front of the child, and the child was asked to place a second object (the "mobile" object) in relation to the stationary object. For each of the pairs of objects mentioned above, each child placed one member in front of, in back of, and beside the other member three times: once when the stationary object faced the child, once when it faced away from the child, and once when it faced to either his right or left side. If front-back features are important in determining judgments of front and back, the children's placements should change when the orientation of the stationary object changes. Our results showed a striking degree of consistency in the children's placements. If we look at *where* the children set the mobile object in relation to the stationary object, all children but one set the mobile object on the front side of the stationary object for the "in front" instruction, on the back side for the "in back" instruction, and on either of the two remaining sides for the "beside" instruction. These placements occurred regardless of whether the front of the stationary object was toward, away from, or to one side of the child. The one child who responded differently—a boy age 6 years, 6 months—consistently placed objects in the same location and facing the same way in reference to *himself:* The changes in orientation of the front of the stationary object evidently made no difference to him.

We also asked how the children *oriented* the front side of the mobile object in relation to the front side of the stationary object. Here too there was strong consistency.

Of all the possible patterns, three occurred frequently enough to be called regular patterns. The mobile object always faced toward the stationary object in the "facing" pattern; the side of the mobile object was always toward the stationary object in the "face-to-side" pattern; and the mobile object always faced in the same direction as the stationary object in the "lined-up" pattern. The lined-up pattern was used most often; 86 percent of all placement patterns were in the lined-up pattern, and about 75 percent of the children made two-thirds or more of their placements in this pattern.

Self-referent Placements

Besides asking the children to place objects in relation to each other, we asked them to place objects in relation to their own bodies. As we had expected, all 80 children made their placements in the appropriate location in relation to their own bodies (but note that this shows only that the children know the fronts, backs, and sides of their own bodies). However, the placements did differ in how the children oriented the object in relation to themselves. Three major patterns of self-referent placements appeared. These correspond to the facing, face-to-side, and lined-up patterns found for the object-referent trials, except that the child takes the place of the stationary object. Together, these three patterns accounted for about 75 percent of the total number of self-referent placements. Now, unlike the object-referent placements, we found that certain patterns were used more often for some objects than for others. The children used the facing pattern most frequently for placing dolls or chairs, and the face-to-side pattern for bugs and vehicles. We suspect that this difference in pattern use depends upon the way in which different types of objects are usually held in play. Wheeled toys are usually grasped by the side and pushed laterally (face-to-side pattern), but chairs, and more obviously dolls, are more likely to be played with face-to-face (facing pattern). Thus, it is likely that the way in which *any* object is used would influence its orientation in a front-back placement; even an adult asked to place a cup "in front" of himself would be unlikely to place it with the handle facing himself. So, although the meaning of "in front of" and "in back of" depends most importantly on the characteristics of the objects, it also is influenced by the individual's typical experience with the objects.

TEST ORDER EFFECT

Half of the children placed objects first in relation to themselves and then in relation to other objects; the remaining children were tested in the opposite order, with object-referent placements first. Somewhat to our surprise, and greatly to our dismay, we discovered that the frequency with which children used the different types of patterns was influenced by test order. This was particularly clear on the self-referent trials. The different use of the facing and face-to-side patterns described above occurred most frequently when the self-referent condition came first. When the object-referent condition came first, children were likely to use the lined-up pattern instead of either of the others. Remember that the lined-up pattern was the typical pattern observed for the object-referent placements. It was as though these children had gotten used to using the lined-up pattern on the object-referent trials, which they now continued to use on the self-referent trials. One might say that they treated themselves as one more object in relation to the mobile object, rather than treating themselves as *users* of the object.

So the expressed meaning of "in front of" and "in back of" evidently depends not only on an object's features and on the ways in which it is typically used, but also on the nature of the child's immediately prior experience in placing objects.

The result which surprised us most was the absence of age differences. Either there is no significant change in understanding of front and back between 4 years, 6 months, and 7 years, 6 months, or our method failed to tap the changes that take place. Yet, the results did begin to address some of the questions we had raised in our discussions. First, the absolute front of a referent object (i.e., the stationary object), appears to specify the locations for front and back placements more strongly than it does the *orientations* of placements. Since the children all knew their own fronts and backs when we asked them, the very high consistency of locations of placements is just what we might expect. Second, we found that what is put in front of what makes a difference, probably because of the nature of prior experience with the objects.

IS "FRONT" THE FACE OR THE BODY?

The difference in placement patterns found for the different kinds of objects led to our second study. The facing pattern which was used for the dolls suggested the possibility of social interaction between the dolls, since dolls—like people—stand front-to-front when they talk to one another. But was the child intending the bodies or the faces of the dolls to be front-to-front? Usually, the face, not the body, is the focus of attention in social interaction. This would suggest that the children's placements of dolls depended more upon face cues than body cues.

The simplest way to find out which had been the basis for placement would be to set the two kinds of cues in competition with each other by turning the head to the side. For our second study, we used the Barbie and Ken dolls which have mobile heads. Our subjects were 40 boys and 40 girls ranging in age from 5 to 10 years. The head and body of either doll could face in the same direction (head and body convergent), or in different directions—to the right or left of the body (head and body divergent).

The answer to our question was clear: The children disregarded the direction of the doll's face. Whether the head and body of both

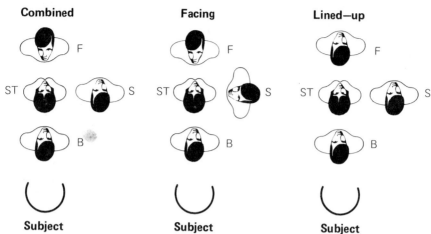

Figure 9.1. *The three placement patterns scored as "regular" (body rather than face as basis for placement). The doll marked ST is the stationary doll. F, B, and S represent the "in front," "in back," and "(be)side" placements of the mobile doll in relation to the stationary doll. Both dolls in each pattern are represented with head and body in convergent alignment. The same patterns appeared regardless of alignment combination. The drawings depict the stationary doll and subject facing in the same direction. The same placement patterns appeared when the stationary doll was turned to either side or toward the subject.*

dolls were convergent or divergent in alignment, the *locations* of the children's placements were the same as they had been in the first study.

We also found the same patterns of orientations of the mobile doll—with one exception. The face-to-side pattern, which we had suspected was specific to wheeled toys because of the way they are played with, was very rare; instead, we found a combined pattern, in which the front placement faced the stationary doll, while back and side placements faced the same direction as the stationary doll. This new pattern, together with the other two, is illustrated in Figure 9.1. The lined-up pattern still accounted for a majority of the placements, although its majority was not as strong (61 percent, compared to 86 percent in the first study).

At the same time, it was clear that children did use the face cues, especially when they could do so and simultaneously use the more basic body cues. One source of evidence came from the children's location of their "beside" placements. Remember that the stationary doll sometimes looked to its right and sometimes looked to its left. A child could use any of the body-based patterns but shift his beside placements from right to left according to the direction in which the stationary doll's head was turned. A substantial number of children did, in fact, make this type of shift. In addition, girls did so more than boys, and older girls more than younger girls. If the use of face cues reflects social responsiveness, it appears that girls were more socially responsive on this task than boys, and social responsiveness increased with age for girls. This interpretation agrees with other research showing greater social responsiveness of girls than boys in a variety of situations.

So we found that the body and not the face defines the front of a person. Why? We think the answer has to do with mobility: Heads are mobile relative to bodies. Therefore, head movements are relatively more frequent and more unpredictable than body movements. Think, for example, of two people sitting with their bodies side by side. Though their heads may frequently change positions in even a few minutes' time, we do not say that the two people change their spatial position with respect to each other, since their bodies remain relatively constant. So if the question is, how does a set of labels evolve to describe spatial relations among persons, the frequency and relative unpredictability of head movements would seem to make the head a poor basis for any consistent labeling system.

SOCIAL MEANING OF FRONT AND BACK

It was becoming clear to us that children's everyday understanding of front, back, and beside was not simply a matter of cut-and-dried spatial judgments, but that these spatial judgments were knit into many different aspects of the children's experience. Since the children in our second study seemed to intend to express a *social* as well as a spatial relation between the dolls when they did use face cues, it next occurred to us that the children's construction of what social scientists call "personal space" (see Robert Sommer's chapter on environmental psychology) might be yet another factor bearing on their understanding of front, back, and beside. The concept of personal space refers to how an individual divides the space immediately surrounding his own body for purposes of social interaction. The area closest to one's own body is a "zone of privacy." Ordinarily, an individual will maintain this distance from others in social interactions, except with those few persons with whom he is intimate. He will become very uncomfortable if this zone is encroached upon by nonintimates. Beyond this zone of privacy is a second zone in which most social interactions take place. Within this zone, distances may vary depending, for example, on how much two people like each other. Finally, there is an outermost zone for formal, public interactions such as speeches. We doubt that children are taught explicitly to maintain these distances. In fact, most adults do not realize that they themselves maintain them, and do not understand why, for instance, they become uncomfortable and want to move away if someone enters their zone of privacy.

Children learn to maintain these distances, and they learn very early. But would children's responsiveness to personal space influence their responses in our task? Would children asked only to put one doll in front of, in back of, or beside another doll put them closer together if the dolls had been described as liking each other, or would they be more likely to use a placement pattern in which the dolls faced away from each other if they had been described as disliking each other? To find out, we decided to provide a social context in the form of short stories about two dolls. We knew from other research that personal space is different for boys and girls. So this time we used four pairings of dolls: both dolls male, stationary doll male, stationary doll female, and both dolls female. Equal numbers of boys and girls made placements with each of these pairings. This procedure lets us see not only how children's concepts of personal space influence their placements of dolls of their own sex, but also whether the children would recognize distinctions among dolls of the other sex, or of boys and girls together.

We also knew, from other research, that personal space is influenced by how well people like each other, and by how well they know each other. We decided to try to emphasize the dimension of liking. In one story, we said (taking the case of two female dolls), "Let's pretend that Sue and Betty are very good friends and that they really like each other. Sue thinks that Betty is really nice, and Betty thinks that Sue is really nice too." In the other story, we said, "Let's pretend that Sue and Betty aren't good friends. They don't like each other at all. Sue thinks Betty is really mean, and Betty thinks that Sue is really mean too."

We decided not to say why the dolls liked or disliked each other, because we feared that our reason might mean different things to different children.

This time we tested 70 boys and 70 girls ranging in age from 8 to 10 years. We chose children this age because we knew they should be responsive to social space on other measures. First, each child made a series of placements without a story to provide us with a neutral measure against which to compare the effects of the stories. Then the child made two more series of placements, one preceded by the "like" story and the other by the "dislike" story. Half the children heard the "like" story before the "dislike" story and half heard it after the "dislike" story. Since our previous studies gave evidence of the effect of prior experience, we expected that the order of stories would be important too. The remainder of the procedure and instructions were the same as in our second study.

We've only begun to analyze the scores, but we already know some things about the results. The major finding is that the children's structuring of personal space clearly influenced their placements. Distance between the dolls was closer for the "beside" placements than for either the "in front" or "in back" placements, which were about the same. This difference perhaps is consistent with the observation that people normally will tolerate closer distances when side-by-side—a position lacking the connotation of intimacy of, say, a face-to-face position.

The major influence on distance, though, was the relationship between the dolls. Dolls that liked each other were nearly always placed closer together than were "neutral" dolls, and dolls that disliked each other were nearly always placed much farther apart than neutral dolls. The results also revealed the sex differences we had expected. Girls placed the dolls closer together than boys did in the neutral condition, and put the dolls farther apart when the dolls disliked each other. The girls' use of personal space thus appears to have been more responsive to variations in our task.

Our hunch that story order would play a role was borne out as well. Children placed the dolls that disliked each other closer when they heard the "dislike" story after the "like" story. Perhaps dolls that first like each other and then dislike each other are seen as "closer" than dolls that have no such history. This interpretation seems to be a reasonably accurate reflection of the course of children's actual friendships. In childhood, even best friends quarrel and, for periods of time, do not speak to one another. It's quite different when two children simply don't like each other. For story order, too, the boys and girls were different. The effect of story order was more pronounced for the girls.

We had expected to find that placement distances also would depend on the sex of the child in combination with the sexes of the dolls. (In our second study, we had controlled for whether a boy or girl placed a boy or girl doll, even though at the time we had no explicit reason to do so. We can see how critical this control was for our third study.)

Consider the girls' scores first. Girls made roughly equally close placements of a male doll in relation to another male doll, or of a female doll in relation to either another female doll, or to a male doll. But they placed a male doll much farther away from a female doll. Perhaps 8- to 10-year-old girls perceive boys as wanting to avoid the close company of girls, though they themselves approach boys and girls about the same way. This seems a reasonable enough account in light of what is generally known about friendship patterns of boys and girls at this age. Boys seem more actively to exclude girls than girls act to exclude boys. Unfortunately, if this sort of account makes any sense in terms of what is known about friendship patterns, the boys' scores throw it into question, since the boy's closest placements were of a male doll in relation to a female doll. Does this mean that boys really do want to approach girls even more than they want to approach other boys? Even more puzzling, the boys' farthest placements were of female dolls in relation to female dolls. Do boys perceive girls as less friendly with other girls than boys are with boys? What we end up with is a series of individually more or less reasonable interpretations which, taken together, do not make sense. We are left to wonder whether or not any of the interpretations of the sex differences are correct.

We were relieved to see, though, that with all this complexity, the effects of the story condition were regular. Whether the subject was a boy or a girl, and whatever the combination of sexes of the dolls, dolls that liked each other were placed closest together, and dolls that disliked each other were placed farthest apart.

We are less far along with the analyses of the placement patterns. Generally, the results agree with those of our previous studies. The lined-up pattern, in which the dolls all face in the same direction, was by far the most frequently used, and the body rather than the face was the basis for placement in most cases. We were very disappointed to find no very strong relation between placement pattern and the relationship between the dolls over the study as a whole. When the dolls liked each other, we had expected, for the in-front placement that the children would make the mobile doll face the stationary doll (as shown in the facing and combined patterns in Fig. 9.1), but face away from the stationary doll when they disliked each other (as shown in the lined-up pattern, Fig. 9.1). There was only a hint of this effect in the results. For the in-back placements, the effect was much clearer. When the dolls liked each other, the mobile doll nearly always faced the stationary doll. But when the dolls disliked each other, they very frequently were placed back-to-back.

We also were encouraged to find a relation between pattern type and distance. A major implication of our assumption that social distance can be expressed both through physical distance and through eye contact (or by turning one's back) is that there should be differences in physical distance between "in front" placements when "in front" is face-to-face (combination and facing patterns) and when "in front" is "face-to-back" (lined-up pattern). This difference appeared: Distances were consistently greater for the face-to-face, or interpersonal, pattern in the control and in both story conditions. This finding, like the finding that "beside" placements were closer than "in front" or "in back" placements, suggests that the children were sensitive to the social prohibition against extreme closeness in face-to-face positions.

So this study gives us additional evidence for a consistency in children's judgments of front, back, and beside. We also have much stronger evidence than we had before that children's spatial judgments are not "merely" spatial, but are complexly interlinked with the children's social experience.

When we first began thinking about the spatial concepts, "front," "back," and "beside," we did not expect that our research would move in this direction. We talked about the spatial setting in which judgments might be made, but it did not occur to us that social settings might also be influential. Instead, the results of our first studies themselves led us in this direction.

CONCLUSION: SOME THOUGHTS ON "PROGRESS" IN SCIENCE

With findings such as these, we are beginning to recognize some new dimensions of Heinz Werner's principle referred to in the early part of this chapter. One is that primitive spatial orientation (the spatial planes of one's own body) evolves into an objective space that has interrelated attributes—perceptual-spatial, social, and linguistic.

These are just some of the directions in which we could go. Doing research is like climbing a many-branched tree. Movement from one position on a limb to another is linear, but at any point, we reach new limbs that we did not and often could not anticipate. But even this simile may be too linear to characterize the situation. It might be better to compare doing research to movement in a catacomb: Any move could carry us off in wholly new directions, or could connect back to where we started from. This is progress—but not in a layman's sense. The layman thinks that scientific progress means diminishing, in some absolute sense, the total fund of ignorance. The scientist knows that the fund of ignorance (and knowledge) is inexhaustible, infinite, and that progress consists rather of discovering new and better questions. Knowing more than you knew before is, in a sense, knowing more about more, and knowing the same thing in a different way. This is why, in the case of our own work, we could summarize our progress by saying, we now know more clearly what we *don't* know than we knew we didn't know before. This can be a very disagreeable state of affairs for people who believe that every question has a definitive, final answer. But for us, uncovering unexpected complexities has been exhilarating. Research wouldn't be fun if the problems one set for oneself yielded their solutions too easily.

When I first started thinking about memory for verbal information, the type of study that usually was reported consisted of having subjects repeat a list of words or nonsense items for a number of trials. A period of time was allowed to elapse ranging from several minutes to a number of hours, after which the subjects were tested to see how many of the items on the list they remembered. Thus, a verbal retention experiment consisted of three stages: First, a learning period followed by a retention interval, and finally a test of the learning. The learning period could have taken 30–60 minutes before the experimenter was satisfied that the learner knew the material thoroughly. In other cases, the experimenter might not require attainment of a criterion of no errors, but might simply run his subjects for a set number of trials. The one constant feature of such experiments was a *retention interval* filled with activity unrelated to the learning task, but designed to keep the subject from rehearsing the list. A typical finding was that as the retention interval became longer, recall of the learning became poorer. In other words, forgetting was found to be directly related to the length of the retention interval. Interest centered on the amount of such forgetting in relation to variables such as the kind of learning materials used, and the similarity of events during the retention interval to those learning materials. During the long history of research on verbal learning, more than enough findings had accumulated to fill a chapter on retention in a textbook.

One day I reflected on the fact that textbooks usually separate the data of such experiments into two chapters—one on learning and another on forgetting. This separation seemed artificial to me. Surely, forgetting did not begin at the beginning of the retention interval but must be present during the learning period itself. Since the appearance of an item on one trial is separated in time from its repetition on the next trial, this interval between items could be viewed as constituting a miniretention interval for that single item. Immediately after a presentation, then, one's recall should be perfect, assuming one had been paying attention. By the time the item appeared again in the

Lloyd R. Peterson is in the Department of Psychology, Indiana University, Bloomington, Ind.

next trial, some forgetting is likely to have occurred, and indeed, the presence of errors indicates that it does occur.

This train of reasoning led me to attempt to measure forgetting over short intervals of time—durations short enough to occur within the "learning" period of a long-term retention experiment. By compressing the three stages of a typical long-term retention experiment into short intervals, one could look at the learning period through a "magnifying glass," so to speak. The traditional learning period might then be shown to contain many miniature retention intervals. Employing such a "microanalysis" of verbal learning, one could see what happened to these individual components in the course of the experiment.

Of course, this was not the first experiment to measure memory capacity over short intervals. Something called the span of immediate memory had been measured for years as a part of many intelligence tests. In a test of immediate memory span, the tester calls out a series of digits at a uniform rate (e.g., 9, 7, 3, 4, 2, 1) and the listener tries to repeat them when the series is ended. Series of various lengths are tested until it is determined how many digits can be recalled immediately after presentation. This number of digits, say seven, is then considered to be the span of immediate memory for that subject. This kind of test was not considered to have much to do with learning, and was mentioned in psychology texts in contexts other than learning.

In my earliest attempts to link short-term retention with learning, I used nonsense syllables, the traditional materials used in verbal learning experiments. I tested the retention of a single syllable over various retention intervals measured in seconds. The three letters were well within the immediate memory span—they could be repeated accurately after a single presentation. But why not introduce a delay between presentation and test and see whether forgetting occurred during the interval? Of course, some other activity would have to be given to the subject during the retention interval so that he would not repeat the letters over and over until the test. Traditionally, retention interval activity took the form of naming colors shown one by one to the subject, or telling the subject to look for certain symbols on a large sheet of symbols. Since the time intervals involved here would be too short for such activities, it occurred to me that a convenient activity for a short retention interval would be counting backward from some number given immediately after the presentation of each syllable. To make the task difficult enough to insure concentration, why not have the subject count backward by three or four until told to stop?

The basic parts of the experiment were easily put together in the living room of a home, and that is where the first experiment was performed. My wife selected a nonsense word made up of three consonants (e.g., BRX). As I lay on a couch with my eyes closed, she spoke three letters at approximately two per second, while I listened. Immediately afterward, she spoke three digits, (e.g., 375) and I started counting backward by three from that number. When she said,

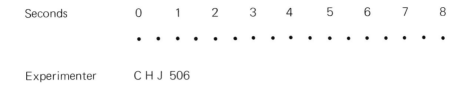

Figure 10.1. *Sequence of events in testing retention of three letters over short intervals of time. (Adapted from Figure 1, Peterson and Peterson, 1959. Copyright 1959 by the American Psychological Association. Reprinted by permission.)*

"Stop," I tried to recall the three letters. To my surprise it was a difficult task when several seconds lapsed from presentation to test. Even on those occasions when I was correct in my recall, I had no confidence that I was right.

After this initial exploratory study, we designed more carefully controlled studies. However, the importance of a crude preliminary study should not be overlooked. Exploratory work can give a rough idea of what it is possible to do in an experiment, with some possibilities quickly ruled out as too easy to be interesting, or too difficult to attempt. Pilot studies cover ground quickly, and one can improvise on the basis of a new finding without requiring elaborate and time-consuming arrangements such as are involved in full scale experiments. Of course, one must go back later and check exploratory findings in order to be sure they are reliable.

We next tried the experiment on college students, using electronic devices to control the duration of the retention interval and to measure the time required for the subject to recall. A metronome was set to sound twice per second, and the experimenter spoke in time with the metronome (see Fig. 10.1). As the experimenter spoke the first digit of the number from which the subject was to count backward, a lever was pressed to start an interval timer which controlled the duration of the retention interval. At the end of this interval, the timer turned on a red light which was the signal to recall the letters. At the same time the timer started a clock measuring time in hundredths of a second. When the subject spoke the third letter of his response, the experimenter pressed a button which stopped the clock. Thus, the apparatus of the lab provided better control over presentations to the subject than was possible in the pilot experiment (a certain amount of practice by the experimenter was necessary to eliminate

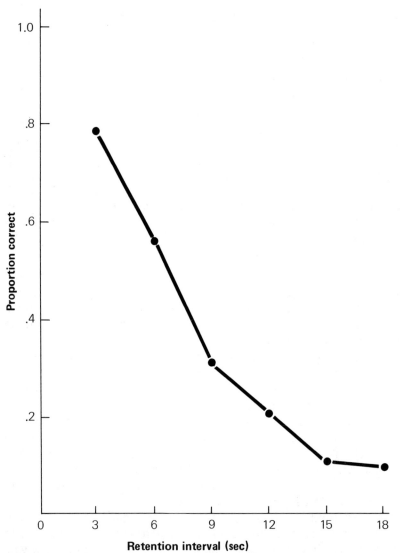

Figure 10.2. *Proportion of correct recalls after several short retention intervals. (Based on data from Peterson and Peterson, 1959.)*

experimenter errors). In later experiments the role of the experimenter was minimized further.

The pattern of remembering in the first full scale experiment is shown in Figure 10.2. It is based on correct recalls that came anywhere in an interval of 15 seconds after the signal for recall. Each point is an average based on eight tests from each of 24 subjects. Note that a considerable amount of forgetting occurred within the first few seconds, and recall was less than 50 percent correct after only 9 seconds.

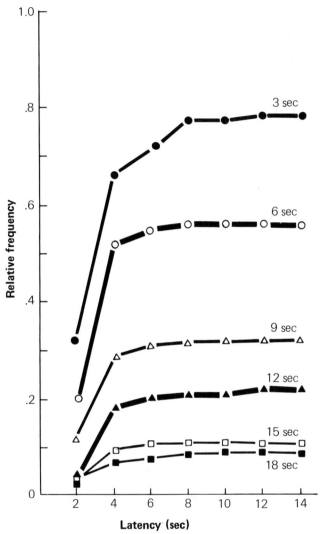

Figure 10.3. *Cumulative proportions of correct recalls as the recall interval lengthened. (Figure 2 from Peterson and Peterson, 1959. Copyright 1959 by the American Psychological Association. Reprinted by permission.)*

Of equal interest to the rapid forgetting demonstrated, was the time that elapsed before the subject spoke the three letters. Figure 10.3 depicts this aspect of recall in a graph. The proportions of correct recalls have been accumulated over successive intervals of time during the recall interval. A separate curve is plotted for each retention interval. Notice that the less time one gives for recall, the poorer the recall will be. One could slice up Figure 10.3 into separate retention curves at each recall interval, and then it would be seen that the height of the retention curve depends on the length of the recall interval. In Figure 10.3 another dimension, time of recall, has been added to the analysis of Figure 10.2.

After thinking about the results of this experiment, it seemed likely that a stronger tie between learning and retention might be found by varying time to rehearse the message. If a single brief presentation resulted in minimal learning, then a greater degree of learning should be obtained with additional time allowed for rehearsal. In terms of retention, longer rehearsal should raise the slope of the retention curve. This is not an inevitable result of rehearsal, and one student of memory had suggested earlier that rehearsal only delays the beginning of the forgetting curve rather than altering the rate of forgetting (Brown, 1958). This point could be tested easily, and we ran an experiment in which subjects were tested after being given a number from which to count backward (1) immediately, (2) after 1 second, or (3) after 3 seconds during which time the message could be rehearsed. The results shown in Figure 10.4 have been plotted from the end of the rehearsal period, so that if rehearsal acts only to delay the onset of forgetting, the three curves should coincide. The data shown are from a group of 24 subjects who rehearsed out loud during intervals provided for that purpose. Clearly, the retention curves for the differing amounts of rehearsal vary from one to the other; the longer the time for rehearsal, the slower the rate of forgetting. This is a learning effect, a slower rate of forgetting being produced by longer time for processing of the message.

It should be emphasized that what happens during the passage of time is what influences recall. The longer the rehearsal time, the longer one remembers. But this is not an automatic effect. One does something to the information. In another comparison, the longer the retention interval, the less one remembers. Does the forgetting result from something that happens with the passage of time, that is, does the arithmetic interfere with memory? One bit of evidence suggests that arithmetic may not produce the forgetting. This evidence comes from Keppel and Underwood (1962), who gave their subjects a visual presentation and permitted them to view it for a few seconds before starting to count backward: On the first test of an experimental session, little or no forgetting was found. However, on the second test of a session some subjects did forget, and the proportion of correct recalls on a third test dropped even more. This forgetting seems to stem from the previous tests given the subjects. Forgetting due to previous experiences is said to be due to *proactive interference*, that is, material presented before the current test interferes with recall of the latest test.

Interference from previous tests shows up in the kinds of errors made in recall. Figure 10.5 shows the source of erroneous responses in an experiment in which six successive tests were given to each sub-

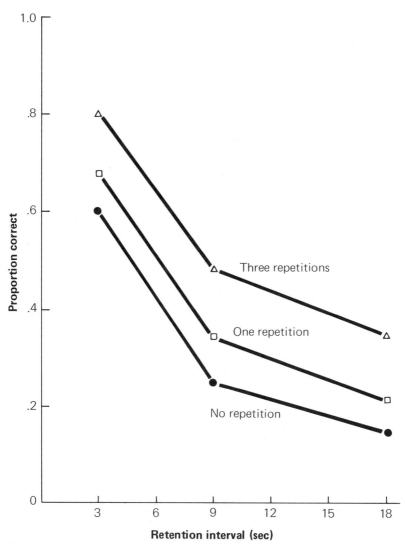

Figure 10.4. *Proportions correctly recalled as a function of varying amounts of explicit rehearsal. (Based on data from Table 1, Peterson and Peterson, 1959.)*

ject. On the sixth test the erroneous recalls were examined, and the proportions of letters which came from each of the five previous tests were calculated. Many of the erroneous letters came from the fifth test; only a few came from the first test. The longer one waited, the less interference there was on recall of a current presentation by a previous presentation. With the passage of time, previous messages competed with the current one to a lesser degree. A similar finding was obtained from a slightly different experiment—if one lengthens the interval between tests, retention improves (Peterson and Gentile, 1965).

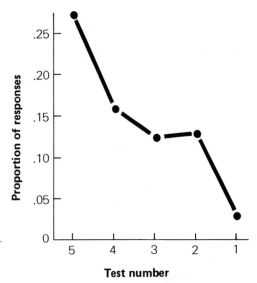

Figure 10.5. *Sources of erroneous letters given during recall of the sixth test of the experimental session. (From Figure 1, Peterson and James, 1967.)*

One aspect of experimental work in any science is that it leads to additional experiments by other workers. Thus, Keppel and Underwood were led to run their experiment by wondering what might be producing the rapid forgetting in our experiment. When they published findings showing that at least some of the forgetting is due to proactive interference, I was stimulated by their results to run other experiments which depended on their findings. Thus, research is a social enterprise and researchers are linked by both formal and informal networks (see the paper by Antrobus, Chapter 14).

Incidentally, in the experiments just reported we had improved apparatus, so that the entire sequence of events constituting a trial was run off automatically. A memory drum used in list-learning studies was modified. As it is generally used, a piece of paper is wrapped around a motorized drum. The drum turns so that one line of typing at a time is exposed through an opening in a shield which limits view of the drum. This enables the experimenter to type a list of words, one under the other, and expose them to the subject's view one at a time at a constant speed (1 or 2 per exposure). A few blank lines appear at the end of the list—these allow the subject to have a few second's rest before the next trial on the list begins. To such a memory drum we added modifications to stop the drum after a set number of exposures and at the same time automatically start the retention interval. The end of the retention interval produced a signal for recall, and after a preset number of seconds the cycle started again.

Our modified memory drum permitted us to investigate another

TABLE 10.1 SAMPLE BLOCK OF OVERLAPPING PRESENTATIONS AND TESTS IN SHORT-TERM RETENTION OF PAIRED-ASSOCIATES

edge	8	law	9
cook	5	mad	3
hose	4	saw	7
saw	7	boat	1
hose		ape	
edge	8	law	9
cook	5	law	
joke	10	mad	3
cook		boat	
note	2	joke	10
note		saw	7
boat	1	edge	
ape	6		

Source: Peterson, 1963, Table 1.

variable influencing memory. Again it was a variable relating retention to learning—specifically, the interval separating repetitions of the same presentation. A standard type of verbal learning, *paired-associate* learning, was modified to provide information on short-term retention after varying intervals between two repetitions of the same pair of associates. Paired-associate learning is one of the aspects of learning a foreign language; one learns equivalent words in the foreign tongue for a large number of English words. In our microanalysis of paired-associate learning, long blocks of overlapping presentations and tests were set up as shown in Table 10.1. "Edge 8" would be seen first, then "cook 5," and so on. Later "cook 5" would be shown again. Still later "cook" would be presented by itself as a test of the subject's ability to recall that "5" goes with "cook." Other pairs were also presented and tested under a variety of conditions. There were two intervals of interest, the retention interval from the last presentation until the test, and the interpresentation interval between first and second presentations of the pair. When retention is plotted at various intervals after a single presentation, one gets a forgetting curve as in Figure 10.6. When a forgetting curve is plotted after two presentations, naturally one expects less forgetting than after one presentation.

Now, the interesting question is whether or not the interval between two presentations of the same pair has an effect on the forgetting curve. At first thought one might predict that the retention curve should be higher when the interpresentation interval was short than it would be when the interval was long. The reasoning would go like

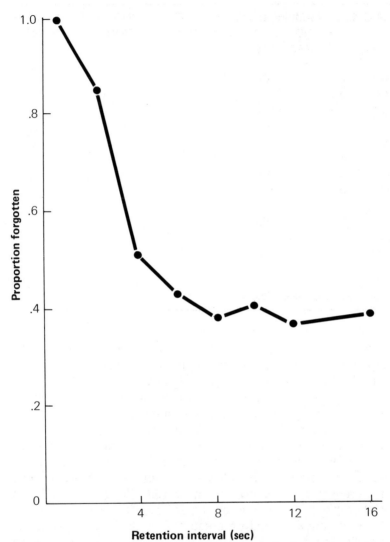

Figure 10.6. *Proportion of forgetting of a paired-associate after a single presentation.*

this: During the interpresentation interval one is forgetting the initial presentation, just as after a single presentation. Surely, the longer one waits before the second presentation, the less total learning will be left at the time of testing. There should be less accumulated learning from two separated presentations than from two presentations massed together.

However, this reasoning leads to an incorrect prediction. In general, retention is better after the second presentation if the interpresentation interval is long. The only exception to this gneralization is

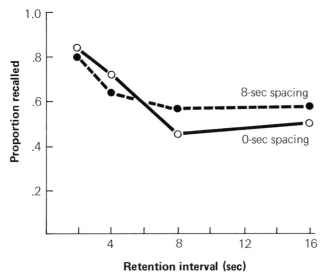

Figure 10.7. *Retention after two massed pairings versus retention after two spaced pairings. (Figure 3 from Peterson, 1963.)*

for very short retention intervals. Figure 10.7 shows that the retention curves for massed and spaced presentations cross. For a short time after the second presentation, spaced presentations yield poorer retention, while at longer retention intervals the spaced presentations provide better retention.

Why should the two curves cross? Two factors seem to be involved, one acting only at short retention intervals, the other dominating the longer retention intervals. One possibility is that long-term recall requires attention during the presentation, and one is more apt to pay attention to a second presentation if the first presentation has not just occurred but took place some time in the past. The matter remains a question for further research.

Common sense suggests that there must be some limit to the length of time one can wait and still have some benefit from a previous presentation. This thought led us to examine a number of intervals between presentations, holding retention interval constant. We determined that there was an optimum length of interval between two presentations, and that if the interval became too long, the effect of the first presentation diminished. The relationship is graphed in Figure 10.8.

CONCURRENT VERBAL ACTIVITY:
DOING MORE THAN ONE THING AT A TIME

Finally, consider an experiment that grew out of the questioning of an assumption. For a long time I had assumed that as long as one kept a subject busy with rapid vocal activity (so he could say nothing

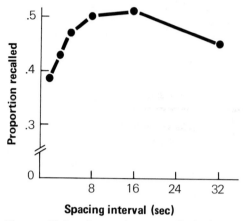

Figure 10.8. *Proportions recalled after a 16-second retention interval with differing amounts of spacing between two presentations. (Figure 4, Peterson, 1966. Copyright 1966 by the American Psychological Association. Reprinted by permission.)*

else) during the retention interval, rehearsal could not occur. One could speak only one thing at a time, and it was only one step further to suppose that only one stream of symbolic activity could be processed at a time. Since a lot of forgetting was found in most of our experiments, this assumption seemed justified, indirectly at least.

I realized that this assumption might not be justified while adding some columns of digits during the preliminary analysis of some data. While doing this I discovered that I could not keep myself from thinking about another matter, and at first, I was annoyed at my inability to concentrate on the addition. When I realized that in spite of my wandering thoughts I was reaching the correct sum more often than not, my concern turned from annoyance at the errors to surprise at the correct sums. The adding seemed to be semiautomatic, in the sense of requiring a minimal amount of attention.

The next step was to try exploratory work on someone other than myself. I looked for a way to measure performance of two symbolic tasks presented concurrently, hoping to avoid dependence on the introspections of the subject. My 12-year-old son was handy, so I instructed him to count softly aloud from 1 to 10 repeatedly and rapidly, while I spoke other digits in his ear. I told him to count loudly enough so that I could hear him, but not so loud that he failed to hear the digits I spoke. As he heard these digits, he was to cumulate their sum and speak the total when I said "stop." After a few practice trials it became apparent that at least one person, a 12-year-old boy, could perform both tasks at the same time with a high degree of accuracy.

Now, this informal finding should not have come as a surprise, since it is well known that individuals can perform two sequences of activity concurrently when one is a routine motor activity. One can talk to a companion while driving a car or light a cigarette while walking down the street. But in these instances only one chain of acts involves verbal activity, while the other is an automatic, highly practiced motor skill. So the question remained whether or not one could perform concurrently two sequences involving symbols. We found initially that given practice, most college students could count aloud rapidly and at the same time solve an anagram (rearrange a set of letters to form a word). Subjects could also recite the alphabet while adding a series of digits. Reciting the alphabet or counting did not seem to slow them appreciably in the solution of anagrams or addition of digits, at least not after a fair amount of practice at such a dual task.

However, there still remained the possibility that memorization of verbal information required a concentration of attention that counting, or adding, or even anagram solution did not require. After all, learning or memorization was really different from these other activities. So I set up an experiment to test the possibility that memorization could occur while the vocal mechanism was busily engaged in irrelevant vocal activity (Peterson, 1969). Subjects were required to perform different tasks while they attempted to memorize nonsense syllables. In one, they read digits aloud as these digits appeared on a memory drum. In another, they added digits which were presented over earphones. In some cases, subjects were asked to perform *both* of these tasks at the same time! They were instructed to rehearse whenever the digits did *not* come over the earphones even though they would be reading digits aloud as they saw them on the memory drum at the same time as they rehearsed. As I suspected, under these conditions, when subjects engaged in dual irrelevant activity, reading aloud and adding, there was more forgetting than in the control condition, when they only read aloud.

I decided to run a third condition in which the subject was asked to rehearse while reading aloud for 3 seconds, after which he went on with both reading aloud and adding. Under this condition, subjects forgot *less* than when they did not have the 3 second rehearsal available. So rehearsal helped even though another stream of symbolic activity went on at the same time.

In this, as well as in other concurrent tasks, one of the tasks, even though it involved symbols, was a highly practiced routine. Symbolic behavior, no less than motor behavior, can become so automatic through long practice that it requires little or no attention.

Note that the subjects had to practice the dual activities involved in these tasks. It is not likely that many subjects attempt dual symbolic activities without explicit instructions to do so. Thus, a single verbal activity during the retention interval remains a reasonable control for rehearsal, particularly if the activity is not highly practiced. For many subjects, counting backward by three or four is not easy, even with some practice. Furthermore, subjects do not always use completely empty intervals for rehearsal (as in an earlier experiment in which we gave subjects time for rehearsal before counting backward but did not specifically instruct them to rehearse). No effect of the empty interval was found. Nevertheless, it is of interest that subjects can, if instructed, perform two symbolic chains of activity concurrently—one being a highly practiced task, and the other requiring more attention.

In conclusion, the experiments that have been described all bear on the theme that it is important to investigate timing of events during a learning task. The effect of lengthening the retention interval has been described; the results of increasing the time available for rehearsal have also been noted. Increasing the duration of the recall interval is likewise found to have a positive effect on retention. Increasing the time between the current test and previous tests results in another positive effect. Changing the time between successive presentations produces more complex results and depends on the retention interval. In all of these manipulations of time, the kinds of events that occur during the passage of time must be considered. Increasing the time for rehearsal does not help recall unless the subject is motivated to do something. Nevertheless, time provides a quantification of the amount of activity. Measurement of the effect of one kind of interval has led to experiments which in turn led to other experiments in which other intervals were measured. Thus, research is a never ending process, since each new finding leads to new questions, which in turn lead to new experiments.

REFERENCES

Brown, J. 1958. Some tests of the decay theory of immediate memory. *Quarterly Journal of Experimental Psychology,* 10:12–21.

Keppel, G. K. and Underwood, B. J. 1962. Proactive inhibition in short-term retention of single items. *Journal of Verbal Learning and Verbal Behavior,* 1:153–161.

Peterson, L. R. 1963. Associative memory over brief intervals of time. *Journal of Verbal Learning and Verbal Behavior,* 2:102–106.

Peterson, L. R. 1966. Short-term verbal memory and learning. *Psychological Review,* 73:193–207.

Peterson, L. R. 1969. Concurrent verbal activity. *Psychological Review,* 76:376–386.

Peterson, L. R. and Gentile, A. 1965. Proactive interference as a function of time between tests. *Journal of Experimental Psychology,* 70:473–478.

Peterson, L. R. and James, L. H. 1967. Successive tests of short-term retention. *Psychonomic Science,* 8:423–424.

Peterson, L. R. and Peterson, M. J. 1959. Short-term retention of individual verbal items. *Journal of Experimental Psychology,* 58:193–198.

Scientists routinely confront challenges and occasionally overcome them. This is the story of one such successful encounter. The challenge arose from the view that adult humans respond to many learning tasks as problems to be solved. According to this theory, the learner actively seeks the solution by testing one hypothesis after the other in an effort to find the solution. If this view is correct, then the hypothesis-testing process is central to learning. Imagine that we are observing a student in some learning situation, with the idea that he is testing out hypotheses in an effort to find the solution; we would like to know as much as possible about this important process of hypothesis testing. However, the problem solver's hypothesis is never visible. It is a subjective state, based on his temporary beliefs about the solution. Because hypotheses are subjective, it would appear that we could never hope to observe or even detect them. But is this inevitably the case? Is there no way to probe for and to detect the learner's hypothesis at any point in the learning task? The challenge we set for ourselves was to find such a probe.

The theory that for several tasks learning proceeds via hypothesis testing is relatively recent. It emerged as a reaction to an earlier theory, one which had been developed in the context of animal (or subhuman) research. Before tracing the development and application of the hypothesis probe, it will be valuable to review these earlier ideas. Let us start with a bit of the animal research upon which this earlier theory was based.

REINFORCEMENT THEORY AND THE
DISCRIMINATION-LEARNING EXPERIMENT

The basic experiment was called "discrimination learning" and was performed as follows: A monkey would be presented with two objects (e.g., a cylinder and a cube) on a tray; a raisin would be hidden under one of these objects (see Fig. 11.1). Let us assume that the experimenter always places the raisin underneath the cylinder. The tray is presented to the monkey, who pushes one of the two objects.

Marvin Levine is on the Faculty of the Department of Psychology, State University of New York at Stony Brook.

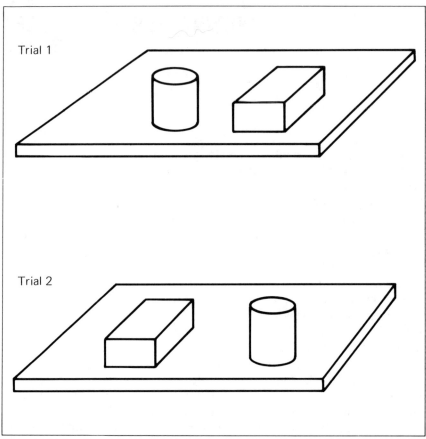

Figure 11.1. *Two trials of the discrimination-learning task used with mon-keys. A raisin might be placed under the cylinder on every trial.*

If he pushes the cylinder, he uncovers and can eat the raisin; if he pushes the block, he receives nothing. This sequence—presentation of the tray, response by the monkey, and possible receipt of the reward —was called a *trial*. The animal received a series of such trials. The only variation from trial to trial was in the location of the objects so that sometimes the cylinder was on the right and sometimes on the left. The two trials shown in Figure 11.1 indicate the two possible stimulus arrangements.

The typical result was that over a series of trials monkeys learn; in other words, they eventually move the cylinder on every trial. If a large group of monkeys received this learning problem, then the "learning curve" could be plotted by showing the proportion of ani-mals who chose the cylinder on each trial. The usual result, repre-sented in Figure 11.2, is that 50 percent of the animals choose the cylinder on the first trial but that, little by little, the proportion of

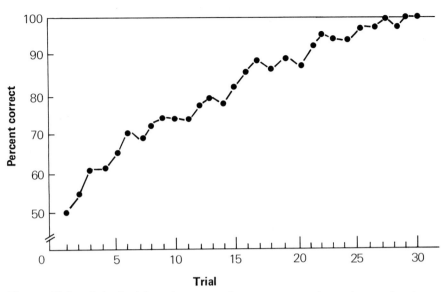

Figure 11.2. *A typical learning curve from a group of monkeys, showing the percentage of animals who are correct on each successive trial.*

rewarded responses increases until, after about 20 trials, every response is correct.

The basic theory that had been used to explain this shift from 50 to 100 percent correct responding was called *reinforcement theory*. According to this theory, learning proceeds because of two fundamental determiners—the reinforced response and the extinguished response. A response which is rewarded is said to be *reinforced* or strengthened, and hence, the probability that it will be made again at the next trial increases slightly. A response which is not rewarded is said to be *extinguished* or weakened, and the probability that it will be repeated at the next trial decreases slightly. In the example just presented, the response of pushing the cylinder, because it was always reinforced, gained strength from trial to trial. Similarly, the response of pushing the cube, because it was not reinforced, became weaker from trial to trial. As a result, the probability of making the correct response gradually increased over the series of trials. According to reinforcement theory, this trial-by-trial increase in the strength of the rewarded response is directly represented in the gradual learning curve (see Fig. 11.2). The discrimination-learning task was important, then, as a moderately complex task which could be accounted for by the simpler underlying processes of reinforcement and extinction. Reinforcement theory, because it relies on concepts developed by Pavlov, is sometimes called *conditioning theory*.

To early conditioning theorists, the theory was presumed to be of general applicability. Although they used animals in virtually all their research, many of these researchers believed that the theory was applicable to human behavior. About two decades ago, similar research was initiated with adult humans and similar theorizing was applied; this change of subject precipitated the controversy over the theory. Before reviewing this development, however, it is ncessary to consider one further detail within the discrimination-learning task. A glance at Figure 11.1 indicates that there are not only two objects which could be baited by the experimenter, there also are two locations—that is, the experimenter could put the raisin always on the left side, regardless of which object was placed there. In such a circumstance, of course, we would tend to find animals going more and more to the left side. Because the task is structured so that the experimenter consistently can reinforce the response to either an object or a location, it is said to have two *dimensions:* form (or object) and position. In the experiment described above, where the experimenter always baited the cylinder, form is said to be the relevant dimension; position is said to be the irrelevant dimension. The existence of this irrelevant dimension poses no problem for conditioning theory, since the baited object is randomly on the right or left. Response to each position is sometimes strengthened, sometimes weakened, so that response to each position maintains a moderate strength. Response to the cylinder, on the other hand, is always gaining in strength. The cylinder, therefore, soon transcends all other aspects of the situation in its ability to evoke the correct response.

Note that other dimensions could be added. Suppose, that on a given trial, one of the objects was red and the other green. Just as the cylinder and block change locations from trial to trial, they also could randomly alternate in color. Color would, then, provide a third dimension. If, in this circumstance, the experimenter still baited the cylinder consistently, color would be an irrelevant dimension and this task would have one relevant dimension (form) and two irrelevant dimensions (color and location). An important point, worth reiterating, is that conditioning theory readily generalizes to tasks with irrelevant dimensions.

When these experiments were first performed with adult humans, it was obvious that the simple two-dimensional task shown in Figure 11.1 was too trivial. College students characteristically make no errors in this task after the second or third trial. The task becomes more demanding, however, if several irrelevant dimensions are added. Typically, at least 4 dimensions (1 relevant and 3 irrelevant) are present in the task, and as many as 12 dimensions have been used in a single problem. In addition to increasing the number of dimensions, other minor details are modified to make the task appropriate for the adult human. Usually, the person is presented with two pictures rather than two objects and he or she indicates choice by touching one of the two pictures. The stimuli for a series of trials in a four-dimensional task

Stimuli
presented

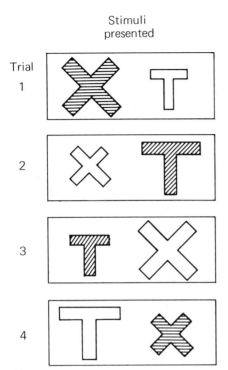

Trial
1

2

3

4

Figure 11.3. Four trials with four-dimensional stimuli. The dimensions are form (X vs. T), size (large vs. small), color (black vs. white) and location (left vs. right). On each trial the subject chooses one of the two pictures and is told "right" or "wrong."

are shown in Figure 11.3. The four dimensions in this figure are form, position, color, and size. As before, the experimenter selects one of these (e.g., color) to be relevant, and further selects one of the two colors to be correct. During the trial, whenever the subject would choose the black form, the experimenter would say "correct"; whenever he would choose the white form, the experimenter would say "wrong." Note, incidentally, the additional adaptation of the procedures to the human subject—instead of giving or withholding a raisin, the experimenter says "correct" or "wrong." Thus, for adult humans, the discrimination task has several irrelevant dimensions; furthermore, the reinforcement is verbal, not material.

So far as conditioning theory was concerned, these variations were inconsequential. The theory still predicted that the correct cue (black, in the example above) would gradually increase in strength, the opposite cue (white) would decrease, and the other cues would tend to maintain an intermediate strength throughout the experiment. The theory was applied to the adult human with some success. The percent of correct responses made on each trial by a group of humans looked very much like the curve in Figure 11.2—it started at 50 percent and gradually increased to 100 percent. Other properties of the patterns of choice made by the subjects were also derivable from conditioning theory. The theorists' faith, that conditioning principles were of general applicability, seemed confirmed.

THE EMERGENCE OF HYPOTHESIS THEORY

A few researchers, the author among them, were troubled by these findings. Conditioning theory seemed to imply that the adult human—the college student, no less—responds rather mechanically. The response is more and more pulled toward the consistently rewarded element in the stimulus pattern. Any internal experience the subject may have, his thoughts about the situation, his attitude toward the form, were considered irrelevant and were ignored. The learner was viewed to be passive. Despite the fact that this view seemed confirmed by the choice-response data from experiments, some of us were skeptical. We felt that a scientist studying adult human behavior has available a source of information unique in the sciences—he himself can be the subject in the experiment and can consult his own experiences about what might be happening. He can, so to speak, get some hunches from the inside about his subject matter (imagine a physicist trying to get information about atomic structure by "feeling" what it must be like to be an atom). When we ran ourselves as subjects in these problems, one thing was very clear. We were not being passive. Rather, we were searching for the solution—trying out first one possibility and if that didn't work (i.e., if it led to a response which was called "wrong"), trying out another. It seemed to us that we were testing hypotheses in an active search for the solution. Furthermore, we began to believe that the correct response was not being strengthened slowly by reinforcement, but that our behavior changed rapidly when we hit on the correct hypothesis.

The attitude of the conditioning theorist was that such internal experiences are irrelevant to science. The primary scientific data were the choices made by the subjects, and these data meshed well with conditioning ideas. If we wanted to replace conditioning theory with some other theory, it would have to be because the behavior of the subjects and their choice of responses warranted the change. What subjects (and scientists) revealed about personal feelings and thoughts had no parallel in any other science and therefore, was nonscientific by definition. Nevertheless, our experiences and the reports of our subjects convinced a few of us that conditioning theory was inappropriate for the adult human. Therefore, even before we had compelling data in hand, we began formulating what has come to be called *hypothesis* (hereafter, abbreviated *H*) *theory*.

Initially, *H* theory had three basic assumptions, which were more or less restatements of our common sense notions. The first assumption was that a subject, when facing a multidimensional discrimination-learning task, had several possible hypotheses he might consider. He chooses one of these as the basis for responding. To take a simple example, a subject facing a stimulus for Trial 1 might say to himself, "I have a hunch the solution is going to be 'black' on this problem. I'll try that." An additional part of this assumption is that the hypothesis dictates the subject's response; hence, the subject whose hunch was that the solution was "black" would choose the picture containing the black figure. The other two assumptions concern the effects of "right" and "wrong," respectively. If the subject's response is called "right," he keeps his hypothesis for the next trial. Thus, "right" is conceived of not as a strengthener of the response, as in reinforcement theory, but as a confirmer of the hypothesis, causing it to be retained. If the subject's response is called "wrong," he gives up his hypothesis and tries a new one. Thus, "wrong" does not weaken the response—it disconfirms the hypothesis, causing it to be replaced.

These three assumptions constituted the core of *H* theory. They reflected our everyday notions about how humans solve problems. They also had implications which could be tested with conventional experimental data. The first important breakthrough came in the fresh analysis of the learning curve performed by two young researchers, Gordon Bower and Tom Trabasso (1963). They argued that the traditional learning curve, with its gradual increase in proportion of correct responses, did not picture the learning process of the individual subject. Consider this learning process from the standpoint of *H* theory. The subject tries a hypothesis (Assumption 1, above). As long as it leads to a correct response, he will keep it (Assumption 2). As soon as it is disconfirmed, he rejects it and tries a new hypothesis (Assumption 3). Note that as long as he is correct, he will keep one hypothesis. When, therefore, the subject finally tries the correct hypothesis, it will lead him to make only correct responses: the correct hypothesis leads to the response called "right"; the subject keeps this hypothesis; it leads again to the response called "right"; etc. The subject, according to this view, will never again make an error. Suppose now that we have selected data obtained from several subjects, all of whom have one feature in common—they all made an incorrect response after Trial 20. According to *H* theory, because they made an error after Trial 20 these subjects had not tried the correct hypothesis during the first 20 trials. (Remember that the correct hypothesis produces only correct responses.) Thus, when one of these subjects was told "right" during the early trials he was merely lucky. He had held the wrong hypothesis, even though it had led to the correct choice. (To see how this could come about, take a specific case. Imagine that the stimuli of Figure 11.3 are presented, and that "large" is the solution. Imagine, further, that Trial 4 is about to begin. If the subject is holding the hypothesis that "white" is the solution, he will choose the

Trial

Subject	1	2	3	4	5	6	7	8	9	10	11
1	+	−	+	+	−	−	+	⊝	+	+	+ ...
2	−	−	+	−	+	⊝	+	+	+	+	+ ...
3	+	+	⊝	+	+	+	+	+	+	+	+ ...
4	−	−	−	+	+	+	−	⊝	+	+	+ ...
5	⊝	+	+	+	+	+	+	+	+	+	+ ...

A

Trial

Subject	...	−7	−6	−5	−4	−3	−2	−1	**TLE**	+1	+2
1			+	−	+	+	−	−	+	⊝	+	+ ...
2					−	−	+	−	+	⊝	+	+ ...
3							+	−	⊝	+	+ ...
4			−	−	−	+	+	+	−	⊝	+	+ ...
5									⊝	+	+ ...

B

Figure 11.4. *A. Each row shows the pattern of right (+) and wrong (−) responses made by one subject. The trial with the last error (TLE) is circled. All responses after this trial were correct. B. Same information as part A of this figure, except that the protocols are now aligned at the TLE. With this arrangement the percentage of correct responses at each trial before the TLE (−1, −2, etc.) may be determined.*

left picture and the experimenter will say "right"; conversely, the answer "black" will lead to the right-hand choice and the experimenter will say "wrong.") According to *H* theory, then, these subjects could never have been holding the correct hypothesis during these first 20 trials, although they should give the correct response about half the time. In general, any error tells the experimenter that prior to that point the subject held only incorrect hypotheses. However, when we see a long run (e.g., 15 trials) of correct responses, then we infer that the subject "has" the solution—that he is holding the correct hypothesis.

Thus, one implication of this theory is that a subject is in two states. At first he is trying out incorrect hypotheses, making correct responses by chance. Then, after some error, he tries the correct hypothesis and from that point on he always chooses correctly. According to this view, learning proceeds by a sudden, dramatic change. The subject goes from not having the solution to having it in one trial.

If this is the true state of affairs, why does the proportion of correct responses gradually increase as in Figure 11.2? Bower and Trabasso argued that it is not the strength of the correct response, but the proportion of people who have the solution which is increasing. This may be understood better by reference to Figure 11.4A. In this figure, we see the protocols for five subjects. A correct response is indicated by a plus and an error is indicated by a minus. The trial at which the last error was made (the TLE or trial-of-last-error) is circled. Assume that *H* theory is right, that prior to the TLE the pluses and minuses occur at random with a plus occurring about half the time. If you take the proportion of pluses, you can see that they would increase over trials, because the number of subjects who have started the criterion run is increasing over trials. Bower and Trabasso were able to derive, therefore, two important implications of *H* theory. One was that the subject learned in a dramatic, rapid fashion. He went from not having the solution to having it. This is now characterized as all-or-none learning. The other implication is that the theory can account for the traditional, gradual learning curve.

Bower and Trabasso, however, went beyond this. They were able to show graphically the suddenness of the learning process. Instead of lining the protocols up at Trial 1, as was done in Figure 11.4A, they lined all the protocols up at the TLE (Fig. 11.4B). According to *H* theory, at each trial preceding the TLE, about 50 percent of the responses should be correct. According to conditioning theory we should see a gradual increase in correct responses. Bower and Trabasso, in the data from several experiments, repeatedly found the same result. A representative example is presented in Figure 11.5. It is clear from these data that the subjects' response sequences reflected the rapid change of state predicted by *H* theory.

PROBING FOR HYPOTHESES

We had, then, a plausible alternative theory and an important datum. My own view was that it would be of immeasurable value to find a probe, a technique for detecting a subject's hypothesis at any stage of the problem. I was confident that such a probe could be developed. If, after all, a hypothesis was something that the subject was "holding," we ought to be able to detect that hypothesis. An obvious solution, of course, comes to mind. If you want to know the subject's hypothesis at some point, just ask him! This easy way out, however, couldn't be taken, for one critical reason. We were still trying to persuade the conditioning theorist that his theory about subjects' choice-responses was wrong. As we saw above, his view was that subjects' statements, having reference to personal, unobservable

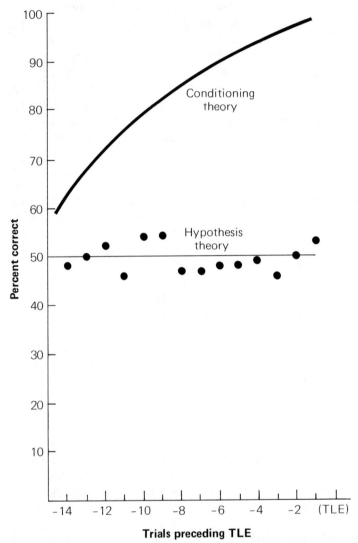

Figure 11.5. *The dots represent the percent of subjects making the correct response at each trial before the TLE (obtained by aligning the protocols as in Fig. 11.4B). The solid lines show the values predicted by the two theories.*

events, were irrelevant and worse, were unscientific. The only legitimate data, the only data to be theorized about, were a subject's choice responses. I felt, therefore, that the most influential probe would be based upon the subjects' choices during the task.

The challenge facing me, then was how to determine a subject's hypothesis at any point in the discrimination-learning task *using choice responses only.* Before reviewing the events that led up to the ulti-

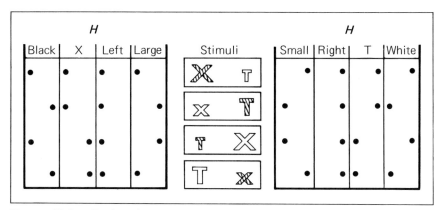

Figure 11.6. Each column contains the pattern of responses correspond-ing to one of the eight simple hypotheses. These patterns will occur, accord-ing to H theory, when the four stimulus pairs are presented consecutively and, following each response, experimenter says "right" (or says nothing).

mate solution, it will be instructive to consider the first probe I de-veloped using choice responses. Consider again the four trials pictured in Figure 11.3 as the first four trials of a problem. Let us imagine a restriction placed on the subject, namely, that he is dealing only with the eight "simple" hypotheses—those corresponding to the eight stimulus values "large is the solution," "black is the solution," etc. (Imagine, that is, that because of our instructions, he doesn't try any bizarre or complicated hypotheses, such as "on odd trials choose 'white'; on even trials choose 'X' "). If we wanted to know with which of these eight simple hypotheses the subject started the problem, we could say "correct" after each of his first four responses regardless of what they are. According to the assumptions of H theory, the sub-ject would start the problem with an hypothesis and, because he was told "correct," would keep it for each successive trial. Suppose, for example, that the initial hypothesis was that black is the solution. The subject would choose (for the Fig. 11.3 stimuli) the left side on Trial 1, the right side on Trial 2, the left again on Trial 3, and the right again on Trial 4. He would respond this way, according to the theory, be-cause he chooses in accordance with his hypothesis ("black is the solution") and, because this hypothesis is being confirmed and re-tained continually. As a result, over four trials he gives us this alter-nating response pattern. Notice, now, something else. None of the other seven hypotheses would produce this alternating response pat-tern. In fact, for the stimuli shown in Figure 11.3, each of the eight simple hypotheses yields a unique response pattern. These stimuli and the corresponding response patterns generated by the eight hy-potheses are shown in Figure 11.6. The first column shows the single-alternation pattern of choices that would be produced if the hypothesis were "black," the second column shows the response pattern produced if it were the form, "X"; etc. Figure 11.6 demonstrates that each of the eight simple hypotheses leads to a different pattern of response. We may, therefore, from the pattern of response, infer which hypothesis the subject was holding. If, to the stimuli in Figure 11.6, the subject (being told "correct" on each trial) chose left-right-right-left we would infer that his hypothesis was "large." This, then, is a probe—a basis for inferring the subject's hypothesis.

There is, however, one objection to the use of this probe. The experimenter must say "right," no matter what the subject does. This represents a change from the basic rules of the experiment, according to which the experimenter would say "right" only when the subject made the correct choice. Subjects typically assume that the experimenter is following this basic rule. They take it for granted, therefore, that being told "right" for several consecutive trials means that they have the solution. If, midway in the problem, the experimenter decides to interpose this probe, the subject will be told "right" for at least four consecutive trials, will think his hypothesis is the solution, and suddenly will be told "wrong." The learning dynamics will be more complicated than we wish at this stage of our science. Because this probe gives rise to this complication, it can be used only once. Furthermore, the problem cannot be continued beyond this single application. The experimenter could not revert to the original right-wrong rule without confusing the subject.

The usefulness of this probe is limited—but it is a probe. It allows us to assess a subject's hypothesis at least occasionally. Bear in mind that the basis for this technique is the assumption the subject keeps his hypothesis when he is told "right."

How could we devise a more general probe, one which would permit us to detect a subject's hypothesis repeatedly, at various points within the task? The solution to this problem was prompted unexpectedly, and came from an unlikely source. In a spare hour I was browsing through some early experimental literature, when an obscure article aroused my interest. The late William Bendig had performed a small experiment dealing with coin tossing. His concern was to verify one facet of conditioning theory, but this is no longer important. Bendig's experiment consisted of the following: He ran two groups of college students. To one group he announced that he was going to toss a coin three times and that he wanted the subject to guess the outcome of the tosses. He had the subjects in this first group write the first guess. Then he tossed the coin, announcing whether it was heads or tails. This procedure was repeated for the second, and then for the third guess. Thus, after each guess the subjects received "feedback" in that they learned whether their guess was right or wrong. To the other group he also announced that they were to guess three coin tosses. This group, however, was instructed to write their three guesses in sequence. Only after the subject wrote all three guesses would Bendig toss the coin three times. This was the entire experiment. One group made three responses, receiving information about the correctness of the response each time. The other group made three responses with no information coming after each response (trials without any feedback or reinforcement have subsequently come to be called *blank trials*).

The question Bendig raised was: What is the relationship between response patterns when subjects receive feedback after each response and when they do not? To put this question another way: If we know how subjects respond when they learn whether they are right or wrong after each trial, can we predict how they will respond during comparable blank trials? Are there some theoretical notions which would lead us to a correct prediction? Bendig showed that the predictions from conditioning theory were not correct. It was, however, a minor criticism which was largely ignored.

The question that Bendig had raised intrigued me, and I began exploring subjects' behavior during blank trials. Using the discrimination-learning task, I ran a few experiments in which subjects receiving occasional sets of blank trials were compared to subjects receiving normal feedback for those trials. The initial phenomenon I discovered was that even though a subject had been instructed that trials without feedback would occur, and that these trials were like tests, he behaved during blank trials as if the experimenter were saying "right." In other words, the subject seemed to retain one hypothesis during a series of blank trials.

To understand this initial insight, consider a subject in Bendig's blank-trial group. He is asked to write down three guesses about coin tosses without any intervening information. Suppose this subject said to himself, "I'll bet he has a two-headed coin" (i.e., the subject's hypothesis is, that the coin was going to come up heads all the time). We would expect this subject to write "heads," "heads," and "heads" again for his three guesses. In other words, the subject has some hypothesis which controls his behavior during this series of blank trials. He retains this one hypothesis throughout and it dictates his response each time. Blank trials, therefore, are almost exactly like reinforced (confirming) trials. In both cases, when the subject is told "right" and when he receives no information, he retains his hypothesis for the next trial.

I verified this hunch about blank trials with the following experiment. Two groups of subjects received virtually identical short problems. In one group each problem ended with four blank trials; in the other group the subjects were always told "right" no matter which response they made for these four final trials. My insight was confirmed by the results: During the four final trials, the patterns of response in the two groups were identical. People receiving no feedback behaved like people being told "right" after each choice. If it is true for reinforced trials. To appreciate the importance of this similarity, retain it after a blank trial.

I was tabulating and studying these data late one night when a crucial implication fairly leaped off the graph: If a subject keeps one hypothesis during a set of blank trials, then we could use these trials to probe for his hypothesis. The logic is perfectly parallel to the logic for reinforced trials. To appreciate the importance of this similarity, refer back to Figure 11.6. Earlier we used this figure to show that the hypothesis could be inferred when the subject was told "right" on every trial. Precisely the same analysis applies when he receives a series of blank trials. When the subject is given a set of four blank trials, his response patterns during this set should reflect his hypothesis. Suppose, for example, that four blank trials are presented at a point in the problem when the subject is thinking that "large" is the solution. We would expect him to choose the large letter on each of these trials. Thus, if the four blank-trial stimuli were like those in Figure 11.6, the subject would respond left, right, right, left. From this pattern of responses, therefore, we could infer that this subject's hypothesis was that "large" is the solution. The beauty of this probe is that it could be applied any place in the problem. Whenever, at any point in a problem, you wish to know a subject's hypothesis, all you have to do is present this series of four blank trials and observe the response pattern.

THE DYNAMICS OF DISCRIMINATION LEARNING

I acquired sufficient additional data to convince myself that response patterns during blank trials did indeed reflect hypotheses. The next step was to test these ideas in formal research. Accordingly, I designed the following experiment: Several four-dimensional discrimination problems were given to each of 80 college students. A blank-trial probe was inserted, and a hypothesis was inferred after every feedback trial. The general design of a problem is shown in Figure 11.7. Before the experimental problems were presented, the subject was instructed about the eight aspects of the stimuli. He was told that one of these would be the basis for correct responding, that he would be informed after every fifth response whether that response was correct or wrong, and that he was to try to make the correct response as often as possible. A particularly important detail about the instructions is that they stipulated the eight possible solutions. This was done to restrict the subject's set of hypotheses and to prevent him from attempting such things as complex sequence solutions or idiosyncratic hunches. Only by assuming that the subject is searching among the

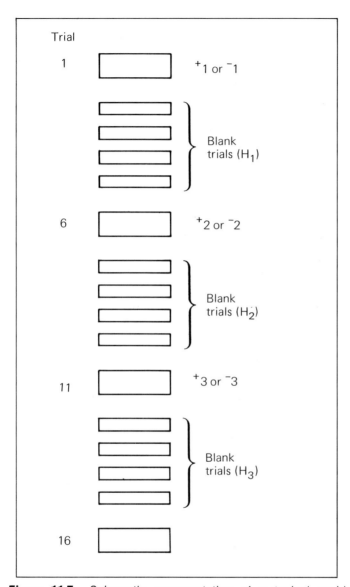

Figure 11.7. *Schematic representation of a typical problem, containing a series of feedback (+ or −) trials each of which is followed by the four-blank-trial probe for the hypothesis.*

eight simple hypotheses could we employ a probe. Another important detail about the instructions is that nothing was said about hypothesis testing or about any special strategy to be employed. The possible effects of suggestion, which might occur were the subject asked to state his hypothesis, were avoided.

The resulting data were studied first to determine whether blank trials could really serve as a probe for the hypothesis. During a series of four blank trials a subject can manifest any one of 16 possible response patterns. Figure 11.6 shows eight of these patterns. Note that the eight columns contain either four responses to one side (the third and sixth columns) or two responses to each side. Any pattern of three responses to one side and one to the other would not be accounted for by *H* theory. To the extent that these eight *inconsistent* (i.e., nonhypothesis) patterns appear, it would be necessary to add further assumptions to account for the choices. If these inconsistent patterns and the hypothesis patterns each occurred about 50 percent of the time (which would happen, for example, if the subject closed his eyes and made his choices randomly) the theory would be totally inapplicable. In this first experiment the eight hypothesis patterns occurred in 92 percent of the probes. The range in several subsequent experiments has been from 90 to 95 percent. The responses during blank trials, therefore, are highly organized in the manner stipulated by the theory. The remaining 5–10 percent of the patterns probably represent mistakes in responding. (Subjects would occasionally blurt out in the middle of a blank trial series something like, "That response was a mistake. Is it too late to change it?")

Another check on the blank-trial probe comes from prediction of the subject's response on each feedback trial, that is, on each trial following the four blank trials. Once we know a subject's hypothesis we should be able to predict his next response. Thus, if we infer from four blank trials that his hypothesis is "large is the solution," at the next feedback trial it is only necessary to see which of the two stimuli is "large" to predict which choice will occur. This prediction is correct about 98 percent of the time. After watching an individual subject for four blank trials, the experimenter can confidently predict the next response.

We now had assurance about blank trials as a probe for a subject's hypothesis. The effects of "right" and "wrong" upon resampling of hypotheses were next investigated. The original form of the theory, we saw, made assumptions about these effects. Also, our everyday language about hypotheses reflects these assumptions: confirmed hypotheses are retained, disconfirmed ones are rejected. Do the data from this experiment conform to these intuitions about hypothesis testing? Consider a particular feedback trial in the problem (e.g., feedback Trial 3, Fig. 11.7). Let us consider only those problems in which subjects were told "correct" at that trial. According to the theory, the hypothesis leading to the response on that trial (i.e., H_2) is confirmed and so should be repeated. Within the data, then, the hypothesis after that trial (H_3) should be the same as that before the trial. This result has appeared in several experiments: The hypotheses before and after a response called "correct" are virtually always the same. By similar analysis, the effects of "wrong" can be determined. According to the theory, disconfirmed hypotheses are given up. If we select those problems in which, for example, the experimenter said "wrong" at the third feedback trial, H_3 should be different from H_2. This result also appears decisively. The hypotheses before and after a disconfirming feedback trial are rarely (less than 2 percent of the time) the same.

There is no evidence for gradual changes in a subject's behavior (remember that conditioning theory held that subjects learn by degrees). After "correct," the subject almost always keeps his hypothesis; after "wrong," he almost never keeps it. Thus, a single feedback makes a radical difference. This unequivocal demonstration of discrete changes in behavior is reminiscent of our common experience of insightful learning. Frequently, we learn something or solve a problem with sudden understanding, as though a light went on. Here, at last, we began to see such sudden changes emerging directly. A final result best illustrates this discrete character of the learning process.

We noted above that, according to H theory, the trial with the last error (the TLE, see Fig. 11.4B) was a pivotal trial. Because that is an error trial, the subject did not previously sample the solution hypothesis. This analysis was investigated directly in the following way: as in Figure 11.4B, all the protocols were aligned at the TLE. However, instead of looking at responses on feedback trials, the hypothesis which preceded each feedback trial was determined. From this the proportion of solution hypotheses which appeared just before the TLE, one feedback trial back (−1), two feedback trials back (−2), etc., was determined. Similarly, the proportion of solution hypotheses which appeared after the TLE was also determined. The curve appears in Figure 11.8 where we see the most dramatic of all the results. The data confirm our intuitions precisely. Prior to the TLE the solution hypothesis is virtually never seen; following that critical trial, this is practically all that occurs. There is no evidence for gradual strengthening. The subject's behavior changes completely at the TLE.

These, then, constituted the first battery of results employing the new probe. It was clear now that we had a viable theory of learning by the adult human. The theory predicted and obtained dramatic, discrete jumps in subjects' behavior. A new probe was developed which functioned almost like a small window into the mind of the subject, permitting us to trace processes which, previously, could only be intuited. It may come as no surprise to you that H theory is currently the dominant theory within the psychology of complex learning by adult humans. It no longer needs to prove itself. The current issues involve, rather, its elaboration: How can the theory be generalized to other learning and problem-solving situations? At what age do children begin to test hypotheses? Is there a difference in the hypothesis-

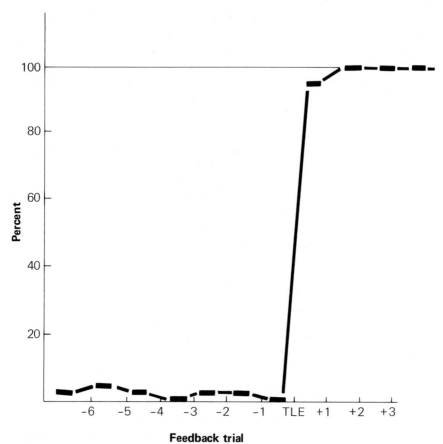

Figure 11.8. *The problems with hypothesis probes were aligned at the last feedback trial on which an error occurred (i.e., at the TLE, see Fig. 11.4B). The curve shows the percent of times the correct hypothesis appeared at each blank-trial set before and after the TLE.*

testing strategies employed by sophisticated and unsophisticated problem solvers? The probe is continuing to play an important role in these developments.

REFERENCES

Bower, G. and Trabasso, T. 1963. Reversals prior to solution in concept identification. *Journal of Experimental Psychology,* 66:409–418.

Gholson, B.; Levine, M.; and Phillips, S. 1972. Hypotheses, strategies, and stereotypes in discrimination learning. *Journal of Experimental Child Psychology,* 13:423–446.

Levine, M. 1966. Hypothesis behavior by humans during discrimination learning. *Journal of Experimental Psychology,* 71:331–338.

Levine, M. 1974. *A Cognitive Theory of Learning.* Hillside, N.J.: Lawrence Erlbaum Associates.

SOME EXTRAORDINARY FACTS
ABOUT OBESE HUMANS
AND RATS
Stanley Schachter

Several years ago, when I was working on the problem of the labeling of bodily states, I first became aware of Stunkard's (Stunkard and Koch, 1964) work on obesity and gastric motility. At that time, my students and I had been working on a series of studies concerned with the interaction of cognitive and physiological determinants of emotional state (Schachter, 1964). Our experiments had all involved manipulating bodily state by injections of adrenaline or placebo and simultaneously manipulating cognitive and situational variables that were presumed to affect a subject's interpretation of his bodily state. In essence, these experiments had demonstrated that cognitive factors play a major role in determining how a subject interprets his bodily feelings. Precisely the same set of physiological symptoms— an adrenaline-induced state of sympathetic arousal—could be interpreted as euphoria, or anger, or anxiety, or indeed as no emotional state at all, depending very largely on our cognitive and situational manipulations. In short, there is not an invariant, one-to-one relationship between a set of physiological symptoms and a psychological state.

This conclusion was based entirely on studies that manipulated bodily state by the exogenous administration of adrenaline or some other agent. My interest in Stunkard's research was generated by the fact that his work suggested that the same conclusion might be valid for endogenous physiological states. In his study, Stunkard had his subjects do without breakfast and come to his laboratory at 9:00 A.M. They swallowed a gastric balloon, and for the next 4 hours, Stunkard continuously recorded stomach contractions. Every 15 minutes, he asked his subjects, "Do you feel hungry?" They answered "Yes" or "No," and that is all there was to the study. He has then a record of the extent to which stomach contractions coincide with self-reports of

Stanley Schachter is in the Department of Psychology, Columbia University. The research reported in this chapter has been supported by National Science Foundation Grant GS 732.

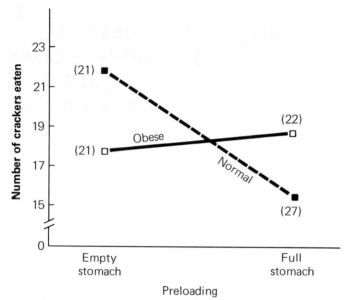

Figure 12.1.   *The effects of preloading on eating.*

hunger. For normally sized subjects, the two coincide closely. When the stomach contracts, the normal subject is likely to report hunger; when the stomach is quiescent, the normal subject is likely to say that he does not feel hungry. For the obese, on the other hand, there is little correspondence between gastric motility and self-reports of hunger. Whether or not the obese subject describes himself as hungry seems to have almost nothing to do with the state of his gut. There are, then, major individual differences in the extent to which this particular bodily activity—gastric motility—is associated with the feeling state labeled "hunger."

To pursue this lead, we (Schachter, Goldman, and Gordon, 1968) designed an experiment in which we attempted to manipulate gastric motility and the other physiological correlates of food deprivation by the obvious technique of manipulating food deprivation so that some subjects had empty stomachs and others full stomachs before entering an experimental eating situation. The experiment was disguised as a study of taste, and subjects had been asked to do without the meal (lunch or dinner) that preceded the experiment.

When a subject arrived, he was, depending on condition, either fed roast beef sandwiches or fed nothing. He was then seated in front of five bowls of crackers, presented with a long set of rating scales and told, "We want you to judge each cracker on the dimensions (salty, cheesy, garlicky, etc.) listed on these sheets. Taste as many or as few of the crackers of each type as you want in making your judgments; the important thing is that your ratings be as accurate as possible."

The subject then tasted and rated crackers for 15 minutes, under the impression that this was a taste test, and we simply counted the number of crackers that he ate. There were, of course, two types of subjects: obese subjects (from 14 to 75 percent overweight) and normal subjects (from 8 percent underweight to 9 percent overweight).

To review expectations: If it is correct that the obese do not label as hunger the bodily states associated with food deprivation, then this manipulation should have no effect on the amount eaten by obese subjects; on the other hand, the eating behavior of normal subjects should directly parallel the effects of the manipulation on bodily state.

It will be a surprise to no one to learn, from Figure 12.1, that normal subjects ate considerably fewer crackers when their stomachs were full of roast beef sandwiches than when their stomachs were empty. The results for obese subjects stand in fascinating contrast. They ate as much—in fact slightly more—when their stomachs were full as when they were empty. Obviously, the actual state of the stomach has nothing to do with the eating behavior of the obese.*

In similar studies (Schachter, 1967; Schachter, Goldman and Gordon, 1968), we have attempted to manipulate bodily state by manipulating fear and by injecting subjects with epinephrine. Both manipulations are based on Cannon's (1915) and Carlson's (1916) demonstrations that both the state of fear and the injection of epinephrine will inhibit gastric motility and increase blood sugar—both peripheral physiological changes associated with low hunger. These manipulations have no effect at all on obese subjects, but do affect the amounts eaten by normal subjects.

It seems clear that the set of bodily symptoms the subject labels "hunger" differs for obese and normal subjects. Whether one measures gastric motility as Stunkard did, or manipulates motility and the other physiological correlates of food deprivation, as I assume my students and I have done, one finds, for normal subjects, a high degree of correspondence between the state of the gut and eating behavior and, for obese subjects, virtually no correspondence.

Whether or not they are responsive to these particular visceral cues, the obese *do* eat, and the search for the cues that trigger obese eating occupied my students' and my attention for a number of years. Since the experimental details of this search have been published (Schachter, 1967, 1968, 1971), and I believe are fairly well known, I will take time now only to summarize our conclusions—eating by the obese seems unrelated to any internal, visceral state, but is determined by external, food-relevant cues such as the sight, smell, and taste of food. Now, obviously, such external cues to some extent

---

*The obese subject's failure to regulate when preloaded with sandwiches or some other solid food has now been replicated three times. Pliner's (1970) recent work, however, indicates that the obese will regulate, though not as well as normals, when preloaded with liquid food.

TABLE 12.1 EFFECT OF QUANTITY OF VISIBLE FOOD ON AMOUNTS EATEN

	Number of sandwiches	
Subjects	One	Three
Normal	1.96	1.88
Obese	1.48	2.32

Source: Nisbett (1968a).

affect anyone's eating behavior. However, for normals these external factors clearly interact with internal state. They may affect what, where, and how much the normal eats, but chiefly when he is in a state of physiological hunger. For the obese, I suggest, internal state is irrelevant, and eating is determined largely by external cues.

As you may know, there have been a number of experiments testing this hypothesis about the external sensitivity of the obese. To convey some feeling for the nature of the supporting data, I will describe two typical experiments. In one of these, Nisbett (1968a) examined the effects of the sight of food. He reasoned that if the sight of food is a potent cue, the externally sensitive, obese person should eat just as long as food is in sight, and when, in effect, he has consumed all of the available cues, he should stop and make no further attempt to eat. In contrast, the amounts eaten by a normal subject should depend on his physiological needs, not on the quantity of food in sight. Thus, if only a small amount of food is in sight but the subject is given the opportunity to forage for more, the normal subject should eat more than the obese subject. In contrast, if a large amount of food is in sight, the obese should eat more than the normal subject.

To test these expectations, Nisbett provided subjects, who had not eaten lunch, with either one or three roast beef sandwiches. He told them to help themselves and, as he was leaving, pointed to a refrigerator across the room and said, "There are dozens more sandwiches in the refrigerator. Have as many as you want." His results are presented in Table 12.1. As you can see, obese subjects ate significantly more than normals when presented with three sandwiches, but ate significantly less than normals when presented with only one sandwich.

In another study, Decke (1971) examined the effects of taste on eating. She reasoned that taste, like the sight or smell of food, is essentially an external cue. Good taste, then, should stimulate the obese to eat more than normals, and bad taste, of course, should have the reverse effect.

In a taste test context, Decke provided her subjects with either

---

TABLE 12.2 EFFECT OF TASTE ON EATING

| | Ounces consumed in | |
Subjects	Good taste	Bad taste
Normal	10.6	6.4
Obese	13.9	2.6

Source: Decke (1971).

---

a decent vanilla milk shake or with a vanilla milk shake plus quinine. The effects of this taste manipulation are conveyed in Table 12.2 where, as you can see, obese subjects drank more than normals when the milk shake was good and drank considerably less when the milk shake had been laced with quinine.

Now, anyone who sees Decke's milk shake data and who is familiar with physiological psychology will note that this is precisely what Miller, Bailey, and Stevenson (1950) found and what Teitelbaum (1955) found in the lesioned hyperphagic rat. For those of you who are unfamiliar with this preparation, let me review the facts about this animal. If you make bilateral lesions in the ventromedial nuclei of the hypothalamus, you are likely to get an animal that will eat prodigious amounts of food and will eventually achieve monumental weight— a creature of nightmares. This has been demonstrated for rats, cats, mice, monkeys, rabbits, goats, dogs, and sparrows. Classic descriptions of these preparations portray an animal that immediately after the operation staggers over to its food hopper and shovels in food. For several weeks, this voracious eating continues, and there is, of course, very rapid weight gain. This is called the dynamic phase of hyperphagia. Finally, a plateau is reached, at which point the animal's weight levels off, and its food intake drops to a level only slightly above that of the normal animal. This is called the static phase. During both the static and the dynamic stages, the lesioned animal is also characterized as markedly inactive, and as irascible, emotional, and generally bitchy.

Now it turns out that though the lesioned animal is normally a heavy eater, if you add quinine to its food it drastically decreases its intake to levels far below that of a normal animal's whose food has been similarly tainted. On the other hand, if to its normal food you add dextrose, or lard, or something that is apparently tasty to a rat, the lesioned animal increases its intake to levels considerably above its regular intake and above the intake of a control rat whose food has also been enriched.

The similarity of these facts about the finickiness of the lesioned rat to Decke's findings in her milk shake experiment is, of course, striking, and many people (notably Nisbett, 1968a, 1972) have pointed to this and other similarities between our data on obese humans and the physiologist's data on the obese rat. In order to determine if there was anything more to this than an engaging, occasional resemblance between two otherwise remotely connected sets of data, Judith Rodin and I decided to treat the matter dead seriously and, where possible, to make a point-for-point comparison of every fact we could learn about the hypothalamic, obese rat with every fact we could learn about the obese human. Before describing the results of our work, I would like, however, to be sure that you are aware of the areas of my expertise. I am not a physiological psychologist. Though I am pretty sure that I've eaten a hypothalamus, I doubt that I've ever seen one. When I say something like "bilateral lesions of the ventromedial nuclei of the hypothalamus," you can be sure that I've memorized it. I make this personal confession because of the dilemma that Rodin, also a psysiological innocent, and I faced in our work. Though we couldn't have succeeded, we attempted to read *everything* about the ventromedial lesioned rat. If you've ever made this sort of attempt, you may have been seized by the same despair as were we when it sometimes seemed as if there were no such thing as a fact that *someone* had not failed to confirm. (I include in this sweeping generalization, by the way, the apparent fact that a ventromedial lesion produces a hyperphagic, obese animal—see Reynolds, 1963, and Rabin and Smith, 1968.) And it sometimes seemed as if there were no such thing as an experiment which *someone* had not failed to replicate. Since I happen to have spent my college physics lab course personally disproving most of the laws of physics, I cannot say that I find this particularly surprising, but if one is trying to decide what is the fact, it is a depressing state of affairs. In our own areas of expertise, this probably isn't too serious a problem. Each of us in our specialties knows how to evaluate a piece of work. In a field in which you are not expert, you simply cannot, except in the crudest of cases, evaluate. If several experimenters have different results, you just don't know which to believe. In order to cope with this dilemma, Rodin and I decided to treat each of our facts in batting average terms. For each fact, I will inform you of the number of studies that have been concerned with the fact and the proportion of these studies that work out in a given direction. To be included in the batting average, we required only that a study present all or a substantial portion of its data, rather than report the author's impressions or present only the data of one or two presumably representative cases. I should also note that in all cases we have relied on the data and not on what the experimenter said about the data. It may seem silly to make this point explicit, but it is the case that in a few studies, for some perverse reason, the experimenter's conclusions simply have nothing to do with his data. Finally, I should note that in all comparisons of animal and human

TABLE 12.3   EFFECTS OF TASTE ON EATING

	Animals		Humans	
Condition	Batting average	Mean F/N*	Mean F/N*	Batting average
Good food	5/6	1.45	1.42	2/2
Bad food	3/4	.76	.84	1/2

*F/N—Fat to normal ratio.

data, I will consider the data only for animals in the static phase of obesity, animals who, like our human subjects, are already fat. In general, however, the results for dynamic and static animals are quite similar.

As a shorthand method of making comparisons between studies and species, I shall throughout the rest of this article employ what we can call a Fat to Normal (F/N) ratio in which we simply get an index by dividing the magnitude of the effect for fat subjects by the magnitude of the effect for normal control subjects. Thus, if in a particular study the fat rats ate an average of 15 gm of food and normal rats ate 10 gm the F/N ratio would be 1.50, indicating that the fat rats ate 50 percent more food than normal rats.

To begin our comparisons, let us return to the effects of taste on eating behavior. We know that fat human beings eat more of a good-tasting food than do normal human beings and that they eat less of bad-tasting food than do normals. The physiologists have done almost identical experiments to ours, and in line 1 of Table 12.3 we can compare the effects of good-tasting food on lesioned animals and on men. You will notice on the left that Rodin and I found six studies on lesioned animals, in this case largely rats. Batting average: five of the six studies indicate that lesioned, static, obese animals eat more of a good-tasting food than do their normal controls. The average F/N ratio for these six studies is 1.45, indicating that fat rats on the average eat 45 percent more of good-tasting food than do normal rats. On the right side of the table, you can see that there have been two human studies, and that both of these studies indicate that fat humans eat more of good-tasting food than do normal humans. The average F/N ratio for humans is 1.42, indicating that fat humans eat 42 percent more of good-tasting food than do normally sized humans.*

*The technically informed reader undoubtedly will wish to know precisely which studies and what data are included in Tables 12.3 and 12.4. There are so many studies involved that, within the context of this paper, it is impossible to supply this information. Dr. Rodin and I are preparing a monograph on this work which will, of course, provide full details on such matters.

Incidentally, please keep in mind throughout this exercise that the left side of each table will always contain the data for lesioned animals, very largely rats, that have been abused by a variety of people named Epstein, and Teitelbaum, and Stellar, and Miller, and so on. The right side of each table will always contain the data for humans, mostly Columbia College students, nice boys who go home every Friday night, where, I suppose, they too are abused by a variety of people named Epstein, and Teitelbaum, and Stellar, and Miller.

In line 2 of Table 12.3, we have the effects of bad taste on consumption. For both animals and men, in all of these studies bad taste was manipulated by the addition of quinine to the food. There are four animal studies; three of the four indicate that fat animals eat less than normal animals, and the average F/N ratio is .76. There are two human studies: one of the two indicates that fats eat considerably less bad food than normals; the other indicates no significant difference between the two groups, and the mean F/N ratio for these two studies is .84. For this particular fact, the data are more fragile than one would like, but the trends for the two species are certainly parallel.

To continue this examination of parallel facts: The eating habits of the lesioned rats have been thoroughly studied, particularly by Teitelbaum and Campbell (1958). It turns out that static obese rats eat on the average slightly, not considerably, more than normal rats. They also eat fewer meals per day, eat more per meal, and eat more rapidly than do normal animals. For each of these facts, we have parellel data for humans. Before presenting these data, I should note that for humans, I have, wherever possible, restricted myself to behavioral studies, studies in which the investigators have actually measured how much their subjects eat. I hope no one will be offended, I assume no one will be surprised, if I say that I am skeptical of the self-reports of fat people about how much they eat or exercise.* For those of you who feel that this is high-handed selection of studies, may I remind you of Stunkard's famous chronic fat patients who were fed everything that, in interviews, they admitted to eating daily, and who all steadily lost weight on this diet.

Considering first the average amount eaten per day when on ad-lib feeding of ordinary lab chow or pellets, you will note in line 1 of Table 12.4 that consistently static obese rats eat somewhat (19 percent) more than do their normal counterparts. The data for humans are derived from all of the studies I know of in which eating is placed in a noshing, or ad-lib, context; that is, a bowl of ordinary food, usually nuts or crackers, is placed in the room, the experiment presumably has nothing to do with eating, and the subject is free to eat or not, as he chooses, just as is a rat in its cage. In two of the three

---

*In three of four such self-report studies, fat people report eating considerably less food than do normals.

TABLE 12.4 EATING HABITS

	Animals		Humans	
Variable	Batting average	Mean F/N*	Mean F/N*	Batting average
Amount of food eaten ad lib	9/9	1.19	1.16	2/3
No. meals per day	4/4	.85	.92	3/3
Amount eaten per meal	2/2	1.34	1.29	5/5
Speed of eating	1/1	1.28	1.26	1/1

*F/N—Fat to normal ratio.

experiments conducted in this context, obese subjects eat slightly more than do normals; in the third experiment, the two groups eat precisely the same number of crackers. For both humans and rats, then, the fat subject eats only slightly more than the normal subject.

Turning next to the number of meals per day, we note on line 2 of Table 12.4 that for both rats and humans, fatter subjects consistently eat fewer meals per day. (A rat meal is defined by Teitelbaum and Campbell, 1958, as "any burst of food intake of at least five pellets separated by at least 5 min. from any other burst [p. 138].") For humans, these particular data are based on self-report or interview studies, for I know of no relevant behavioral data. In any case, again the data for the lesioned rat and the obese human correspond very closely indeed.

From the previous two facts, it should, of course, follow that obese subjects will eat more per meal than normal subjects, and, as can be seen in line 3 of Table 12.4, this is the case for both lesioned rats and obese humans. The data for rats are based on two experiments that simply recorded the amount of food eaten per eating burst. The data for humans are based on all experiments in which a plate of food, usually sandwiches, is placed before a subject, and he is told to help himself to lunch or dinner.

Our final datum on eating habits is the speed of eating. Teitelbaum and Campbell (1958) simply recorded the number of pellets their animals ate per minute. Since there is nothing else to do when you are sitting behind a one-way screen watching a subject eat, Nisbett (1968b—data not reported in paper) recorded the number of spoonfuls of ice cream his subjects ate per minute. The comparison of the two studies is drawn in line 4 of Table 12.4, where you will note an unsettling similarity in the rate at which lesioned rats and obese humans outspeed their normal counterparts.*

*Fat rats do not drink more rapidly than do normals. There are no comparable data for humans.

All told, then, in the existing literature, Rodin and I found a total of six items of behavior on which it is possible to make rather precise comparisons between lesioned rats and obese humans. These are mostly nonobvious facts, and the comparisons drawn between the two sets of experiments do not attempt to push the analogies beyond the point of common sense. I do not think there can be much debate about pellets versus spoonfuls of ice cream consumed per minute as equivalent measures of eating rate. For all six facts in the existing literature, the parallels between the species are striking. What the lesioned, fat rat does, the obese human does.

In addition to these facts, we identified two other areas of behavior in which it is possible to draw somewhat more fanciful, though still not ridiculous, comparisons between the species. These are the areas of emotionality and of activity. Though there has been little systematic study of emotionality, virtually everyone who has worked with these animals agrees that the lesioned animals are hyperexcitable, easily startled, overemotional, and generally bitchy to handle. In addition, work by Singh (1969) and research on active avoidance learning do generally support this characterization of the lesioned animal as an emotional beast.

For humans, we have two experiments from which it is possible to draw conclusions about emotionality. In one of these (Schachter, Goldman, and Gordon, 1968), we manipulated fear by threat of painful electric shock. On a variety of rating scales, fat subjects acknowledged that they were somewhat more frightened and anxious than did normal subjects. In a second experiment, Rodin (1970) had her subjects listen to an audio tape while they were working at either a monitoring or a proofreading task. The tapes were either neutral (requiring the subject to think about either rain or seashells) or emotionally charged (requiring the subject to think about his own death or about the bombing of Hiroshima). The emotionally charged tapes produced dramatic differences between subjects. On a variety of rating scales, the obese described themselves as considerably more upset and disturbed than did normal subjects; they reported more palpitations and changes in breathing rate than did normals; and performance, at either the proofreading or monitoring tasks, deteriorated dramatically more for obese than for normal subjects. Again, then, the data are consistent, for both the lesioned animal and the obese human seem to react more emotionally than their normal counterparts.

Finally, on activity, numerous studies using stabilimeter cages or activity wheels have demonstrated that the lesioned animal is markedly less active than the normal animal. This is not, I should add, a totally trivial fact indicating only that the lesioned animal has trouble schlepping his immense bulk around the cage, for the dynamic hyperphagic rat—who though not yet fat, will be—is quite as lethargic as his obese counterpart. On the human side, Bullen, Reed, and Mayer (1964) have taken movies of girls at camp during their scheduled periods of swimming, tennis, and volleyball. They categorize each camper for her degree of activity or exertion during these periods, and do find that the normal campers are more active than are the obese girls.

All told, then, Rodin and I found a total of eight facts, indicating a perfect parallel between the behavior of the lesioned rat and the obese human. We have, so far, found no fact on which the two species differ. Now all of this has proved such an engaging exercise that my students and I decided to play "real" scientist, and we considered a matrix. We simply listed every fact we could find about the lesioned animals and every fact we could find about obese humans. I have told you about those facts for which parallel data exist. There are, however, numerous holes in the matrix—facts for rats for which no parellel human data have yet been collected, and vice versa. For the past year, we have been engaged in filling in these holes—designing for humans experiments that have no particular rhyme or reason, except that someone once did such an experiment on lesioned rats. For example, it is a fact that though lesioned rats will outeat normal rats when food is easily available, they will not lift a paw if they have to work to get food. In a Skinner box setup, Teitelbaum (1957) finds that at FR1, when one press yields one pellet, fat lesioned rats outpress normal. As the payoff decreases, however, fat rats press less and less until at FR256, they do not manage to get a single pellet during a 12-hour experimental session, whereas normal rats are still industriously pressing away. Similarly, Miller et al. (1950) found that though lesioned rats ate more than normal controls when an unweighted lid covered the food dish, they ate less than did the controls when a 75-gram weight was fastened to the lid. They also found that the lesioned rats ran more slowly down an alley to food than controls did, and pulled less hard when temporarily restrained by a harness. In short, fat rats will not work to get food.

Since there was no human parallel to these studies, Lucy Friedman and I designed a study in which, when a subject arrived, he was asked simply to sit at the experimenter's desk and fill out a variety of personality tests and questionnaires. Besides the usual student litter, there was a bag of almonds on the desk. The experimenter helped herself to a nut, invited the subject to do the same, and then left him alone with his questionnaires and nuts for 15 minutes. There were two sets of conditions. In one, the nuts had shells on them; in the other, the nuts had no shells. I assume we agree that eating nuts with shells is considerably more work than eating nuts with no shells.

The top half of Table 12.5 presents for normal subjects the numbers who do and do not eat nuts in the two conditions. As you can see, shells or no shells has virtually no impact on normal subjects. Fifty-five percent of normals eat nuts without shells, and 50 percent eat

TABLE 12.5 EFFECTS OF WORK ON THE EATING BEHAVIOR OF NORMAL AND FAT SUBJECTS

	Number who	
Nuts have	Eat	Don't eat
Normal subjects		
Shells	10	10
No shells	11	9
Fat subjects		
Shells	1	19
No shells	19	1

nuts with shells. I am a little self-conscious about the data for obese subjects, for it looks as if I were too stupid to know how to fake data. I know how to fake data, and were I to do so, the bottom half of Table 12.5 certainly would not look the way it does. When the nuts have no shells, 19 of 20 fat subjects eat nuts. When the nuts have shells on them, 1 out of 20 fat subjects eats. Obviously, the parallel to Miller's and to Teitelbaum's rats is perfect. When the food is easy to get at, fat subjects, rat or human, eat more than normals; when the food is hard to get at, fat subjects eat less than normals.

Incidentally, as a casual corollary of these and other findings, one could expect that, given acceptable food, fat eaters would be more likely than normals to choose the easiest way of eating. In order to check on this, Lucy Friedman, Joel Handler, and I went to a large number of Chinese and Japanese restaurants, categorized each patron as he entered the restaurant as obese or normal, and then simply noted whether he ate with chopsticks or with silverware. Among Occidentials, for whom chopsticks can be an ordeal, we found that almost five times the proportion of normal eaters ate with chopsticks as did obese eaters—22.4 percent of normals and 4.7 percent of the obese ate with chopsticks.

In another matrix-hole-filling experiment, Patricia Pliner (1970) has demonstrated that obese humans, like lesioned rats, do not regulate food consumption when they are preloaded with solids but, again like the rats, do regulate when they are preloaded with liquids.

In addition to these experiments, we are currently conducting studies on pain sensitivity and on passive versus active avoidance learning—all designed to fill in more holes in our human–lesioned rat matrix. To date, we have a total of 12 nonobvious facts in which the behaviors of lesioned rats paralled perfectly the behaviors of obese humans. Though I cannot believe that as our matrix-hole-filling experiments continue, this perfect parallelism will continue, I submit that even now these are mind-boggling data. I would also submit, however, that we have played this enchanting game just about long enough. This is, after all, science through analogy—a sport I recommend with the same qualifications and enthusiasms with which I recommend skiing—and it is time that we asked what on earth does it all mean? To which at this point I can only answer ruefully that I wish to God I really knew.

On its most primitive level, I suppose that I would love to play doctor and issue pronouncements such as, "Madam, you have a very sick hypothalamus." And, indeed, I do know of one case of human obesity (Reeves and Plum, 1969) accompanied by a precisely localized neoplasm that destroyed the ventromedial hypothalamus. This is an astonishing case study, for the lady reads like a lesioned rat—she ate immense amounts of food, as much as 10,000 calories a day, grew impressively fat and was apparently a wildly emotional creature given to frequent outbursts of laughing, crying, and rage. Now I am not, of course, going to suggest that this lady is anything but a pathological extreme. The only vaguely relevant study I know of is a morphological study (Maren, 1955) of the hypothalami of genetically obese mice, an animal whose behavior also resembles the lesioned rat's, which found no structural differences between obese and normal mice.

Mrosovsky (1971) has been developing a more sober hypothesis. Comparing the hibernator and the ventromedial lesioned rat, Mrosovsky has been playing much the same analogical game as have I, and he, too, has noted the marked behavioral similarities of his two species to the obese human. He hypothesizes that the unlesioned, obese animal, rodent or human, has a ventromedial hypothalamus that is functionally quiescent. Though I would be willing to bet that when the appropriate biochemical and electrophysiological studies are done, Mrosovsky will be proven correct, I do not believe that this is a fact which is of fundamental interest to psychologists. Most of us, I suspect, have long been convinced, psychodynamics notwithstanding, that there is *something* biologically responsible for human obesity, and to be able suddenly to point a finger at an offending structure would not really put us much ahead. After all, we've known about the adrenal medulla and emotion for more than 50 years, and I doubt that this particular bit of knowledge has been of much help in our understanding of agression, or fear, or virtually any other emotional state.

If it is true that the ventromedial hypothalamus is functionally quiescent, for us the question must be, for what function, psychologically speaking, is it quiescent? What processes, or inputs, or outputs are mediated by this particular structure? Speculation and theorizing about the functions of this area have tended to be cautious and modest. Essentially, two suggestions have been made—one that the area is a satiety center, and the other that the area is an emotionality center.

Both Miller (1964) and Stellar (1954) have tentatively suggested that the ventromedial area is a satiety center—that in some fashion it monitors the signals indicating a sufficiency of food and inhibits the excitatory (Eat! Eat!) impulses initiated in the lateral hypothalamus. This inhibitory-satiety mechanism can account for the hyperphagia of the lesioned animals and, consequently, for their obesity. It can also account for most of the facts that I outlined earlier about the daily eating habits of these animals. It cannot by itself, however, account for the finickiness of these animals, nor can it, as I believe I can show, account for the apparent unwillingness of these animals to work for food. Finally, this hypothesis is simply irrelevant to the demonstrated inactivity and hyperemotionality of these animals. This irrelevance, however, is not critical if one assumes, as does Stellar, that discrete neural centers, also located in the ventromedial area, control activity and emotionality. The satiety theory, then, can account for some, but by no means all, of the critical facts about eating, and it has nothing to say about activity or emotionality.

As a theoretically more ambitious alternative, Grossman (1966, 1967) has proposed that the ventromedial area be considered the emotionality center and that the facts about eating be derived from this assumption. By definition, Grossman's hypothesis accounts for the emotionality of these animals, and his own work on active avoidance learning certainly supports the emotionality hypothesis. I must confess, however, that I have difficulty in understanding just why these emotional animals become fat. In essence, Grossman (1966) assumes that "lesions in or near the VMH sharply increase an animal's affective responsiveness to apparently all sensory stimuli [p. 1]." On the basis of this general statement, he suggests that "the 'finickiness' of the ventromedial animal might then reflect a change in its affective response to taste." This could, of course, account for the fact that lesioned animals eat more very good- and less very bad-tasting food than do normals. However, I simply find it hard to believe that this affective hypothesis can account for the basic fact about these animals—that for weeks on end, the lesioned animals eat grossly more of ordinary, freely available lab chow.

Grossman (1967) attributes the fact that lesioned animals will not work for food to their "exaggerated response to handling, the test situation, the deprivation regimen, and the requirement of having to work for their daily bread [p. 358]." I suppose all of this is possible, I simply find it farfetched. At the very least, the response to handling and to the deprivation regime should be just as exaggerated whether the reinforcement schedule is FR1 or FR256 and the lesioned animals do press more than the normals at FR1.

My skepticism, however, is irrelevant, and Grossman may be correct. There are, however, at least two facts with which, it seems to me, Grossman's hypothesis cannot cope. First, it would seem to me that an animal with an affective response to food would be likely to eat more rather than less often per day, as is the fact. Second, it is simply common sense to expect that an animal with strong "affective responsiveness to all sensory stimuli" will be a very active animal indeed, but the lesioned animal is presumably hypoactive.

None of the existing theories, then, can cope with all of the currently available facts. For the remainder of this article, I am going to try my hand at developing a hypothesis that I believe can cope with more of the facts than can the available alternatives. It is a hypothesis that derives entirely from our work on human obesity. I believe, however, that it can explain as many of the facts about ventromedial-lesioned rats as it can about the human obese. If future experimental work on animal proves this correct, it would certainly suggest that science by analogy has merits other than its entertainment value.

The gist of our findings on humans is this—the eating behavior of the obese is under external, rather than internal, control. In effect, the obese seem stimulus-bound. When a food-relevant cue is present, the obese are more likely to eat and to eat a great deal than are normals. When such a cue is absent, the obese are less likely to try to eat or to complain about hunger. Though I have not, in this article, developed this latter point, there is evidence that, in the absence of food-relevant cues, the obese have a far easier time fasting than do normals, while in the presence of such cues, they have a harder time fasting (Goldman, Jaffa, and Schachter, 1968).

Since it is a little hard to believe that such stimulus-binding is limited to food-relevant cues, for some time now my students and I have been concerned with the generalizability of these facts. Given our starting point, this concern has led to some rather odd little experiments. For example, Judith Rodin, Peter Herman, and I have asked subjects to look at slides on which are portrayed 13 objects or words. Each slide is exposed for 5 seconds, and the subject is then asked to recall what he saw. Fat subjects recall more objects than do normal subjects. The experiment has been replicated, and this appears to be a reliable phenomenon.

In another study, Rodin, Herman, and I compared fat and normal subjects on simple and on complex or disjunctive reaction time. For simple reaction time, they are instructed to lift their finger from a telegraph key as soon as the stimulus light comes on. On this task, there are no differences between obese and normal subjects. For complex reaction time, there are two stimulus lights and two telegraph keys, and subjects are instructed to lift their left finger when the right light comes on and lift their right finger when the left light comes on. Obese subjects respond more rapidly and make fewer errors. Since this was a little hard to believe, this study was repeated three times— each time with the same results—the obese are simply better at complex reaction time than are normals. I do not pretend to understand these results, but they do seem to indicate that, for some reason, the obese are more efficient stimulus or information processors.

At this stage, obviously, this is shotgun research which, in coordination with the results of our eating experiments, seems to indicate that it may be useful to more generally characterize the obese as stimulus-bound and to hypothesize that any stimulus, above a given intensity level, is more likely to evoke an appropriate response from an obese than from a normal subject.

Our first test of implications of this hypothesis in a noneating setting is Rodin's (1970) experiment on the effects of distraction on performance. She reasoned that if the stimulus-binding hypothesis is correct, distracting, irrelevant stimuli should be more disruptive for obese than for normal subjects when they are performing a task requiring concentration. Presumably, the impinging stimulus is more likely to grip the attention of the stimulus-bound obese subject. To test this guess, she had her subjects work at a simple proofreading task. In one condition, the subjects corrected proof with no distractions at all. In the three other conditions, they corrected proof while listening to recorded tapes that varied in the degree to which they were likely to grip a subject's attention, and therefore distract him. The results are presented in Figure 12.2 where, as you can see, the obese are better at proofreading when undistracted but their performance seriously deteriorates as they are distracted until, at extreme distraction, they are considerably worse than normals. Rodin finds precisely the same pattern of results, by the way, in a similar study in which she uses the complex reaction time task I have already described rather than the proofreading task. For humans, then, there is evidence, outside of the eating context, to support the hypothesis.

Let us return to consideration of the ventromedial lesioned animal and examine the implications of the hypothesis that any stimulus, above a given intensity level, is more likely to evoke an appropriate response from a lesioned than from an intact animal. This is a hypothesis which is, in many ways, similar to Grossman's hypothesis and, on the face of it, would appear to be vulnerable to exactly the same criticisms as I have leveled at his theory. There are, however, crucial differences that will become evident as I elaborate this notion. I assume it is self-evident that my hypothesis can explain the emotionality of the lesioned animals and, with the exception of meal frequency—a fact to which I will return—can account for virtually all of our facts about the daily eating habits of these animals. I will, therefore, begin consideration of the hypothesis by examining its implications for those facts that have been most troubling for alternative formulations and by examining those facts that seem to most clearly contradict my own hypothesis.

Let us turn first to the perverse and fascinating fact that though lesioned animals will outeat normal animals when food is easily avail-

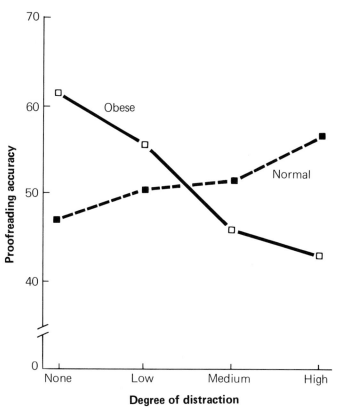

Figure 12.2. *The effects of distraction on performance (from Rodin, 1970).*

able, they simply will not work for food. In my terms, this is an incomplete fact which may prove only that a remote food stimulus will not evoke a food-acquiring response. It is the case that in the experiments concerned with this fact, virtually every manipulation of work has covaried the remoteness or prominence of the food cue. Food at the end of a long alleyway is obviously a more remote cue than food in the animal's food dish. Pellets available only after 256 presses of a lever are certainly more remote food stimuli than pellets available after each press of a lever. If the stimulus-binding hypothesis is correct, it should be anticipated that, in contrast to the results when the food cue is remote, the lesioned animal will work harder than the normal animal when the food stimulus is prominent and compelling. Though the appropriate experiment has not yet been done on rats, to my delight I have learned recently that such an experiment has been done on humans by William Johnson (1970), who independently has been pursuing a line of thought similar to mine.

Johnson seated his subject at a table, fastened his hand in a harness, and, to get food, required the subject for 12 minutes to pull, with his index finger, on a ring that was attached by wire to a 7-pound weight. He received food on a VR50 schedule—that is, on the average, a subject received a quarter of a sandwich for every 50 pulls of the ring. Obviously, this was moderately hard work.

To vary stimulus prominence, Johnson manipulated food visibility and prior taste of food. In "food visible" conditions, he placed beside the subject one desirable sandwich covered in a transparent wrap. In addition, as the subject satisfied the VR requirements, he placed beside him quarter sandwiches similarly wrapped. In "food invisible" conditions, Johnson followed exactly the same procedures, but wrapped the sandwiches in white, nontransparent shelf paper. Subjects, of course, did not eat until they had completed their 12 minutes of labor.

As a second means of varying cue prominence, half of the subjects ate a quarter of a very good sandwich immediately before they began work. The remaining subjects ate a roughly equivalent portion of plain white bread.

In Figure 12.3, you can see the effects of these manipulations on effort. I have arranged the conditions along the dimension of food cue prominence—ranging from no prominent food cues to two prominent food cues—that is, the subjects ate a quarter sandwich and the food was visible. As you can see, the stimulus prominence manipulations have a marked effect on the obese, for they work far harder when the food cues are prominent and compelling than when they are inconspicuous. In contrast, cue prominence has relatively little effect on normal subjects.

Please note also that these results parallel Miller's and Teitelbaum's results with lesioned rats. When the food cues are remote, the obese human works less hard for food than the normally sized human. The fact that this relationship flips when the cues are prominent is, of course, a delight to me, and wouldn't it be absorbing to replicate this experiment on lesioned rats?

Let us turn next to the fact that lesioned rats are hypoactive. If ever a fact were incompatible with a hypothesis, this one is it. Surely an animal that is more responsive to any stimulus should be hyper-, not hypoactive. Yet this is a most peculiar fact—for it remains a fact only because one rather crucial finding in the literature has geen generally overlooked and because the definition of activity seems restricted to measures obtained in running wheels or in stabilimeter-type living cages.

Studies of activity have with fair consistency reported dramatically less activity for lesioned than for normal rats. With one exception, these studies report data in terms of total activity per unit time, making no distinction between periods when the animal room was quiet and undisturbed and periods involving the mild ferment of animal-tending activities. Gladfelter and Brobeck (1962), however, report activity data separately for the "43-hour period when the constant-temperature

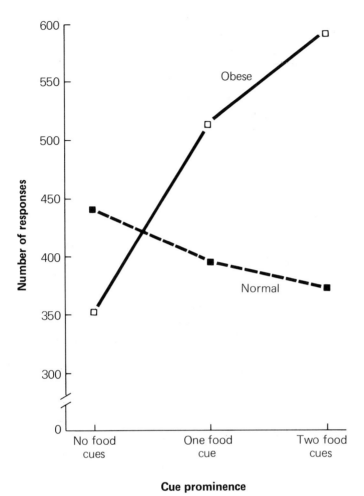

Figure 12.3. *The effect of food cue prominence on effort (from Johnson, 1970).*

room was dark and quiet and the rats were undisturbed" and for the "five-hour period when the room was lighted and the rats were cared for [p. 811]." During the quiet time, these investigators find precisely what almost everyone else does—lesioned rats are markedly less active. During the animal-tending period, however, lesioned animals are just about as active as normal animals. In short, when the stimulus field is relatively barren and there is little to react to, the ventromedial animal is inactive; when the field is made up of the routine noises, stirrings, and disturbances involved in tending an animal laboratory, the lesioned animal is just about as active as the normal animal.

Though this is an instructive fact, it hardly proves my hypothesis, which specifies that above a given stimulus intensity the lesioned animal should be *more* reactive than the normal animal. Let us, then, ask—is there any evidence that lesioned animals are more active than normal animals? There is, if you are willing to grant that specific activities such as lever pressing or avoidance behavior are as much "activity" as the gross, overall measures obtained in stabili-meter-mounted living cages.

In his study of activity, Teitelbaum (1957) has distinguished between random and food-directed activity. As do most other investi-gators, he finds that in their cages, lesioned rats are much less active than are normals. During a 12-hour stint in a Skinner box, however, when on an FR1 schedule, the lesioned animals are more active; that is, they press more than do normals. Thus, when the food cue is salient and prominent, as it is on an FR1 schedule, the lesioned animal is very active indeed. And, as you know, when the food cue is remote, as it is on an FR64 or FR256 schedule, the lesioned animal is inactive.

Since lever pressing is activity in pursuit of food, I suppose one should be cautious in accepting these data as support for my argu-ment. Let us turn, then, to avoidance learning where most of the experiments are unrelated to food.

In overall batting average terms,* no area could be messier than this one, for in three of six studies, lesioned animals are better and in three worse at avoidance than normals. However, if one distinguishes between passive and active avoidance, things become considerably more coherent.

In active avoidance studies, a conditioned stimulus, such as a light or buzzer, precedes a noxious event such as electrifying the floor grid. To avoid the shock, the animal must perform some action such as jumping into the nonelectrified compartment of a shuttle box. In three of four such studies, the lesioned animals learn considerably more rapidly than do normal animals. By this criterion, at least, lesioned animals are more reactive than normal animals.† Parenthetically, it

---

*Of all the behavioral areas so far considered, avoidance learning is probably the one for which it makes least sense either to adopt a batting average approach or to attempt to treat the research as a conceptually equivalent set of studies. Except in this area, the great majority of experiments have used, as subjects, rats with electrolytically produced lesions. In the avoidance learning area, the subjects have been mice, rats, and cats; the lesions are variously electrolytically produced, pro-duced by gold thioglucose injections, or are "functional" lesions produced by topical application of atropine or some other agent.

†Reactive, yes, but what about activity in the more primitive sense of simply moving or scrambling about the experimental box? Even in this respect, the lesioned animals appear to outmove the normals, for Turner, Sechzer, and Liebelt (1967) report that,

> The experimental groups, both mice and rats, emitted strong escape tenden-cies prior to the onset of shock and in response to shock. Repeated attempts were made to climb out of the test apparatus. This group showed much more vocalization than the control group. . . . In contrast to the behavior of the experimental animals, the control animals appeared to become immobilized or to "freeze" both before and during the shock period. Thus, there was little attempt to escape and little vocalization [p. 242].

is amusing to note that the response latencies of the lesioned animal are smaller (Grossman, 1966) than those of the normal animal, just as in our studies of complex reaction time, obese humans are faster than normal humans.

In contrast to these results, lesioned animals do considerably worse than normal animals in passive avoidance studies. In these studies, the animal's water dish or the lever of a Skinner box are electrified so that if, during the experimental period, the animal touches these objects he receives a shock. In both of the studies we have so far found on passive learning, the lesioned animals do considerably worse than normal animals. They either press the lever or touch the water dish more than do normals and accordingly are shocked far more often. Thus, when the situation requires a response if the animal is to avoid shock, the lesioned animal does better than the normal animal. Conversely, if the situation requires response quiescence if the animal is to avoid shock, the lesioned animal does far worse than the normal animal. This pair of facts, I suggest, provides strong support for the hypothesis that beyond a given stimulus intensity, the lesioned animal is more reactive than the normal animal. I would also suggest that without some variant of this hypothesis, the overall pattern of results on avoidance learning is incoherent.

All in all, then, one can make a case of sorts for the suggestion that there are specifiable circumstances in which lesioned animals will be more active. It is hardly an ideal case, and only an experiment that measures the effects of systematically varied stimulus field richness on gross activity can test the point.

These ruminations on activity do suggest a refinement of the general hypothesis and also, I trust, make clear why I have insisted on inserting that awkward phrase "above a given intensity level" in all statements of the hypothesis. For activity, it appears to be the case that the lesioned animal is less active when the stimulus is remote and more active when the stimulus is prominent. This interaction between reactivity and stimulus prominence is presented graphically in Figure 12.4. This is a formulation which I believe fits almost all of the available data, on both animals and men, remarkably well. It is also a formulation which for good ad hoc reasons bears a striking resemblance to almost every relevant set of data I have discussed.

For human eating behavior, virtually every fact we have supports the assertion that the obese eat more than normals when the food cue is prominent and less when the cue is remote. In Johnson's study of work and cue prominence, the obese do not work as hard as normals when there are no prominent food cues, but work much harder when the food cues are highly salient. In Nisbett's one- and three-sandwich experiment, the obese subjects eat just as long as food cues are prominent—that is, the sandwiches are directly in front of the subject—but when these immediate cues have been consumed, they

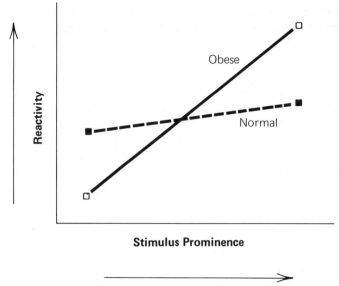

Figure 12.4. *Theoretical curves of relationship of reactivity to stimulus prominence.*

stop eating. Thus, they eat more than normals in the three-sandwich condition and less in the one-sandwich condition. We also know that the obese have an easy time fasting in the absence of food cues and a hard time in the presence of such cues, and so on.

About eating habits we know that the obese eat larger meals (what could be a more prominent cue than food on the plate?), but eat fewer meals (as they should if it requires a particularly potent food cue to trigger an eating response). Even the fact that the obese eat more rapidly can be easily derived from this formulation.

For rats, this formulation in general fits what we know about eating habits, but can be considered a good explanation of the various experimental facts only if you are willing to accept my reinterpretation, in terms of cue prominence, of such experiments as Miller et al.'s (1950) study of the effects of work on eating. If, as would I, you would rather suspend judgment until the appropriate experiments have been done on lesioned rats, mark it down as an engaging possibility.

Given the rough state of what we know about emotionality, this formulation seems to fit the data for humans and rats about equally well. The lesioned rats are vicious when handled and lethargic when left alone. In the Rodin (1970) experiment which required subjects to listen to either neutral or emotionally disturbing tapes, obese subjects described themselves (and behaved accordingly) as less emotional than normals when the tapes were neutral and much more emotional than normals when the tapes were disturbing.

All in all, given the variety of species and behaviors involved, it

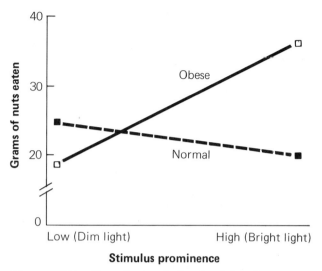

Figure 12.5. *The effects of stimulus intensity on amount eaten (from Ross, 1969).*

is not a bad ad hoc hypothesis. So far there has been only one study deliberately designed to test some of the ideas implicit in this formulation. This is Lee Ross's (1969) study of the effects of cue salience on eating. Ross formulated this experiment in the days when we were struggling with some of the data inconsistent with our external-internal theory of eating behavior (see Schacter, 1967). Since the world is full of food cues, it was particularly embarrassing to discover that obese subjects ate less frequently than normals. Short of invoking denial mechanisms, such a fact could be reconciled with the theory only if we assumed that a food cue must be potent in order to trigger an eating response in an obese subject—the difference between a hot dog stand two blocks away and a hot dog under your nose, savory with mustard and steaming with sauerkraut.

To test the effects of cue prominence, Ross simply had his subjects sit at a table covered with a variety of objects among which was a large tin of shelled cashew nuts. Presumably, the subjects were there to take part in a study of thinking. There were two sets of experimental conditions. In high-cue-saliency conditions, the table and the nuts were illuminated by an unshaded table lamp containing a 40-watt bulb. In low-saliency conditions, the lamp was shaded and contained a 7½-watt red bulb. The measure of eating was simply the difference in the weight of the tin of nuts before and after the subject thought his experimentally required thoughts. The results are presented in Figure 12.5, which, needless to say, though I will say it, bears a marked resemblance to our theoretical curves.

So much for small triumphs. Let us turn now to some of the

problems of this formulation. Though I do not intend to detail a catalog of failings, I would like to make explicit some of my discomforts.

1. Though there has been no direct experimental study of the problem, it seems to be generally thought that the lesioned rat is hyposexual, which, if true, is one hell of a note for a theory which postulates superactivity. It is the case, however, that gonadal atrophy is frequently a consequence of this operation (Brooks and Lambert, 1946; Hetherington and Ransom, 1940). Possibly, then, we should consider sexual activity as artifactually quite distinct from either gross activity or stimulus-bound activity such as avoidance behavior.

2. I am made uncomfortable by the fact that the obese, both human and rat, eat less bad food than do normals. I simply find it difficult to conceive of nonresponsiveness as a response. I suppose I could conceptually pussyfoot around this difficulty, but I cannot imagine the definition of response that would allow me to cope with both this fact and with the facts about passive avoidance. I take some comfort from the observation that of all of the facts about animals and humans, the fact about bad taste has the weakest batting average. It may yet turn out not to be a fact.

3. Though the fact that obese humans eat less often is no problem, the fact that obese rats also eat less often is awkward, for it is a bit difficult to see how food stimulus intensity can vary for a caged rat on an ad lib schedule. This may seem farfetched, but there is some experimental evidence that this may be due to the staleness of the food. Brooks, Lockwood, and Wiggins (1946), using mash for food, demonstrated that lesioned rats do not outeat normals when the food is even slightly stale. Only when the food was absolutely fresh and newly placed in the cage did lesioned rats eat conspicuously more than normal rats. It seems doubtful, however, that this could be the explanation for results obtained with pellets.

4. As with food, one should expect from this formulation that the animal's water intake would increase following the lesion. There does not appear to have been much systematic study of the problem, but what data exist are inconsistent from one study to the next. Several studies indicate decreased water intake; at least one study (Krasne, 1964) indicates no change following the operation; and there are even rare occasional case reports of polydipsia. Possibly my interactional hypothesis can cope with this chaos, and systematically varying the salience of the water cue will systematically affect the water intake of the ventromedial animal. It is also possible that under any circumstance, water, smell-less and tasteless, is a remote cue.

There are, then, difficulties with this formulation. These may be the kinds of difficulties that will ultimately damn the theory, or at least establish its limits. Alternatively, these may mostly be apparent difficulties, and this view of matters may help us clarify inconsistent sets of data, for I suspect that by systematically varying cue prominence we can systematically vary the lesioned animal's reactivity on many dimensions. We shall see. Granting the difficulties, for the moment this view of matters does manage to subsume a surprisingly diverse set of facts about animals and men under one quite simple theoretical scheme.

Since I have presented this article as a more or less personal history of the development of a set of ideas, I would like to conclude by taking a more formal look at this body of data, theory, and speculation, by examining what I believe we now know, what seems to be good guesswork, and what is still out-and-out speculation.

1. With some confidence, we can say that obese humans are externally controlled or stimulus-bound. There is little question that this is true of their eating behavior, and evidence is rapidly accumulating that eating is a special case of the more general state.

I have suggested that stimulus prominence and reactivity are key variables in understanding the realms of behavior with which I have been concerned, and Figure 12.4 represents a first guess as to the nature of the differential functions involved for obese and normal humans. The specific shapes of the curves are, of course, pure guesswork, and the only absolute requirement that I believe the data impose on the theory is that there be an interaction such that at low levels of stimulus prominence, the obese are less reactive, and at high levels of prominence more reactive, than normals.

2. With considerably less confidence, I believe we can say that this same set of hypotheses may explain many of the differences between the ventromedial lesioned rat and his intact counterpart. This conclusion is based on the fact that so much of the existing data either fit or can be plausibly reinterpreted to fit these ideas. Obviously, the crucial experiments have yet to be done.

3. Finally, and most tentatively, one may guess that the obesity of rats and men has a common physiological locus in the ventromedial hypothalamus. I must emphasize that this guess is based *entirely* on the persistent and tantalizing analogies between lesioned rats and obese humans. There is absolutely no relevant independent evidence. However, should future work support this speculation, I suspect, in light of the evidence already supporting the stimulus-binding hypotheses, that we are in for a radical revision of our notions about the hypothalamus.

REFERENCES

Brooks, C. McC. and Lambert, E. F. 1946. A study of the effect of limitation of food intake and the method of feeding on the rate of weight gain during hypothalamic obesity in the albino rat. *American Journal of Physiology,* 147:695–707.

Brooks, C. McC.; Lockwood, R. A.; and Wiggins, M. L. 1946. A study of the effect of hypothalamic lesions on the eating habits of the albino rat. *American Journal of Physiology,* 147:735–741.

Bullen, B. A.; Reed, R. B.; and Mayer, J. 1964. Physical activity of obese and nonobese adolescent girls appraised by motion picture sampling. *American Journal of Clinical Nutrition,* 14:211–223.

Cannon, W. B. 1915. *Bodily Changes in Pain, Hunger, Fear and Rage.* (2nd ed.). New York: Appleton.

Carlson, A. J. 1916. *The Control of Hunger in Health and Disease.* Chicago: University of Chicago Press.

Decke, E. 1971. Effects of taste on the eating behavior of obese and normal persons. Cited in S. Schachter, *Emotion, Obesity, and Crime.* New York: Academic Press.

Gladfelter, W. E. and Brobeck, J. R. 1962. Decreased spontaneous loco-motor activity in the rat induced by hypothalamic lesions. *American Journal of Physiology,* 203:811–817.

Goldman, R.; Jaffa, M.; and Schachter, S. 1968. Yom Kippur, Air France, dormitory food, and the eating behavior of obese and normal persons. *Journal of Personality and Social Psychology,* 10:117–123.

Grossman, S. P. 1966. The VMH: A center for affective reactions, satiety, or both? *International Journal of Physiology and Behavior,* 1:1–10.

Grossman, S. P. 1967. *A Textbook of Physiological Psychology.* New York: Wiley.

Hetherington, A. W. and Ransom, S. W. 1940. Hypothalamic lesions and adiposity in the rat. *Anatomical Record,* 78:149–172.

Johnson, W. G. 1970. The effect of prior-taste and food visibility on the food-directed instrumental performance of obese individuals. Unpublished doctoral dissertation, Catholic University of America.

Krasne, F. B. 1964. Unpublished study cited in N. E. Miller, Some psycho-physiological studies of motivation and of the behavioural effects of ill-ness. *Bulletin of the British Psychological Society,* 17:1–20.

Maren, T. H. 1955. Cited in J. L. Fuller and G. A. Jacoby, Central and sensory control of food intake in genetically obese mice. *American Journal of Physiology,* 183:279–283.

Miller, N. E. 1964. Some psycho-physiological studies of motivation and of the behavioural effects of illness. *Bulletin of the British Psychological Society,* 17:1–20.

Miller, N. E.; Bailey, C. J.; and Stevenson, J. A. F. 1950. Decreased "hun-ger" but increased food intake resulting from hypothalamic lesions. *Science,* 112:256–259.

Mrosovsky, N. 1971. *Hibernation and the Hypothalamus.* New York: Ap-pleton.

Nisbett, R. E. 1968a. Determinants of food intake in human obesity. *Science,* 159:1254–1255.

Nisbett, R. E. 1968b. Taste, deprivation, and weight determinants of eating behavior. *Journal of Personality and Social Psychology,* 10:107–116.

Nisbett, R. E. 1972. Eating and obesity in men and animals. *Advances in Psychosomatic Medicine,* 7:173–193.

Pliner, P. 1970. Effects of liquid and solid preloads on the eating behavior of obese and normal persons. Unpublished doctoral dissertation, Co-lumbia University.

Rabin, B. M. and Smith, C. J. 1968. Behavioral comparison of the effec-tiveness of irritative and non-irritative lesions in producing hypothalamic hyperphagia. *Physiology and Behavior,* 3:417–420.

Reeves, A. G. and Plum, F. 1969. Hyperphagia, rage, and dementia accompanying a ventromedial hypothalamic neoplasm. *Archives of Neurology,* 20:616–624.

Reynolds, R. W. 1963. Ventromedial hypothalamic lesions with hyperphagia. *American Journal of Physiology,* 204:60–62.

Rodin, J. 1970. Effects of distraction on performance of obese and normal subjects. Unpublished doctoral dissertation, Columbia University.

Ross, L. D. 1969. Cue- and cognition-controlled eating among obese and normal subjects. Unpublished doctoral dissertation, Columbia University.

Schachter, S. 1964. The interaction of cognitive and physiological determinants of emotional state. In L. Berkowitz (ed.), *Advances in Experimental Social Psychology,* vol. 1. New York: Academic Press.

Schachter, S. 1967. Cognitive effects on bodily functioning: Studies of obesity and eating. In D. C. Glass (ed.), *Neurophysiology and Emotion.* New York: Rockefeller University Press and Russell Sage Foundation.

Schachter, S. 1968. Obesity and eating. *Science,* 161:751–756.

Schachter, S. 1971. *Emotion, Obesity, and Crime.* New York: Academic Press.

Schachter, S.; Goldman, R.; and Gordon, A. 1968. Effects of fear, food deprivation, and obesity on eating. *Journal of Personality and Social Psychology,* 10:91–97.

Singh, D. 1969. Comparison of hyperemotionality caused by lesions in the septal and ventromedial hypothalamic areas in the rat. *Psychonomic Science,* 16:3–4.

Stellar, E. 1954. The physiology of motivation. *Psychological Review,* 61: 5–22.

Stunkard, A. and Koch, C. 1964. The interpretation of gastric motility: I. Apparent bias in the reports of hunger by obese persons. *Archives of General Psychiatry,* 11:74–82.

Teitelbaum, P. 1955. Sensory control of hypothalamic hyperphagia. *Journal of Comparative and Physiological Psychology,* 48:156–163.

Teitelbaum, P. 1957. Random and food-directed activity in hyperphagic and normal rats. *Journal of Comparative and Physiological Psychology,* 50: 486–490.

Teitelbaum, P. and Campbell, B. A. 1958. Ingestion patterns in hyperphagic and normal rats. *Journal of Comparative and Physiological Psychology,* 51:135–141.

Turner, S. C.; Sechzer, J. A.; and Liebelt, R. A. 1967. Sensitivity to electric shock after ventromedial hypothalamic lesions. *Experimental Neurology,* 19:236–244.

HYPNOTISM IN THE HISTORY OF PSYCHOLOGY

During the late 1940s when I was a student, hypnosis was pre-sented typically as a subtopic within the history of psychology. The standard historical pattern of presentation started with Mesmer, dis-cussed the subsequent controversy over hypnosis as an anesthetic agent in the hands of Esdaile and Braid, and led to its use in psycho-therapy by Charcot and his students through whom the technique was made known to Sigmund Freud. Two points were emphasized. First, hypnosis had promise as an anesthetic agent, but just as it was being accepted by the medical profession, the more reliable chemical anes-thetics were developed. Second, hypnosis had some value in therapy, but since all subjects could not be hypnotized, and symptoms rather than causes were being altered, Freud developed the alternative method of psychoanalysis from which emerged both a new therapy and a new personality theory. The discussion of hypnosis per se was secondary to its historical contribution to psychoanalysis. There were some interesting and curious phenomena such as anesthesia and paraesthesia (false sensations), posthypnotic suggestion, amnesia and hypermnesia (a dramatic improvement in memory), and age regres-sion. However, the state of our understanding at that time did not permit more than a cursory description of these phenomena, and there was no real attempt at explaining them. In effect, our understanding of the mechanism of hypnosis had not advanced much beyond that of Mesmer—and he had been unable to explain the basis for his tech-nique to the French Academy. It was implicit in these discussions that the symptoms and phenomena associated with hypnosis were thought to result from the induction of the hypnotic trance. This con-cept of hypnosis represents what was a rather standard treatment of the topic until about two decades ago. Since then, dramatic changes in our understanding of the mechanism of hypnosis have emerged,

Herschel Leibowitz is Professor of Psychology at Pennsylvania State University. Work on this paper was supported in part by a research grant (MH08061) from the National Institute of Mental Health.

so that the contemporary view of hypnosis, although not quite as mystical, is considerably more fundamental and, consequently, more important to the behavioral sciences.

Stated briefly, the basic assumption from the time of Mesmer was that the trance state was essential, and that all hypnotic phenomena were dependent upon the subject being in the trance state. In a series of well-conceived and carefully executed studies, researchers such as Sarbin and Lim (1963), Hilgard (1965), Barber (1969), and Orne (1959) have demonstrated convincingly and repeatedly that the trance is not always essential to the appearance of classical hypnotic phenomena. Rather, such phenomena frequently have a simpler and more fundamental explanation. For example, studies have shown that subjects who volunteer for an experiment do so with a number of motives—to please the experimenter, to help science, to contribute to a project, to obtain credits toward a grade, to earn money, etc. These factors, which Orne has termed the "demand characteristics" of the experiment, are adequate *in and of themselves* to induce a subject to exhibit essentially all of the phenomena whose appearance was previously thought to require the trance state. Instead of the trance being an essential condition, this impressive experimental literature points to the importance of the subject's willingness to conform to the objectives of the experiment. In a typical study, the behavior of a subject who is asked to pretend or simulate hypnosis without being hypnotized will be indistinguishable from that of those subjects in a true hypnotic state. This is a most interesting literature, and it is important not only because of its relationship to the history of hypnosis, but in reference to experimental methodology with human subjects. (See the chapter by Barber in this book and the references to Hilgard, Orne, and Barber in the Bibliography.)

It is reasonable and logical to ask how our concept of hypnosis could have been incorrect for such a long time. It is fundamental to scientific method that correlation does not necessarily imply causation; in practice, however, it often is difficult to tease out the correct relationships. This is especially true in the present case in which the weight of literally centuries of tradition argues strongly for the causative influence of the hypnotic trance. The critical procedure which demonstrated that the trance is not essential to most hypnotic phenomena is their simulation by nonhypnotized subjects who are instructed to behave as if they were hypnotized. An observer, unaware of which of the subjects are simulating and which are hypnotized, cannot classify them on the basis of observation. The striking similarity of results from simulators is interpreted as demonstrating the non-essential role of the hypnotic trance and the critical importance of the general experimental situation. One reason that most hypnotic phenomena can be successfully simulated by nonhypnotized subjects is that the appropriate behavior is already known to the subject who, in turn, can respond in conformity with the objectives of the experiment. It is not difficult to act like a child under instructions to age regress, since it would be a rare subject in our society who has not had an opportunity to observe the behavior of young children or to recall the appropriate behavior from his own experience. A similar argument could be made for distortion or elimination of perceptual or sensory experences, alterations in memory, posthypnotic suggestions, and other hypnotic phenomena. In effect, this is the contemporary explanation of most hypnotic phenomena, that they simply are the result of the knowledge and willingness of the subject to conform to the desires of the experimenter and the demands of the experimental situation.

HYPNOSIS AND VISUAL ILLUSIONS: AN EXPERIMENTAL STUDY

As an experimental psychologist interested in sensory and perceptual phenomena, I (along with most of my contemporaries) was unaware of the emerging view of hypnosis being developed at the same time I was innocently teaching the old view in my course on the history of psychology. The archaic nature of my understanding was dramatically brought to my attention by a graduate student at Penn State, Michael Parrish, who, after updating me on these recent developments in hypnosis research, raised an interesting and fundamental question. He argued that the classical "hypnotic" phenomena can be produced by nonhypnotized but highly motivated subjects; therefore, a critical test of whether hypnosis involves ingredients other than demand characteristics or task motivation would be to utilize suggestions for which the subject did not know the appropriate response. Specifically, Parrish asked whether there were any perceptual tests which satisfied these conditions. It is not to my credit that I was skeptical and tried to discourage him. However, with encouragement from Professor Richard M. Lundy, he persisted until I reluctantly suggested that some research which we had just completed on two geometric-optical illusions appeared to satisfy the conditions in which they were interested.

We had been involved for some time with the question of whether or not the Ponzo perspective illusion (Figure 13.1c) could be explained simply as a manifestation of general laws of space perception. The theoretical argument derives from the phenomenon of size constancy. As we move about our environment viewing an object at different distances, the sizes of the image formed in our eyes (usually referred to as the retinal image) change continually. However, if you ask a subject to match the size of an object at different distances, the values correspond more closely to their true sizes than to the retinal size. This phenomenon is called size "constancy," in recognition of the fact that perception involves the true or constant sizes of objects in spite of changes in their retinal image dimensions. Constancy is obviously an important stabilizing factor without which visual perception would be chaotic with the dimensions of objects changing continually. Given the importance of depth cues in size constancy, it has been suggested that the Ponzo illusion results from the misapplication of cues, such as perspective, which normally operate to produce size constancy (Gregory, 1973). In Figure 13.1A, the upper log appears larger even though the retinal dimensions of the two are the same. According to the theory, this is because you "know" it is farther away and make an unconscious enlargement correction in the interest of size constancy. In Figure 13.1B, the same correction is made, that is, subjective enlargement of the more distant line; but this is inappropriate and results in an "illusion." This is an appealing theory because it provides a rather simple explanation of at least one illusion: that the error in perception is simply the result of the inappropriate application of a normal mechanism of depth perception.

One way of testing this theory is to determine whether the same variables affect the illusion and size constancy similarly. For example, both size constancy and the magnitude of the Ponzo illusion increase with chronological, but not mental, age. This is an area of research in which we have been involved for some time. In the present context, the relevant point is that we had available stimuli and procedures for studying developmental trends in geometrical illusions and had determined, on a number of occasions, that the Ponzo illusion increases with chronological age.

Figures 13.2 and 13.3 present developmental functions obtained on the same subjects for the Ponzo and for the Poggendorff illusions. The Ponzo illusion was chosen for investigation because of the assumed relationship between converging lines as a cue for depth and the role of learned monocular cues in size constancy. The basis for choosing the Poggendorff illusion was completely atheoretical. It is interesting, easy to administer, and since subjects of various ages were already available, it seemed like a good "bargain" to spend an extra ten minutes per subject and obtain data for the Poggendorff illusion as well. Both of these illusions show rather marked developmental functions. With increasing age, the magnitude of the Ponzo illusion increases. On the other hand, the Poggendorff illusion shows the opposite trend, decreasing with age. Since it was extremely unlikely that any subjects would know of these relationships (the Poggendorff data had not yet been published) these two illusions provided a means of testing whether hypnotic age regression results simply from demand characteristics, or if instead there is something essential or peculiar to the trance state.

Parrish, a former actor highly skilled in hypnosis, in cooperation

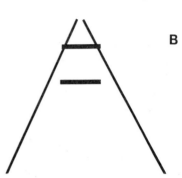

Figure 13.1. *The Ponzo perspective illusion. The horizontal lines are of equal length in both figures. The figure on the right is a geometric form of the illusion often employed in experiments. The photograph on the left illustrates the illusion in a real-life scene. (From Leibowitz, Brislin, Perlmutter, and Hennessy, Science, Vol. 166, pp. 1174–1176, Fig., 28 November 1969. Copyright 1969 by the American Association for the Advancement of Science.)*

with Richard Lundy who is experienced in both clinical and experimental hypnosis, designed the subsequent experiment. It consisted of obtaining illusion magnitudes from college-age subjects under four conditions: (1) awake (2) hypnotized with no suggestion of age regression (3) hypnotized with regression to age 9, and (4) hypnotized with regression to age 5. These conditions were administered in a balanced design to subjects who were highly hypnotizable. Remember that all subjects are not equally hypnotizable, as was mentioned in the opening paragraphs of this chapter. It is important to keep in mind that the subjects in this, as in most hypnosis experiments, are highly selected, representing no more than 10–20 percent of the population.

Figure 13.2 presents the data for the Parrish and Lundy experiments superimposed on the normative data from the previous developmental studies. It will be observed that the college age subjects, either awake or hypnotized, produced age-appropriate responses. With regression to age 9, illusion magnitudes were modified in the appropriate direction with the values falling very close to the developmental functions. With regression to age 5, these were further changed in the age-appropriate directions although the data did not, in either case,

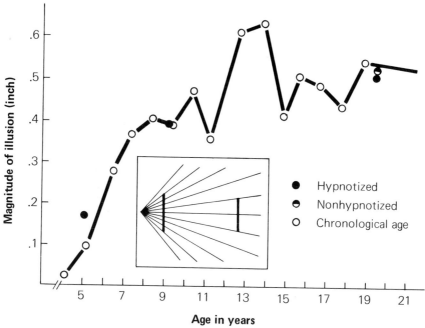

Figure 13.2. *Open circles: the relationship between the magnitude of the Ponzo illusion (insert) and chronological age. Closed circles: the data obtained under hypnosis. (From Parrish, Lundy, and Leibowitz,* Journal of Abnormal Psychology, *1969, 74, 693–698. Copyright 1969 by the American Psychological Association. Reprinted by permission.)*

reach the values typical of children of age 5 (Parrish, Lundy, and Leibowitz, 1969).

An important control in this type of experiment is to ask non-hypnotized subjects to simulate or pretend they are children. Under these conditions, the *nonhypnotized* though highly *hypnotizable* subjects produced illusion magnitudes characteristic of their real chronological age. The hypnotized subjects, on the other hand, produced illusion magnitudes characteristic of the *suggested* age, even though they had no knowledge of what the appropriate magnitude should be.

One implication of those data, with regard to the hypnosis literature, is that there is something to hypnosis which is more than compliance, role playing, or demand characteristics. Obviously, there is no way the subjects in this study could have known what the appropriate age responses should have been. Even if, for some reason, the subjects wished to produce responses typical of children, they could not have known how to modify their behavior on the illusion task. This interpretation is supported by the fact that the simulating group, whose members were instructed to behave like children without being hypnotized—did not produce the appropriate responses.

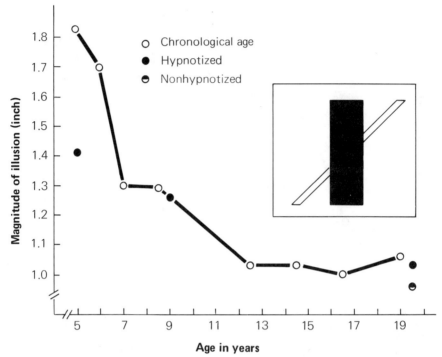

Figure 13.3. Poggendorff illusion. The diagonal line in the Poggendorff illusion (inset) is continuous but appears discontinuous. The graph describes the magnitude of the illusion as a function of chronological age, open circles; superimposed are the data obtained under hypnosis. From Parrish, Lundy, and Leibowitz, Journal of Abnormal Psychology, 1969, 74, 693–698. Copyright 1969 by the American Psychological Association. Reprinted by permission.)

As one would expect, this study was followed by several attempts to replicate it, with generally negative results. At present, we are uncertain as to the explanation of the discrepancies among the results of the different experiments. Differences in the method of selecting subjects, questions regarding the adequacies of the scales used to evaluate hypnotizability, and other methodological differences have not been resolved as of this writing. Whatever the eventual outcome of this controversy, this study has demonstrated a feasible technique for investigating the essential nature of hypnosis. At the same time, interest in this problem provides a convenient framework for discussing the recent advances in hypnosis research and their implications for experimental methodology.

In effect, the lesson to be learned from the recent hypnosis literature is broader, more important, and has wider implications than the study of hypnotic phenomena themselves. It has provided an alternative framework and suggested new ways of interpreting experiments and data. Research on hypnosis has derived from an historical background very different from that of traditional experimental psychology. Thus, it is heuristic because it suggests very strongly that any experiment involving human subjects must seriously consider the interpretation of the situation by the subject himself. In a traditional experiment, the experimenter varies some aspect of the environment (the independent variable), and observes the effect of that manipulation on the subject's response (the dependent variable).

Much of traditional experimental psychology has focused on the specification of the stimulus and the quantification of the subject's response. It is clear from the hypnosis literature that the value of the dependent variable *is* highly related to what the subject assumes is the nature of the experiment, expectations that he implicity or explicitly assigns to the study, and his own motives and goals as a subject. This is not meant to imply that experimenters were not always aware of these organismic factors. But the hypnosis literature has given us a new insight into and new respect for the magnitude of influence of these factors on the results of experiments. An experiment involving human observers may reflect psychological processes and mechanisms which are peculiar to the experiment and which do not necessarily manifest themselves outside of the experimental situation. I believe that the methodological implications of this point of view are the most important lesson experimental psychologists can extract from contemporary hypnosis literature. This point of view is not entirely new. It has been applied in psychopharmacological research in which nonactive or placebo drugs are given to subjects in order to determine whether or not the experimental situation and/or the subjects' expectation of an effect will occur in the absence of an active medicinal agent.

It would be misleading to imply that experimental psychologists have not been aware that factors "within" the subject can influence the results of experiments. However, the hypnosis literature has not only focused attention on the magnitude of such factors, but provided a methodology for their study and control. Researchers in almost every field are often surprised to learn that their discoveries were anticipated by someone in the past. Regardless of the question of priority, the important point is that researchers interested in hypnosis have called attention to and demonstrated the importance of factors that are inherent in experimentation involving human beings as subjects. In view of the role of the behavioral sciences in our society and the fact that they are based to a large extent on such experiments, these developments have both a timely and fundamental relevance to all of us.

MYOPIA AND HYPNOSIS:
AN EXPERIMENTAL STUDY OF A CLINICAL PROBLEM

An excellent example of the interrelation between hypnosis and traditional experimental psychology can be illustrated by studies of the influence of hypnotic suggestion on visual acuity. Visual acuity refers to the ability of the eye to see fine detail. We all are familiar with clinical eye examinations designed primarily to evaluate visual acuity. A typical procedure involves reading a standard eye chart. The smaller the letters which can be recognized, the better the acuity. If an observer can read the 20/20 line on the eye chart, this means that he can read at a 20 foot distance what a "normal" observer reads at 20 feet; acuity is considered to be normal and glasses are not prescribed. However, many individuals in this country cannot read the 20/20 line on the acuity test chart without wearing optical correction either in the form of spectacles or contact lenses. Glasses are prescribed to correct an image that is out of focus or blurred. In the majority of cases, assuming no neurological defect, the optical correction sharpens the image and allows the observer to read the 20-20 line correctly.

There are a number of specific defects which may lead to a blurred image. The most common defect, excluding the inevitable far-sightedness which occurs with age, is myopia (nearsightedness). This refers to a condition in which the image comes to a focus in front of the retina (light sensitive portion of the eye), resulting in a blurred image (see Figure 13.4). People with this condition can see nearby objects clearly, but not distant ones. Millions of individuals in this country suffer from some degree of nearsightedness. As the general illumination is lowered, almost everyone exhibits this defect to some extent "night-myopia."

Historically, the correction of myopia, as well as that of other types of refractive errors, has evolved from the study of optics, a branch of physics, and from physiological optics, which is the application of optical principles to the image-forming properties of the eye. The relevance of this approach is taken for granted and is implicit in the fitting of glasses. Very simply, if the image is blurred, lens power is added or subtracted so as to produce a clear image. For a nearsighted person, a negative lens is added which decreases the refractive power of the eye and allows the image to be focused on the retina (Fig. 13.4). Within a very small and essentially negligible error, this procedure works splendidly.

Given this background, reports that nearsightedness can be improved by hypnosis are puzzling. If the acuity of vision depends upon the sharpness of the optical image, how can hypnotic suggestion, or for that matter any other nonoptical procedure, improve visual acuity? One possibility is that there is some artifact or error in the experiments purporting to show that hypnosis can correct or alleviate

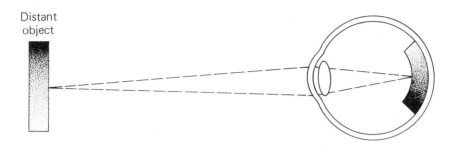

Normal

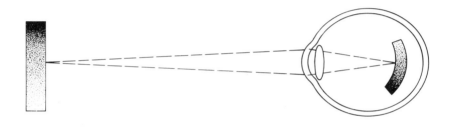

Nearsighted or myopic

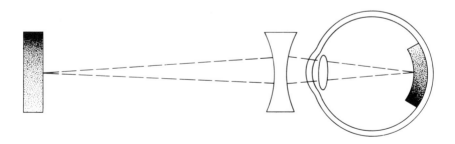

Corrected

Figure 13.4. *Schematic illustration of the image-forming process. Upper: The image is focused on the retina and appears sharp and clear. Middle: Either because the eye is too long, or has too much refractive power, the image is formed in front of the retina and will appear blurred. Lower: If a negative lens is placed in front of the eye, the light will be bent so that a sharp image is formed at the retina.*

nearsightedness. Visual acuity is affected by a large number of factors including the illumination of the test chart, the size of the pupil or opening of the eye, and practice. Many studies which claim to show a relationship between acuity and hypnosis did not control all of these factors. In particular, acuity will improve with practice—a source of variability which must be carefully controlled. Because of uncertainties in the interpretation of previous studies, Charles Graham, then a master's candidate at Penn State, decided to reinvestigate this problem.

In the first phase of Graham's experiment, the effect of hypnotically induced suggestion on the acuity of nearsighted subjects was determined. The experimenters were careful to ensure that all variables known to affect acuity were controlled or kept constant. For example, the usual clinical test chart (Snellen chart) was not used because it has been shown that the various letters are not equally well recognized. Since the object of clinical testing is to determine how well one can recognize these same letters in everyday life, this is not a problem but rather an advantage for a clinician. However, for laboratory studies, a "neutral" test object, such as a Landolt C, is usually used. The subject's task is to indicate the direction of the gap in the circle, thus reducing the effects of past experience and differential familiarity of letters on the results. Illumination was controlled by testing at a very high level so that even slight variations will have no effect on acuity. At these high levels of luminance, when viewing a large area, pupil size remains at a minimal and constant value. Subjects were tested both with and without their glasses, before and after being hypnotized. They were informed that they would be able to see better if they relaxed. The procedure was a rather long one, involving a number of suggestions all of which were administered by Graham, who has a reputation as an excellent hypnotist. To allow for improvement due to training, data were obtained in three consecutive sessions.

The data from Phase I are presented in Figure 13.5 as the minimum resolvable angle—the smallest discernible size of the gap in the test object—both before and after administration of the hypnotic procedure. (Note that the smaller the angle, the higher the acuity.) The three pairs of curves refer to subjects suffering from different degrees of nearsightedness. As this figure demonstrates, acuity improves with practice for both observation conditions. However, all subjects under all conditions apparently were able to see a smaller gap (i.e., better visual acuity), with hypnotic suggestion than without it. The magnitude of the difference depends upon how myopic the subjects are. This improvement is almost a factor of 2:1, which clinically is a significant value (Graham and Leibowitz, 1972).

The findings of Phase I essentially are not new. Rather, they confirm, under conditions of more precise control of experimental variables, the results from a number of previous reports. Fortunately,

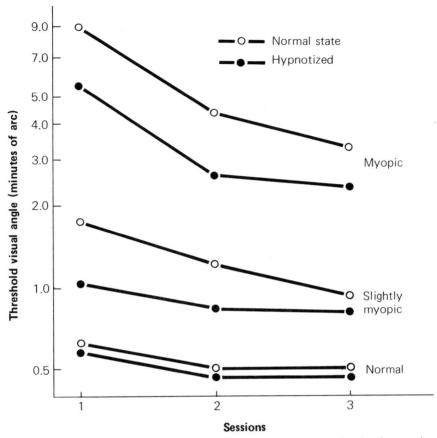

Figure 13.5. *Threshold visual angle (the smaller the angle the better the acuity) for three sessions in which data were obtained with and without hypnotically induced suggestions that the subjects would "see better." (From Graham & Leibowitz, 1972. Reprinted from the July 1972 International Journal of Clinical and Experimental Hypnosis. Copyrighted by the Society for Clinical and Experimental Hypnosis, July, 1972.)*

the contemporary hypnosis literature suggested an important extension of this experiment. As discussed above, a fundamental result of hypnotic research has been the demonstration that phenomena which previously were thought to depend upon the hypnotic trance can also be obtained, under the proper experimental conditions, in the absence of the trance. Subsequently, Phase II of the experiment was designed to determine whether or not the trance state itself was essential in producing the results of Phase I. Therefore, hypnosis was never administered in Phase II; subjects were given "waking instructions," which consisted of suggestions to relax *without* previously inducing the hypnotic trance. Two groups of subjects chosen on the basis of their susceptibility to hypnosis were tested. One group was highly hypnotiz-

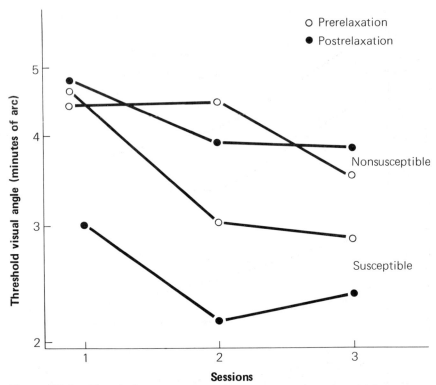

Figure 13.6. *Threshold visual angle for three sessions in which susceptible and nonsusceptible subjects were given waking suggestions that they
would "see better" under relaxation. (From Graham and Leibowitz, 1972.
Reprinted from the July, 1972* International Journal of Clinical and Experimental Hypnosis. *Copyrighted by The Society for Clinical and Experimental
Hypnosis, July, 1972.)*

able while the other was not. Again it should be kept in mind that
studies with hypnotic subjects are confined to the relatively small
percentage of the population that can be hypnotized. Thus, in a
typical hypnosis experiment we are not certain if the personality
characteristic of hypnotizability is responsible for the results, since by
definition, all subjects tested must be hypnotizable. However, with
waking suggestions, one can determine whether hypnotizability per
se is a factor in the results obtained.

The testing procedure was similar to that employed in Phase
I. Nearsighted subjects, without their glasses, were tested in three
separate sessions in the same manner as previously described. The
results are presented in Figure 13.6. Considering first the data for
the nonsusceptible subjects, it will be noted that although acuity
improves with practice, there is no difference between the prerelaxa-
tion and postrelaxation states. However, for the hypnotizable subjects, in addition to the improvement with practice, there is also a

marked difference between the pre- and postrelaxation conditions. The difference is of the same order of magnitude as previously observed with the hypnotic procedure.

The results of Phase II, in line with many experiments in the contemporary literature, indicate that the hypnotic trance per se is not essential to the results obtained. Rather, these results demonstrate that the *hypnotizability* of the subjects is the essence of the improvement. Although this does not resolve the tantalizing question as to the mechanism of the improvement, these results are helpful in pointing the way toward understanding some of the discrepancies in the literature. Specifically, these data show that hypnotizability is a factor in improving acuity by nonoptical means.

Experimenters interested in improvement of visual acuity have attempted to replicate previous studies in which vision was improved by nonoptical techniques. An excellent study of this kind is an experiment carried out by Elwin Marg (1952), a respected professor of physiological optics at the University of California, Berkeley. Marg was interested in reports that vision could be improved by the use of specific training procedures without optical correction. Since the procedure followed by the nonorthodox practitioners is rather long and laborious, Marg chose to use as a measure of the effect of the training procedure the report by subjects that they observed "clear flashes" during training. These clear flashes occur suddenly—the subjects reported that for a moment, everything appears "crystal clear." In Marg's experiment, both the number of clear flashes and any changes in acuity were noted and recorded carefully. His experiment was essentially negative—the number of clear flashes did not increase significantly nor was there any general improvement in acuity (Marg, 1952).

How are we to resolve these differences? Marg's studies were carried out under careful and appropriate experimental conditions. However, it is easy to obtain evidence, albeit of a nonexperimental nature, that vision can be improved by these techniques. There are many instances in which results of carefully controlled experiments appear to be at odds with the experiences and reports of sincere observers. Based on the implications of the Graham experiment, we can now suggest a possible solution to this dilemma. The Graham studies have shown that improvement in acuity by nonoptical means depends on the personality trait of hypnotizability. This leads to the basic question as to whether or not hypnotizability influences the behavior of subjects in situations other than hypnosis experiments. As Hilgard (1965) has pointed out, it would seem logical to assume that there is some generality to this trait, but the evidence to date has not been definitive. Let us assume, however, that hypnotizability is related to other forms of behavior. If this were the case, it would not be unreasonable to conjecture that this trait may differ between the population tested by Marg and that of the unorthodox practitioners. A subject who is hypnotizable may be suggestible, and may respond favorably to the claims by nonorthodox practitioners that cures by unusual techniques can be effected. It would be interesting and important to determine the hypnotizability levels of subjects in these experiments, although it is impossible to do this retrospectively.

Even if there were no differences in hypnotizability among these subject populations, the general experimental milieu or demand characteristics would differ in the two situations. Subjects in university-based studies usually consist of students who often are skeptical and who, by their very nature, are encouraged to disregard mystical and/or unorthodox explanations and procedures. On the other hand, individuals who volunteer to be treated by practitioners whose professional base is outside the usual health care system, probably already have some hopes and expectations that the treatment will work. Thus, even though the experimental procedures might be identical, the motives for serving as a subject and the general expectations of the subjects themselves will differ.

These frankly speculative opinions do not explain the differences between Marg's results and those of other experiments. However, if we consider the implications of the Graham study showing that nonoptical factors, hypnotizability in particular, can influence significantly the results of experimental studies designed to test improvement of visual acuity, a possible basis for the discrepancy has been identified. Future studies should investigate systematically the level of hypnotizability as an experimental variable.

The implications of these data are, of course, broader than the study of visual acuity. Subjects in human experiments come from a variety of sources. In addition to the traditional elementary psychology "volunteer," many studies are based on populations of institutionalized patients, of military and hospital personnel who are required to participate, volunteers who are solicited while walking on public streets, etc. Such population differences will produce not only a wide range of hypnotizability levels in the subjects, but also considerable variation in motives and expectations. A graduate student serving as a subject for his major professor will obviously have a different attitude toward the experiment than someone required to participate as part of his military service. The advantage of the hypnosis literature is that it has focused attention on variables which are absolutely essential to the understanding and conduct of hypnosis experiments, but which also have profound implications for any studies involving human subjects.

HYPNOSIS AND EXPERIMENTAL PSYCHOLOGY: IMPLICATIONS FOR THE STUDY OF HUMAN BEHAVIOR

What lesson can we learn from this brief interlude with experimental hypnosis? First, I think we must be aware constantly of the fact that the behavior of a subject in an experiment is not necessarily typical of his behavior outside the laboratory. Subjects are not passive "black boxes" to be stimulated by experimental psychologists who then discover invariant relationships between stimulus and response by observing their behavior. A human subject is a sensitive, conscious, and easily modifiable organism. His or her expectations of the goals of the experiment or the objectives of a study, and what constitutes success or failure for the subject or the experimenter, can greatly influence the results. If one has any doubts regarding the magnitude of this effect, consider the point made previously that for centuries experimenters insisted that hypnosis was dependent upon the trance state. It is not the trance that is so powerful but rather the interaction between the subject and the experimental situation. One may view the failure of experimental psychologists to discern the correlative rather than the causative relationship between the hypnotic trance and symptoms as an error, as was the case. On the other hand, progress depends on learning from mistakes and the bigger the mistake has been, the more we learn.

Perhaps equally important, the hypnosis literature has provided us with methodology and suggestions for controlling artifacts which may occur in studies with human subjects. One good example is, of course, the simulation group described previously. Similar techniques would involve experimental manipulation of the subject's expectations. This method has been used in memory research in which the behavior of subjects, which was otherwise identical, was termed a "failure" for some subjects, and "success" for others by deliberately manipulating the subjects' understanding of the nature of the experiment. In this case, the subjects' perceptions of their own success or failure were important in determining the memory for the task. Many other possibilities are feasible. The important point is to be sensitive to the role of subjects' expectations and to incorporate these expectations into the experimental design.

THE RELATIONSHIP BETWEEN HYPNOTIZABILITY AND BEHAVIOR

Perhaps the least studied implication of hypnosis research is the role of the personality trait of hypnotic susceptibility. To what extent is the willingness of a subject to be manipulated by the verbal persuasion of another individual a general trait? Is it possible that this trait is confined to the hypnosis experiment? To quote from Hilgard (1965),

> *Many conjectures about hypnosis are highly plausible, so that it is something of a shock to put them to the test only to find that practically none of the plausible conjectures can be proven to be true. There "ought" to be relationships to anxiety, to social*

> *desirability, to conforming tendencies, to social influencibility, to attention, and so on, but such relationships as we find are all very low and unstable, except the criterion of hypnotic susceptibility itself, which is remarkably stable (pp. 339–340).*

Research on "subliminal" perception is illuminating in this regard. During the 1950s, there was much interest in advertising techniques for using subliminal perception. Briefly, "limen" is another word for threshold, or the minimum stimulus energy which can be perceived. At a conversational level, "subliminal" implies that the stimulus is too weak to be seen. A careful analysis of this concept reveals that this is a misinterpretation. Since there is always variability of seeing for weak stimuli, the limen in reality is an arbitrary point on a frequency-of-seeing curve. A stimulus at the limen will be seen 50 or 75 percent of the time depending upon the criterion chosen, while a subliminal stimulus will be seen less often. The subliminal advertising technique involved flashing a weak stimulus, such as "eat popcorn," on the screen of a theater. It was argued that because the stimulus was weak, our natural defenses against the daily barrrage of advertising materials were bypassed, so that one was more likely to act on the advertisement's suggestion. This argument led, in turn, to an interesting discussion among psychologists, who now recognize that we must pay more attention to the distinction between perception and response.

One of the most interesting studies to come from this period is an experiment by Goldiamond and Hawkins (1958) on the tendency of subjects to report the presence of words in a very brief flash of light when none are present. Subjects are shown words under difficult seeing conditions, followed by trials in which no words at all are presented —just flashes of light. The subjects, however, continue to report that they "see" words when none are presented. This experiment represented a sort of historical culmination of research on this problem. It showed that the tendency to report words when none were present was simply a function of the frequency with which those same words had been presented previously. Because the critical trials in the experiment consisted of blank exposures, no perception whatsoever was involved. What was being manipulated was response, not perception. This study focused attention on response processes in perceptual experiments and provided both an empirical and a theoretical basis for rejecting the claims of the subliminal advertisers and, more importantly, for understanding the results of the previous studies. In effect, many of the studies on subliminal perception were misinterpreted because of the failure to distinguish between perception and response, —to realize that what was changing was not perception itself, but the subject's tendency to report a stimulus. (For a general treatment of this problem, see Ericksen and Ericksen, 1972).

Recently, Dr. Robert Miller (1973) studied the effect of hypnotizability on this phenomenon. His study presented blank trials to subjects who previously had been exposed to a number of word stimuli. However, unlike the case in the Goldiamond and Hawkins experiment, Miller knew the hypnotizability level of his subjects. His data demonstrated a predictable relationship between the tendency of subjects to report words when none were presented and hypnotizable level.

Miller's data clearly demonstrate a relationship between hypnotizability and behavior in an experiment not involving hypnosis. As such, they suggest that hypnotizability may have implications broader than the narrow definition of how likely the subject is to respond to hypnotic suggestions. Since the hypnotizability of the subject in previous experiments on subliminal perception or, for that matter, the vast majority of studies in the experimental literature are not known, to what extent was this a factor in determining the results? It is interesting to note that one state legislature was so alarmed by the implications of subliminal perception that it passed a law prohibiting its use. The applications of science to society are, it is hoped, based on the best analysis of a problem, but if a major variable were not even considered in the research literature, any such analysis must be considered incomplete.

We should ask the general question as we did in discussing the improvement of acuity by suggestion, to what extent the results were influenced by the hypnotizability level of the subjects. Many other examples, both within and outside of formal experimental psychology, can be identified. To what extent are a patient's symptoms the result of expectations based on suggestions by friends or on advertisements by drug manufacturers. To what extent can the testimony of a witness in court be influenced by the suggestions of the prosecution or defense attorneys? Clearly, implications of the hypnosis literature are relevant to the behavior of humans whether they are serving in a psychological experiment, watching advertisements on television, or describing their symptoms to a physician.

REFERENCES

Barber, T. X. 1969. *Hypnosis: A Scientific Approach.* New York: Van Nostrand Reinhold.

Eriksen, B. A. and Eriksen, C. W. 1972. *Perception and Personality.* Morristown, N. J.: General Learning Press.

Goldiamond, I. and Hawkins, W. F. 1958. *Vexierversuch:* The log relationship between word frequency and recognition obtained in the absence of stimulus words. *Journal of Experimental Psychology,* 56:457–463.

Graham, C. and Leibowitz, H. W. 1972. The effect of suggestion on visual acuity. *International Journal of Clinical and Experimental Hypnosis,* 20:169–186.

Gregory, R. L. 1973. *Eye and Brain: the Psychology of Seeing,* 2nd ed. New York: McGraw-Hill.

Hilgard, E. R. 1965. *Hypnotic Susceptibility.* New York: Harcourt, Brace, Jovanovich.

Leibowitz, H. W.; Brislin, R.; Perlmutter, L.; and Hennessy, R. 1969. The Ponzo perspective illusion as a manifestation of space perception. *Science,* 166:1174–1176.

Marg, E. 1952. "Flashes" of clear vision and negative accommodation with reference to the Bates method of visual training. *American Journal of Optometry,* 44:230–236.

Miller, R. J. 1973. Psychological differentiation and hypnotizability. Unpublished doctoral dissertation, Pennsylvania State University.

Orne, M. T. 1959. The nature of hypnosis: Artifact and essence. *Journal of Abnormal and Social Psychology,* 58:277–299.

Parrish, M.; Lundy, R. M.; and Leibowitz, H. W. 1969. Effect of hypnotic age regression on the magnitude of the Ponzo and Poggendorff illusions. *Journal of Abnormal Psychology,* 74:693–698.

Sarbin, T. R. and Lim, D. T. 1963. Some evidence in support of the role-taking hypothesis in hypnosis. *International Journal of Clinical Hypnosis,* 11:98–103.

SUGGESTED READINGS

Barber, T. X. 1969. *Hypnosis: A Scientific Approach.* New York: Van Nostrand Reinhold.

Boring, E. G. 1950. *A History of Experimental Psychology,* 2nd ed. New York: Appleton-Century-Crofts, Chapter 7.

Eriksen, B. A. and Eriksen, C. W. 1972. *Perception and Personality.* Morristown, N. J.: General Learning Press.

Hilgard, E. R. 1971. Hypnotic phenomena: The struggle for scientific acceptance. *American Scientist,* Sept.–Oct.:567–577.

Orne, M. T. 1970. Hypnosis, motivation, and the ecological validity of the psychological experiment. In W. J. Arnold and M. M. Page (eds.), *Nebraska Symposium on Motivation.* Lincoln: University of Nebraska Press, 187–265.

THE PRIVATE LIFE OF AN
EYEBALL WATCHER, OR WHERE
IS THE DREAM?
John S. Antrobus

As I sit here watching the surf roll onto the hot sandy beach of Fire Island, I marvel at the lawfulness of the annual activity cycle of research psychologists. All over the Northern hemisphere this sunny July morning there are psychologists, like myself, sitting on the beach or not far from it, writing papers, chapters, and books describing the output of their laboratories during the preceding 10 months. I know psychologists who are writing on the sunny beaches of the Mediterranian, the Black Sea and the Pacific beaches of Hawaii, California, and Oregon. The Eastern Atlantic seaboard of this country is literally packed with psychologist scribes, from the beaches of Wellfleet and Truro of Massachusetts all the way down to Florida. Within easy jogging distance either side of this spot, upon which I sit, I know of half a dozen psychologists who are writing research reports. My next door neighbor is completing his fifth book. During the past 10 months these psychologists have taught, supervised, consulted, administered, and run their laboratories at a feverish pitch. But only in the summer months is it possible to get sufficient consecutive uninterrupted hours to organize one's thoughts and get them coherently onto paper. And if one does not finish by September 15th, the writing will have to wait till the following summer.

If it were not for the fact that my wife, Judy, is writing a particularly exciting book in the area of clinical psychology, she would be joining me in the writing of this chapter for we collaborated on much of the research I will describe here. Judy had always been intensely fascinated with the study of dreams. But it was not until 1959, in Joseph Zubin's graduate course in abnormal psychology at Columbia University, that we heard a presentation on the study of dreams that was to transform the course of our lives. In this class, William Dement described his work with Kleitman and Aserinsky, physiologists at the University of Chicago, who had discovered some remarkably lawful

John S. Antrobus is affiliated with the Department of Psychology, The City College of the City University of New York.

Figure 14.1. *The experimenter monitors the subject's brain waves and eye movements. The electroencephalograph amplifies the electrical potentials being recorded from the subject so that they deflect the pens in the ink-writing apparatus. A roll of moving paper is fed through ink-writing apparatus during the entire night. On a typical night, some 700 or more feet of paper will be used to obtain a continuous record of the subject's brain waves and eye movements during sleep. (From Foulkes, 1966. Reprinted by permission of Charles Scribner's Sons from* The Psychology of Sleep *by David Foulkes. Copyright © 1966 David Foulkes.)*

cycles in the all-night electroencephalographic (EEG) records of sleeping subjects (Dement and Kleitman, 1957a).

Some people seem to think that just because we can measure the EEG we must know what it "means." Not so. As the name implies, the electroencephalograph is a graphic display or line drawing of the electrical activity of the brain—or at least some part of it. Generally, anywhere between 4 and 16 simultaneous graphs are obtained, each drawing or "writing-out" the electrical activity measured at a particular spot on the scalp or forehead (see Figs. 14.1 and 14.2). Beneath each electrode, behind skin, scalp muscle, and skull lie the millions of cells

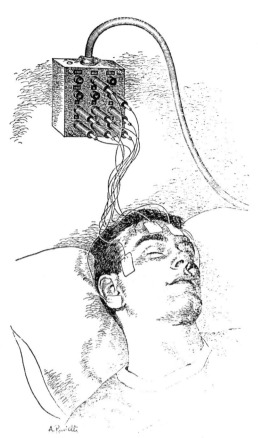

A.Ruselli

Figure 14.2. *A subject in a sleep experiment. Electrodes are tiny metal discs which lie flat over various areas of the face and scalp and which are held in place either by elastic bandages or by collodion-impregnated gauze pads. Wires lead from each electrode disc to a receptacle in a "terminal box" at the head of the subject's bed. From this box a cable runs to an adjacent room where the electroencephalograph produces a write-out of the subject's brain waves and eye movements. (From Foulkes, 1966. Reprinted by permission of Charles Scribner's Sons from* The Psychology of Sleep *by David Foulkes. Copyright © 1966 David Foulkes.)*

of the cerebral cortex, each firing electrical pulses from time to time. Beneath the cortex lie various subcortical neural structures (e.g., the thalamus) which also generate electric pulses. It is the sum of all of this electrical activity that is conducted through bone and tissue and with the aid of an electron-conducting jelly, transmitted to a scalp electrode.

Sometimes, especially during wakefulness, the electric activity appears to be quite different from one electrode site to the next. Each electrode, and therefore, each EEG "channel," shows a different graph, usually of relatively low voltage (less than 50 microvolts) fast

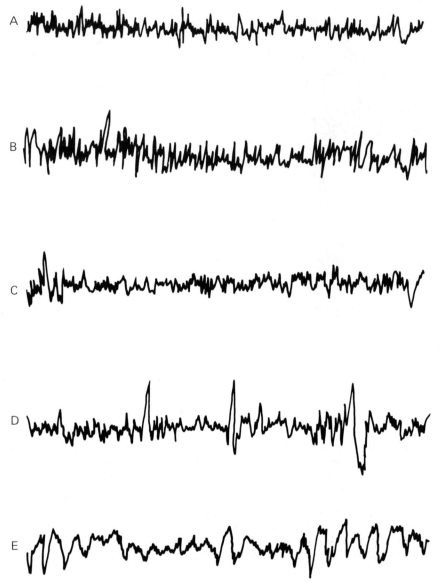

Figure 14.3. *Some examples of waking and sleeping EEG: A. Waking EEG, mostly Beta; B. Waking EEG, mostly Alpha, 8-12 Hz.; C. Sleeping-Stage 1 REM; D. Sleeping-Stage 2; E. Sleeping-Stage 4.*

random activity (see Fig. 14.3A). During certain conditions and states, however, the whole brain seems to pulse synchronously in rhythm. This synchronous EEG activity appears to originate in subcortical structures such as the thalamus. One of these synchronous wave forms, EEG alpha (8–12 cycles/sec, see Fig. 14.3B), has become famous for its association with states of meditation, but it also occurs during drowsiness and when one closes his eyes when wide awake. It generally disappears as one falls asleep.

Aside from EEG alpha, the waking EEG had failed to reveal any changes or stages in the waking state even across large variations in attention, excitement, anger, etc. Since sleep appeared to be a relatively uneventful, unchanging state it was naturally assumed that the sleep EEG would be pretty much the same from one part of the night to the next. However, when Aserinsky and Kleitman first recorded the EEG for an entire 8-hour night they came up with an unexpected phenomenon—a regular cyclic pattern. The brainwaves alternated between periods of predominantly slow (1–2 cycles/sec), high voltage EEG (100–200 microvolts) on the one hand, and fast or mixed frequency (6–30 cycles/sec), low to moderate voltage (5–50 microvolts) EEG on the other (Fig. 14.3C). This latter type of EEG activity was almost indistinguishable from the waking EEG. Yet the subject was sound asleep. Furthermore, this relatively fast, low voltage activity often was associated with rapid eye movements (REM). It got designated, therefore, Stage 1 REM. The remaining stages (Stages 1-without REMs, 2, 3, and 4) of sleep generally are called NonREM (NREM) sleep (see Fig. 14.3D and E). How did eye movements get mixed up with the EEG? Initially, eye movements were picked up by those electrodes on the forehead around the frontal portion of the cortex. The voltage output of the eye movement is so large compared to the EEG, that one couldn't help but see it, even if his primary interest is the EEG itself. Imagine Aserinsky and Kleitman's surprise when they were studying the EEG of sleeping subjects and found flurries of rapid eye movements cropping up in the EEG record. Subsequently, all sleep researchers deliberately measured eye movements by placing electrodes as close as possible to the eyes (Fig. 14.2). (Aserinsky and Kleitman, 1953).

Once the EEG-REM cycle had been established, it was assumed that the REM's would be related somehow to the sleeper watching his dreams. The next obvious step was to wake up a sleeper just after his eyes had begun to move and ask him what had been going through his mind. Let me give you an idea just how obvious that hypothesis was. When Judy turned in her dissertation to the recording secretary at Columbia University, the young lady said: "My, it is about dreaming. How interesting! You know, when we were kids at camp we used to watch the girls dream when they were having a nap." "How did you know they were dreaming?" inquired my wife. "Oh, that was simple. We used to wait until they had been asleep for about half an hour and then we'd go over and we could see their eyes moving under their lids and we knew they were dreaming." Here is the identical hypothesis—generated by an adolescent girl at camp. The girls could see the movements of the eyes without the benefit of 10 thousand dollars worth of sensitive electronic recordings. All they failed to do was to make the systematic awakenings and recordings of the sleeper's reports and publish in a scientific journal. I might add that Ladd, the first president of the American Psychological Association, made the identical observation in 1892, again without the benefit of EEG recordings, which didn't exist at that date. He suggested that the eye movements might be related to dreaming. However, nothing came of his suggestion at the time.

Because of the heavy hand of radical behaviorism in the early fifties, research psychologists rarely asked their subjects what was going through their minds. And so it was left to three physiologists to make the incredible discovery that when awakened from Stage 1 REM sleep, 80 percent of the time sleepers reported dreaming. When awakened from NREM sleep, sleepers reported dreaming only 20 percent of the time. These findings suggested that Kleitman and his colleagues had apparently located the biologic markers for that part of the stream of consciousness we call dreaming (Dement and Kleitman, 1957b).

Listening to Dement's description of this dramatic discovery, Judy resolved then and there that she would do her PhD thesis in this area. Immediately after his talk, she inquired how she might go about learning to operate the equipment and where facilities would be available to run an experiment. Dement, however, had already spent too many nights teaching enthusiastic would-be sleep researchers how to run the EEG, only to find their enthusiasm wither in the face of excruciating demands of successive 10 hour all-night work sessions. Somewhat skeptically, he challenged her, "You learn how to run the equipment first, then come and see me." Two weeks later, after learning the basic elements of electroencephalography from a friendly neurologist, Judy came back to Dement with me as a subject. He taught her some of the special techniques for recording sleeping subjects, such as affixing electrodes on the ear lobes and on the scalp so that they would stay on even through a long night of tossing and turning. From there, off we went to the lab in the basement of Mt. Sinai Hospital in midtown Manhattan. Everything went smoothly. I fell asleep immediately. But sitting in the lonely basement of a vast empty research wing of the hospital and watching my EEG being written out by eight pens, hour after hour, Judy finally gave up and crawled into bed with me at about 4 in the morning. And so began my romance with sleep research.

The soaring euphoria that was shared by the dozen or so active researchers in this continent and in Europe during these early years matches the passions of an intense love affair. Each time one of us made a new finding, no matter how small, we immediately mailed the results to every other investigator in the field, both domestic and foreign. We were a small, intensely loyal family. The fact that we did all our work at night, while the rest of the city slept, added to the sense of mystery surrounding our "secret" society. Above all, we had the strongest physiological handle on mental experience ever known to man. There are few behavioral variables in psychology that exhibit an association which even approaches the strength of the relationship between Stage 1 REM sleep (a physiological variable) and dreaming (a reported mental experience). So encouraging was this high degree of association that many of us hoped that, if we could make our measures a little more precise, we might even push the strength of the association up to 100 percent. There is a certain arbitrariness in all initial delineations of experimental variables, and our definitions of dreaming, Stage 1 REM and NREM sleep were no exception to this rule. Thus it seemed reasonable that we could sharpen the distinction between Stages 1 REM and NREM by redefining as Stage 1 REM sleep those parts of the NREM sleep which yielded dreaming reports. Similarly, certain parts of Stage 1 REM which yielded reports of no dreaming might be redefined as NREM sleep. Moreover, since some dreams were considerably more "dreamlike" than others, careful sharpening of the definition of a dream, or more precise scaling of the magnitude of dreamlike quality, might improve the degree of association with sleep stages reported in the earlier studies.

William Dement was perhaps the strongest advocate of the perfect association model. Perhaps it was his medical background that made him stick to the model for so long. If a pain in the lower right abdomen indicates appendicitis for one patient, it indicates appendicitis for all. Why should it be any different for dreaming and Stage 1 REM sleep?

For a variety of reasons, I expected a lot of ambiguity ("slop," in our jargon), in the process of recalling and describing or reporting the sleep experience. I would expect additional slop in definition of "dreaminess" and in the judgment of how much "dreaminess" is required to make a dream. After all, familiar states such as anxiety and attention are so ambiguously defined as to be practically useless. Why should dreaming—a sleep state—be any better? Further, I expected some persons to report a dream only rarely, while others might have dreamlike experiences throughout the night. These are but a few of the factors which I expected would set a ceiling on the magnitude of the association between dreaming and sleep stages 1 REM vs. NREM. But Dement already had demonstrated that the ceiling was pretty high even with all of these potential and actual sources of measurement error. I had some good ideas about how to reduce the size of many of these sources of error. So I felt that the ceiling must be higher than existing data implied. How much higher, I didn't know, but I set out to find out.

One of the hypotheses Dement proposed was that the dreams reported from NREM sleep were actually remembered from a previous Stage 1 REM period. Regarding the failure to report dreams in approximately 20 percent of the Stage 1 REM awakenings, he proposed that the subjects simply forgot the dream during the process of waking up. The normal person spends 20–25 percent of his sleep (approximately 2 hours a night) in the Stage 1 REM; yet upon awakening in the morning rarely can he recall more than a few fragments of a dream. The massive forgetting of one's dreams was now a well documented rule rather than the exception. Each investigator bit off a different piece of this problem. Don Goodenough at Brooklyn College showed that the percentage of dream reporting in NREM sleep was the same regardless of whether the NREM period had been preceded by a Stage 1 REM period or by wakefulness. That finding effectively laid to rest the hypothesis that NREM dreams were recalled from a previous Stage 1 REM period (Goodenough, et al., 1959).

As you may know, some people say that they dream almost every night, while others insist that they never have had a dream. Judy felt that a careful comparison of the EEG sleep record of these recallers and nonrecallers might give us some clue about how dreams are remembered. Do nonrecallers, for example, spend less than the normal 20 percent of the night in the Stage 1 REM sleep, from which dreams are typically reported? The question was simple and straightforward. The answer required a year of persistent, meticulous hard work, and exhausting strain. The work shift of the sleep researcher generally runs about 10 hours, beginning an hour before the subject's normal sleep time, during which the experimenter must check out the equipment, attach the electrodes to the subject, and put the subject to bed. The shift ends about an hour after the subject has arisen. It is not very difficult to stay up until 1, 2, 3, or even 4 A.M. But to work for 10 hours through the night without a break, constantly monitoring eight wiggling lines that describe the brain activity of the sleeper, tell you whether any electrodes have been pulled off, and whether the equipment is operating properly, is a very demanding task, especially in the dead hours of 5 and 6 in the morning. Then, by the time you have closed the lab and are ready to go home, your body's clock has prepared you for the next day's round of activity. Your body is simply not ready for sleep. You feel worn out, but edgy. Consequently, sleeping in the day time is never a refreshing experience to say the least. I often remember Judy waking up at 7 o'clock in the evening crying from exhaustion as she prepared to go to work while her biological clock was preparing her for sleep.

Once in the lab, things generally went very smoothly, that is, except for a plugged drain in the biologists' lab on the fourth floor. About 4 o'clock one morning, water began to drip through the ceiling. At first it began to drip on a 5 foot stack of EEG records from an earlier sleep study. We found some sterilizing pans and quickly covered the records. Next the water began to trickle around the EEG machine, then on us and finally it began to seep through into the subject's room. We put pots and beakers from the neighboring labs all over the floor, but of course they made so much noise we were afraid the subject would waken. If the subject awakened we would have to throw out the entire night's worth of data, a thought which was absolutely too painful to bear. So we then covered the pots with hospital blankets. What a sight! Then we called the buildings and maintenance staff who arrived about an hour later with a half dozen clanging metal buckets, a tank on wheels, and mops. We nearly chloroformed them on the spot. Unfortunately, there wasn't much that they could do with 3 inches of water across the entire fourth floor of the building, 2 inches on the third floor, and 1 inch on the first floor. It would be hours before the last trickle to our basement in the laboratory would cease.

By the end of the year Judy had run all the subjects and measured the number of minutes of Stage 1 REM sleep in each EEG record. She found that recallers of dreams do indeed have more Stage 1 REM sleep than nonrecallers, but that the difference was of the order of 5 percent, not nearly enough for the very large differences in actual morning recall (Antrobus, Dement, and Fisher, 1964).

So great was our preoccupation with sleep and dreaming that we talked about nothing else. If one of us fell asleep before the other, we would often watch the other person's sleep or see if we could influence it in some way that had not been tried before. One night, for example, I woke up while Judy's fingers were moving back and forth rapidly in her sleep. I put the tips of my fingers against the tips of hers to provide some opposing force to her motion. I waited approximately 30 seconds and then I awakened her. She described playing a portion of a Schubert sonata on the piano, a portion which would have lasted approximately 30 seconds, if actually played. She recalled no experience that would correspond to the period before my fingers were placed against hers. I've often been sorry that we never followed the idea up with systematic experimentation. Wolpert spent several years studying the relationship between fine muscle movements, the electrical activity of muscle groups, and a dream content, but found only occasional instances of association (Wolpert, 1960). Stoyva found no more fine finger movements in deaf subjects who use sign language than in a control group (Stoyva, 1965).

As I've already indicated, there were a number of difficulties involved in getting an accurate report of the subject's sleeping experience. Some subjects simply talked a lot more than others. Some subjects knew that something had been going through their minds but they couldn't remember it. Some subjects took much longer to awaken than others, so that one never knew whether they were reporting what had been going through their minds during the 10–20 secs it took them to awaken or whether they were reporting what had happened while they were sleeping. How nice it would be if we could bypass the verbal report altogether and see what was going on inside of the subject's mind. But that would require magic. What other alternatives might there be? Could the subject report his experience without awakening? How about sleep talking?

Arthur Arkin, a friend and collaborator in several sleep studies, has devoted a great amount of effort to answering this question. He came to one of the first sleep conventions, in the mid-1960s, and asked Judy if she would teach him to identify the sleep stages from the sleep EEG record. Arkin, now an authority on sleep talking, will tell you that nearly all sleep talking occurs during NREM sleep. Also, there are a few people who sleep talk with sufficient frequency to yield many reports in a given night. But it is too costly to run a subject for an entire night simply to obtain one or two fragments of speech. Further, there is some evidence to suggest that a sleeper's speech may be a *response* to what is happening in the dream, but *describes* very little about it. For example, the sleeper may watch somebody about to be run over by a car and call out from his sleep "Watch out!" However, the words "watch out" by themselves provide little information about the actual scene the sleeper was observing. So even a highly verbal talker cannot give us a complete description of what is going on within his mind. Nevertheless, the last word is not yet in. In a 4-year experiment just completed, Arkin and Jorge Farber, a graduate student, found that disrupting the sleep of a nonsleep-talker can produce a sizeable amount of sleep talking. In yet another experiment, he found that sleep talking tends to accompany dreams that have conversation in them.

We decided that we could give up the possibility of getting a verbal report of the sleep experience if we could develop some other procedure for indicating whether or not the subject was dreaming. In other words, could we find a way of teaching subjects to signal us as to the occurrence of a dream without our having to wake them? Extensive research during World War II and in the early 1950s had seemed to demonstrate that such learning was impossible, at least with techniques with which we were currently familiar.

One morning over breakfast at one of the first sleep conferences, I learned from a member of a research team at Walter Reed Hospital in Washington, D. C., that they had had considerable success in teaching subjects to make a motor response continuously almost throughout the entire night. The technique they used was a Skinnerian avoidance conditioning procedure. Subjects were punished with a loud noise if they failed to press a manual switch within a given time interval. Of course, everyone learns to turn over in bed at night without falling out of bed. One also learns to keep the blankets on, in order to avoid getting cold. But this was the first successful experimental training of a motor response during sleep. I think it was probably this experiment that suggested the possibility that we might be able to train subjects to make a motor response while asleep which would indicate whether they were dreaming or not dreaming.

The problem we faced in using this technique was that we could not use an avoidance procedure, because there was no way for us to know whether the subject was or was not dreaming, as we couldn't see inside the subject's head. But we felt it was worth a try even without the avoidance procedure. First, I built a tiny microswitch that could be taped to the side of the index finger and operated by the thumb with the slightest amount of pressure. Judy found four young women who were high recallers of dreams and she motivated them to carry out the experimental procedure. The procedure, for half the group, was to press the microswitch five times if they were dreaming and twice if they were not, and to do this without waking up. The other half of the group was instructed to press the switch twice if they were dreaming and five times if they were not dreaming. Each woman was run for four nights. It was a very difficult and discouraging task for some of those subjects. After wanting so badly to carry out the procedure, several of the subjects wakened in the morning having pressed the switch only once during the entire night. One woman was flabbergasted to find she had not pressed the switch once. She had been dreaming all night of sending smoke signals. In order for our technique to be as good or better than the verbal report technique, subjects would have to make a number of "dreaming" switch presses during Stage 1 REM sleep and "not dreaming" presses during NREM sleep, with few presses occurring in the other two classes (i.e., "dreaming"-NREM sleep and "not dreaming"-Stage 1 REM sleep). The final results showed that most of the switch pressing occurred during Stage 1 REM sleep and most of the presses signaled that the subject was dreaming. You could imagine our surprise upon presenting the results at the next sleep conference, when Charles Tart, then a graduate student in Hilgard's laboratory at Stanford University, told us that he had just performed a similar experiment using hypnosis and obtained pretty much the same results. We both concluded that hypnosis was not a necessary part of the procedure (Antrobus, Antrobus, and Fisher, 1965).

It was about this time that Dement accepted a professorship at Stanford University and Judy inherited his "dream" lab. It was a dream lab in more ways than one, for it was built into a large luxury apartment, overlooking the Hudson River in Manhattan. This arrangement allowed her the maximum flexibility in the distribution of her time between research, administration, and family life. Sometimes it was hard to tell where the laboratory left off and our private apartment began— the living room often was used as a classroom for students and faculty wishing to learn about sleep research, and our kitchen became a cafeteria for just about everyone's subjects and research assistants.

I should add at this point that the experiments which I am describing in this chapter constitute only a small portion of the experiments we were actually carrying out then. For example, Judy became pregnant at this time, and as there were no studies in the literature which showed the effect of human pregnancy with its attendant shifts in hormone balance and the massive sleep disturbance of the latter parts of pregnancy upon the distribution of sleep stages, we ran her in the laboratory once every weekend throughout her pregnancy. We lived to regret the many parties and concerts that we gave up in order to maintain a regular schedule of recording sessions. Immediately after the birth of our first child, we were altogether too distracted to run the postpregnancy control sessions. When we did finally get around to it, we discovered that Judy was pregnant again. I might add that both pregnancies were notable achievements in the annals of sleep research for most of the married sleep researchers at this time were giving up either their night work or their spouses.

It was a happy series of accidents that led us to leave our new-born daughter, Natalia, with relatives in Berkeley while we went on to the next sleep conference at Stanford University. At the end of the conference, Joe Kamiya, now well known as the discoverer of alpha conditioning and a leader in the field of biofeedback research, offered to drive us back from Stanford University to Berkeley. It was during this drive that Joe described his first experiment in alpha conditioning. For the reader who is not familiar with Kamiya's alpha conditioning research, a brief description follows. Alpha, as you recall (see Fig. 14.3), is the name given to a very regular sinusoidal EEG wave of 8–12 hertz (cycles per sec). The alpha waves start at the back of the head over the occipital portion of the cortex and generally move forward toward the frontal regions of the cortex, at times, until the whole surface of the cortex is resonating in the alpha frequency. For most people these alpha waves appear simply by closing one's eyes and disappear when the eyes are open. Alpha waves are common when one is drifting into sleep, but as the sleep deepens, alpha waves tend to diminish. Much of the time alpha waves are mixed with other EEG waves. Therefore, Kamiya and other experimenters studying alpha waves generally use an electronic "filter" which allows through only those EEG waves in the alpha range (8–12 hertz). Kamiya had an automatic timing device which rang a bell every few seconds. When the bell rang, the subject was to say "Yes" or "No." If the EEG machine showed Kamiya that the subject was in an alpha state and the subject, who couldn't see the EEG machine, said "Yes," Kamiya rewarded or reinforced the subject with the word "Correct." If the EEG showed no alpha and the subject said "Yes," Kamiya said "Wrong." Similarly, if the EEG showed no alpha and the subject said, "No," Kamiya said "Correct." And if the EEG showed no alpha and the subject said, "Yes," Kamiya said "Wrong." In this experimental procedure subjects were able to learn to discriminate correctly whether or not they were in the alpha state almost 100 percent of the time (Kamiya, 1962).

The experiment was sufficiently radical that Kamiya's original paper was rejected for publication in the *Journal of Experimental Psychology*. This so discouraged him that he didn't try to get the article into print for almost 10 years. In the meanwhile his fascinating findings were passed around by word of mouth among a smaller group of experimenters. On the drive back from Stanford, the three of us discussed everything from the philosophy of science to the biology of private events. By the time we arrived at Berkeley, Judy and I had designed our next experiment. We would essentially transfer Kamiya's alpha conditioning experiment to Stage 1 REM/NREM sleep. We decided simply to awaken subjects approximately eight times a night, four of the awakenings from REM sleep and four from NREM. Since research on Stage 1 REM and NREM sleep was beginning to hit the popular press at this point, we resolved to make no mention of these technical terms to the subjects. We told the subjects that we wanted to train them to distinguish two types of sleep, type "A" (Stage 1 REM) and type "B" (Stage 2). If we awakened the subject from Stage 1 REM sleep and he said "A," we said "Correct, you may go back to sleep." If he said "B," we said "incorrect."

Our first subject was a young nurse, who remained highly motivated throughout the project. Judy ran her a total of 30 nights, spread over a period of 2 months. The subject was using this "extra" money to finance a vacation back to her home in the Philippine Islands. At the end of each session, she and Judy would calculate how far across the Pacific she had been able to travel with the subject money. When she finally returned from the trip, she brought Judy a dress and me a shirt from her home country. By the end of her 30 sessions in the lab, this young woman had moved from an accuracy of just chance, or 50 percent, to almost 100 percent. Had it not been for her scheduled trip, we might have been able to push her all the way to the top. The next subject, unfortunately, was not able to do as well. She frequently became discouraged and finally dropped out of the project. She seemed less able to articulate her private experience and every time she had a night with a poor record she would say, "I must really sit down now and use the scientific method in order to improve my performance." That's just not the way to learn to discriminate two biological states. The third and last subject started out fairly well and then caught a very bad cold. Despite earlier instructions never to use any drugs, she subsequently admitted that she was taking antihistamines for the cold and was therefore dropped from the study. At this point Judy was in the ninth month of her second pregnancy and shortly thereafter lost the financial support necessary to continue this experiment. The experiment remained a demonstration of a technique which seems to show that REM and NREM sleep could be clearly distinguished, at least by some subjects, without the subject ever once using the word "dream."

You may wonder what the subjects experienced privately as they tried to discriminate the two stages of sleep. Here are some of their comments. "I am almost positive that if you have a good sound dream, no matter how agitating it is, it is type A sleep. . . . The sounder . . . deeper . . . more relaxed . . . sleep is type A and the restless sleep is type B." "You are having type A sleep when you have a vivid dream . . . very clear . . . like a motion picture with a lot of action." "I am not sure if you can call the . . . vague . . . dreams you have in type B sleep 'dreams,' since you are on the verge of waking, they might just be things you are drowsily thinking about." ". . . not just dreaming, but actually being part of the dream, and B was not actually dreaming." "A is deeper sleep, one in which I am probably dreaming. B is lighter sleep. I have often felt as if I were awake when I was called and the answer was B." These comments suggest that the distinction between the Stage 1 REM vs. NREM experience is more complicated than a simple dreaming/not-dreaming dichotomy.

While we were in the middle of analyzing these data, Monroe, Rechtschaffen, Foulkes and Jensen in Chicago published a paper in which two judges were asked to discriminate between Stage 1 REM and NREM reports (Monroe et al., 1965). Unlike our subjects, their judges were discriminating among the typewritten reports obtained from other subjects so that the only information they had was verbal. Moreover, unlike the naive subjects in our experiments, Monroe's judges had considerable experience with Stage 1 REM and NREM reports. One judge, in fact, was highly trained. Presumably, the training would be analogous to hundreds of trials in the experiment which we had just completed. The most notable part of the Monroe experiment was the condition in which judges were given a large number of pairs of reports. Both members of each pair came from the same subject and approximately the same time of night. The judge had to tell which of the pair came from Stage 1 REM sleep. In this condition his judges averaged about 90 percent accuracy, approximately the same as the best subject in our experiment. Although the two experiments differed in a number of respects, it seems reasonably clear that when subjects were able to use all private cues available to them as in our experiment, they could distinguish Stage 1 REM from NREM sleep as well as, but not better than, the judges who had only the verbal reports of the subjects available to them.

Both experiments were carried out to see how well Stages 1 REM and NREM sleep mentation could be discriminated without basing the discrimination on the term dreaming. If people could make a nearly perfect discrimination of the two sleep states using any and all possible features of sleep mentation, we would then conclude that dreaming tells only part of the story. We might say that dreaming provides a good approximation to the distinction between Stages 1 REM and NREM, but additional features must also be considered. The high accuracy of Monroe's judges suggest that this is the case. Monroe and his coauthors do not explicitly test this idea, however. After a detour of several years into some other sleep research issues, now I am returning to this problem with the aid of sophisticated statistical models. Hopefully, the results of this research will soon be available to those whose curiosity about dream research has been aroused by this brief account of our work.

REFERENCES

Antrobus, J. S.; Antrobus, J.; and Fisher, C. 1965. Discrimination of dreaming and nondreaming sleep. *Archives of General Psychiatry*, 12:395–401.

Antrobus, J. S.; Dement, W. C.; and Fisher, C. 1964. Patterns of dreaming and dream recall: EEG study. *Journal of Abnormal Psychology*, 69:341.

Arkin, A. M.; Farber, J.; Antrobus, J. S.; Ellman, S. J.; and Nelson, W. T. 1973. The effects of repeated sleep interruption and elicited verbalization on sleep speech frequency of chronic sleep-talkers: Preliminary observations. *Sleep Research*, 2:105.

Aserinsky, E. and Kleitman, N. 1953. Regularly occurring periods of eye motility and concomitant phenomena during sleep. *Science*, 118:273–274.

Dement, W. C. and Kleitman N. 1957a. Cyclic variations in EEG during sleep and their relation to eye movements, body motility and dreaming. *Electroencephalography and Clinical Neurophysiology*, 9:673–690.

Dement, W. C. and Kleitman, N. 1957b. The relation of eye movements during sleep to dream activity: An objective method for the study of dreaming. *Journal of Experimental Psychology*, 53:339–346.

Foulkes, D. 1966. *The Psychology of Sleep.* New York: Charles Scribner's Sons.

Goodenough, D. R.; Shapiro, A.; Holden, M.; and Steinschreiber, L. A. 1959. A comparison of "dreamers" and "non-dreamers": Eye movements, electroencephalograms and the recall of dreams. *Journal of Abnormal and Social Psychology*, 59:295–302.

Kamiya, J. 1962. Conditioned discrimination of the EEG Alpha rhythm in humans. Paper delivered at the Western Psychological Association Convention.

Monroe, L. J.; Rechtschaffen, A.; Foulkes, D.; and Jensen, J. 1965. Discriminability of REM and NREM reports. *Journal of Personality and Social Psychology*, 2:456–460.

Stoyva, J. M. 1965. Finger electromyographic activity during sleep: Its relation to dreaming in deaf and normal subjects. *Journal of Abnormal Psychology*, 53:339–346.

Wolpert, E. A. 1960. Studies in the psychophysiology of dreams. II. An electromyographic study of dreaming. *Archives of General Psychiatry*, 2:231–241.

INKBLOTS THROUGH THE LOOKING GLASS
Wayne H. Holtzman

"I have answered three questions, and that is enough. . . ."
ALICE'S ADVENTURES IN WONDERLAND

Inkblots are nothing but meaningless blobs of ink splattered on paper. Yet, like clouds and rock formations, inkblots have stirred the imagination of dreamers for centuries. What better mirror of the unconscious than to ask a person to tell you what he sees as he gazes into a complex but "meaningless" stimulus? Surely what comes out must be generated within the person's mind rather than in the realities around him. Even Leonardo da Vinci saw the advantages of using inkblots to study the imagination of artists, poets, and others. But it is only in recent years that serious attention has been given to the study of personality through projective techniques such as inkblots.

The experimental period began with Alfred Binet in 1895. Binet thought of inkblots as a test of imagination for the study of individual differences in intelligence. Three decades later, in 1917, Hermann Rorschach started his famous work. Rorschach, working with mental patients in Switzerland, developed a system of analysis for inkblots which, in its broad outlines, still stands today. While not completely ignoring the content of a person's response to inkblots, Rorschach emphasized the formal aspects of the performance. He stressed the importance of analyzing a person's mode of perception—whether the inkblot was interpreted as a whole or in part; whether the form, color, or shading of the inkblot was primarily responsible for evoking the response; and whether the person reported a static lifeless percept or one imbued with life and action (Rorschach, 1921).

Rorschach had been fascinated by inkblots and other ambiguous art forms since early childhood when he played *Klecksography*, a Swiss game common at the turn of the century. In this game inkblots were made to resemble fanciful things by placing ink on paper and folding it to achieve symmetrical forms. In a fascinating biography of Rorschach, the psychoanalyst Henri Ellenberger analyzed both con-

Wayne H. Holtzman is on the faculty of the Department of Psychology, The University of Texas at Austin.

scious and unconscious aspects of Rorschach's personality and life experiences as they seemed related to his significant, original work on personality theory and inkblot perception (Ellenberger, 1954). Rorschach was primarily trained as a psychiatrist and worked in a relatively isolated mental hospital. Although he never obtained an academic appointment, he longed to be a scientist and completed his advanced medical training and doctoral thesis with high honors. Rorschach died in 1922 at the early age of 37, leaving much of the development of inkblot testing to others. The ten inkblots constituting the Rorschach Test are the same today as they were 50 years ago.

As a young graduate student in psychology, my own fascination with inkblots stemmed from an interest in the unconscious and in the ways in which deeper aspects of one's personality might be expressed. Until World War II, the mainstream of academic psychology looked askance at the Rorschach movement, criticizing its cultist character and lack of scientific discipline. This schism between Rorschach workers and academic psychology grew out of the two completely different traditions that characterized scientific psychology and clinical practice in America and Europe. The academicians were chiefly concerned with the development of general laws to explain sensation, perception, learning, and motivation. Clinicians working with the Rorschach and other psychoanalytically based techniques were mainly interested in a deeper understanding of individual personality. Working outside of academically respectable circles, the Rorschach practitioners developed their own ideas and interpretative systems relying chiefly on intuitive insights and clinical confirmation rather than on hard scientific evidence. However, World War II changed all this with the sudden, urgent need for new devices for psychiatric screening and personality assessment in the armed services. By 1945, the Rorschach technique was firmly established as the leading clinical instrument for psychodiagnosis, a position it holds in some circles till this day.

Like many graduate students in search of an interesting idea on the frontiers of psychology, I seized upon the Rorschach technique as a diagnostic instrument badly in need of scientific evaluation, employing the latest methods of experimentation and control. The outcome of this early activity was a dissertation demonstrating that such personality traits as impulsivity and personal adjustment, based upon peer-group ratings of college students living together, could be predicted by the way in which a person responded to inkblots when asked to tell what he or she saw in them. Overreaction to the color of the inkblots was related to lack of control in social situations. A large number of "clinical signs" that had grown out of earlier experience with the Rorschach proved to be correlated with the degree of personal maladjustment, unhappiness and anxiety of the people in the study.

Spurred on by these positive though modest findings that confirmed some of the earlier clinical hunches about the meaning of inkblot responses, I joined a host of other young investigators interested
in experimental studies with inkblots. Countless studies by graduate
students soon piled up a wave of criticism from which the Rorschach
movement has never fully recovered. While much of this research was
either irrelevant or badly conceived, a growing number of carefully
designed validity studies yielded negative results.

My own enthusiasm was badly shaken by the utter failure of
prominent clinicians, using various projective techniques, including the
Rorschach, to predict which Air Force pilots later became psychiatric
casualties and which pilots performed effectively. After 3 years of hard
work on this Air Force project, we concluded that using psychological
tests to predict personality maladjustment under stress in otherwise
"normal" individuals was too difficult a task. Some researchers interpreted these negative findings as the ultimate in damning evidence
of the "nonsense" sometimes published in the name of projective
techniques and the Rorschach.

Among the most critical attacks upon the Rorschach during this
period was a paper by Zubin (1954) delivered in a symposium, spon-
sored by the Society for Projective Techniques, on failures of the
Rorschach. Zubin strongly criticized the standard Rorschach method
for the lack of an objective scoring system which would be free of
arbitrary conventions and show high interscorer agreement. He challenged current advocates of the Rorschach to provide scientifically
valid evidence of its worthiness for personality assessment and psychodiagnosis. While Zubin may have purposely exaggerated the failures
in order to dramatize the problem, his criticisms and similar attacks
from other scientists had a telling effect upon the attention given the
Rorschach by leading research workers after the mid-fifties.

For many of us, despite these negative findings with the Rorschach, the fundamental ideas underlying the technique were still intuitively attractive and could not easily be set aside. For anyone who
has worked with inkblots or other visual projective materials that are
ambiguously interpreted, it is impossible to deny that an individual
must reveal something about himself, his imagination, his way of organizing percepts in the world around him, and his personality by what
he sees and how he reports his perceptions in a standardized test
situation. If only one could find the key to interpretation of such pro-
ductions, one could learn things about the individual of which he himself is unaware.

One approach views the rich amorphous nature of inkblots as a
mirror of the unconscious in which an individual projects his innermost
fantasies, images, and desires as he tells a psychologist what he sees
in the inkblot and what makes it look like that to him. When viewed
in this way, as a structured depth-interview, the Rorschach can be

analyzed in a purely qualitative manner, stressing the dynamic, symbolic nature of the content, and interpreting the examiner-subject relationship from a strictly phenomenological point of view. This is a useful characteristic of the Rorschach because it is difficult to elicit anything comparable to free associations in a typical interview setting. By providing an "objective" but ambiguous stimulus to the subject, and asking him to associate to it, we can facilitate the flow of material. Furthermore, because the stimulus is ambiguous, we are less likely to elicit the kinds of defensiveness one encounters when a subject is asked a series of questions whose implicit aims are obvious from their phrasing or content.

Associations to inkblots are seen, then, as only one step removed from completely free association in a psychoanalytic session. The skilled clinician listens with his "third ear" carefully tuned to the subtle nuances of the subjects' behavior, mode of expression, and fantasies. From a detailed analysis of such products he infers about the person many things which comprise a personality interpretation when viewed in the context of other relevant information. However, this depth approach leaves little room for scientific scrutiny, since few of the inferences are stated in a form testable by behavioral observations or independent confirmation. Indeed, it can even be argued that elaborate, clinical interpretations of personality from projective protocols often reveal more about the personality of the clinician than about that of the subject.

Quite a different approach is to consider the Rorschach as a psychometric device that yields scores or objective signs which can be examined for their potential value in the assessment of personality. In contrast to a projective technique, a psychometric test is based upon the fundamental assumption that a score obtained on the test reflects a hypothetical "true" score. This "true" score is characteristic of the attribute in question for a given individual, under specified testing conditions at a given moment in time. It is assumed that any deviation of the obtained score from the "true" score represents error of measurement which can be assessed—provided one is willing to make certain assumptions about the nature of such errors. The use of psychometric theory as a basis for assessment of personality also commits one to a trait theory of personality. It is not necessary, however, to think that possession of the trait must be a "fixed" quantity. An individual's "true" score remains invariant only so long as a specific testing condition remains constant and there is no real change in the individual with respect to the trait in question. As soon as one decides to classify and enumerate any characteristics of a person's responses to inkblots, however crude and elementary the system may be, a psychometric frame of reference has been adopted. For example, to classify a given response to an inkblot as a W (whole), meaning that the person used the entire inkblot for his percept, is to assign meaning to the response that transcends the person's idiosyncratic private world and makes it possible to compare him with other individuals who are likewise classified as to inkblot responses. Such symbols of classification can be considered "signs" depicting specified characteristics abstracted from the raw response protocol. In most instances when a series of responses is classified, some types of response will appear more than once. Counting such response frequencies is the first step in the construction of a quantitative scoring system.

Let's take a closer look at how these ideas apply to the Rorschach. The subject is given in 10 inkblots, one at a time, and asked to tell what he sees in them. After he has responded to all 10 plates in what is called the performance phase of the technique, the examiner goes over each response, asking indirect questions about where the percept is in the blot, and what features of the blot make it look that way. All the time, the examiner is busily writing down everything the subject says in order to have an accurate accounting of his free associations. The second phase, inquiry, is designed to provide information useful in scoring the responses. The complex nature of the inkblot permits a wide latitude of location, ranging from small details to the entire blot, and including figure-ground reversals where the white space becomes the figure and the inkblot becomes the background. The use of color, the use of shading, and the imparting of movement to the percept (such as "two people dancing together") are thought of as the determinants of the response. Finally, the conceptual content itself can be categorized as to human, animal, anatomy, explosion, fire, etc. When, by use of vague and indirect questions, a subject is asked to introspect and report to the examiner what the blot suggests, the response often will be "It just looks like it to me"—leaving the examiner about where he started. Even if the subject says that color is playing a part in the concept, do we have any way of knowing, for example in explaining his response, "a bloody thumb," whether the subject would have reported "blood" in the absence of color? How do we know it wasn't the combination of form and shading that suggested a bloody thumb?

Introducing a much more exhaustive inquiry than the usual brief, indirect questioning is one way in which several investigators have tried to overcome this problematic use of determinants. Zubin, for example, developed a system in which inquiry immediately followed the response to each plate presented, rather than having the response follow the showing of all 10 plates. Sixty scales were constructed that could be applied in scoring a single response, provided the inquiry was sufficiently exhaustive. Remember that Rorschach records frequently contain more than 50 responses; thus, the amount of energy invested in the scoring of 60 scales on each response is tremendous. Zubin's system is completely impractical as a standard procedure, yet his exhaustive approach points out the fundamental weaknesses inherent in the standard methods of scoring.

Still another problem in the Rorschach arises from the fact that one person may give 10 or 12 responses to a given card, while giving only one or two responses to the remaining 9, yielding a total of 20–30 responses for the entire set of 10 inkblots. Another individual might give the same number of responses, but spread them evenly over the entire set of inkblots (e.g., two responses to each inkblot). Any of the usual scores will mean something quite different in the two contrasting protocols, even though the total number of responses is constant. Add to this the difficulties arising when the number of responses can vary from less than 10 to over 100, and it is easy to see why most quantitative studies involving the standard Rorschach yield confusing or negative results. Another difficulty with the Rorschach is that the interaction between the examiner and the subject, and variations in style of inquiry used by the examiner, have a profound influence upon the kind and number of responses given. A number of experimental studies have shown that examiner differences can cause disturbing variation in the number of responses and degree of verbosity. When such variation is due to the examiner, the technique cannot be standardized appropriately, nor can meaningful norms be derived from different groups of subjects.

While these serious methodological weaknesses in the standard Rorschach discouraged most experimentally oriented psychologists from further work with the method, it was becoming increasingly clear to me that a fresh point of view was needed urgently. It was apparent that the major limitations in the Rorschach could best be overcome by developing a completely new technique using more inkblots with simplified procedures for administration. How could one develop psychometrically sound scoring procedures for responses to inkblots while also preserving the rich qualitative projective material of the Rorschach? Several clues to the solution of this problem were provided by research completed in the period of intense research activity immediately following World War II. Blake and Wilson (1950) had demonstrated that the first response of a person to each inkblot had all the necessary ingredients for the standard Rorschach scoring system. Why not limit the subject to one response per card and increase the number of inkblots? In spite of its cumbersome nature, Zubin's elaborate rating system demonstrated that a number of variables could be scored for a given inkblot response. However, this required that a simple inquiry be conducted immediately after the response, while it was still fresh in the mind of the subject, rather than going back to it at a later time in the inquiry phase of the standard Rorschach.

Seizing these ideas, we conducted some exploratory work on a small number of cases, asking for a single response and following it with a very simple twofold question—where was the percept represented in the blot and what about the blot suggested the percept? It was estimated that a set of 45 inkblots, requiring only one response apiece, would take no longer to administer than a standard Rorschach in which the 30–50 responses given are followed by the second inquiry phase. Special efforts would have to be made, however, to develop new inkblot materials which have high "pulling power" for responses involving small details, space, and color or shading attributes, to compensate for the tendency to give form-determined wholes as the first response to an inkblot.

Twenty years ago, the idea of abandoning the Rorschach for an entirely new approach to inkblot perception and personality was viewed as heresy by many confirmed Rorschachers. After all, several thousand scholarly articles in learned journals and books had been published using the sacrosanct set of 10 plates. Besides, it would take a great deal of time, money, and effort to produce a new set of inkblots that would be that much better than the 10 selected by Rorschach. Unconvinced by either of these arguments, and driven by a determination to solve the problems of the Rorschach, I embarked in 1953 upon a research program that was to continue up to the present. At a time when funds were hard to come by, I managed to get a faculty research fellowship from the Social Science Research Council of New York. This fellowship made it possible for me to devote more than half my time to the project, and provided a small amount of money for initial experimental work. I was also greatly encouraged by conversations with Gardner Murphy at the Menninger Foundation, where exciting new work on perception and personality was already underway.

It was clear to me right from the start that a new inkblot technique of the kind I had in mind would have several distinct advantages over the standard Rorschach. First, the number of responses per individual could be held to a relatively constant value. Second, since each response would be given to an independent stimulus, the resulting protocol would be much more amenable to psychometric treatment. Third, a fresh start in the production of stimulus materials could result in a richer variety of stimuli capable of eliciting far more information than the original 10 Rorschach plates. And fourth, a parallel form of the inkblots could be constructed easily from item analysis data in the experimental phases of development, and adequate estimates of reliability could be obtained independently for each major variable.

One soon learns that there is more to creating good inkblots than merely splattering ink on a piece of paper and folding it over. After preliminary experimentation with many different inks and types of paper, Pelican water-proof drawing ink and Bassingwork paper were found to produce the best results. These inks have high quality control and accurate color specification. They are brilliant, yet sufficiently transparent to permit complex superimposed stimuli, and they work extremely well with Bassingwork paper, a special lithographic paper used in art work. Half a dozen interested graduate students joined me in experimenting with the production of inkblots and with the limited research funds, I also employed an undergraduate art student who quickly led the way.

Most of the inkblots were made by dropping various combinations of ink and water on Bassingwork paper, folding the paper at the mid-line and applying varying degrees of pressure to different areas of the folded paper to achieve the desired result. Quite a different type of inkblot with unusual texture and lack of structure was produced by first rubbing ordinary printer's ink on a sheet of paper and folding the paper to obtain a symmetrical blot as desired, then pressing the paper against a new sheet of paper and rubbing the two together to transfer the blot. Certain unusual blots were made by placing string or a crumpled handkerchief on a linoleum block, putting a sheet of paper on top of the string and then lightly rolling printer's ink over the surface of the paper. In addition, combining several techniques on the same blot sometimes produced highly effective results.

Each member of our research group constructed many hundreds of inkblots. Those inkblots that a researcher thought were sufficiently interesting to examine seriously were set aside for critical screening by the entire group. Our clinical experience with the Rorschach sensitized us to the stimulus properties of color, shading, symmetry, and form that would be most likely to elicit diverse, rich associations useful in qualitative analyses as well as in quantitative ones. Because of the largely subjective nature of this process, discussion and consensus by team members was important. Blots judged by the group were either rejected or placed in one of three piles: "definitely to be tested out," "questionable, but deserving further consideration," and "probably not much good." Blots finally selected were taken from the first two categories and were approved by all members of the research group. Only about one blot in 50 survived this initial screening.

Using our initial estimate of 45 inkblots as being the maximum number for general use in a standardized procedure, three preliminary forms containing 45 inkblots each were constructed. Our intuition concerning "good" and "bad" inkblots had to be tested by administering the untried inkblots to a variety of subjects. Arrangements were made to obtain samples from two populations: undergraduate college students (presumably normal superior adults) and patients in a state mental hospital. The college students were volunteers. The hospital patients were nearly all psychotic but in sufficiently good contact with reality to serve as subjects.

These two groups of subjects were selected because they represent opposite extremes of several broad variables which presumably are reflected in inkblot performance. Obviously, the ability of a set of inkblots to discriminate between two such widely differing populations

Figure 15.1. *A normal response to this inkblot was "A man's head in the fork of a tree." An abnormal (schizophrenic) response was "The yellow voice is freezing downward."*

is no measure of its real value as a new technique, since almost any procedure will differentiate a group of psychotic state hospital patients from bright, young college students. At the same time, however, any inkblots which failed to differentiate these two extreme groups probably would be poor bets to include in any final version of the test (Fig. 15.1).

Four stimulus qualities of inkblots were given special attention—the proportion of the total inkblot used for a response, the use of texture in the blot as a response determinant, the use of color in determining the percept, and the extent to which figure-ground reversals of white space and the inkblot were obtained. Poor blots were those which did not show a range of differences among subjects in the student group on at least one of these determinants.

The scoring system we devised departed somewhat from the

traditional and it required a new conceptual framework. Leaning heavily on the work of Zubin and others who have developed various scoring systems for the Rorschach, several criteria were adopted for inclusion of a variable as part of the scoring system. First, the variable had to be one which could be scored for any legitimate response. Variables which only rarely occurred were set aside for the moment. Second, the variable had to be sufficiently objective to permit high scoring agreement among trained individuals. Third, the variable had to show some *a priori* promise of being pertinent to the study of personality through perception. And fourth, each variable should be logically independent of the others.

Six variables were selected as particularly important in making the final selection of inkblots—location, form appropriateness, color, shading, form definiteness, and movement. These six variables are closely linked to the stimulus attributes of the inkblot and formed the core of Rorschach's original formal system, making it possible to relate the new technique to the old one. Location is a three-point variable for measuring the amount of the blot used and the extent to which the natural gestalt of the inkblot is broken up by the response. For the use of color as a response determinant, a four-point system was adopted, with 0 for completely ignoring color as a determinant and 3 for use of color as a primary determinant. As with color, the scoring of shading was based solely upon the apparent primacy of shading as a determinant. The scoring of movement followed the work of Sells et al. (1952), in which a five-point scale was adopted varying from 0—no movement or potential for movement—through static, casual, and dynamic movement to 4—for violent movements such as whirling or exploding. Form definiteness referred solely to the specificity of the form of the concept represented in the response, disregarding completely the stimulus characteristics of the inkblot. Form appropriateness, the last of the six major variables used in the initial screening of inkblots, is by its very nature a subjective variable. The goodness of fit of the concept to the form of the blot was rated on a three-point scale independently by at least three judges.

Several other aspects of inkblot perception were recorded systematically in the early stages of the research program. Space was scored whenever a subject gave a response indicating a reversal of the usual figure-ground relationship. We hoped to obtain enough inkblots in which figure-ground reversals occurred to develop space as an interesting and reliable variable. While all 10 of the Rorschach inkblots are highly symmetrical, many of ours were deliberately constructed to accentuate asymmetry in the hope that this imbalance would prove disturbing to some people and provide us with another variable, balance. The last variable considered in the selection of inkblots for the final form of the test is called *pathognomic verbalization* (or V). A primary virtue of the Rorschach in the study of personality is the way in which bizarre and disordered thought processes are made manifest. The ability of unstructured, "meaningless" inkblots to draw out such pathology probably is the major factor accounting for the success of the Rorschach in the clinical study of individuals who have mental and emotional disturbances. In our preliminary studies, all indications of disordered thought processes were considered as signs of the same underlying process. Whenever one or more such signs was noted in a given response, a score of V was assigned to the inkblot.

The reasonably high reliabilities for variables in the preliminary sets of inkblots—correlations in the .80s and .90s—indicated that careful selection of inkblots should yield highly reliable measures of the performance characteristics that are deemed important in the Rorschach. Generally speaking, one way to maximize the reliability of a total score is to select items which have the greatest variance. The mean and variability of each major variable were closely examined for each of the 135 inkblots that had been given in the three preliminary sets to the groups of college students and hospital patients.

Each member of our research team rated each of the 135 inkblots on a five-point scale as to the extent to which it differentiated college from hospital groups, and as to the variability of response on the nine variables initially scored. When merged, these ratings were thought of as crude indices of the desirability of each inkblot for inclusion in the final sets. Pertinent data for each blot were recorded on a small card, together with a schematic colored drawing of the inkblot. By careful study of these cards, pairs of inkblots were discovered for which the scores and their characteristics were almost identical. One blot from each pair was assigned randomly to Form A and the other to Form B. In this way it was possible to obtain two final sets of inkblots, each containing 45 test blots, that were highly matched in terms of original data.

A good psychometric instrument always contains one or two "warm-up" items to help standardize the instructions so that every person taking the test understands what he is supposed to do. Two inkblots were specially chosen as trial blots to be shown the subject before giving him the 45 test blots. One card is very easy, evoking a "bat" response from most subjects. The other card also yields a popular response (human figure) and has just enough bright red color to break any response set for giving only whole responses, and to stimulate the subject into giving color responses when appropriate.

The final order of presentation for the inkblots in each form was arranged so that most of the "best" blots appear rather early in the series. After the two "warm-up" blots, two achromatic blots appear, followed by an inkblot which is predominantly black but has a bright red splotch of color. Thereafter, the order of achromatic and chromatic blots is sufficiently random to minimize undesirable sequential effects.

Construction of the final versions of Form A and Form B completed the first stage of a long research program aimed at producing a standardized instrument. Had we realized the amount of work that would be involved over the next few years before completing the task, we might not have embarked upon it in the first place.

Many thousands of dollars were spent in the expensive, slow process of photoengraving that was required to retain all the subtle shading nuances, blending of colors, and richness of the original blots. Considering the technical difficulties involved in such photoengraving, the printed copies were remarkably similar to the original inkblots. Only after a number of standardized copies of the test were available was it possible to embark on a large-scale standardization program to demonstrate the value of the technique with a large variety of populations. Standardization of a technique involves the specification of detailed procedures for administering and scoring the test, the collection of test protocols from large numbers of individuals representing a wide variety of well-defined populations both normal and abnormal, and the development of extensive statistical information on the reliability and validity of measurement.

Through many personal contacts across the country I was able to secure the cooperation of numerous psychologists who were willing to administer the Holtzman Inkblot Technique to carefully defined samples of subjects. These sites ranged from a veteran's administration hospital for mental patients in New York to a state school for the retarded in Iowa. College students were the easiest to obtain, not only from the University of Texas but also from other colleges nearby. The most difficult, and yet in many ways the most important, populations to obtain were normal, run-of-the-mill adults such as housewives and workmen. We hit upon the idea of testing firemen in the City of Austin. We reasoned that firemen have nothing much to do but sit around all day and wait for a fire. Why wouldn't they be interested in looking at inkblots in the name of science? Housewives were quite another matter. Only by door-to-door sampling in scattered parts of town would it be possible to get anything approaching a representative sample of adult women. By various means, nearly 2000 individual protocols were collected on samples ranging from 5-year-olds to mature adults and from chronic schizophrenic and psychotic depressed patients to mentally retarded children and adults.

Collecting, scoring, coding, and analyzing nearly 100,000 inkblot responses proved to be a formidable task indeed. Had it not been for the highly competent and dedicated psychologists working with me on the research team, it would have been a hopeless task. Joseph Thorpe joined me while still an undergraduate in the early, formative years of the project. He was a seasoned research assistant by the time the main phase of standardization was underway. Then Jon Swartz and finally Wayne Herron joined the research group during the preliminary stages of the standardization program. All three stayed with me throughout the project. Numerous others contributed their time and ideas for one or two years at a time during the period 1956–1961. The conceptual framework, the scoring system and its 22 variables, and all of the many details involved in the collection, scoring, coding, and analysis of data represented a genuine team effort in which no one person could claim any special credit.

Fortunately, computer processing of massive data was possible for the first time at the University of Texas in 1958, just as our program of data collection and analysis was getting underway. A system was devised for key-punching the coded scores for individual inkblot responses on IBM cards for rapid machine analysis. When a batch of protocols had been scored and spot-checked for quality control by a second scorer, they were forwarded for key-punching, using one card for each inkblot response. Thus, the information in one inkblot protocol was stored on 45 separate IBM cards for later analysis. Then the total scores for each of the 22 variables were easily obtained by using a tabulator machine which printed out a summary card containing all necessary information for the entire protocol. The tabulator was used routinely to compute part-scores summed across the odd-numbered inkblots, as well as across the even-numbered items. From these part-scores, split-half reliability coefficients were rapidly computed for each of the 15 populations in the standardization program. Complete matrices of intercorrelations among the inkblot variables were also computed separately for each sample. Over 1.5 million scores were packed into two highspeed magnetic tapes, making it possible to examine all of the basic scoring elements in the standardization data in one rapid sweep through a computer.

Unless two independent scorers can agree highly on how to score an inkblot protocol, the resulting scores always are of questionable value. Consequently, considerable efforts were expended to study the degree of consistency among independent scorers, as well as the extent to which a scorer agreed with himself at two different points in time. Results of this analysis were highly satisfactory for all of the variables. In most cases the interscorer agreement was close to perfect, yielding reliability coefficients in the high .90s.

The odd-even reliability coefficients were also most encouraging, ranging in the .80s and .90s for most variables. These values are about as high as the reliability coefficients obtained for most other highly standardized mental measurements (e.g., intelligence tests). The test was given twice to the same individuals, using Form A on one occasion and Form B on the other; this was done in four studies to obtain estimates of test-retest reliability. Reliability coefficients were generally high, ranging from .49–.81 for major variables, even when an interval of 1 year separated the two testing sessions.

But even more important than the reliability of a test is its validity.

What can be said about the psychological meaning of inkblot variables, even if we assume that they can be measured reliably? How do such variables relate to each other and to independent measures of personality? Are they of value in a differential diagnosis of mental or emotional disorders? The question, "What is the validity of the Holtzman Inkblot Technique?" has no meaning unless the purpose for which the method is to be used is specified. Since conceivably a test may be used for many purposes, it may prove highly valid in one situation and quite invalid in another. After 6 years of research we had developed an instrument worthy of extensive research in a variety of settings. But as yet, we could say little about its utility in the clinical assessment of important personality attributes.

Obviously the most fundamental questions concerning utility in practical situations and validity for the assessment of personality could not be answered until years later, after hundreds of studies had been completed. And yet, just as obviously, it was imperative that the developers of the technique go as far as possible in providing initial validity studies to demonstrate the potential worth of the method.

Three general methods were employed in our research to make a start in providing answers to these fundamental questions. First, intercorrelations were computed among the 22 inkblot variables and factor analyses were carried out for each of the 16 standardization samples to determine the common dimensions underlying inkblot perception and how they may differ in patterning from one population to the next. Second, some of the external correlates of inkblot variables were determined and used as a basis for testing earlier hypotheses taken from the Rorschach, as well as for providing new empirical data bearing upon interpretation of personality. And third, numerous significant differences among well-defined samples were discovered; these shed further light on the meaning of inkblot variables, while also providing a basis for psychodiagnosis of the individual. An example will illustrate the strategy of our approach.

Was it possible to differentiate significantly individuals who were independently classified as chronic schizophrenics, mentally retarded persons, or depressed mental patients? A sample of 100 chronic paranoid schizophrenic patients was carefully matched with 100 control cases of normal adults and with 60 depressed patients of comparable age and education. Using a statistical method known as multiple discriminant analysis, Edward Moseley, a member of our research team, developed a two-stage model for the classification of individuals solely on the basis of responses to inkblots. The first stage consisted of computing a score for each subject, based on the discriminant function for maximizing separation of the three criterion groups. Any individuals who were doubtful cases after Stage 1 were then examined for the distribution of scores on pathognomic verbalization (the inkblot variable dealing with disordered thought processes). This method yielded a high percentage of correct classifications, both in the original samples and in a cross-validation study on completely new cases. The study clearly demonstrated that the technique could be used for psychiatric screening purposes. Further field studies in actual clinical settings, however, would be necessary as a final step before large-scale use of the technique could be applied for this purpose.

Publication in 1961 of a book (*Inkblot Perception and Personality*) completed the 6 years of research necessary to develop the Holtzman Inkblot Technique. The method has been judged sufficiently promising since its publication to warrant extensive translation into other languages and use in a variety of research and practical settings. Over 350 books and articles were published in the years 1961–1974 by many investigators. During this period, our own work moved into different directions: First, the development of techniques for group administration and highly objective methods for computer-scoring and interpretation; and second, the application of the Holtzman Inkblot Technique to the study of personality development in Mexico and the United States.

Since a person is asked to give only one response per inkblot, it is a simple matter to project a slide of an inkblot on a screen in front of a group of people and ask them to write their responses in specially prepared booklets. In a variety of methodological studies, it was found that for most of the inkblot variables, highly similar results for the same persons could be obtained using this more efficient group method. Together with Donald Gorham and Edward Moseley, I developed a system of scoring by machine, which replaced the much more laborious hand-scoring of each inkblot response. Nearly 7000 words were stored in a computer memory and coded for various scoring weights in order to simulate the hand-scoring. Now an entire protocol that would take 20 minutes to score by hand can be done by computer in a matter of seconds. The next step in the use of automatic methods for analysis of inkblot protocols is the development of a computer system for interpreting the responses. While not yet complete, the method shows considerable promise in certain limited areas of personality interpretation. The day may soon come when it will be possible for an individual to receive almost immediate feedback in the form of a "personality interpretation" based on his inkblot responses. One can even visualize a situation in which a person will give his responses at a small computer terminal as the inkblots are placed before him either individually or on a projection screen. Within minutes after completion of the task, the computer will complete the scoring, analysis and interpretation, providing it for the subject (or his psychologist) in a narrative form and also providing a quantitative record of his scores.

Our studies of inkblot perception and personality in two cultures involve the repeated administration of the Holtzman Inkblot Technique, as well as many other perceptual, cognitive, and personality tests, to a large number of normal school children in Mexico and the United States. After 6 years of repeated testing, it is apparent that striking differences exist across the two populations for certain of the inkblot variables, differences that are readily interpretable in terms of the differing life styles and sociocultural premises underlying the two societies (Holtzman, 1974).

It should be apparent by this time that when one embarks upon a program of research in an exciting area where the results are rewarding, the research activity expands almost geometrically. New questions are raised by the solution of old problems. Opportunities arise that never before existed. What may start out as a simple program involving several modest experiments can become a life-time career of research.

REFERENCES

Blake, R. R. and Wilson, J. P., Jr. 1950. Perceptual selectivity in Rorschach determinants as a function of depressive tendencies. *Journal of Abnormal Psychology,* 45:459–472.

Ellenberger, H. 1954. The life and work of Hermann Rorschach. *Bulletin of the Menninger Clinic,* 18:173–219.

Hill, E. F. 1972. *The Holtzman Inkblot Technique.* San Francisco: Jossey-Bass.

Holtzman, W. H. 1974. New developments on the Holtzman Inkblot Technique. In P. McReynolds, (ed.), *Advances in Psychological Assessment,* vol. 3. San Francisco: Jossey-Bass.

Holtzman, W. H.; Thorpe, J. S.; Swartz, J. D.; and Herron, E. W. 1961. *Inkblot Perception and Personality.* Austin: University of Texas Press, p. 417.

Rorschach, H. 1921. *Psychodiagnostics.* P. Lemkau and B. Kronenburg (trans), Berne: Verlag Hans Haber, 1942.

Sells, S. B.; Frese, F. J., Jr.; and Lancaster, W. H. 1952. *Research on the Psychiatric Selection of Flying Personnel. II. Progress on Development of SAM Group Ink-Blot Test.* Project no. 21–37–002, no. 2. Randolf Field, Texas: USAF School of Aviation Medicine.

Zubin, J. 1954. Failures of the Rorschach technique. *Journal of Projective Techniques,* 18:303–315.

SECTION FOUR

APPLICATIONS: PSYCHOLOGICAL RESEARCH AND THE PROBLEM OF RELEVANCE

Science writers are fond of referring to some new experimental finding as being on the "frontiers of science." It is an impressive phrase with an aura of shining virtue. By contrast, discussions of applied psychology are carried out in a much less exhilarating tone, sometimes even a little shamefacedly. Yet, the successful application of scientific knowledge to problems outside the laboratory both validates the work of past scientists, and makes a genuine contribution to society's current problems. Surely, it represents another kind of "frontier."

If science is defined as the search for an understanding of phenomena in the natural world, one measure of the success of a scientific discipline is the extent to which it makes possible the prediction and control of events outside the laboratory. A technology is only as good as the knowledge on which it is based. Bridges, atom bombs, transistors, polio vaccine, vitamin pills—all these attest to the achievements of physicists, biologists, and chemists. Technical applications are perhaps even more important in psychology, a field in which everyone thinks himself a professional. There are many theories of personality, motivation, and social interaction; however, when faced with a case of psychological distress or social disorder, we often must acknowledge that "the psychologist is a professional skilled in the art of applying a technology that does not exist." Still, we persevere.

The relation between science and technology is usually viewed as a one-way street. Basic knowledge is discovered by the scientist, the application of this knowledge is then the task of the technologist. Although this is often the case, the process also may be seen as a two-way street: The need for new materials and new solutions to specific problems may be the impetus for observations in the natural world and hence, a source of knowledge about that world. The technologies of navigation and agriculture must have preceded the sciences of astronomy and biochemistry.

Surely, this is true in Sommer's work on environmental psychology. Indeed, his work is an outgrowth of a very practical problem in what is often called "human engineering." As its name implies, this is a profession which deals with the problems of fitting the environment to the needs and characteristics of people. Sommer's task is that of fitting a specific environment—a state hospital ward—to his subjects, mental patients. As we follow his work we receive an object lesson in the relation between technology and science. It is clear that one can try out a wide variety of furniture arrangements and test their effectiveness by a series of behavioral observations. Although such an approach would work in one specific environment, it does not allow prediction about the effects of such arrangements upon a different population under different circumstances. Principles relating the spatial behaviors of humans to their individual characteristics and social settings were needed. Such principles could be derived only from research on the psychology of personal space. Such research is the product of controlled conditions which only the laboratory can provide and which always involves some degree of abstraction or "irrelevance." Notice the progression in these studies, from the field, where we find observations and simple manipulations in a natural setting, to the laboratory, and the increasing degree of abstraction involved.

Progress in such research often is circular. The data gathered in the laboratory are used to help solve the practical problems facing the applied psychologist. The validity of principles derived from the laboratory is tested by their success in dealing with these practical problems. The results, fed back to the laboratory scientist, provide him with another set of problems which he can study under controlled conditions.

The papers by Buckhout and McConnell illustrate the more traditional relationship between basic knowledge and its application in psychology. In McConnell's case, the Skinnerian emphasis on the control of behavior by behavioral means made it obvious that the principles of operant conditioning might be applied to problems of human behavior. If ever we were to develop a scientifically based technology to deal with disorders of individual and social behavior, it seemed clear that the only likely source of basic knowledge was the experimental psychology of learning. In this sense, the rapid development of behavior modification techniques is the best illustration of the validity of Lewin's dictum (as quoted by Buckhout)—there is nothing so practical as a good theory.

Buckhout's involvement in applied research, like Sommer's, began when he was faced with a very practical problem regarding the behavior of eyewitnesses in a criminal trial. Unlike Sommer, who found himself called upon to apply a nonexistent body of knowledge, Buckhout could draw upon many sources of data on human perceptual processes. However, much of this data had very little to do with what we commonly think of as perception. Instead, it was drawn from research on cognitive processes; learning, memory and attention; psychometrics; test analysis and test construction; and social psychology. Indeed, one of Buckhout's major contributions was his recognition of the need for a breakdown of the usual boundaries between the subdisciplines of psychology. His chapter makes it clear that the development of an applied social psychology involves a shift from the traditional emphasis on individual processes to a concern with the way these processes are integrated into the behavior of individual human beings.

The final paper of this section, Barber's introspective report on responding to hypnotic suggestion, seems to straddle the line between basic and applied research. It could be called an example of basic knowledge in search of an application. As Leibowitz has pointed out in an earlier chapter in this book, Barber's research on hypnosis has helped to remove the aura of mysticism and charlatanism from this topic and bring it back into the main stream of psychological research. In carrying out these studies, Barber has learned a great deal about susceptibility, the influence of authority and complex cognitive processes. An obvious application of such knowledge is in the manipulation of one's own state of consciousness. Indeed, it would not be overstating the case to say that he is developing an "applied psychology of the imagination."

PSYCHO-TECHNOLOGY AND PERSONAL CHANGE
James V. McConnell

I grew up in a small town in Louisiana, the only son of a very religious mother and a very practical-minded father. My first course in psychology was at Centenary College in Shreveport, La., and it blew my mind. The woman teaching the class actually talked about sex openly, right in front of the students! She let us read Freud and other dirty books, and she talked about penises and vaginas and dreams filled with all manner of unconscious symbols that really meant you wanted to have intercourse with somebody. I was 17 at the time, and while I had first-hand evidence that sex actually existed, it was certainly not a topic that was ever discussed around the house. The thought that individals who called themselves psychologists got paid for studying matters sexual convinced me that I wanted to become like them. So I majored in psychology and, as was usual in my life, did so for all the wrong reasons.

All of us are influenced by the people around us, often more than we have any desire to admit. Science itself is not so much the march of ideas across the centuries as it is a catalog of the thoughts and behaviors of individual scientists—most of whom were rather ordinary citizens whose actions were shaped by the people the scientists grew up around. This chapter is the story of my own development as a psychologist. I offer it not as a means of amusing you with a graphic account of all the mistakes I have made, but as a way of illustrating some new and exciting aspects of psychological theory and practice. It is a very personal story because, in order for you to understand the basic processes that underlie anyone's growth and development, you must first single out all of the thousands of environmental inputs that have shaped the person into becoming what he or she presently is.

A year or so after that first psychology course at Centenary College, I entered the U.S. Navy, where I performed menial tasks for the government and learned even more about sex. Once World War II had breathed its final gasps, I returned to Louisiana State University to

James V. McConnell is affiliated with the Department of Psychology, The University of Michigan, Ann Arbor, Mich.

finish my undergraduate education. At LSU I discovered there was a great deal more to psychology than Freud and sex, and that psychology could be a brilliant intellectual exercise besides being a profession that tried to help people who had sexual and other hang-ups.

But what can you do with a BA in psychology? In 1947, the answer was "nothing much." So I took a job announcing at an FM station in New Orleans and spent the next 4 years in radio and television. It was amusing and fairly profitable work, but every time I wrote or spoke a soap commercial, I asked myself, "Does this advertising stuff really work? And if it does, should we be selling it to the highest bidder?" Almost everybody in the broadcast industry seemed convinced that advertising did in fact change people's minds, but nobody could give me any hard data—and nobody wanted to talk much about what the actual consequences of radio and TV commercials might be.

So, when I got the chance, I fled from the hectic land of television to the calm, peaceful, socially-aware world of academia—as it turned out again, for the wrong reasons. I decided that I wanted to help people, so I entered the graduate psychology program at the University of Texas to become a clinical psychologist. I took courses in how to interpret the Rorschach Ink Blot Test, how to administer personality and intelligence tests, how to peer into the deepest recesses of the human spirit. My teachers were sincere, concerned individuals who believed firmly in the rightness of their approach to mending human souls. I made good grades but, at the end of my first year, I was asked to leave the clinical program. I was told that I was a trouble-maker, that my attitude wasn't right. When I asked for a more detailed explanation of my sins, I was informed that I asked too many questions in class. What kind of questions? It seems that, every time a professor stated an everlasting truth about some patient's response to an ink blot, I raised my hand and asked "What data do you have to support what you've just said?"

In the early 1950s, clinical psychology was primarily an intuitive science. Freud, Jung, Rorschach, Horney and other famous people stated what they thought was "the truth" about the workings of the human mind. But the only proof clinicians usually offered for the correctness of their views were their own gut impressions or vague statements about how "patients show improvement when you do thus-and-so." In a very real sense, their comments were similar to those my mother used to give me when I asked her how she knew that people went to heaven or that God had created the earth in just 6 days. Dependence upon the statements of authority or one's own emotions, however, were not the sorts of "proof" that my father usually tolerated. From my mother, then, I acquired the urge to do good to others. From my father, I acquired the urge to be damned sure that what I was doing to others really was *good* in some measurable sense of that word. As you will see, much of my career was spent in trying to reconcile these two very different approaches to understanding the why's and wherefore's of human existence.

The clinicians at Texas reacted to my embarrassing questions about scientific proof underlying their assumptions much the same as did the elders in mother's church—they called me a "smart-ass" and told me to go elsewhere. Of course, they were right. But it took me almost 20 years to learn that criticism usually doesn't help people change for the better, and that verbal punishment and confrontation seldom breed growth, healing, or mental maturity.

So I left clinical psychology (temporarily) not because I lost interest in the workings of the human mind, but because no one seemed to have a handle on how to measure mental events scientifically.

Luckily, I wasn't thrown out of Texas bodily. Rather, I shifted over to social psychology, where Robert Blake and Harry Helson were undertaking some fascinating experiments on "group pressures towards uniformity" (Blake, 1953; Blake, Helson, and Mouton, 1957; Blake and Ramsey, 1951; Helson, et al., 1956).

Picture yourself sitting in a small room with four other people of your own age and sex. You are all subjects in an experiment supposedly designed to test the sharpness of your vision. The experimenter shows you a tiny spot of light that appears to dance about for a few seconds. Then the experimenter asks you to guess how far the light moved. You finish the experiment wondering vaguely what it was all about, but you are convinced that you did a pretty good job of estimating the movement of the light. After all, didn't the other subjects agree with your reports most of the time?

What you didn't realize at the time, of course, was that most of your reports were strongly influenced by what the other "subjects" had to say before you spoke. For the other people in the room were not really subjects—rather, they were "stooges," paid to put psychological pressure on you by giving false reports. If all the stooges reported on a certain trial that the light seemed to move 15 cm (6 in.), then some two-thirds of the "real subjects" (people like you who didn't know what the experimenter was up to) tended to respond that the light moved "close to 15 cm."

The group pressures experiments were begun in the 1930s and 1940s by Solomon Asch and Muzafer Sherif (Asch, 1948; Sherif, 1935). Blake and Helson extended this research tremendously by detailing what sorts of social situations increased or decreased a subject's tendency to yield to the group he or she was in.

My own minor contribution to this work was an experiment showing that the stooges didn't even have to be physically present—if the "real subject" merely heard a tape recording of voices giving judgments about things, the subject yielded as frequently to these artificial social inputs as if the stooges had been sitting next to him. This study earned me a master's degree, along with a great deal of respect for the creativity of Professors Blake and Helson. But it also left me with the same uneasy dissatisfaction that I had felt in radio and television, for the effects of group pressures typically were explained in terms of "attitude change" or "perceptual processes." We still had no way of measuring precisely what the group inputs were, nor any objective way of stating what responses the group made to these stimulus inputs. Nor did we have any real notion of how best to use the information we had in order to help people change their reactions to group pressures.

And so, perhaps again for the wrong reasons, I drifted out of the sometimes fuzzy highlands of social psychology down into what I presumed was the pure and holy valley of biological psychology.

Some time in 1953, another graduate student at Texas almost ruined my life by getting me interested in animal research. The student's name was Robert Thompson, and he was studying how very simple organisms learn what are (for them) highly complex tasks. Thompson was a physiological psychologist who thought that most mental activity could be explained in terms of the flow of electrical energy through neural pathways in the brain. Donald Hebb, the famous Canadian psychologist, had speculated that learning might be a matter of setting up loops or circles of nerve cells, each cell of which fired in sequence. Hebb called these loops "cell assemblies," and stated that each thought a person had, might be stored in the brain by its own specific circle of nerve cells. Since the cells were presumably connected together to form a loop, the firing (or excitation) of any one cell would cause the next neuron in line to become excited. This second neuron would trigger off an electrical response in the third cell; in a fraction of a second, the excitation would circle back to the first cell that fired—much as a rumor might spread among a circle of friends until it looped back to the person who started it. Hebb believed that the sequential firing of the cells ("closing the loop") was the biological equivalent of "thinking a thought" (Hebb, 1949).

The nerve cells in your body are connected to each other at junction points we call *synapses*. According to Hebb's theory, whenever you learn something new, your brain somehow shuffles around the synaptic connections between your nerve cells to form new cell assemblies—much as the telephone company shuffles around its wires and connections whenever it installs a new telephone. According to Hebb, whenever you want to retrieve a memory of something that's happened to you in your past, you are really trying to "call up" the "synaptic telephone number" of the cell assembly that is associated with that memory.

Robert Thompson was much impressed with Hebb's theory—

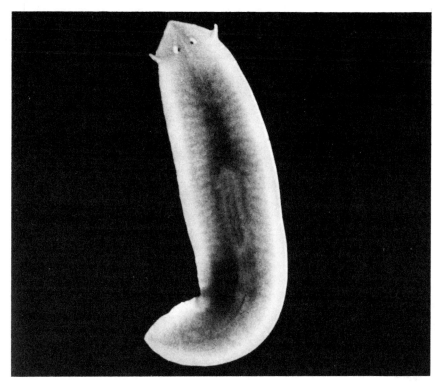

Figure 16.1. *A planarian flatworm. It grows to be about 1 inch long when mature.*

despite the fact that there was little concrete evidence to prove it. He felt that he might be able to add credibility to Hebb's theory if he could show that ordinary flatworms (Fig. 16.1) were capable of learning.

The common planarian—a freshwater flatworm found in ponds and rivers around the world—is the simplest animal to have a true brain and true synapses. Hebb had said that synapses were necessary for learning. Therefore, Thompson reasoned, if flatworms could be taught a few tricks, perhaps the learning of those tricks would demonstrate that synapses were involved in learning. Furthermore, the nervous system of the planarian is so simple that maybe, just maybe, someone might be able to discover a worm's "cell assemblies" some day in the future.

With great enthusiasm, Thompson and I set out to instruct a few inch-long flatworms using a technique called Pavlovian (or respondent) conditioning. We used a water-filled trough about 30 cm (1 ft) long and 1.3 cm (0.5 in.) wide (Fig. 16.2). The trough had metal electrodes at either end that could send a mildly painful current of electricity through the water. Whenever we turned on the current, any

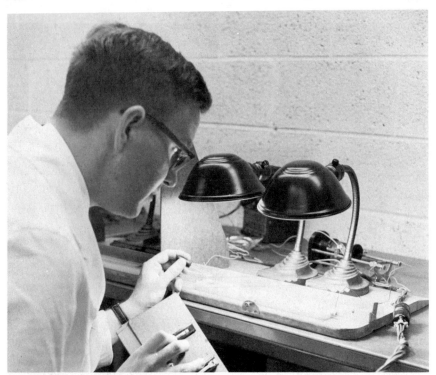

Figure 16.2. *An apparatus for conditioning planarian flatworms. Using an eye-dropper, the animal is placed in a water-filled trough. Light from the two lamps serves as the conditioning stimulus; electric shock passed through the water is the unconditioned stimulus that causes the worm to contract or "scrunch up." As the animal learns, it begins to "scrunch" more and more frequently to the onset of the light, before it is shocked.*

worm crawling along the bottom of the trough would contract vigorously. (To put matters in more colorful terms, when we shocked the worm, it scrunched up.) We mounted a couple of goose-neck lamps above the trough; the onset of the light was a signal to the worm that two seconds later, it would be shocked.

At the beginning of training, the worms mostly ignored the onset of the light, although they always scrunched up when shocked. We hoped that if the planarians were indeed capable of learning, they would eventually respond by scrunching as soon as the light turned on (*before* the shock arrived). Pavlov had trained dogs to salivate "on command" by ringing a bell just before he blew food powder into the dogs' mouths. Could we teach worms to scrunch "on command" by pairing the light with the shock?

As good graduate students always do, we discussed our research with the professor in charge of the animal laboratory at the University of Texas. This noted gentleman thought our plan rather stupid and unscientific because we planned merely to observe the worms and

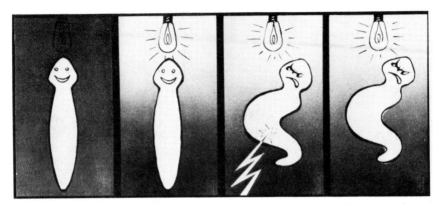

Figure 16.3. *Cartoon showing classical conditioning in the planarian.*

write down their reactions—rather than searching out some way to record the behavior of the worms mechanically. We were refused space in the laboratory and had to do our planarian-training in my kitchen. Each afternoon for several weeks, we sat over coffee and worms; at the end of this time, the planarians, given trials of light-paired-with-shock were scrunching quite regularly when the light turned on. Other worms that were given trials of just light, or just shock, did not show any evidence of having learned anything (Fig. 16.3). Thompson and I assumed (correctly, I am sure) that worms could learn (Thompson and McConnell, 1955).

When I came to teach at the University of Michigan in 1956, my students and I continued the planarian research. We found much more effective ways of training worms using mazes as well as Pavlovian conditioning; we even found techniques for recording the animals' responses mechanically. But mostly we tried to figure out what went on inside the worms when we forced them to change their behavior.

Planarians are peculiar animals. If you cut one in half, the head will grow a new tail and the tail will grow a new head—all in a matter of a few weeks. In 1957 Allan Jacobson, Daniel P. Kimble, and I trained worms (using the light-shock technique) and then cut them in half. We then let the animals regrow their missing parts. A month later, we retested the now-regrown worms (Fig. 16.4). The heads (that had grown new tails) remembered just as much as did worms that had been trained but not cut in half. But what of the tails? They had been forced to grow entirely new brains. Could they be expected to remember anything? We thought not, but to our surprise, the tails remembered even more than did the heads and the animals that hadn't been cut at all (McConnell, et al., 1959).

Later on, we trained planarians and then cut them into several pieces. Each piece replaced its missing tissue and became an intact worm; and each piece showed excellent retention of the original learn-

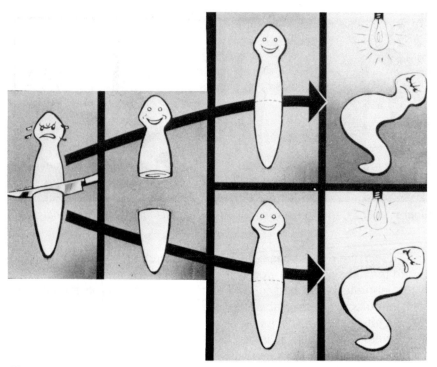

Figure 16.4. *If a trained planarian is cut in half, both the head and tail sections will regenerate into complete animals. If both halves are later tested for retention of the original learning, both head and tail sections "remember" what the original animal learned.*

ing. These experiments—which now have been repeated successfully in dozens of laboratories all around the world—suggested that memories were stored all over the worms' bodies, and not just in the brain (as Hebb's theory might have suggested).

By 1960, we were asking ourselves what the "memory storage mechanism" might be if it weren't entirely "cell assemblies in the brain." We began to suspect that part of this mechanism might involve the creation of new chemical molecules inside the nerve cells. Perhaps these new chemicals act like phone numbers—telling the neurons which synaptic connections to make or break during learning. These molecules could be stored all over the worms' bodies; then, when you cut off a trained planarian's head, it regrew its brain according to the "phone number molecules" it had available. So the tails "remembered" because their synapses were "prewired" to respond the same way the original animal had learned to respond.

In 1960, Reeva Jacobson Kimble, Barbara Humphries, and I pushed the "molecular theory of memory" one step further. We reasoned that if two worms learned the same trick, the new chemical molecules formed in their bodies should be pretty much the same.

So, if we could train a flatworm, take the "new molecule" out of its body and somehow plug this molecule into the body of an untrained worm, the latter might acquire the "scrunch" response without ever having been itself exposed to the light or the shock.

Planarians often are cannibalistic. With this fact in mind we gave "victim" worms the usual light-shock respondent training. Then we cut them in small pieces and fed them to hungry, untrained cannibals. After letting the cannibal planarians have a day or so to digest their meals, we gave them their first exposure to light-shock training. To our delight, the cannibals that ate "educated victims" showed much faster learning than did cannibals that ate "uneducated" or "untrained victims." This research—which again was confirmed in many other laboratories—suggested that some part of the memory process could be transferred from one animal to another (McConnell, 1962). (It also led to proposals about grinding up retired professors and feeding them to freshmen.)

By 1962, we tried to zero in on what molecules might be involved in memory storage. We trained several hundred worms, then put them through a Waring blender, and ground them into a thick paste. Next we performed some chemical magic on the paste and extracted those molecules we guessed might contain the "memory wiring diagrams." Finally, we injected this molecular soup into untrained worms and gave them the usual light-shock training (Fig. 16.5). As a control of sorts, we injected other planarians with "soup" taken from animals given exposure to light only, or shock only, or no training at all. The worms that received "trained soup" learned significantly faster than did worms injected with "soup" from any of the control groups. The experiment was crudely done, for no one had ever before tried to extract "memory molecules" from living tissue—much less inject it into other animals. However, this research did suggest that the "memory storage mechanism" was in part chemical, and other scientists were able to repeat our work successfully later on using rats and mice as well as worms.

As exciting as the "memory transfer" experiments were, they left me unhappy for several reasons. To begin with, the research was always quite controversial. Not all of my colleagues could bring themselves to believe that "memories" might be coded chemically, much less that these coded molecules could be transferred from one animal to another. Although several thousand high school students were able to train planarians with little difficulty—and to perform transfer experiments as well—there were many senior investigators who never got the knack and who complained loudly. The bulk of published (and even unpublished) research supported our early work; but science is a matter of faith as well as facts, and scientists tend to believe what they want to believe even if the facts do not always support their faith (McConnell, 1964).

Figure 16.5. *Using a very tiny needle, one may inject a chemical extract from trained animals into the body of an untrained planarian. If the injectee is tested later, it often shows evidence of having acquired part of the learning "by injection."*

Furthermore, I was disturbed by the notion that what goes on inside your mind could somehow be entirely reduced to chemical changes inside the nerve cells in your body. While this belief, called the *reductionist hypothesis,* fitted well my father's objective view toward behavior, I just didn't feel that all of the richness of human experience could be explained completely and solely in terms of molecules and synaptic connections. Experiments on animals can tell us a great deal about the biology of behavior change; whether or not the mental processes involved in human learning are the same as those involved in animal learning remains an unsettled point.

Finally, my mother's urges to help other people still beat loudly in my brain, and I couldn't picture myself chasing about injecting people with "trained soup." So I began to look around for other things to do.

In 1958, I was named to a committee charged with telling the Department of Defense what kinds of research it should be doing in the field of persuasion and human motivation. Actually, the Department of Defense was interested in learning better ways to control human behavior. But the committee members were all scientists, and "control" was a dirty word to most of us then as now. So our committee talked about "persuasion" and "influence" instead of "control."

I was given the task of writing a paper on how all the hard-nosed research on rats and worms and even people could be used to build a better technology for influencing human actions. Frankly, I had never thought that all the dull and seemingly dusty facts gleaned from lab experiments had much practical (technological) value. But as I went through the literature, I began to see dozens of potential applications. There were a great many studies on advertising, attitude change, politics, and mass persuasion. In most of this work, one person (or a small group of people) tried to influence the actions of a large segment of society all at once. Most of this research involved a communicator, a message, and an audience that received the message. Many books had been written on how the attitudes of the communicator, the stimulus characteristics of the message, and the personalities of the members of the audience affected the persuasive process. But few people seemed to realize there was something important missing from this analysis—namely, some kind of *feedback* from the audience to the communicator. Persuasion was seen as a one-way street: The communicator sent out his or her message, and the audience received this communication—but there was no feedback loop. What was missing was a channel of information flowing back from the audience, telling the communicator about the audience's thoughts, feelings, or reactions toward the message. (I will have more to say about this important point in a moment.)

In addition to these studies on mass communications, there were a great many experiments on group persuasion, where the target audience to be controlled consisted of a handful of people. The group pressures studies of Blake and Helson (and many others) fitted into this category (Blake, Helson, and Mouton, 1957), but so did research on education and group therapy. But again, there were problems with much of this work. As I have said, no one had clearly specified what the stimulus inputs were to the group, much less its behavioral outputs. The fact is that education works—sometimes; so does group therapy—sometimes. But the explanations for the changes that occur when people go to school or enter therapy were seen in terms of *processes* presumed to take place inside people's heads. When you get down to the nitty-gritty, terms such as "learning," "memory," "attitudes," "mental health," and "ego strength" can be terribly difficult to define and measure.

So we had mass persuasion and group influences in abundance. But as I surveyed the field, by far the most exciting research seemed to be that aimed at controlling the reactions of individual subjects. Donald Hebb, in a series of experiments relatively unrelated to his "cell assembly" theory, had shown that people are much more suggestible after they have been isolated completely from their normal environmental inputs for a while (Hebb, 1961). Other research suggested that drugs, hypnosis, and electrical stimulation applied directly to the brain could "persuade" individuals, or make them do things they ordinarily wouldn't do. Studies by Pavlov (1927), Gantt (1945), Liddell (1956), and Masserman (1943) demonstrated that animals can show "neurotic" or "mentally ill" behavior patterns if they are trained in certain ways. The fascinating question raised by such work was this: If "neurotic" behavior can be learned by animals, then might not the response patterns of people we call "mentally ill" in part be learned too? And if we can train normal animals to be "sick," might we not also be able to teach humans with abnormal behaviors to act in a sane and acceptable fashion?

With perhaps the same thought in mind, psychologists Fred Keller (1968) and B. F. Skinner were beginning to adapt animal research into classroom procedures. Skinner, a Harvard professor, had shown that pigeons could be trained quickly to perform highly complex tasks —such as bowling or playing ping pong with each other—if the experimenter made use of a technique called *operant conditioning.* In Pavlovian (respondent) conditioning, the experimenter pairs a new stimulus input (such as a bell) with a stimulus (food) that already evokes the desired response (salivation). Eventually, as Pavlov showed, the bell will call forth the salivation even when the animal isn't given food. The technique is called *respondent conditioning* because the organism is merely trained to respond automatically to certain new stimulus inputs (Skinner, 1962).

In respondent conditioning, the environmental stimuli act on the animal to create the response output that the *experimenter* desires. In operant conditioning, the animal acts (operates) on its environment to produce the stimulus inputs the *animal* desires. For instance, most organisms will look for food when they are hungry. When they perform some action (response) that yields food (a desired stimulus input), the animal tends to repeat the same action whenever it is hungry. In other words, when a rewarding stimulus immediately follows a response, the probability that the animal will repeat the response is greatly increased. As Skinner showed, you can train an animal to perform rather incredible tricks if you are clever enough to give it rewarding feedback (i.e., food) immediately after it does something you want it to do.

When Skinner wished to teach a pigeon to bowl, he began by analyzing in highly specific terms what he really meant by "bowling." In fact, that activity we call "bowling" is really a whole series of muscular reactions that must be performed in a certain sequence. First the bird must learn to approach the tiny ball lying on the floor at the end of the pigeon-sized bowling alley. Then it must bend over and strike the ball with its beak so that the ball is propelled down the alley in the direction of the pins. Obviously, you cannot teach the bird to bowl until you first train it to move toward the ball. So training usually begins by rewarding the pigeon for each "accidental" movement it makes in the general direction of the ball. As the animal's ball-approaching responses become more frequent, the reward is given more and more selectively. Within minutes the animal learns that walking toward the ball will almost always yield it a bit of food. The animal is then persuaded or "shaped" into leaning over, then rewarded for striking the ball with its beak, and finally for aiming the ball down the alley. The whole training procedure often takes no more than 30 minutes.

People are not pigeons, but Skinner reasoned that students could be taught many academic "tricks" rather rapidly if teachers would only break up the material to be learned into chains of responses, and then reward the students for each bit of progress shown. Skinner knew from his own observations of classroom activities that many teachers do not specify what they want from their students; furthermore, instead of rewarding appropriate behaviors, teachers too often attempt to control students by punishing inappropriate behaviors. (As we will see shortly, punishment usually is a poor way to influence what a person does or does not do.)

By 1958, Skinner had developed a technique called "programmed learning" for classroom use. A "program" consisted of a set of related chunks of information about some subject matter (Spanish, history, mathematics, etc.). Each chunk began with one or more factual statements (stimulus inputs) about the subject; the chunk concluded with a question that the student was to answer (response output). The correct answer appeared immediately afterwards in the program so that the student knew at once if he or she was correct. In fact, the statements and questions often were so cleverly constructed that most students got the answers right.

Skinner assumed that the students would feel rewarded for coming up with the correct answers (but we might ask if this "reward" is qualitatively the same as a bit of food). He further assumed that "mentally disturbed" people could be trained in much the same way to display "mentally healthy" behavior patterns, if and only if somebody were smart enough first to define in concrete terms what "mentally healthy" behaviors really were and then worked out "programs" by which mental patients could learn the proper social responses (Skinner, 1958).

As I completed my paper for the Department of Defense, I had a rather wild notion: All forms of personal change (including mass persuasion and politics, education and psychotherapy) really were a matter of making new types of connections between inputs and outputs. In some cases, the inputs and outputs were biological, in some cases they were mental or attitudinal, in other cases they were behavioral. A big company wants you to buy its brand of toothpaste; a politician wants your vote; a teacher wants you to pass an exam; a therapist wants a patient to stop brooding over the death of a loved one, or to react confidently instead of fearfully in social situations; a psychologist wants a worm to scrunch when the light comes on instead of waiting for the shock. In all these cases, the success of a persuasive attempt is always measured in terms of whether or not the desired behavioral, mental, or physiological output occurs. Yet most of the experiments on persuasion seemed aimed at diddling with the processes (attitudes, motivations, personality traits, synapses) that presumably *connected* inputs to outputs.

What would happen, I wondered, if we started paying more attention to *what* people said, did, thought, and felt, and less attention to theoretical explanations of *why* they said, did, thought, and felt these things. Maybe if we focused on how to help individuals change or influence their own inputs and outputs, we might be able to make use of the rather powerful techniques dreamed up by psychologists for controlling organisms in laboratory settings.

In fact, many psychologists had already done so. Skinner and his students had already begun creating "programs" for patients in mental hospitals. British psychologist H. J. Eysenck (1964) had attempted to decrease "insane talk" in some patients by giving them mild punishment whenever they said "crazy" things. Most of all, South African psychiatrist Joseph Wolpe (1969) had begun treating abnormal fears (phobias) using Pavlovian conditioning techniques. Wolpe assumed that a fear of snakes, to take but one example, was probably learned because of some intensely painful experience a person had had in the past. That is, the stimulus of a snake (or the sight of a snake) had been followed immediately by great fear or anxiety (the human equivalent of a "scrunch"). All the biological responses (outputs) that make up the fear reaction (such as sweating, increased pulse rate, trembling, and rapid breathing) became connected to the snake stimulus (input) very quickly. Thereafter, whenever the person saw a snake, or thought about a snake, the fear reaction occurred. Fear isn't a very pretty or pleasant thing. If the person subsequently avoided snakes, he or she was rewarded by not having to live through another fit of panic. This rewarding avoidance kept the individual away from snakes, and also kept the fear conditioning very strong.

The form of treatment that Wolpe pioneered—now called *desensitization therapy* or *counterconditioning*—usually consists of trying to connect a more normal response output to the snake stimulus. It is difficult for most of us to exhibit all the tense "scrunch" signs of panic or anxiety if at the same time we are utterly relaxed and comfortable. So, Wolpe began by teaching his patients to go "completely limp" whenever they wished to. Then, while the patients were deeply relaxed, Wolpe exposed them to the least-threatening snake stimulus imaginable. The patients soon began to react to this stimulus (the mention of the word "snake," for instance) by going limp instead of becoming tense and anxious. As the patients gained experience and confidence, Wolpe would introduce slightly more threatening stimuli (the sight of a real snake 30 feet away, for example), again encouraging the patients to relax instead of falling into panic. After 10 to 20 such training sessions, the snake stimulus frequently became connected to the relaxation response and the persons could often pick up and play with a reptile that only weeks earlier would have sent them screaming from the room.

In the final analysis, there is little practical difference between teaching a worm to scrunch in a fearful reaction to a stimulus it had previously ignored, and teaching a person to ignore a stimulus that previously had evoked flight, panic, or anxiety. Counterconditioning always involves finding a way to elicit the desired behavioral, emotional, or cognitive output reliably; once you can get the organism to produce this output "on command," you can connect the output to just about any stimulus input you desire to. The important practical question is this: Do you think that arguing with the organism, or giving it "insight" into the causes of its fears, would have the same therapeutic success?

My own ideas about therapy in 1958 went somewhat beyond what Skinner, Eysenck, and Wolpe had done, for I wanted to combine conditioning techniques with group pressures, propaganda, attitude change, chemical injections (perhaps even of "memory soup"), hypnosis and reeducation. In fact, I wanted to use any technique that was legal, and in my opinion moral, and nondangerous to get mental patients to think and feel and act "normally." Once they had done so—even to the slightest degree—we could reward them as lovingly and as openly as possible and hence encourage them to continue to think and emote and behave this way.

Unfortunately, most clinical psychologists and psychiatrists reacted to my suggestions as if I were some kind of lunatic, for I seemed to be paying no attention at all to such important "processes" as ego strength, libidinal energy, character, and insight. The prevailing view in those days was that the therapist merely helped the patient work through his or her problems. When the patient understood the problems, the patient presumably would improve. My techniques were too coercive, too controlling, too "inhumane" for most clinical psychologists to stomach. Because my output-oriented therapy appeared to destroy the free will and dignity of the patients, I found it impossible in 1959 to get funds from government agencies to test my ideas.

I did come close to getting some research support once. A friend of mine in New York City, an advertising executive trained in experimental psychology, agreed to introduce me to the president of a private foundation. The three of us were to have lunch at the Colony restaurant one beautiful day in May, 1959, and I was to explain all my wild ideas to the foundation president. Unfortunately for the success of our plans, we neglected to invite my friend's charming French wife. The Colony was at that time one of the most elegant restaurants in the world, and my friend's wife loved its fancy food and the waiters who hovered discreetly at her elbow. My friend insisted it was "business only," and refused to bring her because she would "upset things." But when we arrived, we found her sitting alone at the next table. So of course she had to join us, much to my friend's distress. This glamorous woman seated herself next to the foundation president and moved in on the poor man like a farm wife fattening up a goose for the kill. She spread caviar on bits of toast and plopped them in the man's mouth, she played footsie with him under the table, she cut up his meat for him, she wiped his mouth with her napkin, she batted her long eyelashes at him continuously, she told him wildly funny tales, and flattered him outrageously. And she completely forbade any discussion of business. At the end of the meal, she took the man's arm in hers and walked him back to his office, leaving her husband to pay the very large bill and to mumble apologies to me. I never heard from the foundation president again.

At the very time in 1959 that my wild ideas on psychotherapy were being turned down by the grant agencies, the worms were coming into their own. The National Science Foundation, the National Institute of Mental Health, and even the Atomic Energy Commission coughed up fairly substantial sums for the "memory transfer" research. In my youth I was easily seduced—particularly by money—and so I put aside my questions about whether people might be trained to act sane, and I stuck to my worm lab instead.

There are two important points you must understand about all this. First, in 1959, my ideas about applied psychology (or what I call psychotechnology) were decidedly ill-formed and hazy. The field was in its infancy then, and so was I. Although I sometimes daydream about the contributions I might have made, the facts of the matter are that the real discoveries were made by people like Skinner and Wolpe, Nathan Azrin, Fred Keller, Ted Ayllon, Gerald Patterson, Albert Bandura, and many, many others.

The second point is even more important. It would be easy for me to place all the blame for my failing to get research money on the stupidities of others. The grant committees in 1959 were indeed blind to most of the potentials of behavioral therapy. But whose fault was it that my proposals were turned down? My feeling now is that I was responsible, not they. For I never bothered to look for better ways of winning those people over to my way of thinking. They had something I wanted, so surely it was up to me to find ways to get them to give it to me. They owed me nothing; I at least owed them the most persuasive arguments I could think of.

This second point strikes at the very heart of psychotechnology (applied psychology). In older forms of mentalistic therapy, the responsibility for change almost always is placed on the patient or client.

Mental illness was seen as resulting primarily from bad genes or an insufficiently-developed personality. In short, if you went crazy, it was usually your own fault, and it was your own responsibility to get well. If, during the course of treatment, you refused to respond to some of the suggestions the therapist offered, then you were "showing resistance." There are hundreds of books and thousands of articles on resistance, and typically it is seen as being due to some psychological weakness on the part of the patient.

But isn't this viewpoint something of a cop-out? We learn to think and act and feel as we do, to make the most (or the least) of the bodies and brains we inherit at birth. And what we learn, we can unlearn; and what we haven't learned, we can acquire if we have a good teacher. A therapist must always be a good teacher. If the patient shows resistance, it is typically because the therapist has goofed.

Look at it this way. Skinner showed years ago that pigeons can be taught to bowl. If you yourself tried to teach a bird to bowl, and the bird "showed resistance" to your methods, should you blame this failure on the innate stupidity of the pigeon? Or could it just be that you were incompetent as a trainer? Once you realized that the fault was probably yours, don't you think you'd try to improve your bird-training methods until you found ways that worked?

In similar fashion, we now have ample demonstrations that behavioral and other forms of therapy can help people grow and get well if the proper psychotechnology is used. Therefore, when therapy fails, shouldn't it be the responsibility of the therapist to change his or her way of relating to the patient until the therapist hits upon something that evokes a healthy response from the patient?

From 1959 until I closed my worm laboratory in 1972, most of my research was on the biochemistry of memory. However, my teaching was a different matter entirely. I had this 50-page monograph on persuasion just lying around, so I decided to teach a course called "The Psychology of Influence" that would employ this monograph as a text. I began the class with a discussion of mass persuasion, trying to show the students how they were affected by advertising, public relations, propaganda, and politics. Then we looked at the ways in which inputs from the groups we all belong to could change the way in which we responded to our worlds. Finally, toward the end of the semester, we investigated how drugs, hypnosis, sensory deprivation, therapy, and interpersonal attraction controlled our mental and physical reactions.

For many reasons, the class became relatively popular. To begin with, the material we covered was highly interesting. Most of us want to learn how to be more effective in life, and "effective" usually means "able to influence the behaviors and attitudes of others." We want to learn how to get other people to like us (that is, to shape them into making positive responses toward us), or how to protect ourselves from undue influence from others—or both.

Moreover, as I taught the course repeatedly, my students were kind enough to teach me how to teach them more effectively. When I first began lecturing, I believed that I must show my students how brilliant I was. My usual way of demonstrating "brilliance" was by arguing loudly and viciously with anyone who cared to contradict what I said. If a student challenged me in class, I went to almost any lengths to put the student down. Many class members—the silent ones, chiefly —enjoyed the spectacle and rewarded me with applause and compliments. The only problem was that fewer and fewer students dared to raise their hands in class. I took this as proof of my brilliance; later, it occurred to me that all I was doing was punishing classroom participation. But that was later.

When I began the class, I required the students to pass many examinations and to write several papers. A fair number of the class flunked the exams, so I had to lower the standards "because the kids are dumb." But while I was doing this, Skinner and Keller were pioneering better teaching methods that would almost guarantee that a student would learn whatever subject matter the instructor wanted— if the teacher would only reward the student for learning instead of punishing the student for failing to learn. After lecturing about these new teaching methods for a year or so, I decided it would be amusing to demonstrate some of them in class. So I started giving the students some praise whenever they spoke out in class, and writing encouraging comments to them on their exams and term papers.

Slowly, the whole atmosphere in the class began to change. Students spoke up more often, they wrote better papers, and they did better on exams. Since I taught the course twice each year, and it was a bore to rewrite exams each semester, I started using some questions over again. A few of the students complained that the fraternities kept files of my past exams, hence the frat members had an edge in class. So I put copies of all the exams in the library where anybody could study them.

Some students now complained that this procedure made the exams both too hard and too easy. Since everybody had access to many of the questions that appeared on the tests, everybody got a good score; if I had graded on the usual "curve," giving but a limited number of A grades, then only those students who got a perfect exam score might get an A, while those students who scored 99 percent correct might be stuck with a B.

It was at this point that I began to apply psychotechnology to the philosophy of teaching and grading. I had assumed, as many teachers do, that the purpose of a test was to give the students feedback on their knowledge and performance. Therefore (so this reasoning goes), it is important to point out the students' mistakes and ignorance, and to use grades as a threatening means of motivating the students to correct their mistakes. With this idea in mind, consider psychotherapy for a moment. Do we really want to "flunk" patients who don't do as well as we had hoped, or do we want to change our actions as therapists so that every patient has the maximum chance to demonstrate improvement?

Classrooms are like therapeutic couches. The student has his or her own set of goals, be they good grades, or being entertained, or learning just for the pleasure of learning. If it is the therapist's task to make sure that each patient gets better, isn't it also the teacher's job to see that the students reach their goals? And if the students fail to learn, shouldn't we blame the teacher?

It seemed to me that exams should be used to grade the effectiveness of the teacher's ability to teach, not the students' abilities to learn. Therefore, I reasoned, I wouldn't be happy unless every student in my class had mastered the exam material and got an A—that is, learned as much as humanly possible. With that thought in mind, I set out to discover better ways of encouraging students to achieve the maximal amount of personal change.

There are basically two ways of changing the way people act, think, or feel—by the use of what psychologists often call "feedback" and "feed-forward." The use of feed-forward techniques typically involves the setting up of a model or ideal type of performance—a goal, if you will. The model may be actual, or imaginary—attainable, or merely approachable. Once the goal has been set and agreed upon, the use of rewarding or punishing feedback (information about performance) can help guide the person toward the goal.

A thermostat is an excellent example of a feed-forward/feedback device. When you enter a cold room and turn the thermostat up to 72 degrees, you feed-forward a signal that causes the furnace to turn on. A thermometer inside the thermostat measures the increase in heat (feedback about the performance of the furnace). When the temperature rises to 72 degrees, the feedback from the thermometer exactly matches the setting you made (feed-forward), the goal is reached, and the furnace shuts off.

In efficient classrooms, the teacher typically provides the students with a model of what performance is expected of them—by stating what the final exam questions will be, by putting copies of "ideal" term papers in the library, etc. A more specific model better enables the students to judge their progress toward this fed-forward goal state. Also, the specific model makes it easier for the teacher to provide the students with feedback about their achievement. However, if education is to be most effective, the students must also learn to give the teacher both feed-forward and feedback. Feed-forward usually involves telling the teacher what the students want from the class, and helping set course goals rather than passively accepting all the goal-models imposed by the teacher. Feedback comes when the students evaluate the help they get from the teacher in encouraging them to reach mutually agreed upon goals.

The concepts of feedback and feed-forward apply to therapy as well. Therapy usually involves reeducation of some kind. Respondent conditioning can thus be seen as a form of modeling or "feed-forward." During counterconditioning, the therapist does whatever is necessary to elicit the desired end-state of relaxation. Once the patient can achieve this "model output," the relaxation response can be connected to any stimulus the patient or therapist desires. The "model output" may, of course, be an intellectual or attitudinal response instead of an emotional or muscular reaction. On the other hand, operant conditioning is primarily a feedback technique that guides the organism toward the goal in small steps.

In most forms of effective therapy, I feel sure, the therapist both "models" the changes the patient is expected to make and encourages any movement in the right direction that the patient makes. Just as education works best when the students take care to provide the teacher with encouraging feedback about the teacher's performance, so therapy probably goes fastest when the patient takes the time to point out to the therapist what's going well.

All of these insights literally exploded in my mind during the 1960s and early 1970s. During 1968, for instance, it dawned on me that honey attracts more flies than does vinegar, and that reward encourages better learning than does punishment. The problem with the "modeling" approach to teaching is that once the model has been openly stated, the teacher may find it easier to punish deviations from it (the so-called "law and order" approach to controlling behavior) than to reinforce approximations to it. Punishment certainly has an influence on what we think and feel and do, but its side-effects usually are devastating. When you get back an exam paper with each of your mistakes boldly underlined in red, do you typically have warm and loving feelings toward your teacher? What would your emotional responses be if, instead, the teacher marked all the answers you got right?

We seem most likely to change and accept new ideas, to learn and grow and become better people when we feel nonthreatened— when we feel we have a reasonable chance for success. When the people around you continually point out your faults and punish you for deviating from some model, don't you get rather defensive? And don't you often end up hating those people and wanting to get even? But when people continually encourage you, tolerate your mistakes quietly but give you instantaneous (rewarding) feedback on everything you do that is even half-way right, don't you feel much more secure in your ability to achieve whatever you happen to set your mind to?

By 1970, I determined that every student in my classes really ought to be making an A, or somehow I was a failure as a teacher. To get this level of achievement, I had to worry about some very simple sorts of behavior (just as to teach a pigeon to bowl, you must break up the task into its component behavioral tasks). Most students learn better when they come to and participate in class, when they read the books assigned to them, and when they turn in their papers on time. To get my students to class, I had to give the most interesting and exciting lectures possible. To encourage students to ask questions in class, I had to reward them when they did so rather than cut them down if I thought the questions foolish. So I began doing odd things, like throwing quarters to anybody who raised his or her hand (later in the course, the quarters were given for questions or comments I thought particularly good or appropriate). Sometimes I gave out points rather than quarters; the points could be turned in to take the place of points earned by writing a book report, etc. Rather than penalizing a student for turning in work late, I gave extra points for turning in work early.

Next, I began taking frequent evaluations of my teaching from the students. It soon developed that most of them were much more interested in the sections on behavior modification of individuals than they were in group and mass persuasion. I then reorganized the course and taught mostly what they wanted to learn. By 1970, "The Psychology of Influence" became "Introduction to Behavior Modification," and the enrollment skyrocketed.

During the first year of teaching this class, my assistant Tim Walter and I spent some time trying to find out what most students had as their major goals. Some of them wanted good grades, some wished for individual attention and recognition, while others primarily enjoyed learning more about themselves. But the thing that most students wanted above all was a chance to put into practice the theories regarding human behavior that they learned about in class. So, by early 1971, Tim and I devised a "lab course" in psychotechnology. We began by placing a dozen or so undergraduates in various hospital, prison, and school settings in or near Ann Arbor. Each group of five students was supervised by a graduate student or (later on) by an undergraduate assistant who had already taken the course. We had hoped that our students would be able to perform minor behavioral tasks with mental patients, prisoners, and school kids. What we often got were "minor miracles" instead.

That first fateful semester, we put five students to work in a local mental hospital. One of these students was a young girl, Jane Michener. She worked with a 46-year-old white patient whom I will call Miss B. As we soon learned, Miss B. had been hospitalized for more than 22 years; although the hospital records were confused as to what might be wrong with Miss B., they stated clearly that she had been "nonverbal" for some 20 years. Jane decided that it would be nice to help Miss B. talk again, and even Miss B. agreed with this goal (feed-forward). So Jane tried to engage Miss B. in polite conversation. At the end of 2 hours, Miss B. had said "um-hum" exactly four times. No amount of coaxing could get her to say a recognizable word, much less come out with a complete sentence. The staff members were skeptical that anything could be done; after all, Miss B. was "insane" (wouldn't any sane individual want to talk to his or her fellow humans?).

The second time that Jane saw Miss B., she brought along a bag of gumdrops and other edible goodies. Holding a gumdrop up in front of the woman, Jane asked Miss B. if she wanted it. She said "um-hum" and Jane instantly popped the candy into the woman's mouth. Every time the woman said "um-hum" she was reinforced (positive feedback) with a gumdrop. Within moments, Miss B. was emitting "um-hums" at a rate of several hundred per hour.

Obviously here was a bit of verbal behavior that could be influenced by rewarding feedback. But what about words? Jane resorted to modeling what she wanted from the woman. "Can you say 'gumdrop'?" Jane asked. Miss B. refused. Jane coaxed and wheedled, holding the gumdrop up in front of the woman and saying the word several times. Finally Miss B., perhaps realizing that she now had to do *something* to earn the reward, emitted a response that sounded like "grumdroop."

Now, picture the usual "law and order" approach to such a response. The teacher would say, "I'm sorry, dear, but you didn't say 'gumdrop' clearly and distinctly. You will simply have to practice again and again if you want me to give you a reward." Instead of falling into this error, Jane immediately popped the candy between the woman's teeth and patted her on the back. "You said 'gumdrop' beautifully, Miss B. Now, let's try it once more, and if you say 'gumdrop' again, you'll get another candy."

Within a few weeks, Miss B. was speaking loudly and understandably at a rate of several hundred words per hour. Don't misunderstand; Miss B. wasn't "cured" of her "mental illness," but she had shown a remarkable recovery in one area of difficulty. (Might she not have done even better if the hospital staff were trained to encourage her progress as Jane had?)

Another of our first students, Brian Maifield, worked with a 35-year-old black patient who, if anything, talked too much. This woman, whom I will call Mrs. C., had been hospitalized for several years because (according to the records) she was "paranoid." In fact, the woman showed the classical behavioral symptoms of what is sometimes called paranoia; that is, she talked incessantly about how "they" were out to get her, and how "they" were controlling her mind by whispering evil thoughts inside her head. Mrs. C. was a bright and rather pleasant woman, but the staff complained that she "talked their ears off" and that she "wouldn't obey." When Brian pressed the staff for more specific complaints, it turned out that it wasn't just the *frequency* of her speech that annoyed them, it was *what* Mrs. C. talked about. And about the only time the woman wouldn't obey was in the mornings, when she refused to get out of bed when awakened by a staff member.

Next Brian asked Mrs. C. what she wanted from him. The answer was quick—money. The woman was penniless. What she wanted most at that time was to buy a cheap transistor radio. Why? "Because the radio drowns out the voices in my head," Mrs. C. said loudly. So Brian showed her ways of earning money by acting in appropriate rather than inappropriate ways.

To begin with, Brian promised Mrs. C. a nickel for every morning that she got up on time. Before this "therapy," Mrs. C. never arose when awakened. The first week the nickels were given to her, she made it up 5 days out of 7. The second week she got up on time every day. The third week—without coaching from the staff—Mrs. C. got up so early that she made the rounds with the staff members helping them get other patients out of bed.

Brian had a long talk with Mrs. C. during which they listed all of the speech patterns that most people would admit were "crazy," "disturbing," or "inappropriate." Then they made another list of things that most people would admit were "sane," "pleasing," or "appropriate." Brian then started rewarding Mrs. C. with a penny for each 5 minutes she could converse with him using only "normal" speech. He praised her warmly for everything she said that was appropriate. By the end of the semester, Mrs. C. was able to get through 30 out of 31 5-minute periods in a row without saying anything "crazy." By this time, the staff members were so impressed with her progress that they spent a great deal of time encouraging her. She went home on leave and did so well that she was discharged soon thereafter.

Again, make no mistake; Mrs. C. still had many problems. For instance, when she finally earned enough pennies and nickels to buy the radio, Brian once more asked her why she wanted it. "Because it drowns . . ." she started to say, and then stopped. She looked Brian straight in the eye, smiled broadly, and said, "Because the music is so pretty!" I'd judge from this response that the voices were still there inside her head, but that she had learned not to pay much attention to them. Moreover, she realized that if she didn't punish people with her "crazy talk," they would usually be much more accepting of her. And it was an undergraduate student who helped her learn this very important fact!

The students in the lab course did so well at the hospital that first semester that we were invited to send more students the next year. By 1972, we were placing young men and women not merely in the mental hospital, but in the local school system, in prisons, homes for juvenile offenders, sheltered workshops, in various industrial settings, and in a wide variety of medical clinics and hospital wards. Our rules were simple. Above all else, the student-therapists were to do no harm. And since we required that the students measure the consequences of their own behaviors, they had a pretty good notion at all times of just what it was they were doing. Second, they were never to criticize, punish, or speak negatively about anything or anybody. Third, they were always to try to obtain the informed consent of their clients as to what the goals of the therapy would be. In class, I had learned the great benefits that come from writing an "educational contract" with each student—a contract that specified exactly what the student was going to do, what the teacher was going to do, and what the rewards or sanctions would be for various types of performance. The student-therapists did the same thing with their clients. Except with nonverbal patients, or with children too young to read or write, the students always wrote out a "therapy contract" that was signed by the client, the therapist, the student's supervisor, myself, and by anyone else (such as the staff at the hospital) whose behaviors might influence the outcome of the treatment.

These contracts have a lot going for them, not the least of which is that they keep everything out in the open. They also allow for some relatively objective measurement of the "success rate" of the therapy. I'm delighted to say that, over the years, our students have achieved better than 80 percent success in helping their clients fulfill the "change contracts" that the clients themselves agreed to.

As the behaviorists learned long ago, nothing succeeds like success. For instance, each semester we send five or more students out to work with inmates at a nearby prison. These prisoner-clients are all volunteers who wish to improve their academic skills. We use no punishment, no deprivation, no threats, no coercion. Since we are not usually allowed to bring anything into the prison—not even gumdrops —the students must rely on such social reinforcers as praise and sincere concern for the prisoners' welfare. However, the most potent reward imaginable often turns out to be each inmate's realization that he actually can succeed at the challenging task of learning to read, write, or handle arithmetic.

The students begin by getting to know the prisoners and by finding out what each man likes and doesn't like. Next, the prisoners state their goals—doubling their reading speed, learning to handle complex fractions, increasing the amount of time they spend studying each day, or other academic achievement. Once a contract is written, it is up to the student-therapist to find ways of encouraging the prisoner to change himself. The written contract helps immensely, for it forces us to keep accurate records. And once the prisoner starts charting his own improvement, just looking at the graph's upward movement "turns on" most of these men more than would gumdrops or pats on the back.

Convicts are our society's failures; they've even failed at crime, or they wouldn't be in prison. Over the years, these men have learned that they can't succeed at anything for very long, and their self-attitudes are typically rather poor. Once they discover that they can in fact control their own destinies and achieve their own goals, they sometimes show rather dramatic improvements.

For instance, take the case of Bob P., a young white man with whom we worked. Bob came from a broken home. He had his first brush with the law when he was 7; by the time he was 11 he was shipped off to a reform school for stealing a car. He learned how to drink and fight very well; but he learned little or nothing in school because he seldom was there. In 1972 he landed in the prison near Ann Arbor on an auto theft charge. Although he was 22 at the time, his test scores suggested that he had but the equivalent of a fourth-grade education. Because Bob wanted to be able to read better, he volunteered for our program. Within 6 months he had progressed to the point of almost completing his high school education.

Why this sudden achievement? For several reasons, I believe. To begin with, all his life Bob had been punished for almost everything he did. What a change it was to have someone around who refused to punish, and who rewarded him instead! As Bob learned he could read, his horizons expanded enormously. He began to see the consequences of his behavior toward other people—how they responded to his aggression with aggressive responses of their own. With the encouragement of the lab students, Bob P. learned to control his temper in most situations; he also learned to reward the people around him when they pleased him and to try to ignore them (rather than hit them) when they annoyed him. Bob now plans to enroll in college as soon as he is out of prison, and to take a degree in psychology in order to be able to work in prisons and help other inmates learn the lessons he has learned.

Bob's major problem is with some of the prison authorities. When he arrived at this jail, he was categorized as someone "born to raise hell," a man with a "criminal personality." Now he has changed his way of behaving, but the authorities don't always trust such changes. "Bob's just conning you," one of the officials told me. "He's just pretending to behave himself. Deep down inside, Bob's still the rotten bastard he always was." Only time will tell if this official is right or wrong. It seems likely that the official suffers from what I call the "intuitive fallacy," the belief that you can't judge people by what they do, but rather should judge them according to your gut reactions and emotional prejudices.

At some point in our lifetimes, most of us want to change ourselves. And hardly a day goes by that we don't also wish to make changes in some of the people around us. But before we can create a workable psychotechnology of personal change, we must first answer some fundamental questions about what a human being is.

When Harvard professor William James got psychology going in America back in 1875, he called this new field "the science of mind." The object of psychology—to James and to many thousands of people thereafter—was to explain mental events. The very word *psychology* comes from a Greek term meaning "the study of the mind." Even today, when a psychologist at a cocktail party admits what his or her profession is, the reaction from others is likely to be, "Oh, don't you try to read my mind!"

In the 100 years since James opened the first American psychology laboratory, psychologists have only just begun to learn how to "read people's minds"—and we still don't do it very well. It is only in recent times that most of us have realized that people are a great deal more than their minds, for we have bodies and behaviors as well as thoughts. You cannot hope to understand yourself (or anyone else) unless you are willing to look at the human experience from three different viewpoints at once: We have biological inputs and outputs, cognitive (mental) inputs and outputs, and social inputs and outputs. To ignore any one of these three viewpoints (or levels of analysis) is to limit your comprehension of the complexity of the human organism.

Science is, for the most part, an attempt to determine what kinds of inputs are associated with (or correlated with) what kinds of outputs. Explanations of the processes that appear to link inputs with outputs make up what we call *theoretical* science, but theories are of little value unless they are based on measurable input-output correlations.

Technology, on the other hand, usually boils down to using feed-forward and feedback in an attempt to change or control outputs. If we are to build an effective psychotechnology of personal change, then, we must begin by realizing that there are three different types of outputs that we must bring under control—the biological/emotional, the cognitive/mental, and the social-behavioral. That means, I think, that we must somehow match the type of feedback (input) to the type of output that we wish to influence.

In 1973, while writing the book *Understanding Human Behavior* (McConnell, 1974), it occurred to me that there are three general classes of rewarding inputs (reinforcers) that humans respond to: sensory or biological pleasures (such as food and sex); cognitive or intellectual joys (such as chess and bridge, art and literature, science and mathematics); and social happiness (grades, status, power, family ties, helping others, and interpersonal relationships). Although almost everyone seems to enjoy all three classes of reinforcers, each of us appears to have his or her own unique bias. Some of us really do enjoy sex in preference to chess, while others of us prefer seeing our names in print more than we enjoy an orgasm. Whether our pleasure-biases are learned, innate, or (more likely) a combination of both remains to be seen. But it is quite possible that a strong liking for one or more of these three general classes of inputs is built into our genes and hence helps shape our basic personalities. For it does seem as if much of what we do in life can be explained in terms of our trying to predict and control our preferred types of inputs. The type of feedback a psychotechnologist should use with a particular client, therefore, must depend on the client's own desires, needs, and problems.

Looking back, I see that I would have done better had I paid closer attention to what my students had been trying to tell me all along. For instance, I had at first thought that Jane Michener taught Miss B. to talk using gumdrops as a reward. Instead, Jane had hunted around for a variety of rewarding feedbacks and had tried them all. She modeled the behavior she wanted from Miss B., and then she fed back biological inputs (candy), intellectual inputs (graphs charting Miss B.'s improvement), and social inputs (praise), until Miss B. met the model. However, as Jane told me much later, the "magic moment" in the therapy came when Jane suddenly realized that Miss B. was responding much more to pats on the back and social approval than to gumdrops and graphs. After this breakthrough, Miss B. was sometimes able to set her own models and find her own forms of feedback.

The undergraduates in my lab class typically have done a superb and very humane job of helping the people they work with; but they did so by ignoring those narrow-minded theorists who insist that "people are no more than biological mechanisms," or "you are what you think," or that "group pressures determine your personality." Sometimes a person's problems stem from a mixed-up set of biological inputs and outputs; sometimes the problems are at a cognitive level, sometimes at the level of social interactions; occasionally, all three input-output systems are in disarray. Without quite knowing what they were doing, my students succeeded by making rather shrewd guesses at what was wrong with which system, and by providing positive feedback appropriate to the need at hand.

As I see it, our job for the next few years is that of gaining a much clearer understanding of what the inputs and outputs actually are at each of the three important levels of analysis. Once we begin to measure ourselves in terms of these three systems, we can begin to guess at the biological, mental, and social processes that connect inputs to outputs at all three levels. And it is only when the science of psychology has told us more about these inputs, processes, and outputs that we can build a psychotechnology that will allow us to change ourselves into the human beings that we would all like to become.

And that, surely, is a goal that both my father and mother would have approved of.

REFERENCES

Asch, S. E. 1948. The doctrine of suggestion, prestige, and imitation in social psychology. *Psychological Review,* 55:250–276.

Ayllon, T. and Azrin, N. H. 1968. *The Token Economy: A Motivational System for Therapy and Rehabilitation.* New York: Appleton-Century-Crofts.

Bandura, A. 1969. *Principles of Behavior Modification.* New York: Holt, Rinehart and Winston.

Blake, R. R. 1953. The interaction-feeling hypothesis applied to psychological therapy groups. *Sociometry,* 16:253–265.

Blake, R. R.; Helson, H.; and Mouton, J. S. 1957. The generality of conformity behavior as a function of factual anchorage, difficulty of task, and amount of social pressure. *Journal of Personality,* 25:294–305.

Blake, R. R. and Ramsey, G. V. 1951. *Perception: An Approach to Personality.* New York: Ronald.

Eysenck, H. J. 1964. *Experiments in Behavior Therapy.* Oxford: Pergamon Press.

Gantt, W. H. 1945. Physiological mechanisms and animal experimentation. *Proceedings.* Annual scientific meeting of the Research Committee, American Society for Research in Psychosomatic Problems.

Hebb, D. O. 1949. *Organization of Behavior.* New York: Wiley.

Hebb, D. O. 1961. Sensory deprivation: Facts in search of a theory. *Journal of Nervous and Mental Disorders,* 132:40–43.

Helson, H.; Blake, R. R.; Mouton, J. S.; and Olmstead, J. A. 1956. Attitudes as adjustments to stimulus, background, and residual factors. *Journal of Abnormal and Social Psychology,* 52:314–322.

Keller, F. S. 1968. "Good-bye, teacher . . ." *Journal of Applied Behavior Analysis,* 1:79–89.

Liddell, H. S. 1956. *Emotional Hazards in Animal and Man.* Springfield, Ill.: Charles C. Thomas.

Masserman, J. 1943. *Behavior and Neurosis.* Chicago: University of Chicago Press.

McConnell, J. V. 1962. Memory transfer through cannibalism in planarians. *Journal of Neuropsychiatry,* 3 (supplement 1):542–548.

McConnell, J. V. 1964. On the turning of worms: A reply to James and Holas. *Psychological Record,* 14:13–20.

McConnell, J. V. 1974. *Understanding Human Behavior.* New York: Holt, Rinehart and Winston.

McConnell, J. V.; Jacobson, A. F.; and Kimble, D. P. 1959. The effects of regeneration upon retention of a conditioned response in the planarian. *Journal of Comparative and Physiological Psychology,* 52:1–5.

Patterson, G. and Guillion, M. E. 1971. *Living with Children.* Champaign, Ill.: Research Press.

Pavlov, I. P. 1927. *Conditioned Reflexes.* Oxford: Oxford University Press.

Sherif, M. 1935. A study of some social factors in perception. *Archives of Psychology,* No. 187. New York.

Skinner, B. F. 1958. Teaching machines. *Science,* 128:967–977.

Skinner, B. F. 1962. Two "synthetic social relations." *Journal of the Experimental Analysis of Behavior,* 5:531–533.

Thompson, R. and McConnell, J. V. 1955. Classical conditioning in the planarian, Dugesia dorotocephala. *Journal of Comparative and Physiological Psychology,* 48:65–68.

Wolpe, J. 1969. *The Practice of Behavior Therapy.* Oxford: Pergamon Press.

GUILT BY FABRICATION: PSYCHOLOGY AND THE EYEWITNESS
Robert Buckhout

Science demands precision but not certainty. Law aims at certainty but lacks precision because its quest for certainty glosses over the innumerable variables of individual and situational diversities, which probably will always cause law to be uncertain—(Marshall, 1966)

It's hard to be a social psychologist. Nobody knows exactly what a social psychologist does—especially the social psychologist. He or she must contend both with the popular misconceptions regarding the psychologist among his laymen friends, and with the deep suspicions of his more hard-nosed colleagues who wonder if social psychology is, indeed, scientific. We suffer the problem of dealing with phenomena which are messy—translate as real—and with experiences about which every human being has some opinion. If we spend too much time in the laboratory, we sacrifice reality for rigor. If we work in the field, we trade off control for reality. If we try to achieve both relevance and rigor, we spend more time, more money and risk schizophrenia.

INTRODUCTION

The story of my present work in the social psychology of the courtroom began several years ago in Berkeley, Calif. I had a varied background in experimental research on human engineering problems with the Air Force, stress research, psychophysiology, attitude change, and social influence. At the time in Berkeley, I was interested primarily in applying psychological research techniques to the problems of

Robert Buckhout is with the Department of Psychology, Brooklyn College of the City University of New York.

© Copyright 1974 by Robert Buckhout. Requests for reprints or additional data should be sent to the author at the Center for Responsive Psychology, Brooklyn College, Brooklyn, N. Y. 11210.

I owe more than can be expressed in mere words to a devoted group of undergraduate students who helped me do the research on which this article is based. This group includes Andrea Alper, Susan Chern, Robinsue Frohboese, Richard Harwood, Daryl Figueroa, Ethan Hoff, Carolyn Hogan, Noreen Norton, Vincent Reilly, Betti Sachs, Glenn Silverberg, Miriam Slomovits, and Lynne Williams. I am also indebted to attorneys Leo Branton and Howard Moore who taught me to present psychology in English to a jury.

society. At one point, I was asked to help out a Public Defender whose defendant was accused of rape. This began what I feel has been an exciting learning experience for me and hopefully, a useful contribution to justice.

The young Mexican-American defendant had been accused by three women of raping them in a darkened room some 3 years before.* Working with the attorney and the defendant, I prepared myself to testify as an expert on the social and perceptual factors involved in eyewitness identification. In this particular case there were many obvious factors which tend to contribute to the unreliability of observers. The solid background in the study of memory, learning, information processing and perception which is part of the academic training of most psychologists, is sufficient to analyze a crime in search of these factors. I had the added advantage of some Air Force experience with aerial reconnaissance as well as experimental work on the effects of verbal conditioning.

Habitual television viewers are undoubtedly familiar with the line-up—the formal multiple choice of a witness's ability to identify a suspect in a crime. But the process of identification in this formal setting—which now is rarely done—is only a small part of the socio-dynamic process that a witness to a crime goes through before testifying before a jury. In the rape case, the women had gone through mug books, had given their description of the rapist many times, and had even been shown a driver's license photo of the defendant—whom they declared was not the man. Three years and several lineups later, the police picked up the man on another charge and proceeded to administer a new test—a set of photos—to the victims. This time they identified the defendant.

During the trial, I testified about basic theories of perception, the negative effects of stress on accuracy in reporting, the problem of memory loss over time, the effect of poor lighting on visual identifications, and the powerful effects of social influence on test-taking behavior. In line with Rosenthal's (1966) work on experimenter bias, I observed that the officers administering the identification tests knew they had a man in custody. Furthermore I noted that the women victims were anxious to resolve the case, that the photospread was biased (the defendant's photo stood out), and that having rejected the defendant previously, the victims could be succumbing to suggestion and social influence as demonstrated by their testimony.

The reader may wonder why such unreliable identification testimony became the basis of a jury trial, but, as I was cross-examined, the answer became clearer. The prosecution had a weak case but wanted to ''get'' the defendant who had been in trouble before. Eyewitness identification, with the dramatic pointing out of a defendant in

*People v. Chavez, Superior Court, Alameda County, Calif., May 15, 1970. Testimony of Robert Buckhout.

court, is a pathway to an easy conviction since it impresses juries. I found myself being questioned at length about the perceptual and physiological characteristics of the eye, and being challenged on my assertion that stress leads to observer unreliability. The result was that the jury was divided, and the defendant released. My attorney friends and I had been successful in bolstering the jury's sense of reasonable doubt that the defendant was identified correctly. In turn, I began to focus hard on the problem of eyewitness identification and to develop a research strategy designed to yield information which could be of direct value to the court. But first, following Lewin's dictum that there is nothing so practical as a good theory, I had to develop a conceptual framework for thinking about the problem of the eyewitness in relation to contemporary psychological thinking on perception, information processing, and social influence.

TOWARD A MODEL

If you see an auto accident or witness a murder, and are then asked to describe what you saw, there is no one who can create an instant replay in slow motion for you. You depend upon your memory with all its limitations—a fact which may be of minor importance in your ordinary daily activities. If you are unreliable, if you shade the truth in describing what you saw, it matters little. But, when you are called in as a witness to a crime, the situation escalates in importance. A person's life or an institution's reputation may be at stake. You may be asked to report what you saw in excruciating detail as if you were a videotape recorder.

In court, the written transcript contains your replay of the events. The prosecutor will attempt to show that you have perfect recall; the defense attorney will try to show, by cross-examining you vigorously, that your "tape recorder" is defective. The stakes are high because in modern courts eyewitness testimony is more highly valued than alibi testimony or "circumstantial" evidence. Uncritical acceptance of eyewitness testimony seems to be based on the *fallacious* notion that the human observer is a perfect recording device—that everything that passes before his eyes is recorded and can be "pulled out" by sharp questioning or "refreshing one's memory." In a rare categorical statement by a psychologist, I argue that this is *impossible*—human perception and memory function effectively by being selective. A human being has no particular need for perfect recall; perception and memory are decision-making processes affected by the totality of a person's abilities, background, the environment, his attiudes, motives, beliefs, and the methods used in testing recollection of people and events.

As I work in criminal courts, I'm cognizant of a fundamental clash of conceptions—the nineteenth century vs. the twentieth century view of a person. The nineteenth century view—embodied in psychophysics —asserted a scientific parallel between the mechanisms of the physical world and the mechanisms of the brain. The courts in the United States accept this nineteenth century epistemology quite readily—as does much of the public. However, modern psychologists have developed a conception of a whole human being with an information processing mechanism which is far more complex than the one in the nineteenth century model. Unfortunately, research psychologists, who began by studying practical problems (functionalism), have become more esoteric in their research and less visible in the real world.

I regard the human observer as an *active* rather than a passive observer of the environment; motivated by (a) a desire to be accurate as he seeks *meaning* from the overabundance of information which affects his senses; and (b) a desire to live up to the expectations of others and stay in their good graces, a factor which makes the eye, the ear, and other senses *social* as well as physical organs.

In our laboratory experiments on the physical capabilities of the eye and the ear, we speak of an "ideal observer," by which we mean a subject who would respond cooperatively to lights and tones with unbiased ears and eyes, much like a machine. *However, the ideal observer does not exist.* Stated in other words, the ideal observer is a convenient fiction. Great effort and expense are put into the design of laboratories to provide an "ideal physical environment" free of distractions to enable the observer to concentrate. Such ideal environments can be approached only in a laboratory; in the real world they are seldom, if ever, found. The nonmachinelike human observer copes reasonably effectively in uncontrolled environments with a perceptual capability which fits his nature as a social being.

In a machine we would expect that what comes out (the report) would be a direct function of what goes in (the input or stimulus). However, human perception can be characterized in terms of the phrase, *the whole is greater than the sum of the parts*. This characterization reflects the ability of the human observer to take the fragments of information to which he has time to pay attention (i.e., actively reduce the information), and to reach conclusions based on his prior experience, familiarity, biases, expectancy, faith, desire to appear certain, etc. Most human observers, for example, look at the moon and see a sphere—despite their inability to verify the shape of the unseen side. The conclusion, in psychological terms, is a *decision* efficiently arrived at and independent of the physical evidence which is incomplete (Miller and Buckhout, 1973).

In the eyewitness situation, particularly one involving criminal matters, the fallible human observer is usually in a less than ideal environment. He is subject to factors which we believe inherently limit a person's ability to give a complete account of what took place or to identify the persons involved with complete accuracy (Borchard, 1961).

The section of the paper which follows is a brief outline of the kinds of data which we have obtained from basic research on cognitive and perceptual processes. These processes have implications for the development of an applied science of eyewitness psychology.*

SOURCES OF UNRELIABILITY IN EYEWITNESS IDENTIFICATION
A. The Original Situation
1. INSIGNIFICANCE OF THE EVENTS OBSERVED

In placing the accused at or near the scene of a crime, witnesses are frequently asked to recall seeing the accused at a time when they were not *attaching importance to the event*. They may have been exposed to the scene in passing or as part of the normal routine of an ordinary day. Research on this type of situation dates at least back to 1895, when J. McKeen Cattell wrote about an experiment in which he asked students to describe the people, places and events which they had encountered walking to school over very familiar paths (cited in Murphy, 1949). The reports were incomplete and unreliable; some individuals were highly certain of details which had no basis in fact. My interpretation is that insignificant events do not motivate the person fully to use the selective process of attention, thus making his recall less reliable.

2. SHORTNESS OF THE PERIOD OF OBSERVATION

This obvious source of unreliability acts to reduce the number of features a person can attend to. The tachistoscope (a projector with a controlled shutter which can adjust the duration of time that an image will appear on a screen) is used in controlled research to test recall. Of course, the shorter exposures produce less reliable identification and recall. Fleeting glimpses are common in eyewitness accounts, especially in fast moving, threatening situations. Thus, in the Sacco-Vanzetti case in the 1920s, one of the witnesses gave a detailed and obviously fabricated description of one defendant on the basis of a glance that lasted only a fraction of a second.

3. LESS THAN IDEAL OBSERVATION CONDITIONS

Crimes seldom occur in the well controlled confines of the laboratory. The fast-moving, threatening, chaotic flow of events of a crime in progress conflicts with the perceptual capability of the common observer. Often the presence of a crowd, distance, poor lighting, fast movements, etc. prevent the efficient workings of the attention process. Well established thresholds exist for the eye and the other senses,

*An excellent and thorough review of the literature can be found in Levine, F. J. and Tapp, J. L. The psychology of criminal identification; The gap from *Wade* to *Kirby*. *University of Pennsylvania Law Review*, 1079, No. 5, May 1973. Available as a separate for $0.50 from Foundation Publications, American Bar Foundation, 1155 East 60th St., Chicago, Ill. 60637.

based on research into the limits of efficient functioning of those senses. As those limits are approached, eyewitness accounts can become quite unreliable.

In one case in my experience, a police officer testified that he saw the defendant shoot a victim while standing in a doorway 120 feet away. However, this doorway was so poorly lit that other observers could hardly see a person's silhouette, let alone a face. Independent measures of the lighting of the scene revealed that the light falling on the eye amounted to less than ⅓ of the light from a candle— clearly suggesting that the witness reached his conclusion from factors other than what he directly saw. We felt the officer was either lying or suggesting a person he knew about, who would logically fit the theory being proposed about the crime. We shot some photos recreating the crime to demonstrate that a positive identification was not very probable. The jury members went to the scene of the crime, placed their one black juror in the doorway, and found that they could not identify his features. The jury acquitted the defendant.

B. The Observer
4. STRESS

"I could never forget what he looked like!" This common statement expresses the faith that people have in their memory—even under stress. When a person's life or well-being is threatened, a stress pattern known as the General Adaptional Syndrome (G.A.S.) can be expected to occur in varying degrees (Selye, 1956). This pattern is due to an increase in adrenaline levels and involves increased heart-rate, breathing rate, and higher blood pressure. The end result is a dramatic increase in available energy, making the person capable of running fast, fighting, lifting enormous weight—taking the steps necessary to ensure his safety or survival.

But, if you are under extreme stress, you will be a less reliable witness than you would be normally. Research shows that observers are *less* capable of remembering details, less accurate in reading dials, less accurate in detecting signals when under stress. A person is paying more attention to his own well-being and safety than to non-essential elements in the environment. My research with trained Air Force flight crew members, confirms that even highly trained people became poorer observers when under stress. They never can forget the stress and what hit them; the events, being highly significant at the time, can be remembered. But memory for details, clothing worn, colors, etc., is not as clear. Time estimates are especially exaggerated under stress.

You might test this idea, (if you are old enough) by thinking back to where you were in 1963 when you first heard the news of the assassination of President John F. Kennedy. Chances are you can recall vividly where you were and who you were with. But now describe the clothing of the first person (not a relative or friend) you saw immediately after the news arrived, describe what you were wearing, etc. Then, if you were a witness to the killing of Lee Harvey Oswald on television, try to describe the people next to the killer. These are logical questions—seemingly trivial—but if you were in court, would you be ready to admit that you were too concerned with more important things to pay attention?

5. PHYSICAL CONDITION OF THE OBSERVER

The human senses function much less efficiently when the body has become fatigued or injured, when the person is advanced in age, and when the person has subjected himself to the overuse of alcohol, depressant, stimulant, or hallucinogenic drugs.* We have seen eyewitness testimony reports which physically were impossible to have been accurately made when we compared the person's physical condition to the conditions at the scene of the crime. In one case a witness who was color-blind testified to seeing shades of red, when obviously it was physically impossible for him actually to see red. Color-blindness—principally the inability to see red and green—is an inherited condition which affects approximately 8–10 percent of all men.† In this case, I testified to express doubt about the reliability of the witness' testimony, basing my doubts on the presumption that he was red-green color-blind.‡ The prosecution brought in an ophthalmologist as a rebuttal witness, who argued that I was wrong—the witness was in fact a monochromat—the rarest of color-blindness conditions in which no color perception is possible. The exchange of expert opinions helped to raise the possibility that the witness was perceptually filling in his testimony, in much the same way color-blind people function in society by using inferences rather than the sensations themselves. Specific applied research is needed on the effects of individual differences (sex, wearing glasses, hearing deficiencies, etc.) on the accuracy of eyewitness testimony. Alcohol or drug usage in excess can definitely reduce visual capacity. The sophistication of modern corrective medical techniques suggests a more detailed questioning of eyewitnesses by attorneys over such matters

---

*The evidence of the effects of LSD and marijuana on human perception is not presently complete. The question of dosage levels, as in the case of alcohol, cannot be generalized since humans show wide individual differences in their ability to function with differing amounts of any intoxicant.

†Tests for the common types of color-blindness are easily administered; they can be found in most Introductory Psychology books and are described in Stevens, S. S. *Handbook of Experimental Psychology,* New York: Wiley, 1950. Estimates of the frequency of color-blindness in the population vary considerably. We do know that it occurs primarily in men.

‡*People* v. *Angela Davis,* Superior Court, Santa Clara County, Calif., May 23, 1972, Testimony of Robert Buckhout.

as eyeglasses, hearing losses, hearing aids, artificial pacemakers for the heart, contact lenses, etc., which may affect the witnesses' physical ability to make a reliable eyewitness report.

6. PRIOR CONDITIONING AND EXPERIENCE

Psychologists have done extensive research on how set, or expectancy, is used by the human observer to make judgments more efficiently. In a classic experiment done in the 1930s, observers were shown a display of playing cards for a few seconds and asked to report the number of aces of spades in the display (Postman and Rosenzweig, 1962). Most observers reported only three, when actually there were five. Two of the aces of spades were colored red instead of the more familiar black color. The interpretation was given that since people were so familiar with black aces of spades, they did not waste time looking carefully at the display. Thus, efficiency in this case, led to *unreliable* observation. In many criminal cases, the prior conditioning of the witness may enable him to report facts or events which were not present but which *should* have been. Studies also indicate that white observers show better recognition of white people than of black people when tested with photographs of both whites and blacks whom they have seen before (Laughery, 1970). Recent research supports the proposition that observers have better recognition of people of their own race (Malpass and Kravitz, 1969).

7. PERSONAL BIASES AND STEREOTYPES

Expectancy in its least palatable form can be found in the case of biases or *prejudices* held by a witness. A victim of a mugging may initially report being attacked by "niggers," and may, because of limited experience as well as prejudice, be unable to tell one black man from another ("they all look alike to me"). In a classic study of this phenomenon, observers were asked to take a brief look at a drawing of several people on a subway train (Allport and Postman, 1947). In the picture, a black man was seated and a white man was standing with a knife in his hand. When questioned later, observers tended to report having seen the knife in the hand of the *black* man.

Prejudices may be racial, religious, or based on physical characteristics such as long hair, dirty clothes, status, etc. All human beings have some *stereotypes* upon which they make perceptual judgments; stereotypes which lead not only to prejudice but are a means of making decisions more efficiently. A witness to an auto accident may save thinking time by reporting his well ingrained stereotype about "woman drivers." But these short-cuts to thinking may be erroneously reported and expanded upon by an eyewitness, without his being aware that he is describing his stereotype rather than the events which actually took place. If the witness's biases are shared by the investigator taking his statement, the report may reflect their mutual biases rather than what was actually seen (Tafjel, 1969).

In some of my trial experience, I have encountered eyewitnesses who were biased so much toward the prosecution's case that they were unwilling to acknowledge any doubt about their final identification of a suspect despite their uncertainty in the first identification. In effect they were no more credible in their testimony than were the alibi witnesses in the case. Some banks and airlines issue memoranda to their employees to cooperate with police and prosecutors. This represents responsible citizenship, but also a potential source of bias, since those employees are getting a clear message of their company's strong interest in convicting the accused.

8. NEEDS AND MOTIVES—SEEING WHAT WE WANT TO SEE

The meaning of the phrase "need influences perception," has been demonstrated in numerous experiments in which people report seeing certain things which in fact are not present. Persons who volunteered to go without food for 24 hours were asked to report what they "saw" in a series of blurred slides presented on a screen (Levine, Chein, and Murphy, 1942). The longer they were deprived of food, the more frequently they reported seeing "food" in the blurred pictures. An analysis of the motives of the eyewitness at the time of a crime can be very valuable in determining whether or not the witness is reporting what he wanted to see. In one field study, a student dressed in a black bag which covered him completely, visited classes in a university. The young witnesses were asked to describe the nature of the person in the bag (Buckhout, 1968). Most reports, in the absence of any real evidence, described the "bag" as a black man, a nut, a symbol of alienation, etc. Tests showed that the descriptions were related to the needs and motives of the witnesses. The student in the bag was in fact a white honor student.

9. DESIRE TO BE A PART OF HISTORY

A common behavior, observed by journalists and psychologists, is the tendency for people to claim that they were present when a significant historical event took place near their hometown or city. They make this claim even though they were not physically present or active in the event. Such a story will make them sound interesting and it is usually difficult or impossible to check it out. In one case, a journalist fabricated a charming human interest story about a small town and published it through the newspaper wire services. He visited the town and interviewed citizens who claimed to have played a part in or witnessed this totally fictitious event. In criminal cases with publicity and a controversial defendant, it is not uncommon for volunteer witnesses to come forward. In the Angela Davis case, at least one eyewitness

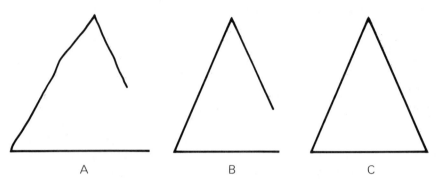

A   B   C

Figure 17.1. *Progression of reproductions from (a) original to (b) 30 days later, and finally to (c) 90 days later illustrating perceptual "filling in."*

came forward a year after the arrest of the defendant, offering testimony which may well have been motivated by a desire to be a part of history.*

C. Testing for Identification
10. LENGTH OF TIME FROM EVENT TO TEST

One of the most stable findings in the psychological research literature is the forgetting of verbal and pictorial information over the passage of time. During this time without practice, a person pays attention to more immediate matters as he efficiently copes with life. Perfect recall of information or faces basically is unnecessary and is found rarely, if ever. The testing of recognition from a lineup or a set of photos will therefore be less reliable, the longer the time that has passed from the event to the test. I assume that social influence has more time to assert itself as time passes.

11. FILLING IN DETAILS WHICH WERE NOT PRESENT

An efficient memory is characterized by certain techniques used to "store" information so that the essence of the information can be recalled when needed. One technique is called "perceptual filling in"—an incomplete or fragmentary image is "cleaned up" by the observer when he is tested later. In research on this phenomenon, subjects first drew an object they were shown. They were then tested on their ability to reproduce the drawing 30 days later and 3 months later (Postman and Rosenzweig, 1962).

As can be seen in the sample result in Figure 17.1, the observers first tended to make the object more symmetrical and later filled it in to make a nice neat triangle. This finding was repeated with many objects—the tendency being for people to "improve" their memory by making their memory seem more "logical." In our analysis of eyewit-

*People v. Angela Davis, ibid.

ness reports in criminal cases, we have seen the reports get more accurate, more complete, and less ambiguous as the witness moves from the initial police report, through a grand jury to actual testimony. The process of "filling in" is an efficient way to remember, but it can lead to unreliable recognition testing, since the witness may adjust his memory to fit the available suspects or pictures. If we rule out lying, it is possible that the witness may be unaware he is distorting or reconstructing his memory. In his very effort to be conscientious, he may fabricate parts of his recall in order to make a chaotic memory seem more plausible to the people asking questions.

Loftus (1974) demonstrated how the semantic value of the words used in asking questions about a filmed auto accident caused witnesses to distort their reports. When witnesses were asked a question using the word "smashed" (as opposed to bumped) they gave higher estimates of speed and were more likely to report having seen broken glass, when, in fact, there was no broken glass.

12. UNFAIR TEST CONSTRUCTION

The lineup and the array of photographs used in testing the eyewitness' ability to identify a suspect can be analyzed as fair or unfair on the basis of criteria which most psychologists can agree on. A fair test should be designed carefully so that first, all items have an equal chance of being selected by a person who didn't see the suspect; second, the items are similar enough to each other and to the original description of the suspect to be *confusing* to a person who is merely guessing; and last, the test is conducted without leading questions or suggestions from the test giver.

All too frequently, I have found that lineups or photograph arrays are carelessly assembled or even rigged in such a way as to make the eyewitness identification test completely unreliable. If, for example, you present five pictures, the chance should be only ⅕ or 20 percent that any one picture will be chosen on the basis of guessing; but frequently, a single picture of a suspect may stand out. In the Angela Davis case, one set of nine pictures used to check identification contained three pictures of the defendant taken at an outdoor rally, two mug shots of other women with different names, one of a 55 year-old woman, etc.* It was so easy for a witness to rule out five pictures as ridiculous choices, that the "test" was reduced to four pictures—including three of Davis. This means that a witness had a 75 percent chance to pick out her picture, whether he had seen her or not. Such a "test" is meaningless to a psychologist and probably tainted as an item of evidence in court.

Research on memory has also shown that if one item in the array of photos is uniquely different (in dress, race, height, sex, photographic

*People v. Angela Davis, ibid.

quality, etc.), it is more likely to be picked out and attended to. Such an array is not *confusing* enough for it to be called a test. When a teacher makes up a multiple choice test, he designs several answers which sound or look alike to make it difficult for a person who doesn't know the right answer to succeed. Police lineups and photo layouts are multiple choice tests. If the rules for designing tests are ignored by authorities, the tests become unreliable.

13. SUGGESTIONS, BIAS AND SOCIAL INFLUENCE IN THE TEST SITUATION

No test, whether with photographs or a lineup, can be completely free of suggestion. When a witness is brought in by the police to be shown a set of photographs, he can safely assume that there is a reason for this; that the authorities have a suspect in mind (or in custody). He is thus under some pressure to pick *someone,* even if the officer showing the photographs is properly careful not to force the issue. The basic books in the field of eyewitness identification (e.g., Wald, 1965) all recommend that no suggestions, hints, or pressure be transmitted to the witness, but my experience with criminal investigation reveals frequent abuse by zealous police officers. Such abuses include remarks about which pictures to skip, saying "are you sure?" when the witness makes what they consider an error, giving hints, showing enthusiasm when the "right" picture is picked, etc. All such errors make us wonder if the identification is based on the witness' memory or on his desire to please—a doubt which clouds the reliability of the test.

In one murder case I worked on, a young witness first could not recognize anyone in a lineup. She was encouraged to try again and again with a videotaped version of the same lineup, until she finally chose the defendant in the case. Under cross-examination she revealed that she had been trying to be sure she picked the same man the police picked. Social pressure plus practice produced this completely unreliable testimony.*

Suggestions can be very subtle. Psychological research has been done on tests where the test giver was merely instructed to smile and be very approving only when a certain type of photograph or statement was picked. Such social approval led to an increase in the rate of picking that type of photograph—even though there was no "correct" answer (Buckhout, 1965). Using a test which measures a *need for social approval,* it has been shown that people who are high in that need (especially those who enthusiastically volunteer information) are even more influenced by suggestion and approval coming from the test giver. It is hard to say "No, I don't recognize anyone," when the pressure is on the person to keep from looking like a fool.

People v. *Fragosa,* Santa Barbara County, Calif., May 1, 1974.

14. CONFORMITY

Are two eyewitnesses better than one? ten? seventeen? Are one-hundred-fifty better than one?

Certainly, the more agreement we find with our fellow man, the more confidence we have in our judgments of reality. But similarity of judgment is a two-edged sword—we can agree in error as easily as we agree in truth. Research on conformity has been an important topic in social psychology for decades. The results of this research indicate that an observer can be persuaded to conform to the majority opinion, even when the majority is dead wrong. In the typical experiment, seven observers are shown two lines and asked to tell which is shorter. Six of the people are in the pay of the experimenter and all say that the objectively longer line is the shorter. After hearing six people say this, our "innocent" subject is on the spot. Astonishingly, the majority of all "innocent" subjects say that the line is short, despite reality, and despite the fact that were the subject alone he would have no trouble telling the correct answer. [McConnell, in Chapter 16, also discusses group conformity.]

A group of my students staged a "crime" in a classroom, asked for individual descriptions and then put the witnesses into groups to produce composite descriptions of the suspect (Alper, et al., 1975; Marshall, Marquis, and Oskamp, 1971). The group descriptions were more complete than the individual reports but there were significantly more errors of commission—incorrect and stereotyped details. The groups concluded incorrectly that the suspect was wearing the standard student uniform—blue dungarees. Thus conformity was achieved around error as well as truth.

15. RELATION TO AUTHORITY FIGURES

The effects of suggestion on the reliability of identification can be greatly increased when figures in obvious authority are doing the testing. In psychological research on suggestion, changing attitudes, and biasing reports, the effects are much greater when we use older, higher status or better dressed people, pretty women, people in uniforms or white coats, etc. In difficult or vague situations, people turn toward the leader, the father, the person in authority, and so on. In some of our perception research, we have found that people will misjudge distances and distort reality in efforts to follow their leader (Marlowe and Gergen, 1966).

In many crimes, several witnesses who work together under a boss, would be hard put to disagree with their boss in public courtroom testimony, or in picking out a photo from a mug book. The process of filling in details can be exaggerated when the boss and his employee share information, and the employee feels obligated to back up his boss and remain in his good graces. Legal history is replete with stories of witnesses (e.g., convicts) who were rewarded by the authorities for "cooperating" by making an identification (Borchard, 1961). One general result of our research is that when we use pressure from authorities, the frequency of attempted identifications—whether correct or not—increases.

In one bank robbery case, we discovered that the tellers were re-warded by their bank for cooperation in giving eyewitness testimony to authorities in trying to convict a robbery suspect. Despite their early sketchy reports, the witnesses became more "certain" of their identi-fication after receiving a letter from their boss urging cooperation. We believe that this type of authority pressure may be one of the main sources of unreliability in eyewitness identification.

16. PASSING ON A THEORY: THE SELF-FUFILLING PROPHECY

"If the data do not fit the theory the data must be disposed of."

This quote is a flip comment (known informally as Maier's Law) made by psychologists about the powerful influence of a theory on observation. In criminal investigations, as in scientific investigations, a theory can be a powerful tool for clarifying confusion—but it can also lead to distortion and unreliability as people cease to be open-minded to the real meanings of facts. The eyewitness who says "some-thing" may be greatly influenced to shape his memory to fit a theory—especially a reasonable sounding and highly publicized theory.

Psychologists, in criticizing their own research, have done re-search in which people were supposed to pick out a "successful" face from a set of photos. There was no correct answer, but the experi-menter dropped hints to his test-givers as to what he thought the results should be. Unconsciously, the test-givers signaled the subjects which photo to pick, producing results which supported their boss's theory. Any test is a social interaction as well as a test. The communi-cation of the theory can even be nonverbal, for example, as the test giver leans toward and smiles at the person who is cooperating with his expectations (see Rosenthal, 1966). This seems to influence the person to be even more cooperative, regardless of the facts. Knowl-edge of the highly publicized theory of Angela Davis' involvement in the Marin County courtroom shootout was, in our opinion, a significant factor in producing questionable eyewitness identifications of the defendant in key locations.

ON TO RESEARCH

So far I've presented the research framework on which I've built my testimony in court as an expert witness. The framework is built on the work of the past, much of which is familiar to a working psycholo-gist, but is hardly the day-to-day conversation of adult Americans who become jurors. Some of the earliest psychologists, notably Münster-berg (1908) had written the essence of this analysis as far back as the beginning of this century. But, there was a nagging gap between the

TABLE 17.1 COMPARISON OF AVERAGE DESCRIPTIONS BY 141 EYEWITNESSES WITH ACTUAL DESCRIPTION OF SUSPECT AND EVENTS

Known characteristics of suspect and events		Averaged descriptions of suspect and events
Duration of incident	34 sec	81.1 sec
Height	69.5 in	70.4 in
Weight	155 lb	180 lb
Age	25 yr	22.7 yr
Total accuracy score	28 pts	7.4 pts

controlled research settings which yield data on basic perceptual processes and some very important questions about perception in the less well controlled, but real world. I felt that this gap could only be bridged by conducting modern empirical research on eyewitness identification in a situation close to that of the real world.

Thus our laboratory and field studies are designed to evaluate eyewitness accuracy and reliability after seeing simulated crimes where we have a good record of the veridical (real) events for comparison. I began with a more detailed version of an experiment which Münsterberg and others had conducted over 65 years ago.

An Experimental Study of the Eyewitness

In order to study the effects of eyewitness testimony in a somewhat realistic setting, we staged an assault on a California State University campus, in which a distraught student "attacked" a professor in front of 141 witnesses. We recorded the entire incident on videotape so that we could compare the veridical event with the eyewitness reports. After the attack we took sworn statements from each witness, asking them to describe the suspect, the incident, and the clothes worn (essentially a free recall process). We also asked for a confidence rating (0–100 percent) in their description. Another outsider, of the same age as the suspect, was on the scene.

Table 17.1 shows a comparison of the known characteristics of the suspect and the averages of the descriptions given by the witnesses. It is clear that the witnesses gave very inaccurate descriptions, a fact which has been demonstrated so often in this type of experiment that professors of psychology use this as a demonstration of the unreliability of the eyewitness. People tend to overestimate the passage of time—in this case by a factor of almost 2½ to 1. The weight estimate was 14 percent higher, the age was underestimated, and the accuracy score—made up of points for appearance and dress—was only 25 percent of the maximum possible total score. Only the height estimate

TABLE 17.2   PERCENTAGE OF WITNESSES IDENTIFYING THE
ASSAILANT (N = 127)

Amount of bias in photo layout	Degree of bias in instructions	
	High	Low
High bias	61.3% (n = 31)	46.9% (n = 32)
Low bias	37.5% (n = 32)	40.6% (n = 32)

was close; but this may be due to the fact that the suspect was of average height. People will often cite known facts about the "average" man when they are uncertain.

We then waited 7 weeks and presented a set of six photographs to each witness individually, creating four conditions in order to test the effects of biased instructions and unfair testing on eyewitness identification. As shown in Table 17.2, there were two kinds of instructions: *low bias* in which witnesses were asked only if they recognized anybody in the photos; and *high bias,* where witnesses were told that we had an idea of who the assailant was, and we made a plea for them to find the attacker in the photos. There were two types of photo spreads, using well lit frontal views of young men the same age as the suspect. In the nonleading photo spread (Fig. 17.2), all six photos were neatly set out, with the same expression on all faces, and similar clothing worn by all men. In the biased photo spread (Fig. 17.3), the photo of the actual assailant was placed crooked in the array, the suspect wore different clothing and had a different expression from the other photos. We thus violated good testing practice for the sake of comparison.

The results, as shown in Table 17.2, indicate that overall only 40 percent of the witnesses correctly identified the assailant; 25 percent of the witnesses identified the wrong man—an innocent bystander who was at the scene of the crime. Of those correctly identifying the assailant, the highest percentage correct was found in the condition where there was a combination of a *biased* set of photos and biased instructions. Even the professor who was attacked picked out the innocent man from the photos. In some of our recent research we have tested the same photo spreads with a group of nonwitnesses to see if they would pick the same person. The biased photo array with the tilted photograph influenced nonwitnesses to pick out suspect number 5. We thus demonstrated how the violation of good testing practices could lead to unreliable eyewitness identifications in a fairly realistic setting.

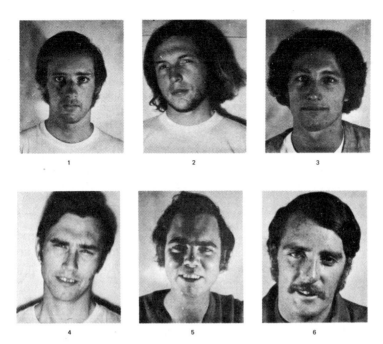

Figure 17.2. *Example of a reasonably unbiased photo-spread lineup used in testing eyewitnesses to an assault. No. 5 was the perpetrator.*

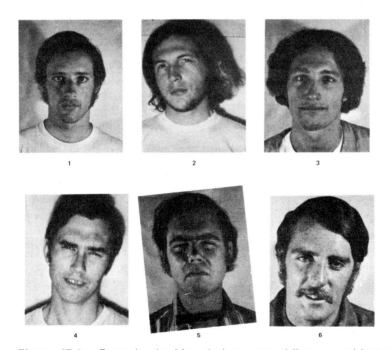

Figure 17.3. *Example of a biased photo-spread lineup used in testing eye-witnesses to an assault.*

Our conclusions in this first study were as follows. First, the reports of over 100 eyewitnesses to a crime were so highly unreliable that if an investigation began to find the person most witnesses described, the likelihood is high that attention would focus on the wrong person. Second, in following police procedures for testing identification through photographs, the presence of biased instructions and leading sets of photos can increase the percentage of witnesses who end up picking the photo toward which the authorities are biased. Third, if the police are biased toward an innocent man, the presence of biased instructions and a leading set of photos could increase the likelihood that the wrong person would be identified (Alper, et al., 1975).

MORE TO DO

Any thoughts I had that this experiment would be a one-time demonstration disappeared quickly as I thought more about human perception and the questions that courts deal with. Unlike publishing an article which occasionally produces a critical letter, my work as an expert witness results in my research (and myself) being cross-examined in depth. In all honesty, I am frequently not able to give a simple answer to a simple question. So much of perception research deals with very complex, basic questions that if I were to generalize from laboratory work, I would have to stretch the data to cover the situations in which real crimes occur. Once again, the research raised more questions than it answered.

There was a delay in my research for a period of 6 months when I moved to Brooklyn College. Here I was to meet and work with a remarkable group of students in what we call the Center for Responsive Psychology. In the past few years we have conducted an intensive series of studies designed to make real world questions answerable in a fairly timely fashion. We publish in the research literature of course; but one of our main activities is the production of a newsletter, *Social Action and the Law*—which is sent directly to lawyers (judges, agencies, law libraries, other researchers, and prisoners.* In the newsletter we attempt to provide short, understandable research reports and analyses of questions from the law (including eyewitness identification) in plain English.

Our team of researchers has become notorious (locally), for staging crimes around the campus. In one study, we staged a live purse-snatching incident in a classroom, followed by the now-familiar questionnaires.† I was concerned with a dilemma posed to us by a number of good, hard-nosed attorneys. They might express it this way:

---

*For details on the newsletter *Social Action and the Law,* write to the Center for Responsive Psychology, Brooklyn College, Brooklyn, N. Y. 11210. One of our issues dealt at length with eyewitness identification.

†A complete report of this experiment can be obtained as Report No. CR–9 from the Center for Responsive Psychology.

TABLE 17.3 PERFORMANCE OF EYEWITNESSES ON TWO LINE-UPS (N = 52)

Positive identification	13.5%
Positive identification impeached	13.5
Look-alike only	13.5
Other mistaken identification only	36.5
Two mistaken identifications	3.8
No identification made	19.2

"Look I'll grant you that a whole bunch of witnesses can't remember much of what they saw in detail, but how come they can still go into court or to a lineup and pick out the guy?"

To express that in psychologese—what we were being asked was why recognition is so much better than recall—as indeed it is. In private, most lawyers and judges agree with us that the accuracy of recall of a crime by witnesses is very poor. But, what I had to do was to break away from my certainty on how *bad* witnesses are and to search for what makes a *good* witness. To do this, we took our whole group of witnesses who had predictably given poor recall data, and gave them a very difficult recognition (lineup) test. Our witnesses would get not only a real lineup (with the actual purse snatcher in the group), but, also a "blank" lineup with a look-alike. The question for the witness was: Would he pick only the correct suspect and avoid a mistaken identification of the look-alike. The strategy is similar to the one employed by the early psychophysicists to catch observers who could be "right" merely by saying "yes" all the time.

We videotaped two lineups (with 5 persons each) and showed them in counterbalanced order to 52 people who witnessed the purse-snatching. The results shown in Table 17.3 tell the story of how few witnesses were completely successful in making a positive identification without ambiguity. An equal number of witnesses picked a second person as well as the correct assailant, while most simply made a mistaken identification.

Our best witnesses had also been among the best performers in the recall test, making significantly fewer errors of commission (adding details which were not present) than those who were unsuccessful on the lineup. The good witness didn't give a particularly complete report (few witnesses do)—but he didn't fill in. We also noted that the good witness expressed *less* confidence than did the witnesses who impeached themselves. Finally, when we compared the written descriptions of the suspect, we found that our successful witnesses gave a significantly higher and thus more accurate weight estimate. This breaks a frame of reference that most of us have held regarding height and weight. When we guess a person's weight we can easily invoke the chart of ideal weight for height and be way off if the person is fat. Our suspect was heavy, and only the successful witnesses had observed that fact in spite of loose-fitting clothing. The others were guessing. (In addition, these witnesses also gave time estimates which were closer to the actual elapsed time, though still overestimated by a factor of 50 percent).

Once again, we note that few witnesses say "I don't know." Eighty percent tried to pick the suspect even though most were mistaken. The social influence of the lineup itself seems to encourage "yes" as a response—a disturbing problem which has driven us back from these rather realistic crimes to the more controlled environment of the laboratory. As we interpreted these results, we wondered if it would be possible to design a test for eyewitnesses which could distinguish a good witness from a poor witness, in a place where we knew the true facts. Pure accuracy measures are not adequate since there are many types of errors, some of which come from the witness' desire to please the questioner with too many details.

THE EYEWITNESS TEST

We finally settled on trying to apply the "signal detection" paradigm (Swets, 1964) to the eyewitness situation. This choice was made because signal detection theory evolved in psychophysics as a means of coping with the empirical fact that the observer's attitude "interferes" with the accurate detecting, processing, and reporting of sensory stimuli. An ideal observer has a clear distinction in his mind as to what a signal (stimulus) is and what it is not. His task usually is to say whether a signal is present or not (e.g., a tone of a particular frequency). The experimenter always presents the subject with some background noise, but only on half the trials will a low strength signal, the tone, also be present. In deciding whether the trial consists of noise alone or contains a signal, the subject employs a criterion which is influenced by factors such as personality, experience, anticipated cost or reward, or motivation to please or frustrate. Because of the arrangement of the experiment, it is possible to count hits (correct "yeses") and false alarms (incorrect "yeses"), thus providing a quantitative estimate of the observer's criterion for judging his immediate experience. A very cautious person might have very few false alarms and a high number of hits, indicating that he uses "yes" sparingly. A less cautious observer might say "yes" most of the time, increasing his false alarms as well as his hits.

In our experiment, we presented 20–25 statements about the crime which were true, and the same number which were false. The witness indicated yes or no and gave a confidence rating as well. We end up with a record of hits and false alarms based on the witness' recall of the crime. These data are combined statistically to produce Receiver Operating Characteristic (ROC) curves as shown in Figure 17.4. The

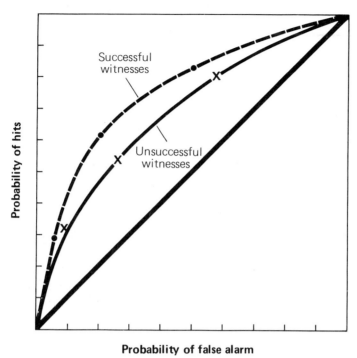

Probability of false alarm

Figure 17.4. *Comparison of ROC curves of successful and unsuccessful eyewitnesses where successful d′ = 1.18 and unsuccessful d′ = 0.74.*

straight line, or "blind man function," would be generated by a person or group whose hits and false alarms were equal—indicating that responses have no relationship to the true facts. The sharper the curve, the more cautious the observer. The greater the area under the curve, the more sensitive was the witness to the difference between a true and a false statement. A single parameter—d′—can be calculated which represents observer sensitivity. This complex function is being used to test various hypotheses on how environmental conditions, stress, bias in interrogation, sex, and social milieu affect the accuracy and reliability of an eyewitness. Our current studies indicate that the witnesses with better ROC curves in the laboratory perform more accurately in recognizing the suspect in a lineup. Thus, we are on the way toward developing a standardized test of eyewitness sensitivity, accuracy, and reliability.

One basic change has occurred in our research strategy. Instead of staging the crimes "live" in the classroom, we are using color-sound movies of carefully staged crimes. In part, we did this for control, but more importantly, the time of the apathetic bystander to a crime appears to have passed. Staging even an innocuous purse-snatching became dangerous for our "perpetrators" as a number of the (bigger) witnesses began to take off in hot pursuit of the purse-snatcher. No research is worth that much realism.

With the ROC curve or the d' parameter as unitary measures of the sensitivity of the witness to crimes, we will explore the extent to which d' changes in response to biasing factors commonly encountered in court cases affecting identifications. In our early studies, we found that witnesses who were ultimately successful in recognizing the suspect in a good lineup had shown high d' scores during recall. People with low d' scores tended to give height and weight descriptions which correlated with their own stature—confirming our belief that when pressured to give a description, witnesses fabricate their responses in the meaningful way that a perception researcher would expect.

We plan to refine the test, giving witnesses the chance to see several crimes. In this way we can check a witness' general reliability and test a number of hypotheses which police officers hold regarding older witnesses, women as witnesses, members of different racial and economic groups, etc. Thus, in one sense, we are just beginning a large research program which came from the real world to be absorbed into the laboratory—and changed the laboratory. Soon we hope to emerge from the laboratory and to bring the results back to the real world where they belong.

EPILOGUE

My role as an expert witness continues to surprise and enlighten me. One incident stands out as an example of how close and yet how far apart are psychologists and lawyers even when discussing eyewitness identification as a common topic.

Toward the end of a bitter cross-examination of my testimony in the Angela Davis case, Mr. Albert Harris, the prosecutor, turned the tables on me by asking if all of my discussion of the unreliability of eyewitness testimony didn't also apply to me. I paused, reflecting for a moment on the obvious fact that as a defense witness I was inevitably cast into an adversary role since my testimony threatened the prosecutor's case. After all, isn't a scientist supposed to be neutral and objective? This is what the judge expects when he allows any expert to testify—an aid to the determination of truth. I blurted: "Yes, I'll testify to being a human being. This is all I have been saying."

I realized what I was doing. I had been an adversary for a psychological view of people—a view which is at odds with what the court expects of a witness. A psychologist *expects* witnesses to be less than perfect and to be susceptible to social pressure. The lawyers are out to win and couldn't care less about whether a witness is perfect, unreliable, or a liar—as long as his testimony fits their side of the battle. I reflect on the fact that I've spent more time on the stand defending psychology and the right of these strange people to testify than I have in giving expert testimony. Invariably, what we are saying about the nature of the human observer will complicate things in court, causing a searching inquiry into the testimony of any witness who might otherwise have been accepted.

In a final angry exchange, Prosecutor Harris picked up on my description of the desire of some witnesses to be a part of history, and asked if this didn't also apply to psychologists who testify as experts in the trials of famous black militants. I very angrily shot back: "Mr. Harris, I could easily redirect that question back to you. . . ."

The audience gasped, the prosecutor sat down, and defense attorney Howard Moore—who taught me a lot about psychological moments in court—yanked me out of there.

REFERENCES

Allport, G. and Postman, L. 1947. *The Psychology of Rumor.* New York: Holt, Rinehart and Winston, pp. 70–72.

Alper, A.; Chern, S.; Harwood, R.; Silverberg, G.; and Slomovits, M. 1975. *Eyewitness Identification: Are Four Heads Better Than One?* To be published in *Bulletin of the Psychonomic Society.*

Borchard, E. 1961. *Convicting the Innocent.* Hampden, Conn.: Anchor Books.

Buckhout, R. 1965. Need for social approval and dyadic verbal behavior. *Psychological Reports,* 16:1013–1016.

Buckhout, R. 1968. Through a bag, darkly. *American Psychologist,* 23: 832–833.

Laughery, K. R. 1970. Photograph type and cross-racial factors in facial identification. In A. Zavala, (ed.), *Personal Appearance Identification II: Psychological Studies of Human Identification and Recognition Processes.* Cornell Aeronautical Lab. Report No. XM–2514–B2, January, 1970.

Levine, R.; Chein I.; and Murphy, G. 1942. The relation of a need to the amount of perceptual distortion. *Journal of Psychology,* 13:283–293.

Loftus, E. F. and Palmer, J. C. 1974. Reconstruction of automobile destruction: An example of the interaction between language and memory. *Journal of Verbal Learning and Verbal Behavior,* 13:585–589.

Malpass, R. S. and Kravitz, J. 1969. Recognition for faces of own and other race. *Journal of Personality and Social Psychology,* 13:330–336.

Marlowe, D. and Gergen, K. 1969. Personality and Social Interaction. In G. Lindzey and E. Aronson, *Handbook of Social Psychology* (2nd ed., Vol. III), Reading, Mass.: Addison-Wesley, pp. 591–665.

Marshall, J. 1966. *Law and Psychology in Conflict.* Indianapolis, Ind.: Bobbs Merrill, p. 104.

Marshall, J.; Marquis, K. H.; and Oskamp, S. 1971. Effects of kind of question and atmosphere of interrogation on accuracy and completeness of testimony. *Harvard Law Review,* 84:1620–1626.

Miller, G. A. and Buckhout, R. 1973. *Psychology: The Science of Mental Life.* New York: Harper & Row.

Münsterberg, H. 1908. *On the Witness Stand: Essays on Psychology and Crime.* New York: Doubleday.

Murphy, G. 1949. *Historical Introduction to Psychology.* New York: Harcourt, pp. 244–245.

Postman, L. and Rosenzweig, M. 1962. *History of Psychology in the Making.* New York: Knopf.

Rosenthal, R. 1966. *Experimenter Effects in Behavioral Research.* New York: Appleton.

Selye, H. 1956. *The Stress of Life.* New York: McGraw-Hill.

Swets, J. A. 1964. *Signal Detection and Recognition by Human Observers.* New York: Wiley.

Tafjel, H. 1969. Social and cultural factors in perception. In G. Lindzey and E. Aronson, *Handbook of Social Psychology* (2nd ed., Vol. III), Reading, Mass.: Addison-Wesley, pp. 326–334.

Wald, P. M. 1965. *Eyewitness Identification in Criminal Cases.* Springfield, Ill.: C. C. Thomas.

ENVIRONMENTAL PSYCHOLOGY
Robert Sommer

My first experiment in environmental psychology was prompted by an internist for an elderly ladies' ward at a state hospital, who asked for help in discovering what was wrong with the place. Upon first seeing the ward, it was easy to be appalled at the lack of privacy in the crowded dormitories, the long straight corridors stretching out to infinity, (see Fig. 18.1), the large impersonal dayrooms, and the smelly cafeteria. It seemed obvious that this setting wasn't doing the patients any good, and in fact, probably was doing them harm. To my surprise very few other people seemed to notice that the place was drab or dingy, nor did they think that it was important enough to mention or change. The staff had become accustomed to the general dreariness, and the patients were nonpersons who apparently didn't have the right to a decent environment.

Ironically, not long before I had been called in, several thousand dollars had been spent to "improve" the ward. The renovation is instructive since it reveals what happens when people receive money unexpectedly. In this case, the institute received the money as a result of a change in the welfare program. The old folks' ward was located in Western Canada where extensive federal, provincial, and local welfare programs were in force. In the 1950s, a bright civil servant deduced that the inmates of institutions were indeed citizens and thus were eligible for federal old age pensions. Seventy-five dollars a month may seem small in absolute terms, but it was a great windfall to all players in the institutional game—custodians, patients, and relatives— since the pensions had accumulated over the years. Some patients had comfortable nest eggs when they were discharged, but if a patient died at the institution, his estate, including the accumulated pension funds, went to his relatives. At this particular hospital, the administration decided to spend some pension funds on amenities for the elderly —curtains framed the windows, the reflection of fluorescent lights danced on the new tile floor, tubular steel chairs with brightly colored plastic seats gave a Mondrian touch to the walls, and several air

Robert Sommer is Professor of Psychology and Chairman of the Psychology Department at the University of California at Davis. From Robert Sommer, PERSONAL SPACE: The Behavioral Basis of Design, © 1969. By permission of the author and Prentice-Hall, Inc., Englewood Cliffs, New Jersey.

Figure 18.1. *Long hospital corridors, sterile and cold, increase the patient's alienation and withdrawal from her surroundings.*

conditioners guarded the windows. Furthermore, a television set was installed in the ward.

There is no record of what the ladies said about the change, since no one solicited their opinions either before the renovation or after it. This is the customary state of affairs in custodial institutions where, in return for the beneficence of free room and board, the grateful inmates are expected to accept their environment as it is. The patients have privileges rather than rights, visitors instead of families. This became painfully evident when I interviewed patients about their wards. The patients were taken by surprise, and the nurses were suspicious—no one had solicited their opinions about the renovations either. The changes were planned and initiated from above, and completed by people who spent no time on the ward. The floor tiles, for example, were all the same pattern and ran the same way, which made the large lounge look even larger and more institutional than it had looked before. This singular style was not due to deliberate planning or economy, but stemmed from inertia and from the inability to

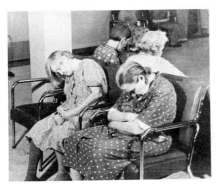

Figure 18.2. *Chairs arranged side-by-side or back-to-back make conversation difficult. The inevitable result will be mutual withdrawal and desocialization.*

realize that floor designs (or color scheme, chair arrangement, etc.) made any difference. Most items were purchased and positioned for ease of maintenance rather than for greater comfort or better therapy. From the standpoint of human relationships, some of the outcomes bordered on the bizarre. Thus, most of the chairs on this ward stood in straight lines along the walls, but in the center, there were several rows back-to-back. Around several columns there were four chairs each facing a different direction! The tragedy was not that these arrangements existed but that they were accepted as normal and reasonable throughout the institution (see Fig. 18.2). To compound the irony, pictures of this ward before and after the renovation formed a major portion of the hospital's application for an improvement award. The pictures revealed such a dramatic improvement in the physical conditions of the ward that the hospital won its award easily.

Despite the good publicity, the ward physician was dissatisfied with the outcome, although he could not specify his reasons. The ward looked better, but the ladies' mental state was unchanged. We visited the ward together, and I took to sitting there alone on long afternoons. Initially I shared his enthusiasm for the new furnishings. There was no denying that it was the best furnished ward in the hospital; as such it was regarded as somewhat of a model to be seen by visitors on tour. It took several weeks of sitting and watching before I could sort figure from ground, and see what *was not* happening as well as what was. With as many as 50 ladies in the large room, there were rarely more than one or two brief conversations. The ladies sat side-by-side in their new chrome chairs against the newly painted walls, and exercised their options of gazing down at the newly tiled floor or looking up at the new fluorescent lights. They were like strangers in a train station waiting for a train that never came. This shoulder-to-shoulder arrangement was unsuitable for sustained conversation even for me.

To talk to neighbors, I had to turn in my chair and pivot my head 90 degrees. For an older lady, particularly one with difficulties in hearing and comprehension, finding a suitable orientation for conversation was extremely taxing. I hardly need add that there was no conversation whatever between occupants of the center chairs that faced different directions.

In retrospect, the reasons for the straight-row arrangement are not difficult to understand. First, there is the lack of explicit principles relating furniture arrangement to social intercourse. Sensitive people intuitively know that there is a connection, and those who want to converse will, consciously or unconsciously, occupy chairs with a suitable orientation and distance. However, this voluntary arrangement is on a prescientific and nonverbal basis and such considerations are unlikely to play much part in the bureaucratic intricacies of institutional architecture and design. Magazines in medical specialties and allied fields devote considerable space to hospital construction and ward design, but the published plans and blueprints reveal only bare walls and rooms. The arrangement of furniture is left to the ward staff who do not realize the therapeutic potential of furniture arrangements. Ward geography is taken for granted, and a chair becomes something to sweep around rather than a necessary tool for social interaction. The same criticism has been leveled at American playgrounds by Lady Allen who pioneered the "adventure playground" in Great Britain. She described the American playground as "an administrator's heaven and a child's hell . . . asphalt barracks yards behind wire screen mesh barriers," built primarily for ease and economy of maintenance.

The inadequacy of the ward arrangement was also apparent when we contrasted it with the conversational groupings in private homes and with the arrangement in the corridor outside the ward. Because of the absence of special visiting rooms (space was short and patients' families had a low priority in the competition for available space), this corridor was used by families and friends during visiting hours. Before the building opened to the public at 8:00 A.M., the custodian arranged the chairs in straight rows shoulder to shoulder against the walls. Several hours later, relatives had moved the chairs into small groups so that they could face one another and converse comfortably. This situation, typical in the corridor, *never* occurred on the ward. Clearly, outsiders (families and friends) arranged their environment to suit *their* needs; the patients, however, were being arranged by the environment.

Certain arrangements of furniture are very efficient from the standpoint of ward chores. It is a sad commentary that more is known about this aspect of furniture arrangement than about its therapeutic use. Nurses often complain about a ward that looks "junky" or cluttered. A quasimilitary arrangement of chairs in neat rows along the wall appears neater, makes it easier to sweep, and allows a survey

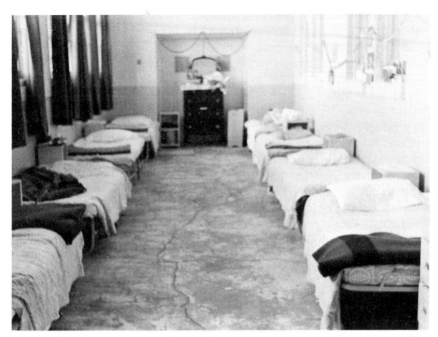

Figure 18.3. *Hospital dormitories like this provide no privacy or possibilities for personalization.*

of the ward at a glance. It takes only a second to look down a continuous row of chairs against the wall, compared with the several seconds required to survey a cluttered room with an irregular seating pattern. Placing chairs along the walls left wide pathways for food-carts and cleaning wagons to pass freely. Food service personnel and maintenance employees often came through this ward because of ease in transit. This "highway" converted the ladies' living space into corridor space that could not be occupied without the risk of injury from the express traffic passing through (Fig. 18.3).

Another factor responsible for the straight-row arrangement was the "institutional sanctity" that prevails whenever people spend long periods of time in any environment. After a while, no matter how unusual or unpleasant it seemed at first, the customary becomes fixed and natural. This can apply to the deafening noises of an auto assembly plant as well as to the straight-row classrooms in schools. Hospitals, too, have a way of seeming right and efficient to their inhabitants, no matter how they appear to outsiders. In the old folks' ward, the staff no longer noticed the odors and clanking of keys that bothered visitors. The same was true of hospital routines, including the fact that patients were awakened every morning at 5:30. The old-line attendants, who were the moral arbiters of the hospital, had decreed that the night shift had a "soft touch" and so should bear the additional responsibility of getting the ladies dressed and ready for breakfast before the day shift arrived. The 83 ladies on the ward averaged 74 years of age, and since there were only two nurses on the night shift, they had to start early in order to get everyone up. The first ladies up and dressed waited for two hours until the day shift arrived and served breakfast. Knowing this, it is not difficult to understand why the ladies were tired and ready for bed at 7:00 P.M. This time schedule produced awkward results when several ladies left the ward to live outside. It was the goal of social service to place as many of the ladies as possible in private homes in the belief that from the patient's standpoint, as well as the cost to the state, this was preferable to living in an institution. Several ladies had to return to the hospital because people objected to their rising at 5:30 A.M. only to sit in the living room waiting for breakfast. Going to bed at 7:00 P.M. did not endear them to households where courtesy dictated a minimum of noise and disturbance while someone sleeps.

Before undertaking our experiment, we spent some time observing seating patterns in a variety of places—homes, bus depots, railway stations, theaters, and hotel lobbies. We became aware of how incorrect our assumptions about public places had been. We had naively believed that hotel lobbies and railway stations were full of people sitting and talking. In actuality, most people sat alone, reading or looking at new arrivals. People who were talking invariably had arrived together. People who came alone, sat alone, and did not interact at all. This provided very little precedent for developing institutional architecture that would bring the residents of this old folks' home into greater contact with one another. The resort hotel might have provided a suitable model, but the usual clientele there is young, active, and eager for new friends and social activities, this in contrast to our population of elderly men and women who were incarcerated—often against their will. Organized games or musical activities might have brought younger people together, but our ladies were, if not infirm, at least sedentary.

After reviewing the various possibilities, we decided that the ladies would be more likely to converse if, instead of sitting shoulder to shoulder, they faced one another. Our initial view, which was modified later, was that the people should be pointed toward one another (like projectiles) in order to maximize conversation. We also felt that the large open areas should be broken into smaller spaces, so that each person could select one or two others with whom to interact. Partitions might have served our purpose, but we decided to start with small tables placed around the ward. This upset the highway patrol no end, since they now had to navigate food carts and cleaning wagons around the tables instead of using the long open stretch they had before. Several of the nurses remarked that the tables made the ward look "junky." Despite these objections it seemed reasonable that we should give the ladies these islands of security around which they might group their chairs. We felt that the ladies were uncomfortable with their chairs out in the oceanic spaces. Square tables have the advantage of letting a person know the boundaries of his territory. This seemed an important consideration for an older person whose sole personal area might be the table space in front of her. With round tables a person never knows where his territory ends and where another's begins.

The dayroom was a large open area that, prior to the study, contained 43 chairs, 4 couches, and 4 small tables. The tables were placed out in the center of the room, too far from the chairs to be useful, and were used for formal activities or for patients whose special diets required them to eat separately. For 2 weeks prior to the beginning of the study, we recorded all interaction that took place in the dayroom. At various times of the day an observer visited the ward and recorded everything that happened during 5-minute periods. So little interaction took place on the ward that longer sessions added little new information. Anything that occurred was recorded on mimeographed floor plans.

After 2 weeks we removed three of the old couches and introduced five additional square tables (30 in. per side), making a total of nine tables. The chairs were moved away from the walls and placed around the tables in various parts of the room. The first 2 weeks following the change formed a stabilization period, in which no interaction counts were taken. During this time the nurses encouraged the ladies to sit at the tables. On the morning when the ladies first discovered the change there were spontaneous comments such as, "Where is our chesterfield? We miss our chesterfield.""This is a nice table, but I don't want to eat all day." and "Is this my chair now?" The last comment reflects the fact that individual chairs were moved to new locations. The maintenance and food service employees complained loudly that the tables and chairs cluttered their route through the ward. An occupational therapist inquired whether we were getting ready to hold a party.

It soon became apparent that if we wanted the ladies to remain at the tables, we would have to make the new locations more attractive. Put another way, we had to provide the ladies with reasons for remaining at the tables. We hoped that this would become less necessary as the advantages of the tables for social intercourse became evident. We imagined that the ladies would initially resist a new furniture arrangement, and endeavored to counteract this by associating the tables with pleasant experiences and objects. Artificial flowers and vases were placed on the tables (later, real flowers were used) and magazines were laid out every day. Even so, it was difficult to persuade the ladies to remain at the tables—they moved their chairs back against the walls at every opportunity. Indeed, the movement of chairs back to the walls continued for some years afterwards and seems to have important psychological significance. Later studies of seating patterns of groups of people, both healthy individuals and patients of various sorts, also showed that people like to sit with their backs to the wall or to other tangible barriers. Partially, this is a result of a search for comfort and the possibility of leaning one's chair back against a solid surface, but in addition, there seems to be a need for security.

A wall location facing out enables one to see what is going on. In a barren institutional environment this is exceedingly important, since the most exciting events are the comings and goings of people. A good vantage point can provide advance information on meals, medication trays, and craft periods. When we mapped room density, we found that the highest concentrations of persons occurred in the small corridor at the entrance to the dayroom. Further observation and interviewing disclosed three major factors responsible for the high density: the certainty of seeing visitors to the ward from this location, its proximity to the dining hall, and the fact that the corridor contained the only windows low enough to permit an outside view.

Our primary concern was to see whether or not the new arrangement would increase interaction between the ladies. The record sheets distinguished between transient verbal interaction (asking a question, shouting at another patient, extending a greeting) and sustained verbal interaction (reciprocated conversations maintained over 2 seconds). Because of the difficulty of deciding what constituted nonverbal interaction (touching hands or giving food), recording was limited to verbal interaction between patients.

We found that in the new arrangement, both brief and sustained interactions almost doubled. Also, there was a remarkable increase in the amount of reading. Before the study was begun, very few magazines were seen in the dayroom respite the fact that large quantities were purchased for the patients or donated each month. One reason for this was that there was no place to store magazines when they were not in use. If a magazine were to be placed on the floor, a nurse was likely to consider this untidy and remove it. The tables now provided places where printed materials could be left without fear of their immediate disappearance. Patients had formerly hoarded magazines, carrying them around in bundles or keeping them under mattresses where they would not be taken away. The same hoarding, which had been a sensible reaction considering the circumstances, appeared when we first laid out magazines on the tables. The first week we supplied 20 magazines a day, which disappeared as rapidly as we put them out. Later, when the ladies found that the magazines were brought to the ward regularly and could be left on the tables safely, hoarding decreased.

At the same time the ward physician was so impressed with the transformation of the ward, that he sent an occupational therapist to the ward to develop a craft program. He felt that craftwork could be done at the tables. None of our interaction recording was done during the craft sessions, but there was an increase in craft activities throughout the day. Like magazine reading, this was a serendipitous outcome of the new ward arrangement; furthermore, it implies that it is difficult to keep change isolated and circumscribed. A hospital ward, like a commercial office or any army barracks, is a social system, and a change in any single element will change other parts too. When one introduces tables into a room, it is likely that the occupants will try to make the tables attractive and functional. Except under highly artificial and restricted laboratory situations, it is unlikely that environmental changes can involve only a single factor. If we study the effects of decreased noise in a commercial office, we might find that it produced lower absenteeism and fewer outside trips. One would thereby be recording interaction among more inhabitants than were present in the office before the change. Initial change produces secondary changes, which then affect the initial change, and it is difficult to determine whether an observable effect resulted from the initial change, one of the secondary changes, or a combination of all.

OTHER STUDIES OF SPATIAL ARRANGEMENTS

This study fascinated me for several reasons. For one, no one had mentioned the physical environment in all my years of graduate work in psychology. None of my professors had ever spoken about the effects of houses, office buildings, parks, or even schools or hospitals on their occupants. Yet Freud was very insistent about the requirements for an analytic chamber, even specifying the angle at which the analyst should sit *vis-à-vis* the patient. To see whether or not this had been a local shortcoming of the schools I attended, I went back and checked the available social science literature—where I found the same lacuna in information. Although the reasons for this lack of interest in the physical environment still puzzle me, I felt sufficiently motivated to devote the next 15 years of my life to the area of environmental psychology. This path has led me to design teams working on schools, offices, prisons, airports, and even bikeways. My belief throughout was that I could contribute *as a psychologist* to the design of physical settings that suited their occupants. I did not want to become an architect or talk like one, though I had to understand enough of their jargon to communicate with them visually as well as verbally.

Over the years, I have also tried to awaken the interests of social scientists in the physical environments as well as develop the interests of designers in the ways that environments affect people. As things turned out, I worked both with laymen, whom I made more aware of how they were affected by their environment, as well as with space managers (hospital administrators, airport terminal managers, school teachers) who were actually responsible for the allocation of space. Often the problem was not so much the way the space was designed, but the inefficiency of its use. The lesson of ecology is that everyone and everything is connected, and if you are going to be effective in environmental work, you will have to learn to deal with the custodian as well as with the banker and the interior designer. The first task in dealing with many environmental problems is to raise consciousness and then to focus this awareness upon specific sources of the difficulty.

The study of chair arrangements led me to examine other institutional settings to see what effect they had upon their occupants. I undertook naturalistic observations in airports, cafeterias, schools, parks, and even beer parlors to see how the arrangement of people affected the kind of interaction that took place. I soon became aware that while natural observation was a valuable tool, it would have to be supplemented by experimental studies of a more basic kind in order to specify the operating variables. More specifically, I decided to undertake some basic studies of human spatial behavior. It seemed necessary to know how close together people sat or stood when they had some freedom of choice, and see how this was related to what they were doing.

In addition to observing and photographing people in various settings, my students and I also undertook *spatial invasions.* Nancy Russo approached women seated in the college library and sat at a distance which violated the customary norms of leaving an empty chair between people. Various sorts of compensatory devices were used by students whose personal space was invaded. Frequently a student placed her hand on her ear and faced away from Dr. Russo, or put her elbows out in a defensive posture. Rarely did the student react verbally to the invasion—she seemed uncomfortable and defensive, and if this failed to move Dr. Russo, the student departed.

We also found a connection between physical distance and social distance. Students were asked to enter a room and discuss a topic with someone who was already seated there. Sometimes the student was told that the other person was a professor in the Psychology Department. Other students were told that the seated person was a fellow student in the class (a peer), and still others were told that the seated person was "a freshman girl who had failed the class the preceding semester and was doing this as a make-up project." These three descriptions were intended to represent points along the status ladder. We had established earlier that in relation to the student, a professor would be of higher status, a fellow student would be of equal status, and a freshman girl doing poorly in school would be of lower status.

When the student entered the room, she found a rectangular

Figure 18.4. *View of experimental setup relating physical distance to social distance.*

table with three chairs on each side, and one each at the head and the foot. Around one of the chairs (see Fig. 18.4) was draped a sweater and on the table in front of it was a pad and a pencil. When the student entered the room, it was logical for her to assume that the other person was seated in the marked chair. Her own location was influenced by the attributed status of the other person. We found that she sat closer to her peer (fellow student) than to either the faculty member or the failing freshman.

We decided to cross validate these results in a questionnaire study with several hundred other college students. Each student was shown a diagram of a small square table surrounded by four chairs. They were asked how they would sit in informal conversation with a person at one of the three status levels (professor, classmate, or freshman doing poorly in school). These results also indicated that they would sit opposite someone of higher or lower status, but corner-to-corner with someone of equal status.

We undertook other studies of interpersonal spacing with different sized groups, some with leaders and some without, some with specific tasks that required competition and others that required co-operation. We wanted to learn some of the principles of interpersonal spacing among interacting individuals who had a free choice of seats, and then apply this information in the design and furnishing of inter-action spaces. These tests showed us that many buildings were poorly laid out from the standpoint of what they were designed to accomplish. Some of the library study areas which were supposed to provide privacy contained long rectangular tables. From the standpoint of privacy, these long tables were "occupied" when one student sat at one corner and another student sat, catty-corner, across. Essentially,

Figure 18.5. *Much of the Pruitt-Igeo housing development, once hailed as a pioneer achievement in redevelopment, has already been torn down. The buildings were marked by high crime and vandalism. The better alternative is smaller units with a territorial quality where access and activity can be set by the residents.*

two students could "occupy" a table with eight chairs. Obviously, this wastes space if the same degree of privacy can be achieved with two four-person tables or with individual carrels. We also found that many lounges (and private homes) were badly arranged from the standpoint of interaction. Like the mental hospital dayroom mentioned earlier, the arrangement of chairs and their fixedness discouraged conversation.

In addition to interpersonal spacing, the distance between people, we also experimented with various physical markers and barriers. The goal of this work was to learn something about human territoriality or the way people mark out and personalize spaces.

Recently this work has been applied by architect Oscar Newman in the design and renovation of public housing projects. Newman was concerned about the high crime rate and vandalism in the public areas of housing projects which seemingly belonged to no one (Fig. 18.5). To avoid this, he changed the projects around to bring these public areas under the visual control of the occupants. With this new arrangement intruders would be scrutinized as a matter of course, and if necessary, challenged. Newman called such territories *defensible space.* What Newman did was to take some of the no man's land and hidden spaces of housing projects and turn them into territories which were visually accessible. When the no man's land was converted into territories, many occupants of housing projects began to plant gardens and take care of grounds which now "belonged" to them (Newman, 1972).

The social sciences finally have discovered the physical environment, and there are all the marks of institutionalization to prove it. At the undergraduate level, there are entire colleges devoted to environmental issues (University of Wisconsin at Green Bay and Huxley College at Western Washington State) and numerous environmental studies programs springing up. Most of the larger schools of architecture and planning now import a social scientist to teach a course in environmental psychology if they do not have a resident social scientist for this specific purpose. In terms of these marks of legitimacy, the practitioners can consider themselves respectable citizens of Academe. There still remains the task of demonstrating that buildings designed with the help of social scientists are more satisfying to their occupants than buildings designed without such help. This seems a rather elementary requirement for a field with a strong research orientation, but it is a task that still remains to be carried out. It will mean that psychologists and sociologists will have to be involved in actual design projects from start to finish, and stay on to complete the necessary postoccupancy evaluation. There will never be an honest field of environmental psychology if it is restricted to federally financed research grants on general issues. This is a sure-fire formula for coming up with results that are interesting rather than helpful. What does it mean to the prospective designer of a college residence hall to know that students are likely to select their friends from among people in adjacent rooms? This is a genuine finding that has been documented in a number of separate studies; still, there is no guarantee that its implications for designers are readily apparent. At the least, someone must help to translate such behavioral findings into terms and applications that have some meaning to designers. I leave open the possibility that this finding has no practical use whatever in designing a new dormitory. On the other hand, I am certain that it does have implications for the resident advisor who counsels students in the dormitory. If a certain student is in difficulty, the advisor might want to discuss the problem with those students who are most likely to know him—the students in the next room. Many of the findings of environmental psychology will have more relevance for the management of spaces than for the initial design process. We will be able to sort out these considerations when we actually apply social science methods in an experimental way on actual design projects. This cannot come from surveys of what people want or from observation of what people do or from lists of needs people have or from summaries of the literature on small group behavior. The presence of social scientists in university schools of design is a healthy development. The next step for these social scientists is to become involved in actual design projects where their insights and findings can be applied and the outcome observed in a systematic way. A few years ago, it was necessary for social scientists to preach to architects about the value of research and the importance of user behavior in the design process. Now it is up to social scientists to demonstrate that fruitful collaboration results in better buildings, more functional city parks, and more humane cities.

BIBLIOGRAPHY

Hall, E. T. 1959. *The Silent Language.* New York: Macmillan.
Newman, O. 1972. *Defensible Space.* New York: Macmillan.
Proshansky, H. M.; Ittelson, W. H.; and Rivlin, L. G. 1970. *Environmental Psychology.* New York: Holt, Rinehart and Winston.
Sommer, R. 1969. *Personal Space.* Englewood Cliffs, N. J.: Prentice-Hall.

RESPONDING TO "HYPNOTIC" SUGGESTIONS: AN INTROSPECTIVE REPORT
Theodore Xenophone Barber

Behavioral scientists try to maintain an objective stance with regard to their areas of inquiry. In attempting to remain objective, they rarely serve as experimental subjects, and in those rare cases in which they take the role of a subject, they usually do not write about their personal experiences. Specifically, in the area of hypnotism, investigators report how their subjects respond to "hypnotic" suggestions but rarely, if ever do they report how they themselves respond. Although objective data are necessary, I believe that the different viewpoints toward hypnotism could be better understood if researchers in this area would describe their own experiences.

With the above considerations in mind, I shall present an introspective report describing and interpreting my personal experiences while I am responding to suggestions. This personal report may help to illustrate some of the major aspects of the theory that my co-workers and I have presented elsewhere (Barber, 1972; Barber and DeMoor, 1972; Barber and Ham, 1974; Barber, Spanos, and Chaves, 1974) and may also show how the theory is harmonious with my own experiences. However, as this theory differs in some important respects from traditional views of hypnosis, it might be useful to discuss the traditional positions in a little more detail and contrast them with our view.

THE TRADITIONAL ANALOGY: THE SLEEPWALKER*

As Hilgard (1969) pointed out, "Hypnosis is commonly considered to be a 'state' perhaps resembling the state in which the sleepwalker finds himself, hence the term 'somnambulist' as applied to the deeply hypnotized person." I believe that the sleepwalker analogy is incorrect and misleading. Let me try to clarify my belief by first describing

Theodore Xenophone Barber is affiliated with the Medfield Foundation, Medfield, Mass.

Work on this paper was supported by a research grant (MH21294) from the National Institute of Mental Health.

*This section on the sleepwalker, as well as the sections on reading a novel and watching a movie and on training in human potentialities, are adapted from material I wrote for a recent book (Barber, Spanos, and Chaves, 1974). I am indebted to Pergamon Press for permission to use the material, and to Drs. Spanos and Chaves for critically evaluating the original manuscript.

the characteristics of the sleepwalker and then those of the responsive hypnotic subject.

A series of studies (Jacobson et al., 1965; Kales et al., 1966; Pai, 1946) indicate that the sleepwalker manifests the following four sets of characteristics:

First, when the sleepwalker arises from his bed at night, the electroencephalogram (EEG) shows that he is sleeping (stages 3 or 4 of sleep). When the sleepwalking episode is brief in duration, the EEG shows that the sleepwalker remains asleep. However, during longer sleepwalking episodes, the EEG shows that the sleepwalker enters light sleep or very relaxed wakefulness.

Second, the sleepwalker shows rigid or shuffling movements, a drastically reduced awareness of his surroundings, a fixed focus of attention, a low level of motor skill, and a blank stare. The sleepwalker rarely replies when someone speaks to him. To get his attention, it is usually necessary to continue talking to him or to interrupt his movements. When the sleepwalker does reply, he tends to mumble or to speak in a vague or detached manner.

Third, when the sleepwalker is told to wake up, he does not awaken. Persistant measures are needed to awaken him. For example, it may be necessary to shake him or to repeat his name over and over, each time more loudly.

Finally, when the sleepwalker is awakened in the morning, or if he is awakened during his sleepwalking, he shows no indication of remembering the episode.

A subject who is said to be "hypnotized" often is termed "somnambulist" with the clear implication that he resembles the sleepwalker. Laymen have commonly assumed that the responsive hypnotic subject resembles the sleepwalker in that he is "half asleep," has a low level of awareness, is detached from his surroundings, has a fixed focus of attention, and shows amnesia on awakening. I believe these assumptions are fallacious. It seems to me that the so-called hypnotized subject differs from the sleepwalker in every important respect.

First, the EEG of the hypnotized subject does not resemble that of a sleepwalker, not even remotely. Judging from EEG criteria, the sleepwalker typically is asleep whereas the subject who is said to be hypnotized is awake. More specifically, responsive hypnotic subjects do not show changes on the EEG that might clearly distinguish them from subjects who are said to be "awake." The EEG of the so-called hypnotized subject varies continually—as it does in any normally awake person—with whatever instructions or suggestions he is given or with whatever activities in which he is engaged (Barber, 1961; Chertok and Kramarz, 1959).*

---

*Other physiological measures also vary in hypnotized subjects in the same way as in control awake subjects. Depending on the instructions or suggestions that the subject receives, both the hypnotized subject and the waking control sub-

Second, some so-called hypnotized subjects may seem to resemble the sleepwalker in that they show a fixed focus of attention, a blank stare, a rigid facial expression, a lack of spontaneity, and a disinclination to talk. However, in the hypnotic subject, but *not* in the sleepwalker, these kinds of characteristics have been produced by suggestions to become relaxed, drowsy, and sleepy and they can be easily removed by suggestions, for example, to be alert.

Third, although the sleepwalker does not awaken when he is simply told to do so, practically all subjects who are said to be hypnotized open their eyes and "awaken" when they are simply told, "The experiment is over" or "Wake up."†

Fourth, sleepwalkers do not remember their sleepwalking. In contrast, if suggestions for amnesia are not given during the hypnotic session, practically all hypnotic subjects remember the events that occurred (Barber and Calverley, 1966; Hilgard, 1966).‡ In addition, it appears that *no* subject has ever forgotten the events occurring during a hypnotic session when he was told, during the session, that he should remember the events (Barber, 1962; Orne, 1966; Watkins, 1966).

---

ject show varying levels of heart rate, blood pressure, skin resistance, basal metabolic rate, respiration, peripheral blood flow, blood clotting time, oral temperature, and so forth (Barber, 1961, 1965, 1970; Crasilneck and Hall, 1959; Levitt and Brady, 1963; Sarbin, 1956; Sarbin and Slagle, 1972; Timney and Barber, 1969). Furthermore, when specific types of suggestions (for example, suggestions of anesthesia) produce physiological changes in subjects who are said to be hypnotized, the suggestions also produce very similar physiological changes in control subjects who are said to be awake (Barber, 1961, 1965). For instance, in both hypnotized subjects and in control subjects, suggestions of anesthesia or analgesia at times reduce respiratory and electromyographic responses to noxious stimulation (Barber and Hahn, 1962).

†In very rare cases, a hypnotized subject does not open his eyes when told that the experiment is over. These rare cases are due to such reasons as the following: The subject may have actually fallen asleep, or he may not have fallen asleep but he (a) wants to remain a little longer in a relaxed or passive condition, (b) has been given a posthypnotic suggestion that he does not want to carry out, (c) is purposely resisting the hypnotist, (d) is testing the hypnotist's ability to control him, (e) is manifesting spite toward the hypnotist, or (f) is attempting to frighten the hypnotist by refusing to awaken (Weitzenhoffer, 1957, pp. 226–229; Williams, 1953).

‡In rare instances, hypnotized subjects who are *not* given suggestions for amnesia, state postexperimentally that they do not remember what occurred during the session. There are several reasons for viewing this apparent amnesia not as a spontaneous occurrence but as due to explicit or implicit suggestions: In many of these cases, the subject had received suggestions for amnesia in a previous hypnotic session and may have generalized those suggestions to apply to subsequent sessions as well. Further, suggestions to sleep were administered during the hypnotic session. Since sleep is followed by amnesia, the suggestions to sleep included the implicit suggestion that the subject is expected to show amnesia on "awakening." Finally, a substantial proportion of present-day subjects believe that "hypnotized" persons manifest amnesia (London, 1961) and that they will be considered poor subjects, the experimenter will be disappointed, and the experiment may be "spoiled" if they state postexperimentally that they remember what occurred.

HYPNOSIS FROM THE
INSIDE OUT: AN ALTERNATIVE VIEWPOINT

Whether or not they use the analogy of the sleepwalker, most traditional theories of hypnosis view the hypnotized subject as being in a special state of mind or consciousness. They further assume that the behaviors which the hypnotized subject displays under hypnosis differ in kind from the behaviors of which he is capable when not in the hypnotized state. They attribute the differences between the two types of behaviors to the differences between the hypnotized and the non-hypnotized state.

My studies of hypnotic suggestability, compounded by my own personal experiences with hypnosis, have led me to a very different set of assumptions. Perhaps the best way to illustrate these assumptions and to show their relation to my own experiences is to present a personal, introspective report of those experiences. Of course, this personal report, in the same way as any introspective report, fails to convey the full flavor of the experiences. Furthermore, this rather matter-of-fact report from a sophisticated or knowledgeable subject lacks the emotional involvement and elaborate descriptions that are proffered by some responsive subjects. However, it is because of my knowledge that the report includes more introspections concerning underlying attitudinal, motivational, and expectancy factors and ongoing cognitive processes than usually are provided by subjects. Therefore it should be helpful in illustrating views on hypnosis which emphasize the importance of these kinds of factors and processes.*

AN INTROSPECTIVE REPORT

An experimenter† enters my office and asks me if I am willing to participate as a pilot subject in an experiment involving responses to suggestions. I agree to participate.‡

Hand Ridigity

The experimenter begins by asking me to clasp my hands tightly with fingers interlaced. He then states, "Your hands are hard, solid, rigid. They are very rigid and solid. They are two pieces of steel that are welded together. They are rigid, solid, stuck together." He continues with these kinds of suggestions for about 30 seconds and finally

---

*I do not know of any other present-day investigator in this area who has presented his own personal report. Our understanding of hypnotism might be enhanced if other investigators, especially those who adhere to the traditional "hypnotic trance" viewpoint, would present their own introspective reports describing, to the best of their ability, their underlying attitudes, motivations, and expectancies, and their ongoing thought processes while responding to "hypnotic" suggestions.

†Dr. R. F. Q. Johnson.

‡This is not the first time I have taken the role of a subject in an experiment involving suggestions (or hypnosis). I have presented one of my earlier introspective reports elsewhere (Barber, 1972).

states, "Try to take your hands apart. Notice that the harder you try, the more difficult it becomes. Try to take them apart. You can't."

Had the experimenter given these suggestions to me 5 or 6 years ago, I would have felt that it was somehow "improper" for me to respond to the suggestions (negative attitude), I would have wanted to be "nonsuggestible" (negative motivation), and I would have believed that it was impossible for my hands to become stuck together (negative expectancy). Consequently, I would not have squeezed my hands together tightly, I would not have focused on the rigidity in my hands and on the idea that they were stuck together, and I would have taken them apart without difficulty.

During the past 5 or 6 years, while conducting many studies in this area, I have slowly changed my own attitudes, motivations, and expectancies toward responding to suggestions. At the present time, I see this type of test situation as a valuable and useful experience (positive attitude). I want to experience those things that are suggested (positive motivation), and I believe or expect that I, and also other investigators, can experience the suggested effects (positive expectancy) if we temporarily put aside critical or analytical thoughts such as "It's impossible for my hands to become stuck together." Since I have positive attitudes, motivations, and expectancies, I cooperate and "think with" or imagine those things that are suggested. When the experimenter first asks me to hold my hands together tightly, I clasp them very tightly. I then let myself think and imagine that my hands are rigid and that they are two pieces of metal that are solidly stuck together. While thinking with the suggestions that my hands are welded pieces of metal, I do not have negative feelings such as "My hands cannot become rigid." When the experimenter states, "Try to take them apart. Notice that the harder you try the more difficult it becomes," I continue to focus my thoughts on the rigidity in the hands and to imagine that they *are* made of welded metal. I pull on the hands but they feel very rigid, like a solid piece of metal. I exert more effort, I am aware that the hands are red and sore, but they do not come apart. Finally, the experimenter states, "Now relax your hands. You can now easily unclasp them." After I relax the hands, I have a feeling of pleasant surprise to see how easily they now come apart.

Age Regression

The experimenter next asks me to close my eyes (presumably to remove distractions) and then gives a series of suggestions along the following lines: "Time is going back . . . You are 6 years old. You are 6 years old and you are sitting in your first grade classroom."

Since I feel that age regression is a worthwhile experience, and since I want to and expect to experience it, I have no reason to contradict his suggestions. There is simply no reason to think about the fact that I am an adult. On the contrary, I think with the suggestions and I imagine and feel myself small and 6 years old. For a few moments, as I begin to feel myself back at the earlier time, I also have a feeling that the ongoing suggestions of the experimenter are bothersome and distracting. However, the experimenter soon stops talking and my thoughts focus on the idea that I am 6 years old. I feel myself as small and my hands feel tiny and I see myself in the second grade classroom. (I presume that I had the fleeting thought that I was in the second grade when I was 6 years old.) I then find myself sitting behind a brown desk and I notice the knife-marks, the round inkwell, and the large yellow pencil on the desk-top. I "touch" the chewing-gum on the bottom of the desk and I "smell" the paste in the room. I look around the room and I notice five large windows and a cloakroom, and I "see" the teacher and children interacting. I then "see" the teacher leave the room, and as soon as she leaves, I wrestle with another boy who sits next to me. The teacher returns and makes me stay in the corner. I feel myself standing there and I feel the need to turn around and look at the others in the class.

Afterwards, when the experiment is over, I report that I felt I was 6 years old and that I was in the second grade. I go on to describe in detail the events that I reexperienced and how I had felt that once again I "saw" my classmates and knew the names of children whom I had not thought about in many years.

Anesthesia

The experimenter next asks me to open my eyes and to "come back to the present" and then gives suggestions of anesthesia as follows:

"Lift your right hand 2 inches above the desk. Imagine novocaine being injected into the hand. The novocaine is beginning to move into the little finger. You begin to feel small changes in the little finger as the novocaine starts to move in. The little finger is beginning to feel a little different, a little numb. Now the novocaine is beginning to move into the second finger. It too feels a little different, it's beginning to feel a little numb and insensitive. Now you notice the novocaine moving into the third finger . . . now the fourth finger . . . now into the thumb. Now you feel the novocaine in all of the fingers. They feel more and more numb, more and more insensitive. Dull, numb, and insensitive. More and more numb, losing all feelings and sensations. Now rub the fingers with the other hand and notice how they feel rubbery, as if they have lost all feelings and sensations. Pinch the fingers now with your other hand and notice how they feel dull, numb, and insensitive."

After a brief pause, the experimenter concludes, "All right now, your hand is normal again—it is no longer numb. It is normal again."

I think with and I focus imaginatively on the ideas that are suggested. I imagine novocaine being injected into the hand and beginning to move into the little finger. As soon as I begin focusing my attention on the little finger it seems to stand off from the rest of the hand and I feel as if there are small sensations in it that resemble those experienced when novocaine is just beginning to take effect. I then focus on the second finger and think with the suggestion that it is beginning to feel a little different and this finger also seems to be set off from the remainder of the hand and to feel somewhat numb. I continue to think with the suggestions as they are given, I imagine novocaine moving into each of the other fingers, and I find it very interesting that each finger in turn seems to feel as if novocaine is moving into it. I also imaginatively elaborate the suggestions, for instance, as I look at the fingers, I think of them as made of wax, then as made of rubber, and then as things sitting out there by themselves, not belonging to me. After a while the experimenter asks me to pinch the fingers with the other hand. As I pinch each finger, I continue imagining that it has been injected with novocaine, and I find that I am not feeling the pinches—the fingers feel rubbery and dead. Afterwards, when the experimenter asks me if I felt the pinches I state that the fingers felt rubbery and insensitive and that I did not feel them.

Auditory Hallucination

The experimenter tells me to close my eyes again and then says, "You are at a large concert hall. You see the orchestra on the stage. The conductor raises his baton and you hear the orchestra begin to play."

I think with the suggestions and I visualize a previous time when I was at a concert. I "see" the concert hall and the orchestra in front of me. When the music begins, however, I am surprised to "hear" a soprano singing "Amazing Grace" and even more surprised to feel that I am listening to my radio. I do not care about this transformation of locus; instead, I listen to the penetrating tones and words of the song and I feel the same way I had felt many times before when I had heard "Amazing Grace" on the FM station—each tone exquisite, penetrating, vibrating throughout my body.

Later, I describe to the experimenter how I "transported" myself from the situation in which I was observing the orchestra to one in which I was listening to the radio and I state that "Amazing Grace" was intense, penetrating, and even carried a tinge of sexual arousal.

Relaxation, Drowsiness, Sleep and Hypnosis

The experimenter next states, "Keep your eyes closed. Feel yourself lying on a large cottony, cushiony cloud. The cloud is made of cotton and you are sinking into it. Soft, quiet, peaceful, and relaxed. Floating easily and gently. You feel a soft breeze and the warm sun. Becoming more and more relaxed, lazy, comfortable, peaceful . . . so relaxed . . . drowsy . . . drowsier and drowsier . . . comfortable, lazy, relaxed . . . drowsy and sleepy . . . drowsier and drowsier . . . sleepier and sleepier. . . . So drowsy, so sleepy, going into a hypnotic trance . . . a deep trance, a deep hypnotic trance."

In tune with the words of the experimenter, I think with the themes of the suggestions. I imagine that I am floating on a cloud made of cotton and I "feel" the warm sun and the breeze touching my body. As I think with the themes of the suggestions, my arms begin to feel limp, my legs loosen, and I feel my head dropping. For a few moments, I become aware that my head is bent forward on my chest, my arms are hanging loosely, and I am breathing very slowly. As I continue thinking with the ongoing suggestions, I feel tranquil and I catch a fleeting thought that it would be so nice to be able to lie down and go to sleep. Somewhat later, I feel very detached and away from things. Toward the end of these suggestions, I feel as if my body has become weightless and as if I am alone and floating very peacefully.

Postexperimental (Posthypnotic) Behavior

The experimenter next asks me to open my eyes. For a few moments after I open them I feel that the experimenter is far away and my surroundings seem dreamlike. This feeling of detachment and tranquility disappears, however, as the experimenter states, "An interesting thing will occur when the experiment is over. When I click my finger, you will cough automatically." He reinforces the suggestion by repeating it.

When the experimenter states that the experiment is over and then clicks his fingers, I find myself clearing my throat and I feel as if the cough came by itself, involuntarily. Apparently, I thought with this suggestion in the same way I had thought with the preceding ones. I did not seem to say to myself, "I will not (or cannot) cough when he clicks." Instead, it seems that I had expected that I would cough and I expected that it would feel automatic.

Looking Back at the Experience

The reader should note that I experienced a series of suggested effects—hand rigidity, age regression, anesthesia, and auditory hallucination—*before* the experimenter told me that I was becoming relaxed, drowsy, sleepy, and was entering a hypnotic trance. Was I hypnotized or in a hypnotic trance when I was responding to these suggestions? When I try to answer this question introspectively, I find that it is not especialy meaningful. I felt that I simply let myself think with, and imaginatively focus on those things that were suggested. Looking back retrospectively, I can also make the following interpretations concerning some of the effects I experienced:

HAND RIGIDITY

I can see now that I produced a strong feeling of rigidity in my hands when I clasped them together tightly and contracted the muscles. Consequently, when I was thinking with and imaginatively elaborating the suggestions, I was focusing on the rigidity that was already present. Also, retrospectively, I can see that in order to have unclasped my hands, when the experimenter said "Try, you can't," I would have had to shift my underlying attitudes and motivations from very positive to very negative. Instead of focusing my thoughts on the rigidity, I would have had to say to myself something like, "That's absurd. Of course I can take my hands apart." Furthermore, to have unclasped my hands, it would have been necessary to remove the muscular contractions by relaxing my hands. However, I had no reason to contradict the suggestions and to relax my hands. Since my underlying attitudes, motivations, and expectancies were quite positive—I perceived the situation as one in which I would have a worthwhile experience, and I wanted and expected to experience the suggested effects—I continued to think of my hands as rigid and to maintain the muscular contractions which prevented me from unclasping them.

AGE REGRESSION

Retrospectively, it seems that it was very easy to focus on the idea that I was a child. I had no reason to say to myself that I was actually an adult and that I was in an experimental situation. As I let my thoughts go with the idea of being a child, I "recreated" scenes of childhood. When the experimenter stated that I was 6 years of age and that I was in the first grade classroom, I "felt" myself sitting in the second grade classroom. I did not care about this contradiction. Although I was thinking and imagining with the *themes* of the suggestions, the particular details did not matter. Just as any other responsive subject, I was carrying out "goal-directed imaging"—I was imagining a situation (the second grade) which was in harmony with the goal of the suggestions even though I was not following the suggestion literally (that I was in the first grade) (Spanos, 1971; Spanos and Barber, 1972). Retrospectively, I felt small, I reexperienced sitting in the second grade classroom, and I felt as if I were again experiencing the same emotions that I had felt when the teacher caught me wrestling with another boy and when I was standing in the corner facing the wall.

ANESTHESIA

Looking back, it seems that the suggestions of anesthesia began when the experimenter asked me to lift my hand above the desk. When the fingers are not touching and moving across an object, they do not seem sensitive. I could easily interpret this actual fact, "not seeming sensitive," as meaning that the fingers were becoming insensitive. Also, by focusing my attention on each finger, while the hand was sitting relaxed above the desk, I could discriminate slight sensations which could easily be interpreted as the kind of sensations which one feels when novocaine begins to take effect. When I rubbed the fingers, and also when I pinched them, the fingers felt rubbery and insensitive. However, when I rub and pinch the fingers now, the feeling of rubberiness and insensitivity is there in a minimal way. It seems, retrospectively, that during the experiment I was magnifying the feelings of insensitivity which normally are present in the fingers when the hand is relaxed and the fingers are not touching anything or being moved across a surface.

When the experimenter stated, "All right now, your hand is normal again—it is no longer numb," I can see now, that the hand did not feel normal immediately; it felt normal only when I moved the fingers a second or two later. In other words, it appears that the feeling of insensitivity is based, in part, on the fact that one is focusing on fingers that are not being moved; if the fingers are in movement it would be much more difficult to experience the suggested insensitivity.

AUDITORY HALLUCINATION

Looking back, it seems that the experimenter's suggestions induced me to hear the music in my head and to feel as if that "internal music" were coming from outside of me. Although the experimenter suggested that I was at a concert hall, I found it more congruent with my previous experience to transport myself to a room in which I was listening to an FM radio and hearing the exquisite notes of "Amazing Grace." As for many responsive subjects, the details of the suggestions were not important to me. I was engaged in goal-directed imagining—I was imagining a situation which was harmonious with the goals of the suggestions, even though I was not imagining what the experimenter had suggested literally. Although responding to this type of suggestion may seem very difficult to some readers, I believe most of us can think about and imaginatively focus on a previous time when we heard music that was especially moving. While focusing on such a previously-experienced situation, we will naturally hear the music in our heads; if we do not have a critical attitude, or if we put it aside, negative thoughts, such as "I am not actually hearing anything," will not arise. In fact, the act of focusing on imagined music or on music in the head is difficult to distinguish subjectively from the act of listening to actual music.

SUGGESTIONS OF RELAXATION, DROWSINESS, SLEEP, AND HYPNOSIS

Retropspectively, it seems that I responded to this set of suggestions for the same reasons that I responded to the preceding suggestions. Since I had positive attitudes, motivations, and expectancies toward the test situation, I thought with and imaginatively focused on the ongoing suggestions and I felt relaxed, drowsy, and then passive and detached.

It should be noted that the suggestions of relaxation, drowsiness, sleep, and hypnosis were given toward the end of the experimental session. However, such suggestions usually are given at the beginning of the experiment and it is commonly assumed that a subject who responds to suggestions for relaxation, drowsiness, sleep, and hypnosis enters a hypnotic trance and that the hypnotic trance gives rise to a high level of responsiveness to subsequent suggestions for limb rigidity, age regression, anesthesia, etc. However, if the suggestions of relaxation, drowsiness, sleep, and hypnosis are placed toward the end of the session, they can be seen to be only another set of suggestions to which the subject may or may not respond. If the subject responds to the suggestions of relaxation, drowsiness, sleep, and hypnosis, he does so for the same reasons that he responded to the preceding test suggestions—he has positive attitudes, motivations, and expectancies toward the test situation and, consequently, thinks with the suggestions and imagines the suggested effects. Let me clarify this further by describing two common events that involve similar processes.

ANALOGIES: READING A NOVEL AND WATCHING A MOVIE

It seems to me that the processes involved in responding to suggestions are similar to those that are present when I am reading an interesting novel or watching a motion picture or stage play. Let me describe each of these analogies in turn.

When I am reading an interesting novel, I think with and vividly imagine the communications from the printed page. To the extent that I become involved in my imaginings, I do not have contradictory thoughts such as "This is only a novel," or "This is only make-believe." Instead, I experience a variety of emotions while empathizing and "living with" the character. At times I may experience sadness to the point of tears. Other times I may smile to myself or even laugh aloud. Along similar lines, Shor (1970) has previously pointed out that, when reading a novel, some individuals "think the thoughts in the story and they feel the emotions." Shor labeled this behavior the *book reading fantasy* and noted the following relevant characteristics:

> . . . the reader creates the fantasy for his own purposes, to satisfy his own motives. The fantasy is not implanted in the mind by the words in the book. The reader is not forced to create the fantasy by the inexorable "suggestive" power of the words. The words do not express themselves with the reader's will held in abeyance. The reader is not too much asleep to control his own mind. He is not an automaton obeying the commands of his master. The words in the book have no ideomotor powers in their own right except insofar as the reader deliberately gives them expression. The reader is deliberately using the words in the book for his own ends (p. 93).

It seems to me that the processes involved in responding to suggestions also resemble those present when I have a variety of emotional experiences while observing a motion picture or a stage play. At a movie, I think with the communications from the screen. As I become imaginatively involved in the action, I do not have negative thoughts such as, "These are only actors," "This is just a story that someone made up," or "This is just a series of lights playing upon a screen." Since I think with the communications, I feel, emote, and experience in line with the intentions of the writer of the screen-play— I feel sad, I weep, I empathize, I feel happy, I laugh, etc. I think with the communications because I am attending the performance in order to have new experiences. My *attitude* toward the movie is that it is interesting and worthwhile to feel sad, to feel happy, to empathize, and to have the other thoughts, feelings, and emotions that the actors are attempting to communicate. Furthermore, I both *desire* and *expect* that the actors will arouse in me new thoughts and emotions. It is misleading to claim that I am having intense experiences and emotions as I observe the movie because I have entered a "hypnotic trance." I have intense experiences while observing a movie, and I have intense experiences when I am responding to suggestions because in both cases, I have positive attitudes, motivations, and expectancies toward the situation and I think with, and imaginatively focus on the communications.

When I am watching a movie, and also when responding to suggestions, I am thinking with and imaginatively focusing on the communications that I receive. However, I am being exposed to different kinds of communications in these situations. The communications from the movie are intended to elicit certain kinds of thoughts, emotions, and experiences. The communications from the experimenter are intended to elicit somewhat different types of thoughts, emotions, and experiences—to feel that an arm is light and is rising, to experience onself as a child, to vividly imagine (or hallucinate) an orchestra playing, etc. When I am responding to suggestions I have different experiences than when I am watching a movie, *not because I am in a different state of consciousness, but because I am receiving different communications.*

It should also be noted that an individual who is part of a motion picture audience may have negative attitudes, motivations, and expectancies toward the performance, and may fail to experience the emotions which the actors are attempting to communicate. He may be attending the movie theater unwillingly and may be uninterested in having new experiences. He may not especially desire nor expect to feel happy, sad, shocked, excited, or empathic. Given these attitudes, motivations, and expectancies, this member of the audience may tell himself "This is just a movie, and I am just watching actors perform their roles." If he observes the movie in this uninvolved and distant manner, he will be aware continually that he is in an audience and that he is observing a deliberately contrived performance. I believe that such an individual closely resembles the subject who is unresponsive to suggestions. Both have negative attitudes, motivations, and expectancies toward the situation which prevent them from thinking with and imaginatively focusing on the communications.

RECAPITULATION

Let me restate a theme that underlies the preceding discussion. Traditionally, it has been assumed that individuals experience suggested age regression, anesthesia, auditory hallucination, etc., when they have been hypnotized or placed in a hypnotic trance. However, since I regard the concept of hypnotized or hypnotic trance as misleading, my viewpoint allows for a broader conception of the capabilities and potentialities of normal human beings. Thus, I postuate that: (a) Age regression, anesthesia, and other phenomena that have been traditionally subsumed under the term "hypnotism" are elicited when an individual thinks and imagines with the suggestions for age regression, anesthesia, etc. (b) A large proportion of individuals have the potential to think and imagine with the themes of the suggestions. However, (c) the potential often remains dormant until the individual's attitudes, motivations, and expectancies are positive in regard to the situation. Let me now present some methods that might prove useful for producing the necessary attitudes, motivations, and expectancies and that might also directly help individuals to think and imagine with the themes of suggestions.

TRAINING IN HUMAN POTENTIALITIES

Since 1969, while conducting group workshops and also while working with a small number of individual subjects, I have been developing a course that I have labeled *training in human potentialities*. The course is not yet complete, and has been evaluated only partially (Chaves and Barber, 1974; Comins, Fullam, and Barber, 1973). However, there are two reasons why I believe it is worthwhile to outline it here: First, the outline should illustrate in a concrete manner how some principles presented in this chapter can be applied and second, others may see the procedures as useful and proceed to evaluate them experimentally.*

*Kinney (1969), Sachs (1971), and Diamond (1972) have recently presented methods for training subjects to become more responsive to hypnotic suggestions. The training procedure presented in this section differs in several important respects and was developed independently from that presented by Kinney, Sachs, and Diamond. However, the methods I use have several features in common with those developed by other investigators. These various methods for training subjects are discussed together elsewhere (Barbar, Spanos, and Chaves, 1974, chap. 11).

Defining the Situation

Typically, I define the training situation as one in which the subject will learn to fulfill his own potentialities. I tell the subject that I can help him learn how to focus his thoughts, how to recall useful material by vividly imagining a previous situation, how to improve his learning proficiency, how to control pain, and how to control his bodily processes by first learning to control his mental processes. I emphasize to the subject that the training he receives in the experimental situation should prove useful in his daily life.

Learning to Control Pain

Although I can begin the training course in various ways, I usually begin by trying to teach the subject how to control pain. I tell him that he will first learn to tolerate a normally painful stimulus and not be bothered by it at all. I also explain to him that the learning will be useful in a wide variety of situations in which he normally experiences pain. For instance, I might state, "It should be useful not only in overcoming the pains and discomforts of daily life, but also in dentistry and (for females) during childbirth. Once you have learned how to control pain, you may be able to transfer or extrapolate what you have learned to other situations in your life in which anxiety, distress, or fear are present."

I then expose the subject for a period of 1 minute to the Forgione-Barber (1971) pain stimulator which brings a weight to bear on the bony part of a finger. Next, I tell the subject that he can control the pain produced by the weight by keeping his mind on other things during the stimulation and also by imagining vividly that the stimulated finger is dull, numb, or insensitive.

Next, I model for the subject. I demonstrate how I can control pain by utilizing the two techniques mentioned above. I place the weight on my own finger and then I state, "I am going to think of other things. I am not going to let myself think of the heavy weight on my finger." While the weight remains on my finger, I verbalize some of the things I am thinking about, for example, "I am thinking back to last summer when I was on the beach. . . . I am sitting on the hot sand. . . . The sun is hot but pleasant. . . . As I enter the water, I find it is comfortably cool. . . . In the distance I see an airplane slowly moving overhead. . . ." I continue for several minutes verbalizing some of the things I am thinking and visualizing, while the weight remains on my finger and I show no signs of pain or distress.

I then state, "I will now try to think of the finger as numb and insensitive. . . . I am imagining that novocaine has been injected into the finger. . . . I am thinking of the novocaine spreading slowly through out the finger and it is becoming dull, numb, like a piece of rubber. . . . I am imagining that the finger is just a piece of matter—a lump of matter without feelings or sensations. . . ." For several minutes I continue imagining numbness and insensitivity, I verbalize my thoughts, and I manifest no signs of pain or distress.

Finally, I remove the weight from my finger and tell the subject that he can control pain by using the same procedures. I ask him to try, to the best of his ability, to think and imagine in the way I have just demonstrated. The heavy weight is then placed on the subject's finger and he practices carrying out the processes of trying to think of other things and then trying to imagine that the finger has become insensitive. Although some subjects find it difficult to think and imagine in this way, other subjects are able to do it rather easily and they succeed in tolerating the pain-producing stimulus.

In further development of this course, I hope to delineate other techniques that subjects can use to control pain. Some techniques that might prove useful include thinking and imagining that the stimulated body part is just a "thing," not an actual part of one's self, and thinking of the sensations, not as pain, but as a variety of unusual sensations with their own unique properties. In further development of the course, I expect to give subjects additional practice in tolerating pain produced by other kinds of stimuli (e.g., pain produced by immersion of a limb in ice water and pain produced by blocking off the blood supply to an arm by means of a tourniquet). When a subject has learned to control pain in the laboratory, I attempt to determine if his learning can be transferred to a situation outside of the laboratory. For instance, I shall ask the subject to try to undergo his next dental appointment without novocaine and try to utilize what he has learned in the laboratory. Thus, he must try to think of other things during the dentistry, or try to imagine that novocaine has been injected and that his teeth and gums have become insensitive. As I continue to develop the course, I hope to discover ways by which subjects can relate what they have learned to other daily situations which involve anxiety or pain.

Learning to Experience a Variety of Phenomena

Usually, I begin the course by trying to teach the subject to tolerate pain. However, I can also begin in other ways, by trying to teach the subject to experience a variety of effects that traditionally have been associated with suggestions and hypnotism.

In teaching the subject to experience a variety of interesting phenomena, I use procedures that are similar to those described above. I first tell the subject that he can fulfill his potentialities by learning to control his thinking and imagining. I then state that he will receive practice in focusing his thinking and imagining on the idea that one arm is very heavy and rigid, the other arm is very light and is rising, his body is rigid and immovable, he feels very thirsty, etc. Next, I model for the subject. I verbalize how I am experiencing a phenomenon, for example, arm heaviness and rigidity, by thinking and imagining that my arm is heavy and rigid. I may also explain to the subject that when I think and vividly imagine that my arm is rigid, the muscles of my arm naturally contract; the contraction of the muscles makes my arm feel heavy and rigid; then by keeping my thoughts on the induced heaviness and rigidity, my arm can feel exceedingly heavy and rigid.

After the subject has attempted to carry out the same kind of cognitive processes, I interview him to determine the extent to which he was able to concentrate on the idea of heaviness or rigidity. If the subject reports that negative thoughts intruded, for example, the thought that "My arm cannot become heavy and rigid," I tell him to try it again while trying to imagine more vividly and that, if he concentrates on imagining, the negative thoughts will disappear.

The same procedures are used to teach the subject to experience other phenomena such as arm levitation, body immobility, thirst hallucination, amnesia, age-regression, and relaxation.

Experiencing Age Regression

I tell the subject that he can heighten his recall of earlier events by vividly imagining a past time. I also give several examples of how this technique is useful in daily life. For instance, I tell the subject that when he is taking an examination and wishes to recall material he had learned previously, he can heighten his recall by imagining and clearly visualizing the concrete situation in which he originally learned the material. I then state: "I will show you how to reexperience a past time. In a moment, I will close my eyes so that I can remove distractions. Then, I will tell myself that I am 10 years old and I will imagine and visualize that I am in the fourth grade classroom. I will then concentrate my thinking and imagining on the idea that I am 10 years old and, when I succeed in concentrating my thinking and imagining around this idea, thoughts that I am an adult in an experimental situation will not arise. Once I begin clearly visualizing the fourth grade, I will let my imagination move and I will let myself go with the events that I imagine."

I then close my eyes. After a few minutes I open them, state that I felt I was 10 years old, and describe how I experienced myself, the teacher, and the students in the classroom. I then tell the subject, "In a minute I will ask you to close your eyes and to think back to the time you were 10 years old. Imagine that you are sitting in the classroom. Concentrate your thinking and imagining on the idea that you are in the classroom, feel yourself in that situation, and then let your imagination move. As you let the teacher, the students, and yourself interact and come alive, thoughts about your being an adult in an experimental situation will disappear."

The subject is then given practice in experiencing himself as a

10-year-old. Subsequently, he is given further practice in experiencing various other age levels.

Experiencing Relaxation

I introduce the training in relaxation by speaking to the subject along the following lines:

"Most individuals are so busy living their daily lives that they rarely, if ever, allow themselves to experience total relaxation. In fact, it is questionable whether most individuals know how to relax. This is unfortunate because the ability to relax completely is very useful in our daily lives. Once we have learned to relax, we are able to remain calm and at ease in many situations that normally produce anxiety or tension. For instance, many individuals become tense or anxious when they meet new people, when they are in a strange or new situation, and when they feel that they are being judged by others. Also, individuals who are alcoholics, or who are obese, or who cannot quit smoking become tense and anxious when they have not had alcohol, or food, or a cigarette for a period of time. Some individuals also have specific kinds of fears, for instance, fear of riding in an airplane, fear of heights, or fear of narrow spaces. If these individuals learned how to relax, they could control their anxiety, tension, or fear. An important fact that has been emphasized by behavior therapists is that anxiety and tension are incompatible with physical and mental relaxation. If a person lets himself relax, he can control or block the anxiety, tension, or fear. In fact, many of the useful effects that are attributed to yoga, hypnosis, Zen, and transcendental meditation appear to be due to the relaxation that is produced by each of these techniques."

I next state that I will now model for the subject, showing him how to relax. I introduce the modeling demonstration as follows:

"I will now show you how to relax. To get rid of distractions, I will first close my eyes. Then I will think to myself that I am becoming very relaxed. I will tell myself that my arms are relaxing, my legs are relaxing, my eyes are relaxing, all parts of my body are relaxing. I will then imagine that I am floating on a soft cloud and that my body feels very, very relaxed. I will continue telling myself that I am completely relaxed and I will imagine scenes, such as floating softly on smooth water, which will make me feel more and more relaxed."

I then model for the subject, demonstrating how to relax. After a few minutes, I open my eyes, report what I was thinking and imagining during the period of relaxation, and then ask the subject to try relaxing in the same way. I may give the subject several practice trials during the session, asking him to relax for longer and longer periods of time. Before the subject leaves, I usually ask him to continue practicing the relaxation technique at home and to try to use what he has learned about relaxation in his daily life whenever he begins to feel anxious or tense.

Experimental Evaluation

The effectiveness of parts of the above course of training have been evaluated experimentally. In one recent experiment (Comins, Fullam and Barber, 1973), the experimenter modeled for one group of subjects, showing them (a) how he thought and imagined those things that he suggested aloud to himself (arm heaviness, arm levitation, hand clasp, and thirst hallucination) and (b) how, consequently, he experienced an involuntary lowering and rising of his arm, an inability to unclasp his hands, and extreme thirst. The subjects who had observed the experimenter responding to the suggestions were then tested on the Barber Suggestibility Scale.* Their scores on the scale were compared with the scores of two random groups of subjects: a control group that had not received any instructions, and a hypnotic induction group that had been exposed to repeated suggestions of relaxation, drowsiness, and hypnotic sleep. Subjects who had observed the experimenter model were markedly more responsive than the control subjects to the test-suggestions of the Barber Suggestibility Scale, and were as responsive as the subjects who had been exposed to the standardized hypnotic induction procedure.

In a second evaluative study (Chaves and Barber, 1974), 120 subjects were first exposed to a pain pretest (a heavy weight was applied to a finger for 2 minutes). Before the pain stimulus was administered a second time (posttest), some subjects were told to imagine pleasant events during the pain stimulation, others were told to imagine that the finger was insensitive, and the remaining subjects were used as controls. Of the subjects who were told to imagine, half were exposed to experimenter modeling and half were not. Those who were exposed to experimenter modeling observed how the experimenter could tolerate the pain when he imagined pleasant events or imagined that his finger was insensitive. Overall, subjects who were told to imagine pleasant events or to imagine that the finger was insensitive reported less pain than the control subjects. Also, the experimenter modeling procedure was effective in producing a further reduction in pain in subjects who reported a high level of pain during the pretest, and who were asked to imagine pleasant events during the posttest.

Although the above two studies evaluated the effects of the experimenter modeling procedure, they did not define the situation to the subjects as one in which they could learn to fulfill their potenti-

---

*The Barber Suggestibility Scale (BSS) is a test for hypnotic-like behaviors without prior induction of hypnosis. The administrator instructs the subject to imagine, successively, eight conditions such as extreme thirst, hands locked in the lap, body immobility, etc. Responses are scored according to predetermined criteria. Raw scores are weighted and averaged to provide a standardized score.

alities. Further studies are planned to test the separate and combined effects of (a) experimenter modeling and (b) defining the situation as training in human potentialities.

REFERENCES

Barber, T. X. 1961. Physiological effects of "hypnosis." *Psychological Bulletin,* 58:390–419.

Barber, T. X. 1962. Toward a theory of hypnosis: Posthypnotic behavior. *Archives of General Psychiatry,* 7:321–342.

Barber, T. X. 1965. Physiological effects of "hypnotic suggestions": A critical review of recent research (1960–64). *Psychological Bulletin,* 63: 201–222.

Barber, T. X. 1969. *Hypnosis: A Scientfic Approach.* New York: Van Nostrand Reinhold.

Barber, T. X. 1970. *LSD, Marihuana, Yoga, and Hypnosis.* Chicago: Aldine-Atherton.

Barber, T. X. 1972. Suggested ("hypnotic") behavior: The trance paradigm versus an alternative paradigm. In E. Fromm and R. E. Shor (eds.), *Hypnosis: Research Developments and Perspectives.* Chicago: Aldine-Atherton, pp. 115–182.

Barber, T. X. and Calverley, D. S. 1966. Toward a theory of "hypnotic" behavior: Experimental analyses of suggested amnesia. *Journal of Abnormal Psychology,* 71:95–107.

Barber, T. X. and DeMoor, W. 1972. A theory of hypnotic induction procedures. *American Journal of Clinical Hypnosis,* 15:112–135.

Barber, T. X. and Hahn, K. W., Jr. 1962. Physiological and subjective responses to pain producing stimulation under hypnotically-suggested and waking-imagined "analgesia." *Journal of Abnormal and Social Psychology,* 65:411–418.

Barber, T. X. and Ham, M. W. 1974. *Hypnotic Phenomena.* Morristown, N. J.: General Learning Press.

Barber, T. X.; Spanos, N. P.; and Chaves, J. F. 1974. *Hypnosis, Imagination, and Human Potentialities.* New York: Pergamon Press.

Chaves, J. F. and Barber, T. X. 1974. Cognitive strategies, experimenter modeling, and expectation in the attenuation of pain. *Journal of Abnormal Psychology,* 83:356–363.

Chertok, L. and Kramarz, P. 1959. Hypnosis, sleep, and electroencephalography. *Journal of Nervous and Mental Disease,* 128:227–238.

Comins, J.; Fullam, F.; and Barber, T. X. 1973. Experimenter modeling, demands for honesty, and response to "hypnotic" suggestions. Medfield, Mass.: Medfield Foundation.

Crasilneck, H. B. and Hall, J. A. 1959. Physiological changes associated with hypnosis: A review of the literature since 1948. *International Journal of Clinical and Experimental Hypnosis,* 7:9–50.

Diamond, M. J. 1972. The use of observationally-presented information to modify hypnotic susceptibility. *Journal of Abnormal Psychology,* 79: 174–180.

Forgione, A. G. and Barber, T. X. 1971. A strain gauge pain stimulator. *Psychophysiology,* 8:102–106.

Hilgard, E. R. 1966. Posthypnotic amnesia: Experiments and theory. *International Journal of Clinical and Experimental Hypnosis,* 14:104–111.

Hilgard, E. R. 1959. Altered states of awareness. *Journal of Nervous and Mental Disease,* 149:68–79. Reprinted in T. X. Barber, et al. (eds.),

Biofeedback and Self-Control: An Aldine Reader. Chicago: Aldine-Atherton, 1971, pp. 763–774.

Jacobson, A.; Kales, A.; Lehmann, D.; and Zweizig, J. R. 1965. Somnambulism: Allnight electro-encephalographic studies. *Science,* 148:975–977.

Kales, A.; Jacobson, A.; Paulson, M. J.; Kales, J. D.; and Walter, R. D. 1966. Somnambulism: Psychophysiological correlates. I. All-night EEG studies. *Archives of General Psychiatry,* 14:586–594.

Kinney, J. C. M. 1969. Modification of hypnotic susceptibility. Doctoral dissertation, Stanford University, Ann Arbor, Michigan: University Microfilms, 70–10, 476.

Levitt, E. E. and Brady, J. P. 1963. Psychophysiology of hypnosis. In J. M. Schneck (ed.), *Hypnosis in Modern Medicine.* (3rd ed.) Springfield, Ill.: C. C Thomas, pp. 314–362.

London, P. 1961. Subject characteristics in hypnosis research: I. A survey of experience, interest, and opinion. *International Journal of Clinical and Experimental Hypnosis,* 9:151–161.

Orne, M. T. 1966. On the mechanism of posthypnotic amnesia. *International Journal of Clinical and Experimental Hypnosis,* 14:121–134.

Pai, M. N. 1946. Sleep-walking and sleep activities. *Journal of Mental Science,* 92:756–783.

Sachs, L. B. 1971. Construing hypnosis as modifiable behavior. In A. Jacobs and L. B. Sachs (eds.), *The Psychology of Private Events.* New York: Academic Press, pp. 61–75.

Sarbin, T. R. 1956. Physiological effects of hypnotic stimulation. In R. M. Dorcus (ed.), *Hypnosis and Its Therapeutic Applications.* New York: McGraw-Hill, Chapter 4.

Sarbin, T. R. and Slagle, R. W. 1972. Hypnosis and psychophysiological outcomes. In E. Fromm and R. E. Shor (eds.), *Hypnosis: Research Developments and Perspectives.* Chicago: Aldine-Atherton, pp. 185–214.

Shor, R. E. 1970. The three-factor theory of hypnosis as applied to the book-reading fantasy and to the concept of suggestion. *International Journal of Clinical and Experimental Hypnosis,* 18:89–98.

Spanos, N. P. 1971. Goal-directed fantasy and the performance of hypnotic test suggestions. *Psychiatry,* 34:86–96.

Spanos, N. P. and Barber, T. X. 1972. Cognitive activity during "hypnotic" suggestibility: Goal-directed fantasy and the experience of nonvolition. *Journal of Personality,* 40:510–524.

Timney, B. N. and Barber, T. X. 1969. Hypnotic induction and oral temperature. *International Journal of Clinical and Experimental Hypnosis,* 17:121–132.

Watkins, J. G. 1966. Symposium on posthypnotic amnesia: Discussion. *International Journal of Clinical and Experimental Hypnosis,* 14:139–149.

Weitzenhoffer, A. M. 1957. *General Techniques of Hypnotism.* New York: Grune and Stratton.

Williams, G. W. 1953. Difficulty in dehypnotizing. *Journal of Clinical and Experimental Hypnosis,* 1:3–12.